# Grammar for Teachers

Andrea DeCapua

# Grammar for Teachers

A Guide to American English for Native
and Non-Native Speakers

 Springer

*Author*
Andrea DeCapua, Ed.D.
College of New Rochelle
New Rochelle, NY 10805
adecapua@cnr.edu

ISBN: 978-0-387-76331-6        e-ISBN: 978-0-387-76332-3

Library of Congress Control Number: 2007937636

Printed on acid-free paper

9 8 7 6 5 4 3 2 1

springer.com

# Preface

*Grammar for Teachers: A Guide to American English for Native and Non-Native Speakers* is a result of my frustrations over many years of teaching graduate-level structure courses and not being able to find an appropriate grammar text for the pre- and in-service teachers enrolled in these classes. The students in these courses have represented a variety of teaching backgrounds: ESL and EFL teachers, native and non-native speakers of English, and mainstream content-area teachers with ESL students in their classes, to name a few. Some of these students have had a strong knowledge of English grammar, but often have difficulties in applying their knowledge to real-life discourse. Other students' exposure has been limited to lessons in "correctness," and are generally unaware of which language features are central to teaching ESL/EFL learners. Some students are resistant to taking this course, but are required to do so, whether to satisfy specific degree requirements, for state or professional certification, or for other reasons. A few students have had some linguistics, many not. The challenge has been finding a way to convey the essentials of American English grammar clearly, to engage students actively in their own learning and understanding of grammar as applicable to ESL/EFL learners, and to motivate them to undertake perceptive analyses of grammatical elements and structures, and of ESL/EFL learner needs and difficulties.

The overall aim of *Grammar for Teachers* is to make grammar accessible and comprehensible. The text assumes no prior knowledge and can be used with active and prospective teachers who have little or no background in grammar, linguistics, foreign languages, or other related fields. It is also intended for those users whose exposure to English grammar has been primarily limited to prescriptive rules of what speakers should say and write with little or no consideration of the concerns and problems ESL/EFL learners face in learning and using English. The text encourages users to develop a solid understanding of the use and function of the grammatical structures in American English so that they may better appreciate the language difficulties of ESL/EFL learners. The underlying premise is that teachers of ESL/EFL learners need to understand how English works from a practical, every day approach of "What does the learner need to know in order to produce X." When teachers understand the grammar of American English and the problems and needs of ESL/EFL learner, they are in a better position to teach and explain elements of grammar.

The text reviews essential grammar structures clearly and concisely, while avoiding jargon or technical terms. The text approaches grammar from a descriptive rather than a prescriptive approach and focuses on the structures of grammar of greatest importance to ESL/EFL learners. *Grammar for Teachers* encourages users to tap into their own, generally subconscious, knowledge of the grammar of English and make it a conscious knowledge that they can apply to their own varied teaching settings. The text strives to make the study of grammar interesting and relevant by presenting grammar in context and by using authentic material from a variety of sources. Discussions of areas of potential difficulties for ESL/EFL learners are included throughout the text. *Grammar for Teachers* also explores differences in forms accepted in formal versus casual or informal writing and speaking based on the types of questions and concerns learners are likely to have.

In each chapter, users of the text work through numerous Discovery Activities that encourage them to explore for themselves different elements of grammar and to consider how these elements work together to form meaningful discourse. Additional Practical Activities at the end of each chapter provide more practice on structures presented in that chapter. Included in the Practice Activities are samples of relevant learner errors and error analysis exercises. These exercises expose users to authentic ESL/EFL learner discourse at different levels of proficiency and from many different native languages, and afford them opportunities to practice focusing on specific errors at any given moment.

# Acknowledgments

I especially thank the students at New York University, The College of New Rochelle, New York and Long Island University, Purchase Campus who used various drafts of the text over the years and provided feedback. Special thanks are due to Helaine Marshall, at Long Island University, Purchase, New York Campus and Will Smathers, New York University who piloted earlier versions of the text. Their comments, insights and suggestions were invaluable. Thanks also to Judy Hausman, Susannah Healy, Betsy Reitbauer, Cheryl Serrano, and Walter Oerlemann for their help and encouragement.

# Contents

# Chapter 1
# What is Grammar?

## Introduction

> When I think of grammar, I think of word usage – which, of course, everyone
> butchers.
> I despise grammar. I find the rules trite and boring. Grammar (and its enforcers)
> need to loosen up and enjoy life more!
> Grammar makes my stomach churn.

These comments will strike a chord with many users of this textbook. The term
*grammar* does not bring pleasant memories to the minds of many people. The term
grammar frequently brings to mind tedious lessons with endless drills, repetition,
and other generally mindless practice, focused on mostly obscure rules of how people are supposed to write and speak. For native speakers of any given language,
grammar often represents to them the great "mystery" of language, known only to
language specialists or those of older generations, the ones who really know what is
"right". Many feel that "grammar" is something that they were never taught and that
feel they therefore "don't know." Grammar is also often linked to both explicit and
implicit criticisms of people's use or "misuse" of language, which may have created
a sense of resentment or frustration with the notion of grammar.

## Grammar as a Set of Rules

The idea that grammar is a set of rules, often seen as arbitrary or unrealistic, is only
one narrow view of grammar. Such a view is based on the belief that:

- grammar must be explicitly taught;
- grammar is absolute and fixed, a target or goal that speakers need attain in order
  to be "good" speakers or writers of the language;
- grammar is inherently difficult and confusing, its mysteries only apparent to
  teachers, language mavens, or linguists.

A. DeCapua, *Grammar for Teachers,*
© Springer 2008

**Discovery Activity 1: Making Decisions on Grammaticality**

Look at the sentences below.

a. In your opinion, label each sentence as **G** for grammatical, **N** for ungrammatical, and **?** for "not sure" or "don't know".
b. For those sentences you labeled as **N**, identify the element or elements that you think are ungrammatical and explain why you think they are ungrammatical.
c. For those sentences you labeled as **?**, if you can, discuss why you are unsure.

1. _____ She had less problems with the move to a new school than she thought she would.
2. _____ She lays in bed all day whenever she gets a migraine headache.
3. _____ My sister Alice, who is older than me, still lives at home.
4. _____ Everyone needs to buy their books before the first day of class.

## Discussion: Discovery Activity 1

In all of these sentences there is a difference between casual English and formal English. In formal English, particularly when written, there are rules that speakers are taught that must be followed in order for sentences to be considered "correct." In the first sentence, *few* should be used only with nouns we can count, such as apples, pens, or days while *less* should be used with nouns we can't count, such as math, water, or beauty. According to this rule, the sentence should be *She had fewer problems with the move to the new school than she thought she would* (see Chapter 3).

In the next sentence, there is a formal grammar rule distinguishing between *lie* and *lay*. *Lie* is a verb that is not followed by an object, while *lay* is a verb that is followed by an object. Compare these two sentences:

| | |
|---|---|
| Cats lie on beds | lie = resting or sleeping |
| Cats lay mice on beds. | lay = put |

Another way to differentiate these two similar verbs is to describe *lay* as an action verb and *lie* as a non-action verb. According to the rule that tells us that *lie* doesn't take an object but *lay* does, Sentence (2) needs to be rewritten in formal English as:

*She **lies** in bed all day long whenever she has a migraine headache.*

Adding to the confusion between *lie* and *lay* is the fact that the past tense form of *lie* is *lay*. (The past tense of *lie* is *lay*). As the distinction is becoming less and less common, even "serious" publications interchange the two forms, which illustrates how language, and what is considered acceptable, gradually changes:

> Goldmann and Wermusch detected the dried-up river bed of this branch, which had discharged into the sea west of the present-day city of Barth. The two concluded that large parts of Vineta must **lay** buried in the silt of the lagoon north of Barth.
> [Bryasac, S. (2003 July/August). Atlantis of the Baltic. *Archeology*, 64.]

In Sentence (3) there is a grammar rule that dictates *I* needs to be used here, not *me* because *than* compares two nouns in subject position as in:

> *My sister Alice, who is older than **I**, still lives at home.*

Nevertheless, for many users of English, *I* after *than* sounds stilted or affected in spoken English and in informal written contexts, such as e-mail or personal correspondence.

In Sentence (4) *Everyone needs to buy their books before the first day of class,* the discussion of which pronoun to use is a subject of controversy. Traditional grammarians for centuries have argued that the singular male pronoun is the grammatically correct form because words such as *anyone* or *anybody* are singular, even though they refer to plural concepts. The choice of the male pronoun *his* was based on the assumption that the male pronoun encompassed reference to females.

While such an argument may be true of Latin and other languages such as Spanish or German, there is no basis for this in English. In Spanish, all nouns are either masculine or feminine. In the case of Latin or German, all nouns are masculine, feminine, or neuter. The plural form, when reference is made to both sexes, is the male plural form in all of these languages.

English, in contrast, does not classify its nouns according to gender, except in a few instances where they clearly refer to a specific sex such as *girl* or *father*. In addition, English plural nouns are gender neutral (*we, our, ours, you, your, yours, they, their, theirs*), unless the antecedent (preceding noun or noun phrase) specifically indicates gender.

The use of "his" after such pronouns as *anyone* or *everybody* is an artificial construct of traditional grammarians, derived from early English grammarians who wrote the first grammars based on "logical" Latin. Guided by the "logic" of Latin, they concluded that since *-one* and *-body* are singular and since a male pronoun should encompass reference to all persons, *his* was the "logical" or "correct" choice.

Although grammarians have insisted that speakers use "his" for centuries, the tendency has been to use the plural pronoun form *their* and to avoid any reference to gender. In fact, in the last several decades, it has become generally unacceptable in American English to use the singular male pronoun after such words as *each, everyone, somebody*.

Following the rise of the feminist movement and the changes in the status of women in society, some modern grammarians, in response to the gender controversy have begun recommending the use of *he or she*, while others urge using plural nouns and pronouns in order to avoid the problem. Instead of *Everyone needs his book*, the sentence can be reworded as "all students need their books." Another strategy is the use of "a" instead of "his" as in: *Everyone needs a book*.

***What was the Purpose of this Discovery Activity and discussion?***

## Language and Change

This brief activity and discussion highlight the differences between how people actually express themselves and how language experts say they should. Moreover, even among so-called language experts there is not uniform agreement as to what is "correct" or acceptable. One reason for such controversy is the nature of language: It is a living, fluid entity that changes in response to changes in society.

Societal changes are reflected in language. For example, the change in women's status is reflected in changes in acceptable pronoun reference, as illustrated in Sentence (4) of Discovery Activity 1. Societal changes can also be seen in the new words adopted into the language. Think of the enormous number of new words related to computers and the Internet that have entered languages around the world. Language changes reflect the greater changes of a society.

Frequently, changes in grammatical use or even new word adoption are considered "degeneration" or "degradation" of the language with calls to avoid sloppiness and carelessness in language. George Orwell, author of *1984* and *Animal Farm* wrote:

> A man may take to drink because he feels himself to be a failure, and then fail all the more completely because he drinks. It is rather the same thing that is happening to the English language. It becomes ugly and inaccurate because our thoughts are foolish, but the slovenliness of our language makes it easier for us to have foolish thoughts.
> [Orwell, G. (1966/1953). Politics and the English language. In: *A collection of essays* (p. 156). New York: Harcourt Brace Jovanovich. Also available on line at: http://www.privateline.com/ Orwell/orwell.html]

In some countries there are even official language academies charged with maintaining the "purity" and "integrity" of the language. In France, for instance, L'Académie française has been the arbiter of the French language for several centuries. Upset by the increasingly Anglicization of French (i.e. the adoption of English words into French, particularly in the sciences and technology), the French government passed a law in the mid-1990s essentially outlawing the adoption of foreign words into French and requiring instead the use of newly-created or adapted French words.

Yet even with such an academy dictating proper usage, the French language spoken at the beginning of the 20th century is different from that spoken at the beginning of the 21st. A language that does not change does not have any living native speakers, as in the case of Latin or Sanskrit. Thus many argue that changes in language are an indicator of the viability and vitality, of that language.

While American English has no equivalent academy acting as "protector of the language," it does have manuals of style, language mavens, and others weighing in on the grammaticality of a form or the acceptability of new words and usage. However, since there is no single official arbiter of American English, there is often disagreement among "experts," particularly in areas that many regard as involving the finer or "more obscure" points of grammar.

Discovery Activity 2 will help expand our discussion of grammaticality.

---

**Discovery Activity 2: More Decisions on Grammaticality**

Look at the sentences below.

a. Based on your opinion, label each sentence as **G** for grammatical, **N** for non-grammatical, and **?** for "not sure" or "don't know".
b. For those sentences you labeled as **N**, identify the element or elements that you think are ungrammatical and explain why you think they are ungrammatical.
c. For those sentences you labeled as **?**, if you can, discuss why you are unsure.

1. _____ Jackie says she don't know if they can come.
2. _____ I'm not going to do nothing about that missing part.
3. _____ We sure don't have any problems with the phone company.
4. _____ Shoppers are used to standing on long lines at this store.

---

## Discussion: Discovery Activity 2

Before you look at the discussion, think about your initial reactions to each of these four sentences. Were any of your reactions different from your reactions to the sentences in Discovery Activity 1? If so, how and why? If you are a non-native speaker of English, ask a native speaker to complete this activity. Compare your responses. If they are different, think about why this might be so.

For many native speakers of American English, Sentences (1) and (2) represent forms of non-standard English are considered markers of low socioeconomic and/or marginalized social status. In other words, these are *stigmatized* language forms that are recognizable to the general population as "incorrect" American English, in both spoken and written forms. This is in contrast to the examples in Discovery

Activity 1, where even highly educated speakers produce such sentences, except in the most formal contexts.

Sentences (3) and (4), on the other hand, represent regional variations in the United States that speakers from other parts of the country find unusual or curious. Outside the New York City metropolitan area, most people stand *in line* and not *on line*. Outside most of the south, most speakers do not use *sure don't*. Neither Sentence (3) nor Sentence (4), however, carries the stigmatizing effect that Sentences (1) and (2) do.

Discovery Activity 2 illustrates some further differences in the concept of "grammar." On the one hand, there is something most users of a language recognize as a "standard." They may not be able to articulate all the rules and usages, but they can recognize what is and is not acceptable and can generally point to the reason why. For example, standard language users may not know the rule, "Use third person *–s* in singular present tense verbs," but they do know that "he or she" uses "doesn't" and not "don't." The difference between the sentences in Discovery Activity 1 and Discovery Activity 2 is that those in 2 are clearly recognized by the majority of users as "incorrect" English.

Teachers of ESL/EFL learners need to recognize that learners of English often produce sentences such as (1) and (2), not necessarily because they are speakers of non-standard English, but because they have not yet mastered the standard forms. Even if students have been consistently introduced to and practiced the standard forms, it generally takes a significant period of time to master these forms.

## Linguists and Grammar

Linguists have a very different approach to the notion of grammar. From the linguist's point of view, grammar is not a collection of rules, often obscure, arcane, and often illogical, that must be taught, but rather a set of blueprints that guide speakers in producing comprehensible and predictable language. Every language, including its dialects or variants, is systematic and orderly. Languages and their variations are rule-governed structures, and are therefore "grammatical." In other words, all languages consist of patterns, or "grammars," that make sense of the features of a given language that include the arbitrary symbols, sounds, and words that make up that language.

Consider the following string of words. How many sentences can you come up with using these words and only these words?

the, came, girl, baskets, home, with

Most native speakers, using only their intuitive knowledge of grammar, will come up with this sentence:

The girl came home with baskets.

Some native speakers may come up with this variation:

> The girl with baskets came home.

What they do is use grammar to put this seemingly random string of words into a comprehensible sentence. Any other combination of words would produce sentences that would sound strange to English speakers because they would not be grammatical; i.e. fit the blueprint of how words are combined in English to make sentences.

While this is true for native speakers, ESL/EFL learners need to learn explicitly which words fit together in a string according to the rules or patterns of English. For them, their intuitive knowledge is valid for their own native language, which uses patterns different from, and often contrary to, English.

## Language is Rule-Governed

### What does "rule-governed" mean?

This interpretation or definition of grammar is what is meant when linguists say languages are rule-governed, systematic, and organized or *grammatical*. Children, as part of the process of acquiring their native language, learn without formal instruction what belongs with what in order to form coherent, intelligible, and meaningful sentences. They learn the grammar of their language and with this grammar they can create an unlimited number of new and original sentences. Even when the sentence elements are new and unique, ones that native speakers have never before seen, they can use and adapt them according to the patterns of their language.

Consider this excerpt from *Jabberwocky* by Lewis Carroll:

> Beware the Jabberwock, my son!
> The jaws that bite, the claws that catch!
> Beware the Jubjub bird, and shun
> The frumious Bandersnatch!

The poem is famous for consisting of nonsense words mixed in with normal English words. What makes the poem so vivid and effective in many respects is the ability of the author to evoke images based on the grammatical knowledge of the native or highly proficient non-native speaker. *Jabberwock* for instance, is preceded by *the*, a word, called a definite article, that in English precedes a noun. Both that clue and the fact that *Jabberwock* is capitalized, tell us that this nonsense word is a noun, specifically a proper noun or a name noun similar to *Chicago* or *Italy*.

Now let's look at the word *Jubjub*. Like *Jabberwock,* this word is capitalized and preceded by *the*. However, we know intuitively that *Jubjub* does not have the same sentence function as *Jabberwock*. Why is this so?

After *Jubjub* we see the word *bird*. This is a word that we call a noun, specifically a noun that names a thing; in this case a thing that flies, has wings, and a beak. From the position of the word *Jubjub* before this noun *bird*, we know that

*Jubjub* is describing something about *bird*. Since *Jubjub* is written with a capital *J*, we can guess that it is telling us specifically what kind of bird is being referred to. In other words, *Jubjub* is functioning as an adjective before the noun *bird*. Because of its sentence position, *Jubjub* has a function similar to *Siberian* as in *Siberian tiger.*

Similarly, we can guess that *frumious* is another descriptive word, describing something about the proper noun *Bandersnatch*. The sentence position of *frumious* before *Bandersnatch* is one clue. A different type of clue telling us something about *frumious* is the ending *–ous*. This is an ending that is found in other words that describe nouns, such as *famous, gorgeous, voluptuous, egregious,* and *pretentious.*

Native and highly proficient non-native speakers of English can understand and appreciate this poem without ever before having seen such words as *Jabberwocky* or *frumious*, and without necessarily knowing what the terms *noun* or *adjective* mean because they know the grammar of English. The rules they are using to understand this poem are below their level of awareness. Few speakers, whether native or highly proficient non-native speakers, are conscious of which "grammar" rules they are applying or using to understand this poem.

Since languages differ in the types and applications of rules, however, ESL/EFL learners need to learn the new patterns of the language they are studying. They need to begin by becoming aware that there *are* differences in how languages are patterned, and then work toward the goal of being able to subconsciously produce the new language without explicit reference to rules.

In Discovery Activity 3 you will have the chance to see how much you know about English grammar.

---

**Discovery Activity 3: Follow-Up: Jabberwocky Excerpts**

Here are more excerpts from Lewis Carroll's *Jabberwocky*. Using the previous analysis as a starting point:

1. What conclusions can you draw about the italicized words?
2. Explain why you reached the conclusions you did.

> And, as in *uffish* thought he stood,
> The Jabberwock, with eyes of flame,
> Came whiffling through the *tulgey* wood,
> And burbled as it came!
>
> One two! One two! And through and through
> The *vorpal* blade went *snicker-snack!*

   [Carroll, L. (1871). *Through the looking glass and what alice found there.* Available on line at: http://www.jabberwocky.com/carroll/jabber/jabberwocky.html]

## Discussion: Discovery Activity 3

You may not have been able to explain exactly why you came to the conclusions you did regarding the different highlighted words in this activity; nevertheless, you were probably able to give some description as to the functions of the words. This ability is part of your knowledge of the underlying patterns, or grammar, of English.

Based on sentence position and endings, you probably concluded that *uffish*, *tulgey*, and *vorpal* are descriptive words (adjectives) describing the nouns following them. *–ish*, *-y*, and *–al* are common adjective endings. In Chapter 2 we will examine word endings in more detail.

| -ish | -y | -al |
|------|------|------|
| waspish | smelly | logical |
| smallish | rainy | biographical |
| standoffish | crazy | nautical |
| greenish | jumpy | educational |

Although *snicker-snack* is not recognizable as an adverb based on word ending, its sentence position identifies it as such. It comes after the verb *went* and is describing something about the verb. We can also say that the alliteration of the sounds of the word easily bring to mind a sound such as a sword might make.

## Language as a Set of Rules versus Language as Rule-Governed

Discovery Activity 3 demonstrates that there are two very different conceptions of *grammar*. There is one school of thought that views grammar as a collection of rules that must be learned in order to use language "correctly." Users of language who do not adhere to the rules are using an "inferior" or "sloppy" form of the language. The correct rules must often be learned and practiced, and may at times be contrary to what even educated native speakers use in formal language contexts. This is the **prescriptive** school of grammar.

There is another school that sees grammar as a blueprint of language. As a blueprint of language, grammar guides speakers in how to string together symbols, sounds, and words to make coherent, meaningful sentences. This type of grammar knowledge is intuitive and reflects the innate ability of speakers to learn and use their native language. Children, for instance, do not memorize rules as they learn to speak; what they actually learn are the rules or patterns governing their language. Grammar is what allows language users to create and understand an unlimited number of new and original sentences. Furthermore, no language has only one grammar; each language has subsets of grammar, which are generally referred to as dialects. These subsets are often considered substandard forms, yet they are also just as rule-governed as the standard variety. This is the **descriptive** school of thought. A more in-depth look at the two different schools of thought follows.

# Prescriptive versus Descriptive Grammar

*What are some examples of the differences between prescriptive and descriptive grammar?*

## Prescriptive Grammar

A key distinction between how linguists view grammar and how others do is the distinction between *prescriptive* and *descriptive* grammar. Prescriptive grammar is the grammar taught in school, discussed in newspaper and magazine columns on language, or mandated by language academies such as those found in Spain or France.

Prescriptive grammar attempts to tell people how they should say something, what words they should use, when they need to make a specific choice, and why they should do so—even if the rule itself goes against speakers' natural inclinations. At times, prescriptive grammar rules are overextended to the point that speakers *hypercorrect*, that is, they apply the grammatical rules in situations where they should not.

Take, for instance, the use of the pronouns *I* and *me*. For many years English teachers in the United States railed against the incorrect use of *me*, the object pronoun, in subject position as in:

(1)  **Me** and John are going to the store.
     *or*
     John and **me** are going to the store
(2)  **Me** and Sue had lunch.
     *or*
     Sue and **me** had lunch.

There is a prescriptive grammar rule in English specifying that pronouns in subject position must be subject pronouns (*I, you, we, he, she, it, they*). According to this rule, speakers' use of *me* in (1) and (2) is incorrect because *me* is actually the first person *object* pronoun. In addition, the subject pronoun *I* should follow any other noun subject or subject pronoun. Thus, from a prescriptive point of view, Sentences (1) and (2) must be:

(1a) John and **I** are going to the store.
(2a) Sue and **I** had lunch.

In the last several decades, many native speakers, attempting to avoid the incorrect use of *me* tend to hypercorrect the use of *me* by substituting *I*, even in cases where *me* is called for because it is in object position. Consider the following samples of actual speech:

(3) They couldn't have raised all the necessary funding without input *from* **John** and **I**, even coming in at the last minute as we did.

**John** and **I** are objects of the preposition *from*. The prescriptive grammar rule requires the use of *me* and not *I*.

(4) He really shouldn't have been put into that class, but *between* **you** and **I**, the principal didn't have any other choice.

**You** and **I** are the objects of the preposition *between* and again, as in Sentence (3), and *me* rather than *I* must be used.

(5) The driver gave **the boys and I** good directions on how to find the back entrance to the restaurant.

**The boys and I** are the objects of the verb *give*. As in Sentences (3) and (4), *me* is the correct choice and not *I*.

What we see in Sentences (1) through (5) is a difference in *prescriptive* grammar rules and *descriptive* grammar rules. Prescriptive rules (sometimes referred to as usage rules) are those rules that explain what users of a language are *supposed* to do. These are often the rules that:

- are explicitly taught and learned in formal school settings.
- often require conscious effort to remember and apply.
- are often learned incompletely or insufficiently, leading to hypercorrection as in Examples (3), (4), and (5).

Change is vital to a living language. As the substitution of *I* for *me* in the object position becomes increasingly widespread, it may well become an accepted language form in the future, except perhaps for the most formal of contexts.

## Who versus whom

*How is the difference between* **who** *and* **whom** *related to prescriptive grammar versus descriptive grammar?*

An example of a change that has become more widespread and accepted is the loss of the distinction between *who* and *whom*. Most native speakers of English do not make this distinction consistently. A prescriptive grammar rule maintains that *whom* is the object form of *who* as in:

(6) The author, **whom** I met last year, signed several copies of the text.
(7) *For* **Whom** *the Bell Tolls* was written in 1940 by Earnest Hemingway.

In Sentence (6), *whom* is the object of the verb *met*. In Sentence (7), it is the object of the preposition *for*.

For many, if not most speakers of American English, the rules governing the use of *whom* seem bothersome, and require attention and effort as the form is generally not used in informal speech and is essentially reserved for formal edited writing. In spoken and written English, native speakers commonly produce such sentences as:

(8)  **Who** did you see last night at the movies?
(9)  The person **who** you really need to talk to is not here right now.

From the perspective of prescriptive grammar, the correct form in Sentences (8) and (9) is *whom*, not *who*. In both sentences *whom* is functioning as an object and not as a subject. In Sentence (8), *who* is the object of the verb *see* and in Sentence (9), *who* is the object of *you really need to talk to*.

Thus, from a prescriptive perspective, these sentences should be:

(8a)  **Whom** did you see last night at the movies?
(9a)  The person to **whom** you really need to talk is not here right now.

The distinction between *who* and *whom* is a prescriptive grammar rule requiring conscious attention and effort which is often incompletely applied. Thus, language users, in an effort to use "correct" grammar produce sentences such as:

(10)  (waitress to customer): **Whom** ordered the steak rare?
(11)  The references of all applicants **whom** will be walking clients' dogs will be checked.

In both sentences, the correct form is *who*, not *whom*. In Sentence (10), *Who* it is the subject of the verb *ordered*. In Sentence (11), it is the subject of *will be walking*.

Learners of English who have begun their study of the language in their home countries are often more aware of the difference in use between *who* and *whom* because their instruction has been more prescriptive. Also, since their exposure is frequently limited to classroom instruction, they may have had less exposure to more informal forms of English.

### *How much emphasis needs to be placed on the distinction between who and whom in the ESL/EFL classroom?*

There are several factors to consider in answering this question. For example, are the students preparing to take certain exams that test knowledge of prescriptive rules? If the answer is yes, then the ESL/EFL teachers must place more emphasis on this distinction than if the answer is no.

Additionally, how much does not observing this distinction between *who* and *whom* interfere with understanding? Since native speakers routinely do not observe this distinction, the answer is very little. As we will see in later chapters, there are more serious learning issues that do interfere with comprehension on which ESL/EFL teachers need to focus.

## *Descriptive Grammar*

Descriptive grammar rules, in contrast to prescriptive rules, describe how adult native speakers actually use their language. From this perspective, grammar is what organizes language into meaningful, systematic patterns. These rules are inherent to each language and are generally not conscious rules. However, they are readily observable for those interested in looking. Descriptive grammar, unlike prescriptive grammar, does not say, "this is right" or "this is wrong."

Some people think that descriptive grammar means saying that everything is right and nothing is wrong. What we must consider is the purpose for which a speaker is using language. If a person is at a white-collar job interview or sending in a college application, using stigmatized language forms is inappropriate. On the other hand, if the person is among a group of peers, using a different variety of language is part of in-group acceptance and identity. This is not to say that there should be no grammar rulebooks, manuals of style, or standards of usage; on the contrary, there is a need for standards, especially in formal language contexts and when we are teaching English to non-native speakers. What ESL/EFL teachers must do is develop an awareness, especially as learners become more proficient, that there are variations of prescriptive grammar rules, some of which are more acceptable in certain contexts than others.

### *Why do I as an ESL/EFL teacher need to know the difference between prescriptive and descriptive grammar?*

ESL/EFL teachers need to understand what learners need to know in order to learn English. The needs of these learners are very different from those of native speakers. Native speakers and textbooks geared to them focus on prescriptive grammar. ESL/EFL learners, on the other hand, need to learn structures and forms that native speakers know as part of their innate knowledge of English. The vast majority of what ESL/EFL learners need to learn is descriptive grammar. ESL/EFL teachers must also consider why students are learning the language, which errors are more serious than others, and on which aspects of grammar to focus. In this text we will be focusing on the grammatical rules and grammatical structures that ESL/EFL learners need to learn in order to communicate in English.

### *Why do I need to know grammar?*

For teachers of ESL/EFL learners, a knowledge of how English works is essential. Teachers need to be able to talk about how sentences are constructed, about the types of words and word groups that make up sentences, and about the functions of these words and word groups within sentences and in larger contexts.

With this knowledge, teachers can help their students understand the language and know what their students need to learn in order to acquire it. Without knowing the essential components, as well as the complexities of the language in question, it is difficult to understand what learners actually need to know in order to learn the new language.

### What do you mean by the "complexities of language?"

The next two Discovery Activities introduce a few of the structures and forms that we will discuss in greater detail throughout the book. These are examples of the "complexities" that native speakers know intuitively, yet that ESL/EFL learners need to learn explicitly. After you have finished Discovery Activity 4, check your answers with those found at the end of the chapter in the section labeled "Answer Key."

---

**Discovery Activity 4: Verbs**

Look at the following sentences.

a. Find the verbs and underline them.
b. How would you explain these verbs in these sentences to a learner of English?

1. Many people don't like meat.
2. Do you drive to New York?
3. She's lived in the country since last year.
4. I'm about to buy a new car.
5. The flight is leaving in the next 20 minutes.

---

After you have checked your answers to Discovery Activity 4, try Discovery Activity 5. Think about how you would explain the italicized words to an ESL/EFL student. Discuss your answers with your classmates; then compare your responses with those found in the Answer Key. This will then conclude our introduction to grammar.

---

**Discovery Activity 5: Other Parts of Speech**

Look at the following sentences.
How would you explain the italicized words in these sentences to a learner of English?

1. The child painted a *big, beautiful, wooden* box. *but not*:
   The child painted a *wooden beautiful big* box.
2. *The* pencil I have doesn't have *an* eraser.
3. That is a *stone* fence.
4. Mary drove *fast* but stopped *quickly* at the red light.

---

# Summary

| Linguists versus Grammarians | |
|---|---|
| **A linguist's definition of grammar is** | **A grammarian's definition of grammar is** |
| • a system or the "blueprints" for creating language | • the written rules governing when to use which forms or structures |
| • the shared rules (patterns) in native speakers' minds that allow them to generate unique utterances; native speakers' shared mental rules | • something you follow in order to use the language correctly |
| • there are different grammars shared by different groups of speakers; because all languages and variations are systematic in their generation of utterances; all grammars are viewed as valid | • that one particular variety of grammar is considered the "standard" |
| • descriptive | • prescriptive |

| **A linguist's purpose in examining grammar is to** | **A grammarian's purpose in examining grammar is to** |
|---|---|
| • understand the mental or subconscious rules shared by different groups of native speakers. These rules are learned as part of the process of growing up as a native speaker of a given language. | • focus on discrete items and specific rules of use ("usage rules"). |
| • describe the system and blueprints. | • determine what word, phrase or construction is or is not correct according to a particular usage or style book, or person (usually self-appointed "language mavens" or "language gurus"). |
| • understand the shared elements (rules) that make variations still belong to one language versus another different language; i.e. what makes English not German or Chinese. | |
| • learn which variations are used by which groups and in which situations. | • determine grammar "rules" which must often be taught. These rules often exist on a continuum of acceptability because language changes and some usage or style books, or language gurus are more reluctant to accept change than others. |
| • understand which variations are less-acceptable or stigmatized in which situations and why. | • debate what must be used when and why based on what a particular usage or style book, or person determines is correct. |
| • learn which changes are taking place and why. | |

| Standard American English |
|---|
| • is that which most style and usage books and speakers recognize as "correct." There is no language academy or formal government institution decreeing or legislating "correctness" for American English. |
| • exists on a continuum of "correctness." Not all style and usage books, and not all "language gurus" agree on what is "correct" because language changes. Some grammarians are slower to accept change than others. |

(continued)

---
**Standard American English**
---

- Only languages that no longer have native speakers do not change. These are referred to as "dead" languages. Examples of this are Latin and Sanskrit.
- The English that is taught to non-native speakers is recognized as Standard English because the grammar, for the most part, reflects formally educated native speakers' shared rules.

---

## Practice Activities

### *Activity 1: New Words*

Many new words have entered the English language in the last decade. Can you find at least 5 and discuss how they entered the language and whether they are considered standard or slang words. For example, *Internet* and *to boot up* have recently entered the English language to describe computer use.

As another example, the popular Harry Potter series by J.K. Rowlings has made *muggle* a commonly accepted term designating ordinary people without special magical powers. Although there was such a word in the English language prior to the publication of the first Harry Potter book, it was an obscure term with very different meanings. The new and popular meaning of *muggle* has come about through literary means.

### *Activity 2: Language Intuition*

1. Look at the following list of nonsense words and English words. On a separate sheet of paper, create 5 original sentences using only these words but all of these words in each sentence.

    mishiffen a drinking keg gwisers some were stoshly frionized

2. Ask at least 2 other people to make up 1–2 sentences using these words.

    - They must use all of the words in each sentence.
    - When they finish writing the sentences, ask them if they can tell you why they wrote the sentences as they did.

3. Compare your sentences with those you collected from your informants.

    - How many sentences were the same?
    - How many were different?
    - Were there any sentences that surprised you or that you found unusual? Why or why not?

4. Bring your sentences, the sentences your informants wrote, and their comments to class. Compare these with those other classmates gathered.

5. What insights did you gain into the idea of "language as a system" or "language as a set of blueprints?"

## Activity 3: Nouns

Look at the following sentence.

> Some mishiffen gwisers were stoshly drinking a frionized keg.

a. Which two words refer to things (nouns)?
b. What clues are there to help you decide which words refer to things (nouns)?
c. Which words do you think are describing the things (nouns) in this sentence?

## Activity 4: Prescriptive Grammar

1. On a separate sheet of paper, write 5–10 sentences you consider to be "incorrect" grammar, for example, using *ain't* instead of *isn't* as in *She ain't on time*.

   a. Share this list with at least 3 other native or near-native speakers of English.
   b. Ask them to tell you which sentences they find incorrect and why.
   c. Bring the results to class, discuss how your informants' evaluations compared to your own, and why.

2. Compare your list and those of your classmates.

   • Do they list errors different than errors such as Sentences (a), (b), and (c) below made by ESL/EFL learners Discuss why or why not.

   a. She no like pancakes.
   b. She go when?
   c. She move to farm last year.

## Activity 5: Gender and Pronoun References

Write a reflective essay on the following situation. Use the questions below to guide your thoughts.

As a teacher you have conscientiously taught the use of the singular male possessive pronoun in such sentences as **Everyone** *needs to bring* **his** *book to class tomorrow* or **Anyone** *who wants* **his** *grades can come to my office on Friday.* Several students come to you with the situations below:

• Student A was watching a movie. The student notices that everyone in the movie said such phrases as **Someone** *has to share* **their** *room* or **no one** *goes out without paying* **their** *parents* and asks you why they are using these forms.

- Student B shows you some pages from an English novel. In one part the author has written *If **each** and **every** person had **his** way, there would be chaos.* In another part the same author has written: *Her mother called, "**Someone** has left **their** bag at our house."*

1. How do you explain the differences to them? Consider the differences between prescriptive and descriptive grammar. Take into consideration any standardized testing these students might be taking.
2. How might you deal with issues related to prescriptive versus descriptive grammar?
3. What differences, if any, do you see in addressing this issue when teaching ESL/EFL learners vs. native speakers?
4. What changes (if any) would you make in your teaching? Justify your decision.

## Answer Key: Chapter 1 Discovery Activities

### *Discussion: Discovery Activity 4*

1. Many people *don't like* meat.

   In English, to form a present tense negative sentence, we need to use what is commonly called an *auxiliary* or *helping* verb, or *do*. (See Chapter 5). In many languages, in contrast, the negative is formed by simply adding a negative word:

   |          | affirmative                    | Negative                           |
   |----------|--------------------------------|------------------------------------|
   | Spanish  | Tú caminas. (You walk)         | Tú **no** caminas. (You do not walk.) |
   | German   | Ich laufe. (I walk)            | Ich laufe **nicht.** (I do not walk.) |
   | Chinese  | Ni xi huan. (You like it)      | Ni **bu** xi huan. (You do not like it.) |

2. *Do* you *drive* to New York?

   In English, to form a question in present tense, we need to use what is commonly called an *auxiliary* or *helping* verb or *do*. (See Chapter 5). In many languages questions are formed by inverting the subject and the verb:

   |          | affirmative                 | question                      |
   |----------|-----------------------------|-------------------------------|
   | Spanish  | Tú caminas. (You walk).     | Caminas tú? (Do you walk?)    |
   | German   | Du sitzt. (You sit).        | Sitzt du? (Do you sit?)       |

   In other languages, a word is added at the end of a sentence to indicate that it is a question:

   |          | affirmative                | question                           |
   |----------|----------------------------|------------------------------------|
   | Chinese  | Ni xi huan. (You like it.) | Ni xi huan **ma**? (Do you like it?) |

3. She*'s lived* in the country since last year.

She's **lived** is a contraction for *she has lived*. This is a verb form that refers to indefinite time or time in the recent past. We will see exactly what this means in Chapter 6 when we examine time, tense, and aspect.

4. I'*m* about to buy a new car.

Compare these two sentences:

    (a) I am hot.
    (b) I am about to leave.

If you ask yourself whether the verb *am* in Sentence (a) refers to the same time as the verb *am* in Sentence (b), you will note that it doesn't. The time referred to in the two sentences is different because of the phrase *about to*. This phrase changes the time of present tense *am* to indicate that an immediate future action is taking place. (See Chapter 5).

5. The flight *is leaving* in the next 20 minutes.

Normally we would say that *is leaving* refers to something happening now. However, as in Sentence (4), the addition of a phrase, *in the next 20 minutes,* changes the time reference to the immediate future. (See Chapter 6).

## *Discussion: Discovery Activity 5*

1. The child painted a *big, beautiful, wooden* box.

Adjectives (descriptive words) follow a certain order when there is more than one. Saying *The child painted a wooden, beautiful, big box* sounds awkward to native and highly proficient native speakers because it does not follow normal English word order for multiple adjectives. (See Chapter 4).

2. *The* pencil I have doesn't have *an* eraser.

*The* and *an* are used before nouns. *The* refers to a specific object; *an* refers to an unspecified object and is used before a vowel sound as in *eraser, orange, ink, apple.*

Many languages do not have determiners; thus, ESL/EFL learners whose native languages do not have determiners experience difficulties both in remembering to use *the* and *a/n* and in choosing between *the* and *a/n*.

3. That is a *stone* fence.

In English we often use two nouns together. The first noun describes something about the second noun. We can say *stone fence, wooden fence, iron fence, garden fence* and each time describe a different type of fence. (See Chapter 3).

4. Mary stopped *quickly* at the red light.

*Quickly* describes the action word (verb) in the sentence. Such words are generally labeled adverbs (See Chapter 4). *Quickly* belongs to the subcategory of adverbs often called "manner adverbs" because they describe how something is done. They often, but not always, end in *–ly*:

happily    angrily    jokingly    sadly    loudly

*Fast* is an example of a manner adverb that does not end in *–ly*. Less proficient ESL/EFL learners find it confusing that we can say *Mary stopped quickly,* but not *\*Mary stopped fastly*. *Fast* is also an example of a word that has the same form as an adjective and as an adverb (See Chapter 4).

# Chapter 2
# Morphology

## Words and Their Parts

## Introduction

Chapter 2 is divided into two sections. Section 1 focuses on word classes and includes a brief introduction to some of the basic parts of speech to aid in our discussion of the next section. Section 2 focuses on morphology, which is the structure and form of words.

## Section 1: Word Classes

For many people, words are the center of language. This comes as no surprise if we consider that the most obvious, concrete and recognizable parts of any language are its words or its *lexicon*. In any given language there are tens of thousands of words, although most speakers will know and use only a relatively small number of them.

A primary concern of grammarians is the classification of words into groups or categories. Traditional English grammar, based on Latin, adopted terminology and classification systems that often do not reflect the actual grammar of English. However, in order to discuss the different elements and structures of English, we need to employ some sort of terminology, so we continue to use the traditional labels and classification systems which have their usefulness in that they provide a common vocabulary for discussing the words of language. For example, you have probably learned that different words are classified into *parts of speech* and many grammar texts still use this classification.

However, many grammar texts prefer to think of parts of speech in terms of *form* and *structure* classes. The form classes are composed of the major parts of speech: nouns, verbs, adjectives, and adverbs. These are the words that carry the content or meaning of a sentence. The structure class words are composed of the minor parts of speech: prepositions, pronouns, determiners, conjunctions, qualifiers and other subsets. These structure words generally accompany specific form classes. For example, determiners, or articles, such as *the* or *a/an* typically occur before a noun such as *dog, bed, battle*.

A. DeCapua, *Grammar for Teachers*,
© Springer 2008

Try Discovery Activity 1 to see how much you know about the different word classes (or parts of speech), even if you are not always sure of the labels.

---

**Discovery Activity 1: Introduction to Parts of Speech**

Look at the following words.

> system in big communicate between confidentiality relevant obey under shatter blizzard warn weary beside rebellion happy

1. On a separate sheet of paper, make 4 columns. Label these columns **Group A, Group B, Group C** and **Group D** as you see below.
2. Without using a dictionary or any other reference tool, try to place the different words that you think belong together in the different columns. The first four words have already been done for you as a sample.
3. After you have categorized as many words together as you can, explain why you grouped them as you did.

| Group A | Group B | Group C | Group D |
|---------|---------|---------|-------------|
| system  | in      | big     | communicate |

4. Now take your paper and make two new columns, **Group A** and **Group B.**
5. Using the new list of words below, try to place the different words that you think belong together in the different columns. There are just two groups this time.

- As you group this new list of words, consider whether any of the words can belong to more than one group. Try to explain why or why not.

> harm remind cancer cup scream date struggle queen poison announce style write

---

## Discussion: Discovery Activity 1

Your grouping of the words in the first list probably looks like this:

| Group A | Group B | Group C | Group D |
|-----------------|---------|----------|-------------|
| system          | in      | big      | communicate |
| confidentiality | between | relevant | obey        |
| rebellion       | under   | weary    | shatter     |
| blizzard        | beside  | happy    | warn        |

Each of these four groups represents a word class. Even without knowing the labels for each group, you should have been able to place the words in the list together with other words performing the same function. Group A consists of *nouns*; Group B consists of *prepositions*; Group C of *adjectives*; and Group D of *verbs*.

Your grouping of the words in the second list should look like this:

| Group A | Group B |
| --- | --- |
| harm | harm |
| | remind |
| cancer | |
| cup | cup |
| scream | scream |
| date | date |
| struggle | struggle |
| queen | |
| poison | poison |
| | announce |
| style | style |
| | write |

Here Groups A and B again represent different word classes. Group A represents words that are verbs and Group B words that are nouns. Some of the words fit into both groups; for example *harm* can be either a verb or a noun. You can *harm* (verb) someone or you can suffer *harm* (noun).

While you may recognize that a word can fit into more than one group, you may not be able to do so without thinking of a sentence or *context* for that particular word. In English, the group or class to which a word belongs is not always obvious without context, as you were most likely aware of when doing Discovery Activity 1.

Unlike many other languages, English does not always rely on word endings or word forms to determine part of speech. The form of a word in English does not necessarily tell us the function of that word. However, context and sentence position are key to clarifying the function of a word or phrase in English because word order is highly fixed. As we saw in Chapter 1, words need to be placed in a certain order. This helps us to understand their function and meaning. These are two central themes we will revisit throughout this text: Form in English does not necessarily equal function; and, word order is fixed, meaning that words in English have to occur in a particular sequence.

## Context and Function

### *How are the sentence position of a word and its function related?*

As the *Jabberwocky* activities and discussion in Chapter 1 illustrated, the sentence position of some of the nonsense words told you their function. The context let you guess what word class some of these words belonged to.

The following sentences illustrate again the importance of context in assigning function and/or class. In both sentences you can see that the same word appearing in different contexts has a different function:

(1) She made a **wish** on a star.
(2) They **wish** to learn more about effective research practices.

In Sentence (1), *wish* is a noun, while in Sentence (2), *wish* is a verb. In subsequent chapters we will be analyzing the clues that help us decide which function words have in different contexts.

## Word Plays and Context: An Additional Illustration

Newspaper headlines are famous for using short, catchy phrases with words that have different meanings depending on context. A reader's attention is caught by the headlines, which often play on the different meanings of words. The actual meanings only become clear after reading the articles themselves.

### Discovery Activity 2: News Headlines

- Look at the newspaper headlines.
- Underline the words you find ambiguous, i.e. have more than one meaning.
- Explain what these different meanings are.

1. City Fires Director for New Look
2. Kidnapped Child Found by Tree
3. British Left Waffles on Gibraltar
4. EMT Helps Raccoon Bite Victim
5. Kids Make Nutritious Snacks

## Discussion: Discovery Activity 2

In order to see the double meanings implied by the headlines, consider the questions below: How you answer determines what words you might want to insert to clarify the exact meaning.

1. Who has the "new look"? The director or some thing or place in the city?

   - If the director has a "new look," perhaps you want to write: City Fires Director for *His* New Look.
   - If the city is meant to have a "new look," e.g. be revitalized, perhaps you would write: City Fires Director *in Order to Get a* New Look.

2. Can a tree find a child or is the reference to the place where the child was found?

   - Since it is unlikely that a tree can find a child, you may want to choose to re-write the sentence as: Kidnapped Child Found *Sitting* by Tree.

3. Did the British leave an edible food item or are the leftists indecisive?

   - In this case the writer is probably referring to the verb form of *waffles*.
   - In order to convey the verb form meaning, you could re-write the headline along these lines: British Left Waffles on Gibraltar *Decision,* or British Left Waffles on *Decision* About Gibraltar.

4. Did EMT personnel help the raccoon or the victim?

- Similar to #2, it is unlikely that the medical personnel helped a raccoon bite its victim. You might like to re-write the headline this way: EMT Helps Victim *Bitten by* Raccoon or *Raccoon Bite Victim helped by EMT.*

5. Are the kids the snack or do they prepare them?

- As in #s 2 & 3, the writer is not likely to be equating children with good things to eat; therefore, you may want to choose an alternative verb for make: Kids *Prepare* Nutritious Snacks.

The writers of these headlines have deliberately played on the different meanings of the words to create humorous, attention-getting titles by omitting important words. The actual meanings are within the articles, which provide the context for the correct meanings.

### *Tell me again why I need to focus on context with my ESL/EFL learners? Shouldn't I just focus on their mastering a form and then worry about context?*

Teachers need to be aware of what learners need to know about a language and why they need to know it. Reflect again on our discussion in Chapter 1 of native speakers' innate knowledge of grammar and Discovery Activity 1 of this chapter. Context lets native and near-native speakers "know" the function of a word without necessarily knowing *how* they know it or without knowing *the labels* for what they know. ESL/EFL learners, on the other hand, don't have this type of knowledge because they are *learners* of English.

As Discovery Activity 2 highlighted, context is critical in determining meaning. Whether "left" refers to the past tense of "leave" or to the term describing political persuasion becomes clear only in the reading of the text. Words without context can be difficult to understand. Similarly grammar taught without context may have little meaning for ESL/EFL learners.

Isolated grammar rules with isolated sentences may be necessary at very low levels of English proficiency to introduce learners to a particular form. However, ESL/EFL learners need to use forms and structures in meaningful and relevant contexts as often as possible.

The next Discovery Activity highlights again the importance of context in understanding meaning and function.

### Discovery Activity 3: Context

Look at the following pairs of sentences.

- Think about how context alters the function and meaning of the words in each pair.
- Consider how in English form is not equal to function. Use the questions below to help you.

I.   a)   I **practice** my **talk** every morning.
     b)   I **talk** every morning before the **practice**.
II.  c)   I **present** many speeches.
     d)   I gave her a nice **present**.
     e)   The students are all **present.**

1. Are the two words, **practice** and **talk,** the same in sentences (a) and (b)?
2. What differences and similarities are there between **practice** and **talk** in sentences (a) and (b)

   • How are they similar?
   • How are they different? Do they have the same function in both sentences?
   • Do they have the same form? Why or why not?

3. How do **practice** and **talk** differ in the two sentences?
4. What differences and similarities are there between **present** in Sentences (c), (d) and (e)?

   • Does **present** have the same function in both sentences?
   • Does it have the same form? Why or why not?

## *Discussion: Discovery Activity 3*

The purpose of this activity is to highlight the importance of context in understanding the meanings and functions of individual words. Words that look the same may have different meanings and functions depending upon where they occur in a sentence.

• In Sentence (a), **practice** is an action word (verb) referring to what *I* (the subject) is doing. **Talk** refers to a "thing" (noun).
• In Sentence (b), the opposite is true. **Talk** is an action word (verb) referring to what *I* (the subject) is doing. **Practice** refers to a "thing" (noun).
• In Sentence (c), **present** is an action word (verb) referring to what *I* (the subject) is doing.
• In Sentence (d), **present** refers to a thing (noun).
• In Sentence (e), **present** is describing something about *the students*. It is being used as an adjective.

In spoken English, there is a difference between **present** in Sentence (c). The action word **present** in Sentence (c) is accented on the second syllable: pre sent′. **Present** in Sentences (d) and (e) is accented on the first syllable: pre′ sent. There is also a phonological shift that ESL/EFL learners need to be aware of. The "s" of *present* has a "z" sound when functioning as a verb and an "s" sound when functioning as a noun or adjective.

The next part of the chapter will introduce the parts of speech. Different chapters will explore these parts of speech or word classes in greater depth.

## Parts of Speech or Lexical Categories

As we mentioned earlier, English words fall into two main categories: form class words, which include the major word classes, and structure class words, which include the minor word classes.

The **major** category is the larger of the two categories. This category consists of the word classes commonly labeled nouns, verbs, adjectives, and adverbs (although not all linguists agree that adverbs belong in the major category). These major word classes are comprised of the words that carry the content or essential meaning of an utterance. They are often referred to as **content** or **form** words.

The **minor** category includes the minor word classes generally known as prepositions, pronouns, conjunctions, and determiners. These words serve primarily to indicate grammatical relationships and are frequently referred to as **structure** words.

Take a look at the following sentence:

(3) **Victoria ate** a **banana** at the **table**.

This sentence consists of seven words: four content words and three structure words. If you saw only **Victoria, ate, banana, table,** you could probably make an accurate guess as to the sentence's intended meaning because these four content words are crucial for conveying sentence meaning.

The three structure words, *a, at,* and *the* show the grammatical relationships of the content words; *a* before *banana* tells us Victoria ate one thing, *at* tells us where Victoria ate the banana, and *the* specifies the thing, namely a specific table.

The minor category includes fewer words than the major category, as we will see in the next section. However, the structure words that comprise the minor category, are more difficult for ESL/EFL learners to master. Note that the structure words are more limited in number than the form words, but it is the structure words which cause more difficulties for ESL/EFL learners.

## *Open Word Classes*

The major category is vast. It is so large because we frequently create new English words. Thus, the major word or form classes are called *open classes* because new words enter the language constantly. English is a language that readily borrows and invents new words, which generally enter the language as nouns, verbs, or adjectives.

*How do new words enter the English language?*

Often new words enter via informal language (slang or jargon) and with increased use become accepted into standard English.

(4) The girls **dissed** Ashley during lunch.
(5) People like to include **emoticons** in their e-mails.

The verb **dis** (or diss), meaning to make fun of, show disrespect to, or disobey, is used primarily in informal speech. It is a shortened form of "disrespect" and has come into standard American English from African-American English via rap music.

Let's take another example. **Emoticons** refer to the icons used to display emotions in computer communications. The original emoticons consisted of keyboard characters such as :-) for happy or :-( for sad, but now also include ASCII glyphs. It is an invented word that combines the *emot* of *emotion* with the word *icon*.

Technology is a common source of new vocabulary. Words such as *mouse, surf, e-mail,* and *blog* are other examples of words that have taken on new meanings or been invented in relation to the computer.

---

### Discovery Activity 4: To Word is Human

There are many new words that have entered the English language.
Look at the list below of words that have entered English in the last 50 years or so.

1. How many of these words do you recognize?
2. For those words you recognize, explain where you have seen and/or heard them.
3. How comfortable do you feel using each word? Explain.

(a) blading
(b) go postal
(c) spam
(d) televangelist
(e) cassette
(f) microwave
(g) to Google or to google

---

## Discussion: Discovery Activity 4

(a) blading: This is a shortened version of "rollerblading," itself a new word that came into English with the invention of rollerblades. It falls into the same group of words and follows the same grammatical rules and formation as other such words referring to sports activities: *go blading, go swimming, go riding, go fishing.*

(b) go postal: The phrase originated in the 1990s when there were several instances of disgruntled United States postal workers shooting fellow employees. It has taken on the meaning of becoming violent or going berserk, the latter itself a borrowed expression first entering standard English in the early 1800s.

(c) spam: Originally a proprietary name registered by Geo. A. Hormel & Co. in the late 1930s to refer to a canned meat product, the meaning expanded to include Internet junk mail in the 1990s.

(d) televangelist: Derived from *tel* + *evangelist* to mean an evangelist holding religious broadcasts via television, which became popular starting in the early 1970s.

(e) cassette: First used in the early 1960s to refer to a small flat closed case with two reels and a length of magnetic tape.

(f) microwave: Although the term entered the language in the early 1930s, it came into common use in the mid-1960s/early 1970s as microwave cooking became popular.

(g) to Google/google: In the late 1990s a new search engine, Google, was developed and quickly became one of the largest and most popular search engines on the web. The name is sometimes used as a verb, "to google" meaning "to search the web." "To Google" is an example of a proper noun (the name of something) becoming a verb. Although generally written with a capital "G," we also see it written with a small "g."

One thing you may have noticed in doing this activity is that there are many common words that speakers may not recognize as being "new." Second, new words are not necessarily always "informal" or "slang." Finally, words can take on new meanings to meet the evolving needs of language users.

## Closed Word Classes

The second category, which consists of the minor or structure word class words, are referred to as closed word classes. These classes are considered "closed" for several reasons. First, they consist of small numbers of words that change very little over long periods of time and have been in the English language for centuries. Despite the fixed number of structure words, it is these words, along with the inflectional morphemes, that cause the most learner difficulties.

Structure words are among the most common and frequently used English words. They include:

- prepositions (e.g. *in, on, at, of, from*),
- determiners (e.g. *a, an, the, this, that, these, those*);

- coordinator (e.g. *and, but, or*)
- pronouns (e.g. *it, his, you, them, mine, herself*)[1]

Second, words in the closed classes are fixed and invariant which means they do not have other forms. There is only one form for the preposition *in*. In contrast, a noun, which is an open class word, can be plural or singular (e.g. *dog* or *dogs*).

Third, these words occur only in a narrow range of possible positions within a sentence and they must always accompany content words. There is no flexibility in word order. *The* must always precede a noun. It cannot follow a noun. We cannot choose to say *dog the* but must say *the dog*.

Finally, closed word classes have little lexical or semantic function. The job of these words is to establish logical relationships between the different parts of sentences.

### *What does "to show logical relationships in a sentence" mean?*

For example, if we say, *I went **to** the store* this sentence has a different meaning than if we say, *I went **by** the store*. The only difference between the two sentences is the change of prepositions from *to* to *by*, but it is these words which indicate a difference in the relationship between *I went* and *the store*.

Because English depends on word order to show grammatical relationships, these structure words are essential sentence elements. Discovery Activity 5 further illustrates how prepositions function to signal grammatical relationships.

---

**Discovery Activity 5: Prepositions and Grammatical Relationships**

The following pairs of headlines have different meanings.

1. Explain how the inclusion or omission of a preposition changes the meaning of each pair of sentences.
2. Discuss what this tells us about prepositions and grammatical relationships.

*Political Headlines:*

   (1a) Iraqi Head Seeks Arms
   (1b) Head of Iraq Seeks Arms

*Agriculture Headlines:*

   (2a) Angry Bull Injures Farmer with Axe
   (2b) Angry Bull Injures Farmer Axe

---

[1] See Appendix E for more complete lists.

*Headline News*:

    (3a) Man Struck by Speeding Car
    (3b) Man Struck Speeding Car

*Local News:*

    (4a) Police Help Fire Chief
    (4b) Police Help to Fire Chief

## Discussion: Discovery Activity 5

(1a) One part of a body in search of other body parts!
(1b) The political leader trying to buy weapons.
(2a) The farmer was in possession of an axe. (A quick reading could also lead one to read the headline as the bull having the axe.)
(2b) The farmer's family name is "Axe."
(3a) The car hit the man
(3b) The man hit the car
(4a) The police assist the fire chief
(4b) The police aided in the dismissal of the fire chief from his job.

As you saw in Discovery Activity 5, the addition or deletion of a preposition in the headlines in alters the meaning. The activity illustrates the importance of the role of structure words in establishing grammatical relationships. This role grows even more important as the complexity of the discourse increases. For ESL/EFL learners, some of the structure word classes can be among the most difficult to master.

    We will now continue with a look at the traditional parts of speech that make up the major word category.

## Overview: Major Parts of Speech

The next section is a brief overview of the major parts of speech comprising the major word category and provides the basis for our discussion on morphology.

## *Nouns*

The traditional or standard definition of a noun is a word that refers to *a person, place,* or *thing.* On the surface, this definition has merit. We can easily come up with words that fit this definition of a noun:

| Person  | Place    | Thing  |
|---------|----------|--------|
| boy     | city     | car    |
| teacher | school   | lesson |
| pilot   | airport  | wheel  |
| nurse   | hospital | bed    |
| swimmer | beach    | towel  |

If we expand *thing* to include two subcategories, tangible or (concrete) and intangible (or abstract) things, the list expands quickly:

| Tangible | Intangible  |
|----------|-------------|
| car      | philosophy  |
| wood     | adolescence |
| water    | justice     |
| horse    | anger       |
| medicine | suggestion  |

We can also differentiate another subcategory, that of proper nouns. Proper nouns are those nouns that name a person, place, or thing, and that are typically written with a capital letter:

| Person            | Place       | Thing         |
|-------------------|-------------|---------------|
| Dr. Smith         | Chicago     | Pacific Ocean |
| Jane              | Afghanistan | Mt. Everest   |
| Professor Jones   | Europe      | Lake Tahoe    |
| President Lincoln | Montana     | Erie Canal    |
| Ms. Peters        | Everglades  | The Sphinx    |
| Spaniard          | Pyrenees    | Spanish       |

The basic definition of nouns works well to a certain point, and will provide a starting point in determining which words are nouns. However, as we will see in Chapter 3, it will be necessary to revise this definition to account for nouns that do not fit neatly into this initial definition.

## Adjectives

Adjectives are usually characterized as descriptive or modifying words because of their function in a sentence. Words such as *beautiful*, *hard, happy*, and *tall* come readily to mind. These are the content words that function to create descriptive images or add color and flavor. Multiple adjectives can be found in a sentence:

(5) He had never seen such a harsh, boring, yet beautiful and magical landscape.

The adjectives **harsh, boring, beautiful,** and **magical** all describe the noun *land-scape.* The author has chosen to use pairs of opposing adjectives to fix the contradiction of the landscape in the reader's mind.

Other types of adjectives and words used as adjectives will be examined more closely in Chapter 4.

## Verbs

The first association many people make with the term "verb" is that of action, as in *run, drive, listen,* or *identify.* Verbs also refer to the state of something, as in *be (am, is, are),* or *feel.* English verbs may also indicate time. *We eat sandwiches* and *We ate sandwiches* refer to different times.

A sentence must always contain a verb. A verb and a noun are enough to form a complete sentence:

(6) I run.      They walk.      We listen.

A sentence can be long and complex, and yet still contain only one verb:

(7) The long hot sultry day notwithstanding, the boys **wore** long, heavy shirts, denim pants, thick cotton socks and work boots.

(8) Scrambling reluctantly up the slippery slopes of the muddy ravine, the strong-willed horse, although most decidedly fearful of the rider's whip, **tossed** his head relentlessly.

English verbs can be difficult for ESL learners to identify since they often have noun forms that are exactly the same, as we saw in Discovery Activity 1. Learners might also think *scrambling* is a verb, and while it is a verb form, it is not a verb here (see Chapter 12). Context and structural clues help determine whether the verb or noun form is being used. The forms, functions, and structural characteristics of verbs will be examined in Chapters 5 and 6.

## Adverbs

The common definition of an adverb is a word that describes or modifies a verb, an adjective, or another adverb. However, as we will see in Chapter 4, adverbs are difficult to characterize because the label *adverb* refers to many different kinds of words that perform a variety of functions. Essentially, adverbs can modify anything in a sentence. Adverbs are generally grouped into subcategories, according to their function, as for example we see in the following table.

| manner | frequency | time and place |
|--------|-----------|----------------|
| quickly | often | now |
| happily | always | here |
| silently | sometimes | later |

There are other words and subgroups of adverbs; unlike the other parts of speech we have looked at however, there is not complete agreement as to which words should be classified as adverbs or placed in separate classes. The fact that the line or division between adjectives and adverbs is not always clear-cut also clouds the issue. Some adjectives end in –*ly*, the common adverb suffix (e.g. deadly, lonely, kindly), while some adjectives and adverbs have the same form (e.g. early, fast, far). Compare for instance:

| adverb | adjective |
|--------|-----------|
| Judy walks *fast*. | Judy is a *fast* walker. |
| Jason rises *early*. | Jason is an *early* riser. |

(See Chapter 4 for further discussion).

At this point we will end our overview of the parts of speech comprising the major word categories and turn to look at morphology, the structure and form of words.

## Section 2: Morphology

In Section 1 we discussed how words may look alike but have different meanings and/or functions that only become clear through the context in which they are used. In Section 2, we examine the parts that make up the words of English.

Many words that users think of as being a single word are actually more than that. The smallest unit of meaning is called a *morpheme*. A morpheme can be a single word or other independently meaningful units. For example, consider the word "book." There is no smaller form of this word; in other words, this *book* cannot be broken into any other units. It is a single morpheme. Now consider these words:

bookworm        bookish        books

Most language users will easily recognize *bookworm* as two words (a compound word) consisting of *book* + *worm*. The other two words may be more difficult to recognize as actually consisting of two parts.

*Bookish* can be broken down into *book* + *ish*, and *books* into *book* + *s*. Most language users would probably not consider –*ish* and –*s* meaningful units. Nevertheless, although –*ish* and –*s* are not "words," they are independently meaningful units. They change the meaning (and sometimes the class) of a word. Both *book* and *bookworm* are nouns. *Bookish* is an adjective that describes a person as in "He's a bookish person."

Likewise, *books* can be broken down into two parts, *book* + *s*. Adding –*s* to certain words (nouns) indicates that there is more than one, as in *books, computers, days, shoes, pens,* and *geraniums.* This plural –*s* can also be added to *bookworm* to form *bookworms. Bookworms* now consists of three meaningful units: *book* + *worm* + *s*.

### Discovery Activity 6: Decoding Morphemes

Look at the following words.

1. Break the words down into the smallest possible meaningful units.
   blizzard
   frighten
   teacher
   often
   truthful
2. When you have finished, think about whether or not it was easy to find the smallest possible meaningful units. What reasons can you give for your answer?
3. When you have finished, check yours answers in a dictionary.

## Discussion: Discovery Activity 6

In addition to introducing you to learning how to distinguish morphemes, Discovery Activity 6 also showed that there are two kinds of morphemes, *bound* and *free*.

## Bound and Free Morphemes

### *What are* bound *and* free *morphemes?*

We call words such as *blizzard, never, amaze,* or *grace* **free morphemes** because they are meaningful units that can stand alone. They do not need to be attached or bound to another morpheme in order to have meaning.

Endings (suffixes) such as *–ful, -ment,* or *–er,* or markers (inflections) such as *–s* need to be attached or bound to other meaningful units. Since they cannot occur alone and function only as parts of words, they are called **bound morphemes.** Frequently several morphemes, both bound and free, occur in the same word as in:

undeniable      un + deny + able

*Undeniable* consists of two bound morphemes *–un* and *–able* and the free morpheme *deny.* (The "y" changes to "i" in accordance with English spelling rules.)

backpacks      back + pack + s

*Backpacks* is a compound word consisting of two free morphemes *back* and *pack* and the bound morpheme –*s*.

There are many compound words or words consisting of two free morphemes in English. Usually the –*s* bound morpheme can be attached to these words.

| compound word | + –*s* |
|---|---|
| firehouse | firehouses |
| workshop | workshops |
| schoolbook | schoolbooks |
| lifestyle | lifestyles |

### Are suffixes and prefixes morphemes?

We saw above that -*able* attaches at the end of *deny* and *un*- attaches to the front of *deny*. -*able* is a suffix and *un*- is a prefix. Both are bound morphemes. As a group, these morphemes are called **affixes**. We further distinguish what kind of affixes they are by where they occur. If they come before another morpheme, they are called **prefixes**. If they come after, they are called **suffixes**. Some common affixes are:

| prefixes | | suffixes | |
|---|---|---|---|
| *dis-* | disinherit | -*less* | groundless |
| | disclaimer | | fearless |
| | disregard | | thoughtless |
| *inter-* | interdependent | -*ness* | kindness |
| | international | | blindness |
| | interchange | | happiness |
| *bi-* | bisect | -*ate* | graduate |
| | bipartisan | | frustrate |
| | binary | | congratulate |
| *un-* | unclear | -*able* | reasonable |
| | unsure | | debatable |
| | unreal | | changeable |

## Derivational and Inflectional Morphemes

### Are there different types of bound morphemes?

Bound morphemes can be divided into two groups: **derivational** morphemes and **inflectional** morphemes. Derivational morphemes are lexical morphemes. They somehow either change the class a word belongs to or change the semantic meaning of a word. We have looked at such words as *undeniable* and *renewal,* which have derivational morphemes.

Inflectional morphemes, on the other hand, are grammatical morphemes and do not change the class to which a word belongs nor its semantic meaning. They provide grammatical information about a word. For example an "s" added to a noun such as *chair* in English changes that noun from a singular word to the plural word *chairs*.

## Derivational Morphemes

Derivational morphemes are lexical morphemes. They have to do with the vocabulary of the language. These morphemes form an open set to which new words or word forms are frequently added. Derivational morphemes can come at the beginning (prefix), or at the end (suffix) of a word, and more than one can be added to a word:

> Disagreement: **dis** + agree + **ment**
> *dis-*: prefix meaning opposite
> *-ment*: suffix that changes the word class to a noun and that refers to an action, process, or means.

The addition of a derivational **suffix** often, but not always, changes the part of speech of a word.

| Noun | → | Adjective | Verb | → | Noun |
|---|---|---|---|---|---|
| child | | child**ish** | realize | | realiz**ation** |
| face | | face**less** | establish | | establish**ment** |
| trend | | trend**y** | conform | | conform**ity** |

Sometimes a derivational **suffix** will only change the meaning of a word, but not the class:

| Adjective | → | Adjective | Noun | → | Noun |
|---|---|---|---|---|---|
| economic | | economic**al** | fellow | | fellow**ship** |
| politic | | politic**al** | progress | | progres**sion** |

Derivational **prefixes** only change the meaning of a word, never the class:

| Adjective | → | Adjective | Verb | → | Verb |
|---|---|---|---|---|---|
| forgettable | | **un**forgettable | appear | | **dis**appear |
| essential | | **non**essential | finish | | **re**finish |

It is not always easy to divide words into morphemes, since some of them are not recognizable today as individual parts of words. Many of these morphemes have their origins in Latin and Greek word forms that are unfamiliar to most people today. The English word *correlation*, for instance, consists of the morphemes *cor + re + lation*. Most modern speakers of English would have difficulty identifying the three morphemes. The morpheme *cor* is actually a derivative of *com*, meaning "together," *re* meaning "back or again" + *latus*, meaning "brought."

Breaking down words to such a degree is not very important for ESL/EFL learners. The most important point in teaching derivational morphology is to help learners to recognize the more common affixes and their functions. Learning the meanings of derivational morphemes can be a powerful tool for developing one's vocabulary, whether the person is a native speaker or an ESL/EFL learner. For example, having learners understand that the suffix -tion usually tells us that the word is a noun can be helpful in deciphering new words. Teaching ESL/EFL learners common derivational morphemes is also more productive than learners trying to memorize long lists of vocabulary words.

## Inflectional Morphemes

Inflectional morphemes, in contrast to derivational morphemes, are a small closed set of eight grammatical morphemes. These eight add little or no content, but serve a grammatical function such as marking plural or tense. Inflectional morphemes change the form of a word without changing either the word category it belongs to or its meaning:

cat    →    cat**s**
walk   →    walk**ed**

The addition of "s" to the noun *cats* indicates that more than one cat is being referred to. The "ed" at the end of "walk" indicates a past action.

The eight English inflectional morphemes are:

| The 8 English Inflectional Morphemes | | | |
|---|---|---|---|
| **Morpheme** | **Grammatical Function** | **Attaches to** | **Example** |
| -s | plural | noun | desks, chairs, boxes |
| -'s | possessive | noun | the boy's hat, the cat's tail |
| -s | third person singular | verb present tense | She drives. He talks. It walks. |
| -ed | regular past tense | verb | He talked. |
| -ed | regular past participle | verb | She has walked. |
| -ing | present participle | verb | She is driving. |
| -er | comparative | adjective/adverb | taller, faster |
| -est | superlative | adjective/adverb | tallest, fastest |

Inflectional morphemes are always the last morpheme of a word. They are always suffixes. Only one inflectional morpheme can be added to a word. The only exception to this is noun plural –s plus possessive. In written English, this is reflected by moving the apostrophe to after the –s:

(9) The boy**'s** book = a book belonging to one boy.
(10) The boys**'** book = a book belonging to more than one boy.

Inflectional morphemes are essential for the correct production and understanding of grammatical or structural elements of utterances. The crucial difference between following pair of sentences, for instances, is reflected only by the additional of one inflectional morpheme.

I walk to school.    **versus**    I walk**ed** to school.

*Do ESL/EFL learners have trouble with these 8 inflectional endings?*

▶ *Learner difficulties*

Although English has relatively few inflectional morphemes, some of the most frequent learner errors are in the correct use of these inflections. ESL/EFL students for example, will frequently omit the third person singular '*s* or the omit the past tense –*ed* and produce sentences such as:

*she like cats.
*we walk home yesterday.

You will note that the two sentences above are preceded by an asterisk (*). Throughout the text, when you see an asterisk before a sentence, it means that the sentence following it is incorrect or ungrammatical.

The omission or incorrect use of these eight inflectional morphemes is another central focus of this book. We will see more examples of the difficulties ESL/EFL learners have with these inflectional morphemes in later chapters.


# Redundancy in Language

In most languages, there is a feature that we call *redundancy*. The term redundancy refers to any feature that provides the same grammatical information that another one already provides. In other words, when more than one grammatical clue or marker is required to reveal grammatical information, it is called redundancy.

Discover Activity 7 will help you understand the notion of redundancy more clearly.


**Discovery Activity 7: Redundancy**

Examine the following two sentences.

1. Which of the two sentences is incorrect or ungrammatical in Standard American English?
2. Underline those elements in the sentence you choose that make it ungrammatical.

   (a) Yesterday, two teachers expressed their feelings about John's grade.
   (b) Yesterday, two teacher express their feeling about John's grade.

## Discussion: Discovery Activity 7

The second of the two sentences (marked with an *) is an ungrammatical Standard American English sentence.

(a) Yesterday, two teachers expressed their feelings about John's grade.
*(b) Yesterday, two teacher express their feeling about John's grade.

In Sentence (b), the nouns *teacher* and *feeling* have not received the plural inflection –*s*. Even though the sentence provides other clues that indicate the nouns are plural (e.g. *two, their*), Standard American English still requires this plural –*s* inflection.

The number *two* and the –*s* inflection on *teachers* both serve to indicate that *teachers* is a plural noun. Either one of these markers would be enough to mark the noun as plural, but English requires both markers in order for the sentence to be grammatical, even though the sentence would be understandable with only one of the two plural markers.

Another example of redundancy is the use of *yesterday* and the past tense inflection –*ed* to indicate the past time reference of this sentence. While the use of the *yesterday* is enough to show past time reference as in (a), the lack of the past tense inflection –*ed* causes the sentence to be an ungrammatical English production because it does not meet the redundancy requirements of the language.

*Why do I have to understand inflectional endings and what do they have to do with redundancy in terms of teaching ESL/EFL?*

▶ *Learner difficulties*

For ESL/EFL learners, the inflectional endings require at least some explicit language instruction. These inflectional endings are not always obvious to ESL/EFL learners, especially if something comparable does not exist in their native language so they need to be exposed to the idea that words must change form in certain instances.

Another reason that ESL/EFL learners need explicit instruction regarding these forms is that they may not "hear" the inflectional endings because the sound of them is reduced. By this we mean that inflectional endings do not receive stress in a word, so learners may not always be aware of them. For example, the past tense –*ed* of the verbs in the following paragraph is barely pronounced in natural speech.

When Margaret *arrived* at work, she noticed that her left tire was low. She called a mechanic who d*iscovered* a nail in the tire. He *pulled* the nail out and *patched* the hole.

Furthermore, as we have just discussed, English requires redundancy. We saw this illustrated in Discovery Activity 7, where the sentence required the use of the past *-ed* together with the time marker, *yesterday*, and the plural inflection *-s* together with the plural word *two*. As other languages do not necessarily have equivalent forms and structures, learners from such languages may have difficulty mastering the use of inflectional derivations. ESL/EFL learners who are speakers of languages that do not have tense markers find it difficult to remember to use the *-ed* past tense inflection on a verb. They instead tend to rely on time adverbs such as *yesterday* or *last month* to indicate past time reference. Similarly, such learners may also have difficulty remembering to use the *-s* plural inflection on nouns when the sentence includes such plural markers as *two* or *many*.

## Summary

Word classes are grouped into two categories, closed and open

| Closed | Open |
|---|---|
| • structure or grammatical words<br>• provide information as to the grammar or organization of a sentence<br>• have little or no lexical (content) meaning<br>• the number of words is relatively fixed; new words are rarely added | • content words<br>• have grammatical function, e.g. subject of a sentence<br>• convey important lexical (content) meaning<br><br>• new words are constantly being added<br>• and/or formed following the grammatical constraints of English<br>• derivational endings can provide new meaning or change the word class of a word meaning |
| • do not share any formal features such as specific derivational endings that make them identifiable as members of particular word classes. There is nothing, for example about the form of the words *a, an, the* to identify them as articles, nor about the form of the words *by, without, from,* or *on* to identify them as prepositions. | • often share derivational forms that make them identifiable as members of particular word classes. For example, words ending in *-ment* are nouns as in *basement, replacement, advancement, management*. |

Morphemes

---
**Morphemes are the simplest unit of a word**

---

- They cannot be divided into smaller units, e.g. *work, for, 's*
- There are open class and closed class morphemes
- Open class morphemes can take derivational and inflectional morphemes
- There are free morphemes and bound morphemes.

  - Free morphemes are words that can stand on their own, e.g. *board, live*
  - Bound morphemes must be attached to another word. e.g *-s (boards),
    -able (livable)*

---

Derivational Morphemes

---
**Characteristics of Derivational Morphemes**

---

- They can change the part of speech or word class to another, e.g. the addition of
  the suffix *–able* changes a noun to an adjective: reason → reasonable, measure →
  measurable
- They can remain the same part of speech but change the lexical meaning, e.g. the
  addition of the prefix *un–* simply changes the meaning to "opposite": conscious and
  unconscious are both adjectives but with the opposite meaning; home and homeless
  are both nouns but with different meanings through the addition of the suffix *-less.*
- More than one derivational morpheme can be added: unworkable → un + work +
  able

---

Inflectional Morphemes

---
**Characteristics of Inflectional Morphemes**

---

- They provide grammatical information to open class words, e.g. plural of nouns, possessive of nouns, tense and aspect of verbs, and comparison and contrast of adjectives
  and adverbs.
- Inflectional morphemes come only at the end of words, e.g. wide → wid**er**; sing →
  sing**s**.
- Only one inflectional morpheme can be added, except the possessive "s" after a plural
  noun. This second "s" is only obvious in written English. e.g. The boys' dog = One
  dog belonging to more than one boy.
- These are the most difficult morphemes for ESL/EFL learners to master.

---

## Practice Activities

### Activity 1: Identifying the Major Parts of Speech

Look at the paragraph and answer the questions.

> During the respectful, appreciative buzz of voices that followed the speech, General Montero raised a pair of heavy, drooping eyelids and rolled his eyes with a sort of uneasy dullness from face to face. The military backwoods hero of the party, though secretly impressed by the sudden novelties and splendors of his position ...
>
> (Conrad, J. (1994). *Nostromo.* (p. 109) London: Penguin Books.)

1. Identify the major parts of speech in the following paragraph. Write N for noun, V for verb, Adj for adjective, and Adv for adverb.

   **N     V     Adv**

   *Example*: The boy rode quickly.
2. Think about which major part or parts of speech occur most frequently.

   • Do you think this is typical? Explain.

#### Optional Follow-up

3. Find another paragraph in a book, magazine, or newspaper. Identify the major parts of speech in the paragraph you selected.

   • Do your findings support or not support your response to #2? Explain why, if you can.

### Activity 2: Redundancy

In Discovery Activity 8, we saw how English requires redundancy. However, such redundancy is not true in all languages. Some languages have no inflectional morphemes.

1. Discuss what kinds of problems ESL/EFL learners who come from languages without inflectional morphemes might have in learning and using English inflectional morphemes for tense (*-ed*) and plural (−*s*).

### Activity 3: Derivational Morphemes

1. Look at the words in the list below.
2. On a sheet of paper, write the derivational morphemes for the words in the list.
3. Explain which derivational morphemes you found that identify the class to which a word belongs.
4. Discuss the meaning of each derivational morpheme you identified.

- Limit your examination to common derivational morphemes. Do not look at obscure and/or forgotten roots.
- Keep in mind that you are looking for derivational morphemes that will help your students decode meaning and function.

*Example*:

partnership: partner + ship     The suffix *-ship* is only used with nouns. *-ship* refers to     position or skill as in *professorship* or *penmanship*.

a) partnership
b) unhappy
c) biology
d) brutalize
e) journalist
f) terrible
g) positive

## Activity 4: More Decoding of Morphemes

It is not always easy to distinguish morphemes, especially bound versus free. Try this activity if you would like more practice in distinguishing morphemes.
    Examine the following list of words.

1. Identify the different morphemes that make up each word.
2. Label the different morphemes as **B** for bound and **F** for free.

*Example*:

breakwaters     break = F     water = F     s = B

a) neighborhood
b) fashionable
c) forecasters
d) aorta
e) bartend
f) usually
g) renewal
h) inaccessibility

# Chapter 3
# The Noun Phrase

## Nouns, Noun Signals, Pronouns

## Introduction

Chapter 2 introduced the basic definition of a noun as a person, place, or thing. In this chapter we will examine in more detail what constitutes the word class *noun* with a view to expanding our understanding of what a noun encompasses. We will also discuss different types of nouns and various noun signals, word classes that are closely associated with nouns and that help us identify what words are functioning as nouns. The chapter is divided into four parts. Section 1 discusses identifying nouns. Section 2 examines different types of nouns. Section 3 considers some of the structure classes that signal nouns; and Section 4 reviews pronouns, that is, words which substitute for nouns.

## Section 1: Identifying Nouns

### *Context and Function*

One of the most important concepts to which we will be returning to throughout this book is that, in English, identifying the class membership of content or lexical words is not always easy because form is not always equal to function. In Chapter 2, for instance, we saw that some words fit into more than one class. Let's review this concept by looking at the two sentences below with the word *harm*, which, depending upon context, can change its function.

In Sentence (1), *harm* is a noun referring to a thing. In Sentence (2) *harm* is a verb referring to an action. Context is what allows us to distinguish the class to which the word *harm* belongs.

(1) The **harm** was minimal.                                      (noun)
(2) The drug **harmed** more than it helped.                      (verb)

In Sentences (1) and (2), the context shows us two different functions of *harm*, based on its different sentence positions.

A. DeCapua, *Grammar for Teachers*,
© Springer 2008

- In Sentence (1), *harm* follows the noun signal *the* and comes before the verb *was*. *Harm* is in what we call **subject** position.
- In Sentence (2), *harm* is no longer in subject position. Instead, we see that *harm* comes after the noun *drug*, the subject of the verb, *harm*.

Some words, as we will see, clearly belong to one class. However, even if a word clearly belongs to a particular class, this does not automatically guarantee the function of that word. The words *rich* and *poor*, for instance, are words that fit our definition in Chapter 2 of a descriptive word or an adjective:

(3) Plants grow in *rich* soil.
(4) Plants don't grow in *poor* soil.

In both Sentences (3) and (4), the adjectives *rich* and *poor* describe the noun *soil*. They tell us in what kind of soil plants grow or do not grow. In the next two sentences, however, *rich* and *poor* are still adjectives, but they are functioning as something else:

(5) The *rich* have a good life.
(6) The *poor* have a hard life.

In Sentences (5) and (6), the adjectives *rich* and *poor* are in the sentence position where we normally expect a noun (to the left of the verb) and are indeed functioning as nouns and as the subjects of the verb *have*.

As Sentences (1) through (6) illustrate, in English membership in a particular form class does not automatically determine grammatical function because the same form may have different functions. Remember, form is not necessarily equal to function.

In addition, as we saw in Chapter 2, form classes are open classes to which new words are continually added. Often new words are added by shifting, meaning words change move from one form class to another.

## *Semantic Clues*

### *What clues are there for helping us to identify nouns?*

The standard definition of a noun as a person, place, or thing is what is called a *semantic* definition because it categorizes words by definition. When we categorize words by what they mean, we consider what semantic properties they have in common. *Astronaut* and *firefighter* are classified under this definition as nouns because they refer to people, *city* and *New York* because they refer to places, and *plant* and *lamp* because they refer to things.

The notion of semantic clues refers to shared properties of words. In other words, certain types of words can be grouped or classed together because they have shared intrinsic meanings. In Chapter 2 in Discovery Activity 1, you were able to group different words together without necessarily knowing the names of different word classes. There were certain inherent properties or characteristics in the different words that allowed you to place them together in specific groups. Words such as *listen, speak,* and *sit* all carry the idea of some type of action. Words such as *bird, tree,* and *pencil* bring to mind a concrete object or thing.

Words that carry the core semantic properties are called *prototypical* words. The word *bird* for most people conjures up an image of a creature with a beak, wings, feathers, and the ability to fly. This is a prototypical bird, regardless of whether a person's exact mental image is a robin, crow, cardinal, or parrot. The word *bird*, however, encompasses a vast number of birds that do not necessarily share all these avian features, such as the ability to fly as in the case of ostriches or penguins. Ostriches and penguins are still birds, just not prototypical examples of birds.

However, while native speakers and highly proficient non-native speakers may be able to rely on semantic clues in classifying words as nouns, this is generally not the case for ESL/EFL learners—especially if their language is unrelated to English—and they must rely on other clues to help them determine which words are functioning as nouns.

### *What other clues are there for helping us to identify nouns?*

There are three other types of clues we can use to help us identify nouns: structural ones, which we will introduce here briefly and discuss later in Section 3, and derivational and morphological clues to which you were introduced in Chapter 2.

## *Structural Clues*

Another way to identify word function is to consider structural clues such as sentence position, which we saw in our discussion of context, and the co-occurrence of other words. For example, nouns characteristically occur after articles such as *the*:

the book
the water
the computer

Such structural clues help us identify the class membership of words that look identical but occupy different functions in a sentence:

(7) I drank the water.
(8) I water the plants.

In Sentence (7), *water* is preceded by *the*, a structural clue indicating that water is functioning as a noun in this particular context. In Sentence (8), *water* occurs after the subject pronoun *I*. Its placement in this sentence occurs where we normally expect an action word or verb, namely before, or to the right of, the subject. Such a structural analysis allows us to account for and understand the (occasional) use of adjectives as nouns in the sentences we saw earlier:

(9) The *rich* have a good life.
(10) The *poor* have a hard life.

The structural clues of Sentences (9) and (10) define the function of the adjectives in these two sentences as nouns, without changing their class membership; *poor* and *rich* remain adjectives. In Section 3 of this chapter we will examine structural clues in greater detail.

## Derivational Clues

In Chapter 2 we saw how certain derivational endings provide us with clues to identifing class membership and we discussed how learning common derivational endings is a valuable tool for helping learners of English identify new words and their word class membership. We saw for instance, that the suffix *–ment* generally signals nouns as in *amazement, settlement,* or *movement.*

## Morphological Clues

Also in Chapter 2 you were introduced to inflectional endings and we saw that certain inflectional endings go with nouns. These inflectional endings are the -*s* for regular plural formation and the *'s* to show possession. The -*s* is also referred to as the *genitive case.*

|  | Function of "s" |
|---|---|
| (11) I have books, pencils, pens, and folders. | plural *s* |
| (12) I have Justin's car. |  |
| The cat's whiskers are long. | possessive (genitive) *'s* |
| The girl's jacket is here. |  |

- In Sentence (11), *books, pencils, pens,* and *folders* are all plural nouns marked by the inflectional –*s*.
- In Sentence (12), *Justin's, cat's,* and *girl's* all have the possessive *'s.*

Thus, words that are plural or take the possessive *'s* provide derivational clues in identifying them as nouns. However, as we will see in Section 2, not all nouns can form the plural. In addition, a concern for ESL/EFL learners is how to distinguish the plural –*s* from the third person singular present –*s*. Finally, as we discuss below, not all nouns can take the possessive *'s* inflection.

## *What exactly does the possessive 's inflection tell us?*

### *Possessive 's*

As we saw in Sentence (12), the possessive *'s* identifies that word as a noun. Traditional definitions of *'s* define this inflectional ending as something added to certain nouns to show possession or ownership. In reality, the *'s* indicates more than possession or ownership. It can also convey the meaning of originator or inventor as in:

Darwin**'s** theory of evolution
Edison**'s** light bulb
Stephen King**'s** novels

Possessive *'s* can also describe something related to a characteristic as in:

the soldier**'s** courage
the killer**'s** obsession

It can also be a description in itself as in:

children**'s** literature
the women**'s** movement

### *Can all nouns can take the possessive's?*

Not all nouns can take the possessive *'s* to indicate possession or ownership. Nouns that can take the possessive*'s* are generally those referring to:

- people
- time
- animals
- collective nouns

Nouns that generally do not take the possessive*'s* are **inanimate** nouns, although there are certain inanimate nouns that do take the possessive*'s*. These are generally collective nouns that refer to groups of people such as *company, team, committee,* or *government*.

Most inanimate nouns take "of phrases" to show possession, as in *the back of the desk* and not *\*the desk's back*. However, like many other examples in English that we will see, there are many exceptions to this "rule." We say, for instance *the book's cover*.

Consequently, while ESL/EFL learners may want to know exactly when they can or cannot use the possessive *'s*, there is no hard and fast rule for them to follow, just general guidelines. When ESL/EFL learners do use the possessive*'s* where native speakers would not, such errors are not serious. They generally do not cause misunderstandings and are rarely stigmatized by native speakers.

At this point we will leave our brief overview of clues for identifying word as nouns and turn to Section 2 to explore the different types of nouns.

## Section 2: Different Types of Nouns

*Why can we say* an animal *but not* an advice?

## *Count and Noncount Nouns*

One way to classify nouns is by categorizing them as *count* or *noncount* nouns. Simply put, count nouns refer to those nouns that can be counted. Noncount nouns are those nouns that cannot be counted in English.

### Count Nouns

Count nouns have both singular and plural forms, e.g. *animal, animals,* or *book, books.* Plural count nouns take a plural verb and are replaced with plural pronouns:

(13) **Books** *are* interesting.        → **They** *are* interesting.
Some **animals** *live* in the wild.        → **They** *live* in the wild.

### Count Nouns and Plurals

Only count nouns have plural forms. The regular plural is the *-s* inflection affixed or attached to the end of a count noun. Although most count nouns in English take the plural *–s* inflection, there are a few exceptions. There are also count nouns that do not have plural forms such as *one sheep, two sheep,* or *ten deer, fifteen deer,* and words that always end in *s* but are not plural as in *series* or *genius.* There are a number of irregular nouns that change the internal vowel, add irregular plural endings, or undergo other spelling changes.

| Regular plural *s* | | Irregular plural ending | | Internal vowel change | | f → ves | |
|---|---|---|---|---|---|---|---|
| pawn | pawns | syllabus | syllabi | goose | geese | Leaf | leaves |
| forest | forests | basis | bases | mouse | mice | wife | wives |
| picture | pictures | phenomenon | phenomena | foot | feet | shelf | shelves |

Irregular plural nouns are generally nouns that follow older patterns of English or are nouns that have been borrowed from Latin or Greek and thus take the Latin or Greek plural formation. In the case of words that have been borrowed from Latin or Greek, there is a tendency for them to adopt over time the regular English plural *–s* inflection. Therefore, we see words such as *syllabus* that actually have two plural forms, the original *syllabi* and the English *syllabuses.* Since these exceptions are limited, they are not difficult for ESL/EFL to learn.

**Discovery Activity 1: Nouns and "s"**

1. Look at the following list of words.
2. Identify which nouns are plural and which ones are nouns that simply end in *s*.

*Example:*

    linguistics: noun that ends in "s"
    fans: plural word

| | | | |
|---|---|---|---|
| genius | chess | jeans | news |
| clothes | parts | fans | alias |
| admirers | scissors | | |
| syllabus | summons | | |

## Discussion: Discovery Activity 1

As this Discovery Activity illustrates, not all nouns that end in "s" are plural. Words such as *jeans, clothes,* and *scissors* are nouns with only plural forms; other words such as *genius* and *syllabus* simply end in "s" with no plural meaning attached to this "s". Since there are relatively few words that follow this pattern, it is not difficult for learners of English to become familiar with the most common of these and use them correctly.

### Noncount Nouns

Noncount nouns refer to things we cannot count, such as abstract concepts, general nouns, or units. We will look shortly at the types of noncount nouns in greater depth, but for now, just keep in mind this broad definition. Noncount nouns have only one noun form, e.g. *relaxation,* but not *\*relaxations*; *rice,* but not *\*rices*. Because noncount nouns cannot be counted, they cannot occur with *a/n* or precise numbers, such as *two, three,* etc.

Noncount nouns always take a singular verb because there is no plural form. They are replaced by a singular pronoun.

    **Advice** *is* helpful.    →    **It** *is* useful.

Look at the box below to help clarify the difference between count and noncount nouns. If you look at the words in the left-hand column, you will notice that you can add a number before each one. You can also add the inflectional *–s* plural ending. If you look at the right-hand column, you will see that you can't add any numbers or the plural *–s* inflection. We can't say *\*3 advices*.

| Count | Noncount |
|---|---|
| cookie | advice |
| answer | information |
| letter | air |
| wall | input |
| map | weather |
| drawer | harm |
| calendar | recreation |

In Discovery Activity 2, see how well you can distinguish between count and noncount nouns. For this activity, the answers are not provided because you can check the words in a dictionary. If there is no plural form given, you know it is a noncount noun.

---

### Discovery Activity 2: Count versus Noncount Nouns

Look at the words below.

1. If the word is a count noun, label it **C**.
2. If the word a noncount noun, label it **NC**.

*Example:*

   cat   **C**   happiness   **NC**

| | | |
|---|---|---|
| carrot | knowledge | garbage |
| chalk | anger | scanner |
| muscle | language | health |
| soap | raindrop | sadness |

---

### *What about a loaf of bread or a slice of bread? Aren't these count nouns?*

The noncount noun, e.g. *bread* is still a noncount noun. What has happened is that we have added a quantifiying phrase, *a loaf* or *a slice*, before the noncount noun, *bread*.

Many noncount nouns can be quantified, that is made countable, by adding certain phrases before them: ***a grain of*** *sand,* ***three bottles of*** *water,* ***a piece of advice***. When one of these phrases comes before a noun, we call the entire group of words a noun phrase.

| phrase + | noun | = noun phrase |
|---|---|---|
| a/the bit of | information | a/the bit of information |
| a/the loaf of | bread | a/the loaf of bread |
| a/the piece of | cheese | a/the piece of cheese |

In Discovery Activity 3, try adding an appropriate quantifying phrase to the noncount nouns. For most of the noncount nouns in the Discovery Activity, you will find that there is more than one possibility. You can compare your answers with those at the end of the chapter under the section labeled "Answer Key."

---

### Discovery Activity 3: Adding Quantifying Phrases to Noncount Nouns

1. On a separate sheet of paper, write at least one quantifying phrase that you can use with each noncount noun below.

*Example:*
bread: a slice of/a loaf of/a piece of

1. ham
2. paper
3. butter
4. water
5. hair
6. wisdom
7. intelligence
8. grass

---

*Is there any way to classify or categorize different types of noncount nouns?*

Subcategories of Noncount Nouns

In looking at the noncount nouns in Discovery Activity 3, you will notice that they differ in a basic way in what they refer to. *Wisdom,* for instance, is something we refer to as an abstract concept. *Water,* on the other hand, is a liquid. To help ESL/EFL learners understand noncount nouns, we generally classify them into three major different subcategories: **abstract, mass**, and **collective nouns**.

*What is the difference between an* **abstract, mass**, *or* **collective** *noun?*

**Mass nouns** include those nouns that cannot be counted or that refer to larger units or categories. These include nouns such as *furniture, cheese,* or *grass.* The noun *furniture,* for instance, is the larger unit or category including items such as tables, chairs, sofas, beds, and similar items. Mass nouns also include nouns that refer to undifferentiated substances, such as liquids, gases, and solids, such as *water, oil,* and *bread.*

**Abstract nouns** refer to nouns that refer to ideas, concepts, emotions, beliefs, precepts, or intangible phenomena such as *intelligence, hate, fear,* and *honesty.* These cannot be counted because they do not refer to anything that has substance or that we can touch.

**Collective nouns** include words that refer to sets, units, or categories of things. Examples of such nouns include *audience, press, committee,* or *faculty. Audience* or *faculty* can be thought of as a set or category, for instance, because each word refers to a group of persons or individuals.

In American English collective nouns generally take a singular verb, but in British English they take a plural verb.

| Collective Nouns | |
| --- | --- |
| **American English** | **British English** |
| The *press has* become intrusive. | The *press have* become intrusive. |
| The *committee meets* today. | The *committee meet* today. |

At the end of this chapter you can find a chart listing the common types of noncount nouns.

### What exactly is something "countable?"

### ► Learner difficulties

This can be a difficult concept for ESL/EFL learners. Native speakers are generally not consciously aware of the distinction between count and noncount nouns. As part of their innate knowledge of the grammar of English, they have no difficulty using these different nouns in a systematic, rule-governed manner. This distinction between count and noncount nouns, is however, a problematic area for non-native speakers for a variety of reasons. Conceptualizing which nouns are count or noncount is difficult for speakers whose native languages have different ways of looking at nouns. In some languages, nouns are categorized according to whether they are animate or inanimate; in other languages nouns are categorized according to shape and size. In many languages nouns are not categorized at all.

For some ESL/EFL learners, using phrases such as *a bit of* or *a piece of information* make this word countable in their minds. Other ESL/EFL learners conceptualize a noncount noun such as *information* or *advice* as countable, whether because of their native language or another reason and produce such utterances as *\*informations* or *\*advices*. Remember, as we saw earlier, knowing which type of noun a given word is, is important because it affects other sentence elements, such as verbs, determiners, and quantifiers.

### What else do I need to teach my ESL/EFL learners about nouns?

Look at the following sentence.

(14) Michale Chiarello was introduced to flavored **oils** in the kitchen of his *nonna*, who would put a spoonful of olive **oil** infused with dried tomatoes in her tomato sauce.
[Gugino, S. (2006, Novermber 30). Tastes: Flavored oils. *The Wine Spectator,* p. 19.]

You will probably be wondering why *oil*, which is generally categorized as a noncount noun, has a countable counterpart, *oils*. This is an example of what we can call a "crossover noun."

## *Crossover Nouns*

### *What exactly is a crossover noun?*

This term refers to nouns which have both count and noncount meanings. In the sentence above, *flavored **oils*** refers to different oils that are flavored by a variety of herbs and spices. *A spoonful of **oil*** refers to the general liquid and is preceded by the quantifying phrase *a spoonful*.

Similarly, when we refer to *gas* as in *The car needs gas,* we are using this noun in its noncount sense. When scientists refer to the different types of this substance, they talk about *gases* and use this noun in a count sense as in the phrase *the gases surrounding Jupiter*.

In short, a crossover noun is count when such nouns are used to describe **members** of a set, category, class, or group. It is noncount when used in its **general sense** to name a set, category, class, or group.

### *Does this explanation cover all examples of crossover nouns?*

In some instances, noncount nouns and count nouns may have somewhat different meanings. Speakers may refer to the metal *iron* and be using the word in its noncount sense; however, when they press their clothes, they use *an iron*, which is a count noun.[1]

### *Is it easy for ESL/EFL learners to understand crossover nouns?*

The difficulty with crossover nouns for nonnative speakers is that while the grammatical explanations governing count versus noncount usage may be clear, the actual use of count and noncount nouns may be more difficult. With practice, ESL/EFL learners can usually grasp the idea of such countable items as *chair, table, sofa* as all concrete things comprising part of the noncount category *furniture*. They can usually also understand that a sign in the supermarket advertising *chicken* refers to a type of food while a picture of a barnyard will show the individual creature *a chicken*.

While crossover nouns are generally not a concern for beginning or intermediate level language learners, as these learners become more proficient and encounter more sophisticated vocabulary, they will encounter more crossover and also less commonly used crossover nouns. *Yarn,* when referring to the material is a noncount noun, but its use to describe a type of entertaining story or tale is less common. Moreover, the count meaning of *yarn* is not obviously related to the noncount meaning, even though speakers may refer to the idiom *spinning a yarn,* which has historic roots in the noncount meaning.

Discovery Activity 4 practices distinguishing count, noncount and crossover nouns. As you complete this activity, think about using the different words in

---

[1] Although the modern iron has nothing in common with the metal, the count noun derived from the fact that the original instrument for pressing clothes was made from iron.

different contexts. When you have finished, compare your answers to those in the Answer Key at the end of the chapter.

---

**Discovery Activity 4: Count and Noncount Nouns**
Look at the list of nouns below.

1. Which ones are only noncount nouns?
2. Which ones can be used as both count and noncount nouns?

- Discuss whether or not they have different meanings if they have both count and noncount uses.
- Discuss which phrases, if any, can come before any of the noncount nouns to make them countable.

*Example*: *bread*

- noncount noun
- We can say *a loaf or loaves of bread* to refer to one or more units.
- We can also say to *a slice or slices of bread* to refer to individual pieces of bread.
- can also be used as a count noun and made plural: *That bakery sells breads from around the world,* which refers to the different types, groups, or units of bread that are baked in different countries.

(a)  sense
(b)  coffee
(c)  hair
(d)  concern
(e)  music
(f)  thunder
(g)  experience

---

***Why is this distinction between count and noncount nouns important?***

Native speakers are generally unaware of these two categories of nouns. It is part of their innate grammar knowledge. However, ESL/EFL learners must learn and understand the difference between count and noncount nouns because this difference influences other sentence elements. For example, count nouns can occur alone or with determiners, such as articles and expressions of quantity, e.g. *a few, several, some*. Different structure words signal different types of nouns.

Look at the chart below to see how the count noun *animal* takes different noun signals than does the noncount noun *advice*.

| Structure Words Accompanying Count and Noncount Nouns | | | |
|---|---|---|---|
| **Animal** | | **Advice** | |
| **an** animal | *an, the* | **the** advice | only *the* |
| **the** animal | | | |
| animals | plural *-s* | advice | no plural form |
| **this** animal | | **this** advice | |
| **that** animal | *this, that* | **that** advice | only *this, that* |
| **these** animals | *these, those* | | |
| **those** animals | | | |
| **many** animals | *many* | **much** advice | *much* |
| **a few** animals | *a few* | **a little** advice | *a little* |
| **few** animals | *few* | **little** advice | *little* |
| **Three** animals | *exact number* | advice | *no numbers* |

As you can see from the chart, count and noncount words are preceded by different structure words. Because knowledge of count and noncount nouns is part of their innate grammar, native speakers automatically know which structure words go with which type of noun. ESL/EFL learners, in contrast, must learn both what count and noncount nouns are and which structure words accompany which type of noun. This now brings us to Section 3 of the chapter.

## Section 3: Structure Words that Signal Nouns

### *Noun Signals*

There are certain words that precede nouns and therefore act to signal a noun. In this next section, we will consider some of the structure class words that signal nouns. We begin with articles, turn then to look at demonstratives and conclude with quantifiers. All three types of noun signals are often classified as *determiners*.

### *Articles*

| the | a/n |
|---|---|

English has two articles, *the* and *a/n*. When articles combine with nouns, they form *noun phrases*:

| Article + | Noun | = Noun Phrase |
|---|---|---|
| a | cat | a cat |
| an | elephant | an elephant |
| the | creature | the creature |

**The Definite Article** *the*

English has one definite article, *the*. The definite article both signals a noun and tells us that a specific noun is being referred to. It does not refer to something general. For example, compare these two sentences:

(15) We like movies
(16) We like *the* movies at Cinema I.

In Sentence (15), we do not put *the* before *movies* because we are referring to movies in the general sense of a type of activity we enjoy. In Sentence (16), we do put *the* before *movies* because we are referring to the specific type or genre or selection of movies shown at this movie theater.

*The* may be used with a singular or plural noun. It may be used before singular count nouns to refer to a type of person or a thing in general when referring to a category or type. *The* is also used with certain place names such as *the United States, the City of New York, the University of South Florida, the Golden Gate Bridge,* and *the Library of Congress.*

Try Discovery Activity 5 and see how well you do in recognizing the function of *the*. You can check your answers with those at the end of the chapter in the Answer Key.

**Discovery Activity 5:** *the*
Look at the following excerpts.

1. Describe how *the* functions in these excerpts.

**A.**

The boys met **the** professor outside **the** main door of **the** Bristol Library at five p.m., as they usually did. All three of them were hungry, so they went to **the** center of town to find a restaurant.
[Bellairs, J. (1990). *The secret of the underground room* (p. 62). New York: Puffin Books.]

**B.**
**The** computer is to **the** typewriter what **the** typewriter was to **the** pencil.

**The Indefinite Article** *a/n*

English also has an indefinite article that speakers use when referring to something that is not specified, something that is vague, uncertain, or undefined. It is used with a singular count noun.

This indefinite article has two forms, depending on the initial vowel sound of the word following the indefinite article. If the noun or adjective begins with a vowel sound, then we use the form **an** as in *an icicle* or *an early meeting*. If the word begins with a consonant sound, we use the form *a* as in *a cup* or a *happy girl.*

It is important to point out to ESL/EFL learners that the initial letter of the word does not necessarily indicate that the word has a vowel or consonant sound. Consider these words:

*hour        herb        home        horse*

All four words are written with an initial "h, which, however, is not pronounced in all of them." In *hour* and *herb*, the "h" is not pronounced in American English and must therefore be preceded by *an*. *Home* or *horse*, on the other hand, are both written and pronounced with the initial *h* consonant.

At lower levels of proficiency, ESL/EFL learners need to practice distinguishing between words spelled with a vowel but pronounced with a consonant sound and words spelled with a consonant but pronounced with a vowel sound so that they can correctly choose between *a* and *an*. While they may make some errors in choosing between *a* and *an*, especially as beginning language learners, these are not major errors.

The next Discovery Activity illustrates a much greater concern for ESL/EFL learners: When do we use articles and for what purpose?

**Discovery Activity 6: Articles**
Look at the following sentences.

1. Underline all the articles (*a, an, the*) Explain the use of each article.
2. Discuss whether or not you could substitute one article for another, e.g. use *the* in place of *a/an*.

- If yes, discuss how the meaning of the sentence would change.
- If no, discuss why you cannot substitute one article for another in this instance.

   To drive a nail, hold it upright and tap it gently with a hammer, then take your hand away. Holding the hammer near the end of its handle, simply lift it, swinging your forearm from the elbow and let the weight of the head drop the hammer.
   [Reader's Digest. (1973). *New complete do-it-yourself manual* (p. 23). Pleasantville, New York: Reader's Digest.]

## *Discussion: Discovery Activity 6*

This excerpt is from a how-to guide. Since the intent is to explain home repair and maintenance procedures, the selection begins with nonspecific, general reference to the things used (*a nail, a hammer*) in hammering a nail:

   To drive **a** nail, hold it upright and tap it gently with **a** hammer, then take your hand away.

Once reference has been made to something, it becomes a specific or definite thing in the mind of the speaker. Consider:

> Holding **the** hammer near **the** end of its handle, simply lift it, swinging your forearm from **the** elbow and let **the** weight of **the** head drop **the** hammer.

If this "something" has different parts to it (e.g. *hammer*), then these parts are also something specific or definite (e.g. *the end of its handle*).

Because this how-to guide is explaining to the reader how to accomplish a particular task, *the* is also used before anything belonging to the reader's body used in this task (e.g. *the elbow*).

In this selection substituting *a/n*for *the* would sound awkward or wrong to a native speaker because of the reference to specific things.

### *This doesn't seem that complicated, so why do many ESL/EFL learners have problems with articles?*

To answer this question, compare the use of the articles *a/an* and *the* in Discovery Activity 6 with their use in the following sentences:

> **A** collection of lines in **an** image can narrow **the** odds even further. For example, **a** set of parallel lines or near-parallel is seldom **an** accident. Nonparallel lines in **the** world rarely project near-parallel lines in **an** image.
> [Pinker, S. (1997). *How the mind work* (p. 244). New York: Norton.]

In the first sentence, *a* and *an* can be replaced with *the*, although the meaning changes:

> **The** collection of lines in **the** image can narrow **the** odds even further.

Now, rather than referring to any collection or any image, the writer has a specific collection and image in mind, possibly those found on the page of the text in which this passage appears.

In the phrase *the odds*, however, *the* cannot be changed because *the odds* is a set expression or idiomatic phrase, adding another potential area of confusion to language learners.

We can also change the next sentence:

> For example, **the** set of parallel lines or near parallel is seldom *an* accident.

Notice that *the* can replace *a* before *set*. The meaning changes from general to specific. In the next part of the sentence, we cannot change *an accident* to *the accident* because there is no previous reference to make that accident a specific one.

Let's now see how we might change the last sentence:

> Nonparallel lines in **the** world rarely project near-parallel lines in **the** image

As in the previous sentence, *the* can replace *a* before *image* in this new context. *The world*, cannot, however change to *a world*. Here, from a native speaker's perspective, there is a particular world, i.e. *the* world in which we live. For nonnative speakers of English, particularly for those whose languages do not have articles, this is often a difficult perspective to comprehend and internalize.

Discovery Activity 6 and this discussion illustrate the complexity of information an ESL/EFL learner must keep in mind when trying to use articles correctly—not an easy task, especially when the learner's language does not have articles.

### *Are articles only used with count nouns?*

So far we have seen examples of article use with count nouns. For noncount nouns we can also use an article, but only *the:*

(17) I want fruit.
(18) I want the fruit by the sign.

In both Sentences (17) and (18), *fruit* is a noncount noun. Sentence (17) does not include *the* before *fruit*, but Sentence (18) does. Why is this?

- In Sentence (17), the speaker is referring to the general class or category known as *fruit*. The speaker is using *fruit* in a generic sense.
- In Sentence (18), the speaker is not referring to any fruit in general, but specifying a particular kind or instance of this category, namely *the fruit by the sign*.

As our brief examination of articles demonstrates, article usage is complicated. It is particularly difficult for ESL/EFL learners whose native language does not have articles. These learners face the greatest difficulties in correct article usage in English since they must learn to understand both the concept of articles, as well as the nuances and subtleties of article usage. Such learners have great difficulty, even at the most advanced levels, in choosing which article to use in which situation.

There are many books that offer detailed rules governing the use of articles, but learners often find these confusing and hard to learn. Offering learners frequent opportunities to practice the use of articles in a variety of contexts and to discuss their difficulties with them when they make repeated errors of the same type can help learners improve their use of articles.

Let us turn now to look at another structure class, the demonstratives.

## *Demonstratives*

> this, that, these, those

Demonstratives are another group of words signaling nouns. Demonstratives precede nouns and indicate relative location or position. The class consists of four words: *this*, *that*, *these*, and *those*. The choice depends on whether the noun is singular or plural and is relative to the speaker's mental and/or physical perception. Noncount nouns, since they have no plural forms, can only take the singular demonstratives *this* or *that*.

When speakers refer to *this book*, they are generally thinking of one book (as opposed to several or many books) physically close to them or of one book in particular which they have been discussing. When speakers refer to *this idea*, they are referring to a mental distance. When speakers refer to *those houses*, they are not referring to houses close to them, but rather to houses farther away, either physically or mentally. In addition to referring how far or close something is in the mind of the speaker, demonstratives can also refer to time, to preceding text, and to a new entity.

Discovery Activities 7 and 8 practice demonstratives. The first, Discovery Activity 7, is easier and uses teacher-made sentences. The second Discovery Activity is more difficult since it uses authentic excerpts.

**Discovery Activity 7: Demonstratives**
Look at the following sentences.

1.  Underline the demonstratives *this, that, these, those*.
2.  Discuss the use of *this, that, these, those*.

(a)  I enjoyed reading this book by Brown, but I didn't really like that one by him because I didn't think the ending was very good.
(b)  Those boys hanging out by supermarket are not nearly as friendly as these boys are.
(c)  Have you seen this new movie reviewed in the paper?
(d)  I haven't seen it, but I saw that movie with Russell Crowe reviewed last week.

## Discussion: Discovery Activity 7

- *Sentence (a)*
  The speaker is differentiating between two things, one physically closer than the other one by *this* and *that*.
- *Sentence (b)*
  The speaker is again indicating relative physical location of two groups of people by the use of *those* versus *these*.
- *Sentence (c)*
  *This* is used to identify something the speaker has just seen.
- *Sentence (d)*
  Since it is a response to the question the speaker poses in (c), *that* refers to something different, previous, and farther in the past.

In Discovery Activity 7, the use of the demonstratives can be quite easily explained by the notion of distance. Things that are close to the speaker, whether physically or mentally, are referred to as *this* (singular) or *these* (plural). Things that are farther away from the speaker are referred to as *that* (singular) or *those* (plural). This is the type of explanation generally presented to low-level language learners and certainly quite effective in that it can be easily demonstrated visually.

However, as learners become more proficient in English, they need to become aware of the metaphorical uses of these demonstratives. Frequently, they are used to refer to *mental* or *perceived* distance, which refers to the distance in the mind of the speaker. Since this is a psychological reference, it is a subjective type of distance and one that can be more difficult for learners to grasp. You will find examples of this in Discovery Activity 8, which is more challenging than Discovery Activity 7. You can find the answers to Part I of Discovery Activity 8 in the Answer Key. Compare your answers to Part II with those of your classmates.

**Discovery Activity 8: More Demonstratives**

**Part I**

Look at the following excerpts.

1. Underline the demonstratives *this, that, these, those.*

**A.**

College does seem to have a substantial net effect in the area of critical thinking. However, research on that topic has often not been controlled for age...

[Abbott, A. (2003, October). The zen of education. *The University of Chicago Magazine, 96*, p. 54.]

**B.**

"There's no telescreen!" he could not help murmuring...

"Ah," said the old man, "I never had one of those things."

[Orwell, G. (1949). *Nineteen eighty-four* (p. 82). New York: Signet.]

**C.**

Learning to configure a firewall isn't easy if you are not technically literate, but these devices will become increasingly necessary.

[Grossman, W. (2003, November). The spam wars: How should the internet deal with junk mail? *Reason, 42.*]

**D.**

Winston came across to examine the picture. It was a steel engraving of an oval building with rectangular windows, and a small tower in front..... "I know that building," said Winston finally.

[Orwell, G. (1949, 1984). *Nineteen eighty-four* (p. 83). New York: Signet.]

**Part II**

Look at the demonstratives you underlined.

2. Discuss the use of *this, that, these, those*.
3. Compare the use of *this, that, these, those* in this activity with their use in the previous Discovery Activity 9b.

   • Could you explain the demonstratives in the same way? Explain why or why not?

The last structure class words we are going to examine in Section 3 are quantifiers.

## *Quantifiers*

> some, many, much, few, a few, little, a little, a lot of, no, less

Quantifiers are another group of words that precede nouns and act as a signal that the following word is a noun. Quantifiers function to indicate a general number or quantity. When we talk about *many books*, we are talking about a large number of books rather than a small number. When a speaker says "*I have less time than I thought*," the hearer knows that this person is referring to a small quantity or amount of time.

Some quantifiers, such as *many* or *fewer,* can only be used with count nouns and others, such as *much* or *less,* only with noncount nouns. Still others, such as *some* can be used for plural count nouns or noncount nouns. Both *a lot of,* and *lots of* may substitute for either *much* or *many* in most (but not all) cases, particularly in spoken and less formal written forms of English. Consider the chart below:

| | |
|---|---|
| (19a) The Botanical Gardens has *many* flowers. | *flowers* is a count noun; use **many** or *a lot of* |
| (19b) The Botanical Gardens has *a lot of* flowers. | |
| (20a) Did it take *much* effort to collect these flowers? | *effort* is a noncount noun; |
| (20b) Did it take *a lot of* effort to collect these flowers? | use **much** or *a lot of* |

Native speakers generally use *a lot of* in spoken English. In more formal writing, however, *a lot of* is considered too informal and is avoided. Nonnative speakers of English often find it easier to use *a lot of* rather than *much* or *many* since *a lot of* can be used for either count or noncount nouns.

This next Discovery Activity asks you to decide on the grammaticality of sentences with *much* or *many* and then to think about why you made the decisions you did.

---

**Discovery Activity 9: Much, Many**

Look at the following sentences.

1. Mark the sentences that sound ungrammatical to you with an asterisk.*

    (a) The Botanical Garden has many flowers from all over the world.
    (b) Did it take much effort to collect these flowers?
    (c) Much of the plants were donated by collectors.
    (d) Many time has been devoted to gathering the plants and flowers.
    (e) Has the Botanical Garden received many support from the town?
    (f) It is encouraging that many people support the gardens.
    (g) Much dollars have been raised during the fundraising campaign.

2. Look at all the grammatical sentences containing *many*.

    - How can you describe the nouns following *many*?
    - What grammatical feature(s) do they have in common?

3. Look at the grammatical sentences containing *much*.

    - How can you describe the nouns following *much*?
    - What grammatical feature(s) do they have in common?

4. Look at the ungrammatical sentences you marked with an asterisk and the grammatical sentences you described in (2) and (3).

    - What generalizations can you make about the use of *many* and *much*?

---

## Discussion: Discovery Activity 9

English requires the use of *much* with noncount nouns and *many* with plural count nouns. This rule of grammar is one that native speakers generally adhere to quite closely, albeit unconsciously. When they encounter *much* + a plural count noun such as *much cats* or *much schools*, they are struck by the construction, although they may not be able to articulate why. Sentences (c), (d), (e), and (g) are ungrammatical because they violate this rule:

- In Sentences (c) and (g), *plants* and *dollars* are plural count nouns and need to be preceded by *many*.
- In Sentences (d) and (e), *time* and *support* are noncount nouns that require *much*.

▶ *Learner difficulties*

> Native speakers of English are generally unaware that a rule distinguishing between *much* and *many* exists because they intuitively know which one precedes which type of noun. For ESL/EFL learners however, the correct use of *much* and *many* requires understanding the concept of count versus noncount nouns and knowing which noun belongs in which category.
>
> For these learners, the problem is compounded by the fact that *much* and *many* occur far less frequently than do *a lot of* or *lots of*, both of which can be used with count and noncount nouns.

The next Discovery Activity looks at *less* and *fewer.*

> **Discovery Activity 10: Less, Fewer**
>
> Look at the following sentences.
>
> 1. Mark the sentences that sound grammatical to you with a **G.**
> 2. Mark the sentences that sound ungrammatical to you with **UN.**
>
> (a) Fewer students than expected registered for night classes in spring semester.
> (b) During the long winter months, there are fewer daylight hours and less people like to travel at night.
> (c) When there is less demand for classes, the university hires less teachers.
> (d) With less classes offered, students have less choices.
> (e) With fewer choices, students have less options in courses they can take toward graduation.

## Discussion: Discovery Activity 10

In this Discovery Activity, unlike in the previous one, native speakers may have difficulty deciding which sentences are ungrammatical. The "rule" governing the use of *fewer* versus *less* states that *fewer* comes before plural count nouns and *less* before noncount nouns. In contrast to the rule governing the use of *much* and *many,* native speakers often use *less* before count nouns. This mixing of the two forms is readily observable, including supermarket checkout lines, where one can see signs announcing registers designated "10 items or less."

Earlier in this chapter we posed the question of why the distinction between count and noncount nouns is important for ESL/EFL learners. As our exploration of different noun signals in Section 3 has again demonstrated, certain structure words accompany either count or noncount nouns. Thus, we see that understanding this distinction helps learners make appropriate language choices.

We now turn to the last part in this chapter, Section 4, in which we examine pronouns.

## Section 4: Pronouns

The most common definition of a pronoun is a word that replaces a noun. While this is true in many cases, when we examine pronouns more closely, we see that they can replace a noun or a noun phrase.

### *What is a noun phrase?*

A noun phrase includes a noun and all of its modifiers. These modifiers include determiners and adjectives, as you can see in the chart below.

| Noun Phrase + Verb | Pronoun + Verb |
|---|---|
| (20) *Jerry* reads. | |
| (21) *The boy* reads. | |
| (22) *The little boy* reads. | ⟶ **He** reads. |
| (23) *The happy little boy* reads. | |

As we see in Sentences, (21), (22), and (23), the noun phrase, regardless of the actual number of words it contains, can be replaced by the pronoun *he* in exactly the same way that *he* replaced *Jerry* in Sentence (20).

For extra practice, Discovery Activity 11 asks you to change noun phrases into pronouns. This is a teacher-made activity with no authentic excerpts, so you may find it very easy. If you are sure you know what noun phrases are and do not feel you need this activity, continue on to the next section.

**Discovery Activity 11: Pronouns**

Look at the following sentences.

1.  Underline the noun phrases.
2.  Substitute a pronoun for the underlined noun phrases.

(a) Lauren was married yesterday.
(b) The bride was elegantly dressed.
(c) The lovely white gown looked stunning.
(d) The nervous bridegroom wore black.
(e) The younger sisters and brothers were excited.
(f) A cousin was the flower girl.
(g) A well-organized, lavish reception was held later.
(h) My mother, my father, my older brother, and I were invited.

## Discussion: Discovery Activity 11

1. *Lauren* was married yesterday.
   **She**
2. *The bride* was elegantly dressed.
   **She**
3. *The lovely white gown* looked stunning.
   **It**
4. *The nervous bridegroom* wore black.
   **He**
5. *The younger sisters and brothers* were excited.
   **They**
6. *A cousin* was the flower girl.
   **She**
7. *A well-organized, lavish reception* was held later.
   **It**
8. *My mother, father, brother, and I* were invited.
   **We**

A pronoun may replace a single noun as in Sentence (1), but it also may replace noun phrases (see Chapter 8). As Sentences (2) through (8) illustrate again, regardless of how long the noun phrase is, it can be replaced by a single pronoun.

In this particular activity, we replaced all the noun phrases with one type of pronoun. This type of pronoun is called a **subject** pronoun because it is the subject of the verb of the sentence.

## Types of Pronouns by Function

### What are the different types of English pronouns?

There are several different types of pronouns, each type serving a different function in the sentence. In this section, we will look at four types of pronouns: subject, object, possessive, and indefinite.

## Subject Pronouns

In Discovery Activity 11, you replaced all the noun phrases with *subject* pronouns. Pronouns that are found to the **left** of the main verb are called subject pronouns because they tell us who or what the doer of the verb is, or who or what is described by the verb.

| Subject Pronouns | |
|---|---|
| **singular** | **plural** |
| I | we |
| you | you |
| he, she, it | they |

As you look at this chart, you will notice that in English we use eight subject pronouns, although there are only seven different pronoun forms. The second person pronoun *you* can refer to either a singular or plural person; context is what indicates whether the singular or plural pronoun *you* is intended. Again we see that in English form does not equal function.

In southern regions of the United States many speakers frequently use *you all* or its contracted form *ya'll,* for second plural pronoun formation. Another dialectal variation for plural *you* found in some parts of the United States is *youse*. While *you all/ya'll* is an accepted variant in the American South, *youse* is considered nonstandard and is a stigmatized form.

## *Object Pronouns*

*Object pronouns* are another type of pronoun. These are pronouns that replace nouns or noun phrases in object position in the sentence. Object position means that the noun or noun phrase receives the action of the verb:

| | **Function** |
|---|---|
| (24a) **The girl** reads. | **noun phrase** in *subject* position |
| (24b) **She** reads. | *subject* pronoun |
| (25a) The girl reads **books**. | **noun phrase** in *object* position |
| (25b) She reads **them**. | **pronoun** in *object* position |

In Sentence (24a) *The girl* is the subject of the verb *reads*.

- The noun phrase *The girl* answers the question *Who reads?*, a question that helps tell us who (or what) the subject of the verb is.
- Since *The girl* is in subject position and refers to a single female person, the subject pronoun *she* can replace *The girl* (Sentence 24b).

In Sentence (25a), *books* is the object of the verb *reads*.

- The words *books* answers the question *What does the girl (or she) read?*, a question that helps tell us what (or who) the object of the verb is.
- Since *books* is in object position and refers to a plural object, the object pronoun *them* can replace *books* (Sentence 25b).

Like the subject pronouns, there are eight object pronouns, although there are only seven different forms. The object pronoun *you* is the same for both singular and plural. Note that the object pronouns *you* and *it* are identical in form, although not in function, to their subject pronoun counterparts.

| Object Pronouns | |
|---|---|
| **Singular** | **Plural** |
| me | us |
| **you** | **you** (no change) |
| him, her, it | them |

Because *you* and *it* have the same pronoun form in both subject and object positions, low proficiency ESL/EFL learners sometimes become confused as to the function of these two pronouns.

### Possessive Pronouns and Possessive Adjectives

Possessives comprise a third group of pronouns. This group is generally divided into two subgroups, based on the function of the possessive pronouns in a sentence. The first subset is generally known as *possessive adjectives* and the second set as *possessive pronouns*.

The distinction between the two groups lies in what does or does not follow. Possessive adjectives are followed by a noun or noun phrase (Sentence 26). Possessive pronouns stand alone (Sentence 26a).

(26) This is **my** *book*        versus        (26a) It is **mine**.

Possessive pronouns, like any pronoun, replace a noun or noun phrase. In Sentence (26a), *mine* replaces the noun phrase *my book* in Sentence (26).

Possessive adjectives and possessive pronouns are similar because they both refer to possession or ownership. They differ, however, in their function:

- Possessive **adjectives** form *part* of a noun phrase.
- Possessive **pronouns** *replace* noun phrases.

Possessive adjectives are not actually pronouns because they do not replace nouns or noun phrases. In Sentence (26), for instance, *my* is modifying or describing something about *book*. *My* is not replacing *book*. Nevertheless, since the use of possessive adjectives closely parallels that of possessive pronouns, possessive adjectives are usually grouped together when presented to ESL/EFL learners.

The table below shows the different forms of the possessives.

| Possessive Adjectives | Possessive Pronouns |
|---|---|
| my | **mine** |
| your | yours |
| his | his |
| her | hers |
| its | its |
| our | ours |
| their | theirs |

Use Discovery Activity 12 to practice distinguishing between the possessive adjectives and the possessive pronouns. If you are comfortable in your ability to distinguish them, proceed to the next section.

**Discovery Activity 12: Possessive Adjectives versus Possessive Pronouns**

Look at the following sentences.

The **possessive adjectives** are **bolded**.
The **possessive pronouns** are *italicized*.

1) Discuss why you think the italicized words are called possessive pronouns.
2) Compare the underlined and italicized words in Set A and in Set B.

- How are they similar?
- How are they different?
- Why do you think they are considered two subsets within the same category?

**Set A**

(a) I like **my** car.
(b) You lost **your** book.
(c) The man sold **his** computer.
(d) That woman knows **her** priorities.
(e) That dog hurt **its** paw.
(f) We want **our** share.
(g) They forgot **their** appointment.

**Set B**

I like *mine*.
You lost *yours*.
The man sold *his*.
That woman knows *hers*.
_____
We want ours.
They forgot theirs.

## Discussion: Discovery Activity 12

The underlined possessive adjectives in Set A are part of noun phrases. They are describing, or modifying, the nouns they precede, as illustrated in the following table.

| Possessive Adjective | + Noun | = Noun Phrase |
|---|---|---|
| my | car | my car |
| your | book | your book |
| his | friend | his friend |

Since the italicized words in Set B replace noun phrases, the words in this set are called possessive pronouns. The one exception is Sentence (e), where the possessive adjective *its* has no corresponding possessive pronoun form. We cannot use *its* as a possessive pronoun.

**Why do ESL/EFL learners have difficulties with possessive adjectives and possessive pronouns?**

▶ *Learner difficulties*

For learners of English, difficulties in the use of possessive adjectives and possessive pronouns arise for several reasons. First, there are the similarities in form between the subject and object pronouns. The possessive pronouns and the possessive adjectives are also similar in form, which often make them confusing for ESL/EFL learners.

Second, English pronoun forms distinguish between gender when the pronoun refers back to a female or male subject. In *Amanda sees her brother* or *Tom brought his friend*, the possessive adjectives *her* and *his* refer to *Amanda* (female) and *Tom* (male) respectively.

In some languages where all nouns have gender, the possessive adjectives and pronouns change according to the noun they are modifying or replacing, and not to the subject as in English. Contrast these French and English sentences:

| | |
|---|---|
| (27) Amanda sees **her** *book*. | Amanda = female person<br>pronoun, *her*, agrees with *Amanda* |
| (28) Amanda voit **son** *livre*. | *livre* = masculine noun<br>pronoun, *son,* agrees with *livre* |

Learners whose native languages have patterns similar to French may have trouble choosing the correct possessive adjective form in English.

## *Reflexive Pronouns*

Reflexive pronouns are a little different from the pronouns we have explored up to now because reflexive pronouns do not substitute for a noun or noun phrase. Instead, reflexive pronouns are generally used to refer back to the subject, as in Sentence (29). They can also be used for emphasis as in Sentence (30), (31), and (30a). In addition, when a reflexive pronoun is used with *by*, it usually means "alone" as in Sentence (32).

| | |
|---|---|
| (29) *The actress* admired *herself* in the mirror. | *herself* refers back to *The actress* |
| (30) *I myself* would never do that. | *myself* is used for emphasis. It can |
| (30a) *I* would never do that *myself*. | immediately follow the subject (30) or come at the end of the sentence (30a). |
| (31) The teacher wants *us* to present the projects *ourselves*. | *ourselves* is also used for emphasis, but it refers back to the **object** *us*. |
| (32) *Joe* can't answer the question by *himself*. | *by* + relative pronoun = alone |

### *What are the forms of the reflexive pronouns?*

The reflexive pronouns vary according to person and number (singular/plural) as in the chart below:

| **Reflexive Pronouns** | |
|---|---|
| I | **my**self |
| you | **your**self |
| he | **him**self |
| she | **her**self |
| it | **it**self |
| we | **our**selves |
| you | **your**selves |
| they | **them**selves |

The singular forms all end in *–self*; the plurals in *–selves*. Note that there are two forms for "you" in the reflexive: the singular *yourself* and the plural *yourselves*. This is one instance where English does make a distinction between the singular and plural "you."

### *What kinds of difficulties do ESL/EFL learners have with the reflexive pronouns?*

▶ *Learner difficulties*

Less proficient learners, particularly those who speak languages that do not have the same pronoun distinctions as English, often confuse the use of the object pronoun and the reflexive pronoun, producing such sentences as:

*She looked at *her* in the mirror.

## *Indefinite Pronouns*

*Indefinite pronouns* comprise another subclass of pronouns. These pronouns are called indefinite because they do not refer to something definite, that is something known or specific. Some grammar books call these pronouns compound pronouns because they are formed by combining two separate words, as you see in the chart below.

|        | -body     | -one     | -thing     |
|--------|-----------|----------|------------|
| some-  | somebody  | someone  | something  |
| any-   | anybody   | anyone   | anything   |
| every  | everybody | everyone | everything |
| no     | nobody    | no one*  | nothing    |

*Note that *no one* is the only indefinite pronoun spelled as two words.

These indefinite pronouns take the singular third person verb form, as we see in this article title:

(29) Is Anybody out There? Detection devices are in the works for rooting out extraterrestrial life

[Brownlee, C. (2006, January 21). *Science News, 16*(3), 42.]

Or on this web page from the American Museum of Natural History in New York City:

(30) Biodiversity: Everything Counts!

[(2006, December 17). Retrieved from: http://ology.amnh.org/biodiversity/]

In prescriptive, formal English, these indefinite pronouns are followed by a singular possessive pronoun. As we discussed in Chapter 1, under the most traditional rules of formal English, this singular possessive pronoun must be the masculine form *his*. With attempts toward more inclusive language, there has been acceptance of the use of *his or her* or *his/her*. In casual spoken and less formal written forms of English, these indefinite pronouns are often followed by the more neutral plural possessive form *their*.

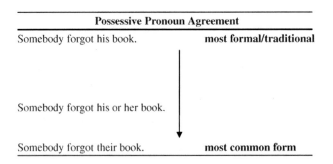

|                                  |                          |
|----------------------------------|--------------------------|
| **Possessive Pronoun Agreement** |                          |
| Somebody forgot his book.        | **most formal/traditional** |
| Somebody forgot his or her book. |                          |
| Somebody forgot their book.      | **most common form**     |

## ► *Learner difficulties*

The use of the singular possessive pronoun is an area with which native speakers and ESL/EFL learners both have difficulty although the underlying reasons are different. Generally, native speakers require specific instruction in the use of the singular pronoun after the indefinite pronouns. English is a relatively gender-free language and since speakers do not know to whom an indefinite pronoun is actually referring, there is a (natural) preference to use the gender neutral plural form.

For ESL/EFL learners, the misuse of possessive pronouns with indefinite pronouns is part of the general difficulties they have in learning pronoun usage. In addition, the more learners are exposed to native speakers' actual use of English, the more they become confused between what they hear and read, and what they have been taught in terms of appropriate or correct pronoun usage with indefinite pronouns.

Nevertheless, for both ESL/EFL learners and native speakers, it is important to draw a distinction between informal and formal language, whether written or spoken. In addition, for test-taking purposes, learners must be aware of the "correct" use of formal forms.

# Summary

**To identify nouns we use**

- semantic clues
- structural clues
- morphological clues

**There are three categories of nouns that learners of English need to learn**

- count
- noncount
- crossover

**Determiners tells us how many or which items the noun or noun phrase is referring to. They act as noun signals**

| Examples | Type |
|---|---|
| the, a/an | articles |
| my, your, his, her, its, our, their | possessive adjectives |
| this, that, these, those | demonstrative adjectives |
| some, many, much, few, a few, little, a little, a lot of, no | quantifiers |
| one, two, three, fifteen, forty, one hundred | ordinal numbers |
| first, second, twentieth | cardinal numbers |

## Functions of Nouns Discussed in Chapter 3

| Function | Example |
|---|---|
| subject of verb | The **cat** meowed.<br>**Students** study hard.<br>Meg **likes** books. |
| direct object of verb | Meg likes **books.**<br>The boys hit **the ball.**<br>The policeman stopped **Jack.** |

| | Subject pronouns | Object pronouns | Possessive adjectives[2] | Possessive pronouns | Reflexive pronouns |
|---|---|---|---|---|---|
| | | | **English pronoun chart** | | |
| 1st person singular | I | me | my | mine | myself |
| 2nd person singular | you | you | your | yours | yourself |
| 3rd person masculine, singular | he | him | his | his | himself |
| 3rd person feminine, singular | she | her | her | hers | herself |
| 3rd person neuter, singular | it | it | its | (not used) | itself |
| 1st person plural | we | us | our | ours | ourselves |
| 2nd person plural | you | you | your | yours | yourselves |
| 3rd person plural | they | them | their | theirs | themselves |

[2]Remember that although technically possessive adjectives are not pronouns, they are generally classified and taught together with the possessive pronouns because of their closely related function, meaning, and forms.

| Common types of noncount nouns[3] | |
|---|---|
| abstract | information, advice, help, homework, love, hate, health, behavior, work, patience, experience, fun, beauty, democracy |
| solids | bread, meat, pasta, ice cream, cotton, silk, wool, iron, wood, glass, chalk, soap, detergent, butter, margarine, yogurt, cheese, chocolate, garlic |
| liquids | oil, vinegar, soup, water, milk, coffee, juice, wine, beer, vodka, shampoo, conditioner, lotion, gasoline, blood |

(continued)

| Common types of noncount nouns[3] | |
|---|---|
| grains/powders | rice, cereal, wheat, flour, sugar, salt, pepper, baking soda |
| gases | air, oxygen, carbon dioxide, smoke, smog, steam |
| classes or categories | furniture, food, fruit, luggage, baggage, transportation, mail, jewelry, trash, equipment |
| weather | weather, rain, snow, sleet, hail, ice, fog, haze, wind, thunder, lightning, sunshine, humidity |
| fields of study | linguistics, education, sociology, mathematics, engineering, biology, chemistry, social work, business, psychology |

[3]Some of these may be crossover, e.g. *democracy* or *meat*.

## Practice Activities

### *Activity 1: Nouns and Verbs*

The words below can function as both nouns and verbs.

1. On a separate sheet of paper, write pairs of sentences contrasting their use.
2. Explain which words provide clues to the function of the words in your sentences.

    *Example:* badger

        A *badger* lives underground.
        That mother *badgers* her children.

- In the first sentence, the article *a* before *badger* and its initial sentence position indicate that *badger* is being used as a singular noun. It is part of the subject noun phrase *a badger*.
- In the second sentence *badger* is a verb. It is found to the right of the subject noun phrase, in the sentence position usually occupied by a verb.
- Another clue is the inflectional *–s*, which is attached to present tense singular verbs in English.
- Although learners could confuse this *–s* inflection with the plural *–s* inflection attached to nouns, the placement of *badger* in a sentence will help them determine that it is a verb.

    1. fall
    2. mail
    3. time
    4. drink
    5. color

## *Activity 2: Articles*

Part I

1. Read Excerpt A and Excerpt B.
2. Underline all the articles (*a, an, the*)
3. Discuss whether or not you could substitute one article for another, e.g. can you use *the* in place of *a*/an?

   - If yes, discuss how the meaning of the sentence would change.
   - If no, discuss why you cannot substitute one article for another in this instance.

   **A.**

   There's much you can do to keep the plumbing in your home functioning well, as this chapter shows. Beginning with an overall description of a home plumbing system, the chapter goes on to describe the basics of repair and maintenance, showing how to deal with everything from a leaky faucet to an overflowing toilet.

   > [Reader's Digest. (1973). *New complete do-it-yourself* (p. 197). Pleasantville, NY: Reader's Digest.]

   **B.**

   ... lines that are parallel in the world, such as the edges of a telephone pole, almost always project near-parallel lines. So if there are near-parallel lines in an image, the odds favor parallel edges in the world.

   > [Pinker, S. (1997). *How the mind works* (p. 244). NY: Norton.]

Part II (optional follow-up)

4. Compare the use of articles in Excerpt A and Excerpt B.

   - What similarities and/or differences do you see?

5. Consider article use from the perspective of speakers whose native language has no articles.

   - What do you think they might such learners of English find difficult?

6. Discuss how you might use an excerpt such as one of these for teaching purposes.


## *Activity 3: Count and Noncount Nouns*

Nouns in English can be classified into two broad categories, count and noncount nouns.

1. Discuss how you might explain the difference between count and noncount nouns to ESL/EFL student at a low to intermediate level of proficiency.
   There are also many nouns in English that are crossover nouns. These are nouns that have both count and noncount meanings.
2. Look at the list below.

- On a separate sheet of paper, make three columns. Label the first column **Count Nouns,** the second column **Noncount Nouns,** and the third column **Crossover Nouns.**
- Write the nouns listed below into the appropriate column.
- For those nouns you listed under the column **Crossover Nouns,** discuss the differences between the count and noncount meanings.

experience      sense    poverty      idea    yarn    fear    flour        vapor
foliage anger        difficulty    water    concern        blood    skylight

## Activity 4: Crossover Nouns

The sentences in the excerpts below include both count and noncount nouns.

1. Label the nouns that are count with **C.**
2. Label the nouns that are noncount with **NC.**
3. Label the nouns that are crossover, that is which ones have both count and noncount meanings with, **CR.**
4. Discuss the nouns you have identified as **CR:**

- Identify any clues you used in labeling any word as a crossover.

*Example:*

**CR**                                                                    **C**
Emotions, in particular, are often governed by cultural expectations.

*Emotion* is a crossover noun. When we talk about the general category of strong feelings, *emotion* is noncount noun; when we refer to specific strong feelings such as love, hate, or anger, *emotion* is a count noun. A clue that helps identify the count usage in this sentence is the plural *–s* ending of *emotions*.

1. Unlike turkeys, chickens are not native to North America. However, they were easily transported from Europe and became a staple food in early settlements like Jamestown in Virginia. Ubiquitous and easy to raise, chicken became an important part of the Southern diet.
   [The World of Food. (2006, September 30). *Wine Spectator, 31*(8), p. 68.]
2. Like Italian food, Italian olive oil is distinguishable by region. Oils from Tuscany are considered the benchmark.
   [The World of Food. (2006, September 30). *Wine Spectator, 31*(8), p. 100.]
3. Spain produces an extraordinary range of wines.
   [The World of Food. (2006, September 30). *Wine Spectator, 31*(8), p. 108.]

## *Activity 5: Error Analysis*

The following excerpts were written by learners of English. There are four types of errors in each paragraph:

(a)  article usage (*the, a/n*)
(b)  quantifiers (*much* vs. *many*)
(c)  singular vs. plural
(d)  personal pronoun use

Ignore *any other* **errors**, even though this may be difficult. Focus only on the four types of errors listed above.

1.  Underline and correct each error you find.
2.  Compare your responses with your classmates.

*   When you compare your responses with other native speakers, you may find some disagreement. For example, native speakers do not always agree in their use of *the*. This underscores again that the use of the article *the* is very difficult for ESL/EFL learners even native speakers may have different interpretations and disagree in the use of *the*.

    *Example:*

    Today there is the e-mail and the snail mail.
    Today there is *the* e-mail and *the* snail mail.

In this sentence, the learner is adding the article *the* before a noncount noun that is being used in a very general or generic sense.

**A.**

Snail mail is the nickname of regular mail. In the recent years more and more people use the e-mail. There are advantage and disadvantage of e-mail though. Unfortunately, the e-mail also has it bad points because the senders can never send gifts or touchable stuffs to your friend and family.

**B.**

Working women in America face much kind of problems. The pressure from work affects her families. The women don't have the much opportunities the men do. Men have the more opportunities in the workplace. And the women earn fewer money—they earn about 75 cents for every dollar earned by the men. But American women face many problems when they work. They have much kind of pressure from work and from her families. They must work better than the men. The American women must take care of her children and do many houseworks when she gets home from his job.

## C.

I think there are numerous benefits to travel in groups with a tour guide. There is many informations about new places, but I need a specific one. Tour guides can give me good advices. People who want to travel alone should have many experiences about traveling. I don't have experiences, so I don't prefer to travel alone.

## Answer Key: Chapter 3 Discovery Activities

### *Discussion: Discovery Activity 3*

Possible expressions of quantity include: (note that not all in the list will work with all the different noncount nouns in the activity.)

- a pound of
- a slice of
- an ounce of
- a sheet of
- a cup of
- a piece of
- a bit of
- a great deal of
- a blade of

### *Discussion: Discovery Activity 4*

- *Sense, coffee, hair, concern,* and *experience*: both count and noncount. When used as count nouns, they refer to individual faculties, pieces, items, interests, or events.
  - *Pam has an acute sense of smell:* refers to Pam's ability to smell.
  - *Llyod's experiences abroad proved invaluable:* refers to the events Llyod experienced.

- *coffee:* both count and noncount. It has become common for speakers to use such expressions as *a coffee, two milks, three sugars.* These expressions have become a type of shorthand for underlying longer expressions, which include the actual descriptive phrases making them countable:

| | | |
|---|---|---|
| ○ a cup of coffee | → | a coffee |
| ○ two containers of milk | → | two milks |
| ○ three packets of sugar | → | three sugars |

- *music:* noncount. May be used with a noun pharses such as *type of music* or *piece of music.*

- *thunder:* noncount. While *thunder* is noncount, it is often referred to in a count-able form through the addition of the noun phrase *clap of* as in *I heard a clap of thunder.*

## Discussion : Discovery Activity 5

*Excerpt A*

- *the* before *professor, main door,* and *center of town* serves to identify each spe-cific or particular noun.
  - ○ When the author refers to *the professor,* he is referring to a particular pro-fessor, one of the main characters of the book, and not just any person who happens to be a professor.
  - ○ *The main door* is a specific door in the author's (and reader's) mind.
  - ○ *the center of town* refers to the specific part of town in which the story is taking place.
- *the Bristol Library:* an example of *the* + place name.

*Excerpt B*

- *the* before *computer, typewriter,* and *pencil:* these nouns are the labels or names for different types or kinds of items.
  - ○ *The computer* and *the typewriter* refer not to a specific computer or typewriter, but to that kind of machine.
  - ○ *The pencil* refers not to a specific instrument, but to a kind of writing imple-ment.

## Discussion: Discovery Activity 8

*Excerpt A*

- *That* refers to the previously mentioned topic from which the writer is distancing himself/herself.

*Excerpt B*

- *Those* refers to telescreens, items this speaker feels outside of or far away from his own personal experience of such a thing.

*Excerpt C*

- *These* refers to *a firewall* (or *such devices* since *a firewall* itself is singular).
- Unlike in Excerpt A, the writer is not distancing himself/herself from the object or topic.

*Excerpt D*

- The reference to *that building* is similar to Excerpt A, where the speaker is refer-ring to a perceived mental distance

# Chapter 4
# Adjectives and Adverbs

## Introduction

This chapter focuses on two closely related word classes: Adjectives, which we explore in Section I and adverbs, which we investigate in Section II. The chapter examines the differences and similarities of these two word classes and also considers the issues in categorizing the various subclasses of adverbs.

Adjectives and adverbs generally differ in form, but not always. Some adjectives and adverbs have no "typical" derivational endings, and some adjectives and adverbs have derivational endings typical of the other class. Key to distinguishing between the two classes is their function: adjectives modify nouns and, as we saw in Chapter 2 and will examine more closely in this chapter, adverbs can modify just about anything else in the sentence.

## Section 1: Adjectives

### *What role do adjectives play in a sentence?*

Adjectives comprise a rich, picturesque category that gives flavor to the written and spoken languages. Unlike structure words, adjectives do not provide grammatical meaning to a sentence. Instead, adjectives are content words that provide imagery and character to discourse by describing the nouns in a sentence.

## Identification of Adjectives

### *How can I identify adjectives?*

As with nouns, we can use semantic, morphological, and structural clues to identify adjectives.

A. DeCapua, *Grammar for Teachers,*
© Springer 2008

## Semantic Clues

When we say that we use semantic clues to help us identify the function of a word, we mean that the meaning of a word itself provides a clue to its use. For example, *long, small, hot,* and *great* are descriptive words that describe something. These words are descriptive adjectives that fall into a group of what are referred to as *prototypical adjectives.*

### *What is a* prototypical adjective?

Prototypical adjectives are those adjectives that are generally easily identified on the basis of their inherent characteristic of describing nouns. Such adjectives are often called "best example" adjectives and are the kinds of adjectives native speakers will generally think of when they are asked to list adjectives.

As we noted in our discussion of nouns in Chapter 3, while native speakers may be able to rely on semantic clues in classifying words as adjectives, it is usually difficult for learners of English to rely on semantic clues and they must use other clues to help them determine which words are functioning as adjectives.

Try Discovery Activity 3 if you would like more practice in identifying prototypical adjectives. After this Discovery Activity, we will look at morphological and structural clues, which are more productive for ESL/EFL learners in identifying adjectives.

---

**Discovery Activity 1: Prototypical Adjectives**

1.  Read the sentences.
2.  Write in the first adjective that comes to mind to complete each sentence.

   (a)  The _____ boy refused to put away his toys.
   (b)  The _____ dog bit the man.
   (c)  Some _____ birds flew over my head.
   (d)  The engineers failed to realize the _____ impact the project would have.

3.  Evaluate your adjectives and those of your classmates.

   • Are there any morphological clues, that is, suffixes that identify these words as adjectives? If yes, what are they?
   • Would you consider these adjectives "best example" or prototypical adjectives? Why or why not?

## *Discussion: Discovery Activity 1*

The purpose of Discovery Activity 1 is to illustrate how much you, as either a native speaker or a highly proficient non-native speaker, know about adjectives. Compare your responses to another classmate or friend. Think about the words you chose. What are they telling or describing about each noun?

Whether or not you know all the rules governing the use of adjectives, you intuitively know which words describe nouns. You are relying upon a subconscious knowledge of the semantic properties of adjectives to complete the sentences in this Discovery Activity. However, as we pointed out in our discussion of nouns and semantic properties, morphological and structural clues are generally more useful to ESL/EFL learners.

## Morphological Clues

### *Derivational Endings*

Morphological clues, such as the derivational endings discussed in Chapter 2, offer clues as to which words are adjectives. Remember that in Chapter 1 you were able to identify some of the nonsense words in the poem *Jabberwocky* as adjectives based on their derivational endings (morphological clues) and/or on their sentence position (structural clues).

#### *What are some of the typical derivational endings for adjectives?*

In Chapter 2 we saw that derivational morphemes are affixes (prefixes and suffixes) that attach to words to make new words and/or change their word class. Some of the suffixes we examined were those that indicate adjective class membership such as *–ous* (e.g. *gorgeous*) and *–ful* (e.g. *helpful*). Although not all adjectives can be identified on the basis of morphological endings, many can be.

Discovery Activity 1 reviews some common derivational endings of adjectives. If you are feel that you are strong in this area, you can move on to the next section.

---

**Discovery Activity 2: Adjectives**

**Part I**

Look at the following excerpts.

1. Underline all the adjectives you find.

**A.**

Love him or hate him—as many do in light of . . . revisionist views of Columbus—it is impossible to downplay the importance of Columbus's voyage . . .

[Davis, K. C. (2003). *Don't know much about history: Everything you need to know about American history but never learned* (p. 4). New York: HarperCollins.]

**B.**

Autocratic and conservative, he tyrannized his workers. Ford's attitude was that workers were unreliable and shiftless.

[Davis, K. C. (2003). *Don't know much about history: Everything you need to know about American history but never learned* (p. 338). New York: HarperCollins.]

**Part II**

Look at the adjectives you underlined.

1. Discus which morphological clues helped you identify the adjectives.
2. Were you able to use morphological clues for all the adjectives? Why or why not?

## *Discussion: Discovery Activity 2*

As you can see in Discovery Activity 2, many adjectives can be identified by their morphological endings. Common adjective suffixes include:

| -ist | -ible/able | -ic | –ive | -less |
|------|------------|-----|------|-------|
| revisionist | impossible | autocratic | conservative | shiftless |
| journalist | reliable | academic | active | helpless |
| lobbyist | considerable | basic | selective | jobless |

As we discussed in Chapter 2, learning about derivational endings is very helpful for ESL/EFL learners in both helping them identify word classes and in building their vocabulary. However, learners of English need to be cautioned that some suffixes can identify words that belong to more than one class. A good example of this here is *–ive*, which is included in the above chart as identifying adjectives. This *–ive* suffix can also serve to identify nouns. Consider the sentence:

(1) He is a *conservative*.

In this sentence, *conservative* is a noun, meaning someone who belongs to a conservative party or movement. Likewise the word *relative* can be either an adjective or a noun as in:

(2) It is a *relative* problem.
(3) My *relative* lives nearby.

Something that is *relative* refers to a type of comparison or relation to something else. When we refer to someone connected to us by blood or marriage, we refer to the noun, a *relative* of ours. The form of the two words is identical, but their function is different, which we can tell from the sentence position of *relative*. In Sentence (2), *relative* comes before a noun, and in Sentence (3), *relative* is to the left of the verb, which is the normal sentence position for a noun subject.

## Inflectional Clues

### Are there any inflectional clues to help us identify adjectives?

Just as only plural count nouns can take the inflectional *–s* ending, there are inflections that adjectives take. As we saw in Chapter 2, adjectives and adverbs can take the *–er* and *–est* inflections to show the *comparative* and *superlative*. When we compare two things, we use the comparative. When we compare more than two things, we use the superlative. We can identify many adjectives by their ability to take the comparative suffix *–er* and the superlative suffix *–est*, (with some spelling changes).

**Adjectives and inflectional endings**

| Adjective | Comparative *–er* | | Superlative *-est* |
|---|---|---|---|
| cool | cool**er** | (than) | The cool**est** |
| mad | mad**der** | (than) | The mad**dest** |
| lean | lean**er** | (than) | the lean**est** |
| happy | happ**ier** | (than) | the happ**iest** |
| little | litt**ler** | (than) | the litt**lest** |

*Sample Sentences:*

a. It is **cool** today.
b. It is **cooler than** yesterday.
c. It is **the coolest** day of the year.
d. On a separate sheet of paper, write your own sample sentences:

   i. long
  ii. green
 iii. busy

Note that in addition to the *–er*, we must include *than*, and in addition to the *–est*, we must use *the* before the adjective.

## Why do we say more beautiful *and not* *beautifuller?

Generally, for adjectives with two syllables or more we add the *more* and *most* before the adjective to form the comparative and superlative forms.

**Adjectives and *more/most***

| Adjective | Comparative *more* | | Superlative *most* |
|---|---|---|---|
| beautiful | **more** beautiful | (than) | **the most** beautiful |
| gorgeous | **more** gorgeous | (than) | **the most** gorgeous |
| enthusiastic | **more** enthusiastic | (than) | **the most** enthusiastic |

*Sample Sentences:*

a. That is a **beautiful** house.
b. That house on the corner is **more beautiful than** the one across from us.
c. The house over there is **the most beautiful** of them all.
d. On a separate sheet of paper, write your own sample sentences:

    i. delicate
    ii. expensive
    iii. priceless

The most common exception to this rule is words that end in –y or those that end in the suffix –le, (e.g. *pretty* or *little*). These words usually take the morphological inflections –er and –est (*prettier, littler*). *Than* still follows the comparative when the two items being compared are explicitly referenced. The superlative *most* is preceded by *the*.

There are also some irregular comparative and superlative forms:

**Irregular adjectives**

| Adjective | Comparative | Superlative |
|---|---|---|
| good | better (than) | (the) best |
| bad | worse (than) | (the) worst |
| little | less (than) | (the) least |

*Sample Sentences:*

a. I have **little** money.
b. She has **less** money than Sandra.
c. Alex has **the least** amount of money.
d. On a separate sheet of paper, write your own sample sentences:

    i. good, better, best
    ii. bad, worse, worst

Descriptive adjectives can also be used to compare two like nouns or noun phrases. In such cases we use the form *as* + adjective + *as*:

(4) The man was *as tall as* the door.
(5) Avery is *as blonde as* her mother.

The *as* + *adjective* + *as* form is often used in similes when two unlike things are compared:

(6) My cat is *as loud as* a lion.
(7) She has eyes *as clear as* glass.

### Can all adjectives be compared?

There are some adjectives that cannot be compared. These are generally adjectives from technical fields, e.g. *biological* or *psychological*, or what some grammarians call *absolute terms*, e.g. *chief* or *perfect*. Many grammar books label adjectives that can be compared as *gradable* adjectives to distinguish them from adjectives that cannot be compared.

### What kinds of problems do ESL/EFL learners have with these inflections?

▶ *Learner difficulties*

Conceptually, ESL/EFL learners usually have little difficulty understanding the comparative and superlative forms. In practice, they may confuse which adjectives take the *–er/est* endings and which ones require *more/most*. At times they add both an inflectional ending and *more/most*. Remember that a large number of learner errors occur in the use of inflectional morphemes.

(8)*We had a *boringer* class than last time.
(9)*Her crying is *the most loudest* of all my babies.

As we will also see in our study of verbs in Chapters 5, 6, and 7, whenever there are two or more parts to a particular structure, ESL/EFL learners will often omit one or more of these elements. For example, they may omit the *the* of the superlative:

(10)*It is *oldest* book I own.

Or, in comparing two like nouns (*as* + *adjective* + *as*), learners may forget to use the second "as:"

(11)*Mr. Jones is *as tall* Mr. Smith.

Less serious errors also occur in spelling changes, which occur at times when the inflectional endings are added.

(12)*I am *busyier* this semester.

Although these spelling changes need to be learned (see Appendix C), ESL/EFL learners, have fewer difficulties with these than with the use of *-er/-est, more/most* and *as + adjective + as*.

The next Discovery Activity looks at adjectives that have common derivational endings and those that do not. You can check your answers to Part I in the back of the chapter in the section labeled "Answer Key." Discuss your responses to Part II with your classmates.

**Discovery Activity 3: More Adjectives**
**Part I**

Look at the following excerpts.

1. Underline all the adjectives you find.

**A.**

After everyone took a bite of the delicious creamy cake, we looked around to see who had it.
  [Kline, S. (2003). *Horrible harry and the holiday daze* (p. 19). New York: Viking.]

**B.**

As Tad walked by the little empty chapel in the woods and past its small, old graveyard, he heard voices . . .
  [Young, R. (1993). *The scary story reader* (p. 66). Little Rock, AR: August Horror.]

**C.**

Many museums display giant ant colonies that you can watch through big windows.
  [Gomel, L. (2002). *The ant: Energetic worker* (p. 21). Watertown, MA: Charlesbridge.]

**Part II**

Look at the adjectives you underlined.

1. Discuss whether you were able to use derivational clues for all the adjectives? Explain why or why not.
2. Were you able to use inflectional clues for any of the adjectives you identified?

In addition to the morphological clues we have been discussing, we can also use structural clues to help us in our identification of adjectives.

## Structural Clues

Consider the sentence:

> (13) Belinda darted behind *a* **big** *rock*.
> [Herrman, G. (1999). *Tooth fairy tales* (p. 69). New York: Bantam.]

In Sentence (13), the position of *big* between the article *a* and the noun *rock* is a structural clue indicating the adjective function of the word *big*. As you will remember, since word order in English is very fixed, the sentence position of a word tells us what a word is functioning as.

### *Do adjectives only occur before a noun as in Sentence 13?*

Adjectives can occur in three positions:

- before a noun
- after certain verbs
- after certain nouns

The most common place for adjectives to occur in a sentence is before a noun. Many grammar books refer to this position as *prenominal*. In Excerpt B of Discovery Activity 3, for instance, *little* and *empty* occur before the noun *chapel*. These adjectives give us descriptive information about *chapel*. Their sentence position before *chapel* is an indicator of their function as adjectives.

Adjectives can also come after certain verbs, especially the verb *be*. This position is often referred to as the *predicate* position. Verbs that are followed by adjectives are often called *stative* or *linking* verbs. These verbs refer to mental states, attitudes, perceptions, emotions, or existence. They "connect" the subject with something after the verb. (See Chapter 6).

> (14) "My friends *were* **right**," Belinda said aloud . . .
> [Herrman, G. (1999). *Tooth fairy tales* (p. 71). New York: Bantam.]
> (15) When the air *feels* **hot** enough, a few ants stretch their legs and antennae.
> [Gomel, L. (2002). *The ant: Energetic worker* (p. 16). Watertown, MA: Charlesbridge.]

Adjectives that come after a linking verb describe or modify the noun phrase that is to the left of the verb. In Sentence (14), *right* is describing something about *My friends*. In Sentence (15), **hot** is describing something about *the air*.

Most adjectives can come either before a noun or after a linking verb. A few, however, can only occur in certain positions, as illustrated in the following chart:

| Adjective position | Examples |
|---|---|
| prenominally (before the noun) | Betsy bought a **huge** house. |
| *or* | |
| after a stative verb | Her house is **huge**. |
| | The coat feels **small**. |
| prenominal position only | Rob ate the **entire** hamburger. |
| | *The hamburger was **entire**. |
| predicate position after a stative verb only | Meg looks **asleep**. |
| | *The **asleep** girl is Meg. |

In addition, some adjectives occur after the noun they are describing. This is often called *post-nominal* sentence position. Most of the nouns that have adjectives following them have to do with units of measurement:

| Adjectives in Post-nominal (after the noun) Position | |
|---|---|
| | The quake caused a crack five inches **wide**. |
| Units of measurement | They have a pool twelve feet **deep**. |
| | The rapids run two miles **long**. |

### *Why should I know so much about adjective sentence position?*

For native speakers and highly proficient non-native speakers, adjective sentence position is not an issue. However, ESL/EFL learners do need to learn both basic positions and the exceptions. How difficult this will be for learners depends greatly on their native language. If, for instance, normal adjective position is similar to English, as in Chinese, they will have fewer difficulties than Spanish speakers where the position is different.

In doing Discovery Activity 4, think about our discussion of structural clues and ESL/EFL learners. What kinds of things need to be pointed out to them?

### Discovery Activity 4: Adjective Position

Look at the following sentences.

1. Underline the adjectives.
2. Decide which sentences sound correct.
3. If the sentence sounds incorrect, explain why.

    a. He was a mere boy when he left home.
    b. He was mere when he left home.
    c. She cried out with a sharp shriek.
    d. Her shriek was sharp.
    e. A cold rain hit their faces.

f. The rain was cold as it hit their faces.
g. The story was an utter fabrication.
h. The fabrication was utter.

## Discussion: Discovery Activity 4

- Sentences (b) and (h) are incorrect because the adjectives in these sentences are examples of the limited number of adjectives that cannot be used after the verb in predicate position.
- Sentences (c), (d), (e), and (f) the adjectives *sharp, cold* can, like the majority of English adjectives, come before the noun (prenominal position), or after the verb *be* (predicate position).

As we have discussed previously, in English word order is important. For the most part word order is fixed and not very flexible The vast majority of adjectives in English come before the noun, or after a linking verb; therefore, teachers need to focus primarily on these sentence positions, particularly at lower levels of proficiency.

The next Discovery Activity is intended for extra practice if you still have questions about identifying adjectives, otherwise, move on. The answers to Discovery Activity 5 are in the Answer Key.

**Discover Activity 5: Identifying Adjectives**

Look at the sentences.

1. Underline the adjectives you find in each sentence.

- Discuss the clues you used to help identify the adjectives.

2. Circle the noun or noun phrase each adjective is modifying.

*Examples:*

1. The large dog barked loudly.
   The *large* dog barked loudly.

   - adjective: *large*.
   - It modifies or describes the noun *dog*.
   - It comes between the article *the* and before the noun *dog*.
   - We can add *–er/–est*.

2. The salesclerk is busy.
   The salesclerk is *busy*.

- *busy* modifies or describes the noun phrase *the salesclerk*.
- An adjective after the verb *be* modifies the noun before the verb.
- *–y* at the end of a word often indicates membership in the adjective class.
- We can add *–er/-est*.

(a) The new students had excellent scores on the tests.
(b) Some of the concerns we had were important.
(c) Some parents are unhappy with the current changes in the curriculum.
(d) Although their home is humble, they are content to live as they do.
(e) The cold, snowy weather over the long weekend kept many people at home and resulted in slow sales for retailers.
(f) When the viewers saw the movie, they were ecstatic over the ambitious plot and the stupendous special effects.

## Order of Adjectives

*If I have more than one adjective, do I have to put them in a certain order?*

Back in Discovery Activity 3 in Excerpts A and B, we saw that two or more adjectives can appear together:

*delicious creamy* cake
*small old* graveyard

The order of adjectives in English is not random; different types of adjectives occur in a certain order. The exception to this is with adjectives of general description and those of physical state (size, shape, color), where their order may be reversed.

(16a) They own an **enormous, long-handled** cutting knife.
(16b) They own a **long-handled, enormous** cutting knife.

(17a) She has a **round yellow** sofa.
(17b) She has a **yellow round** sofa.

When the adjective order is reversed, as in the sentences above, the speaker generally wants to emphasize or draw attention to the first adjective in the sequence.

Native speakers and highly proficient non-native speakers know intuitively the order in which adjectives should occur when more than one is used. The order of adjectives is not something they have difficulty with, nor generally even think about. However, the order of a string of adjectives is something that ESL/EFL learners need to learn. Much of this knowledge is gained through practice, but a chart such as the one below detailing the order of adjectives can be helpful for learners at lower levels of proficiency.

Although changes in normal adjective order do not interfere with sentence meaning or comprehension, such changes do lead to awkward and/or strange-sounding sentences. Note that this chart provides only general guidance and not hard-and-fast rules of word order.

## Adjective Types

| opinion | general description | size | shape | color | place of origin/type | material | use or type | NOUN |
|---|---|---|---|---|---|---|---|---|
| | fierce | | | | Siberian | | | tiger |
| | new | | sleeveless | | | woolen | | dress |
| unusual | | | oval | | | | | frame |
| | | | | black | | leather | | patch |
| | | enormous | long-handled | | | | cutting | knife |
| beautiful | | large | round | green | | china | serving | dish |

## Sample Sentences and Practice

1. The children admired the **fierce Siberian** tiger.
2. She wore a new **sleeveless woolen** dress.
3. That is an **unusual oval** frame.
4. They own an **enormous, long-handled cutting** knife.
5. Her aunt bought a **beautiful, large, round, green china serving** dish.
6. Write your own sample sentences:

   a. I like to watch _____ _____ movies.
   b. They live in a _____ _____ house.
   c. The _____, _____, _____ dog belongs to Joe.

7. Discuss how the adjectives in your sample sentences fit in the above chart.

### *Is there any special punctuation I need to tell my students about?*

When there are more than two adjectives, a comma may be necessary to separate them, particularly if they are adjectives of opinion, general description, size, shape, or color. As a rule of thumb, we do not use commas between adjectives referring to place of origin or type.

In cases where you are not sure whether or not to use a comma, a simple test is to use "and" where you think the comma should go. If you can insert "and" between two adjectives, we usually need to add a comma:

(18a) I saw a boisterous, rowdy crowd of boys in the park.

(18b) I saw a boisterous **and** rowdy crowd of boys in the park.

(19a) The zoo has clever, mischievous Capuchin monkeys.

(19b) The zoo has clever **and** mischievous Capuchin monkeys.

but not:

*(19c) The zoo has clever, mischievous, Capuchin monkeys.

*(19d) The zoo has clever **and** mischievous **and** Capuchin monkeys.

*(19e) The zoo has clever, mischievous **and** Capuchin monkeys.

Discovery Activity 5 allows you to practice sorting adjectives into categories. As you will see when you do this activity, it is not always easy to distinguish between some of the categories. Keep in mind that the chart above is only meant as a guideline or introduction to the order of adjectives. When you have finished, compare your answers to those in the Answer Key.

---

### Discovery Activity 6: Adjective Word Order

Look at the following sentences.

1. Underline the adjectives.
2. In sentences where there are two or more adjectives, discuss whether you could change the word order of the adjectives.

*Example:*

The large spotted dog barked loudly.
The *large spotted* dog barked loudly.

(a) Do you own any light cotton dresses?

(b) The pirates' swift ship outran the ponderous tanker.

(c) Her elderly mother received a box of expensive Swiss chocolates for her birthday.

(d) Mr. Branch was a little squat man with bushy black hair.

(e) Rapunzel's long golden hair was wrapped in a priceless silk scarf.

(f) The flower consists of delicate blossoms on a slender green stalk with broad rectangular leaves.

(g) The busy young architect displayed his plans on a drawing board.

3. On a separate sheet of paper, make a chart like the one below. Place each of the adjectives you have identified into the categories on your chart.

The words from the example have been done for you.

| general description | size | shape | color | place of origin | material | use |
|---|---|---|---|---|---|---|
| | large | spotted | | | | |

# Special Types of Adjectives

In this section, we will look at two special types of adjectives: nouns that function as adjectives and participial adjectives.

*One of my students asked me if "school" in "school bus" is an adjective like "small" as in "small bus." How can it be an adjective if it's a noun?*

## *Nouns Functioning as Adjectives*

In English, as we have seen, class membership is no guarantee of function. Nouns, for example, frequently function as adjectives. In other words, one noun can come before another noun to modify it. Consider the following sentences:

(20) The horse jumped over the **stone** *wall*.
(21) The **train** *station* is on the next block.

In Sentences (20) and (21), **stone** and **train** are both nouns describing what kind of *wall* and what kind of *station*. In these sentences, **stone** and **train** are functioning as adjectives because they are modifying the nouns they precede. We know, however, that while they may be functioning as adjectives, **stone** and **train** have not changed word class membership because they do not share the features or characteristics of other adjectives, but rather the features inherent to nouns.

*What are these features?*

Both **stone** and **train** are count nouns that take the plural –s inflectional ending common to most regular count nouns. If you remember from our discussion of nouns and inflections in Chapter 3, only count nouns can take the plural –s inflectional ending. Adjectives cannot take this inflectional ending.

In English we cannot say *\*stones wall* even though there may be many stones in that wall, or *\*birds coop* even though there are many birds in a bird coop. The –s plural inflection can only attach itself to nouns and only when the nouns are functioning as nouns. When nouns function as adjectives, they lose their ability to take the plural inflection.

Try the next Discovery Activity to see how well you are able to identify nouns functioning as adjectives. Remember that nouns modifying other nouns do not change their class membership, only their function. You can find the answers in the Answer Key at the end of the chapter.

---

**Discovery Activity 7: Nouns functioning as Adjectives**

Look at the sentences.

1. Underline the nouns functioning as adjectives.

(a) I race across the baseball field, past a bunch of houses that line my street, and to my tree house in our backyard.
(b) Right when I sat down, Vince asked, "Are you wearing a pajama top to school?"
(c) Then I mess up my hair even worse than Brian's and make a fish face to go with my new, crazy hairdo.
(d) "I'll have the school counselor work with Vince to teach him the skills he needs to be a better friend.

[Ludwig, T. (2006). *Just kidding*. Berkeley, CA: Tricycle Press. No page numbers.]

*A noun modifying another noun and thus functioning as an adjective – Is this a difficult concept for ESL/EFL learners?*

▶ *Learner difficulties*

Conceptually, understanding that the first noun is modifying the second noun is not that difficult for language learners. However, adding the *–s* plural inflection to the modifying noun is an error that ESL/EFL learners may make. This is especially common if a plural inflection is required in their native language for adjectives modifying plural nouns.

For such learners, *stones walls* would be logical because in their language the adjective (*stones*) has to take a plural inflection because the noun (*walls*) has a plural inflection. Once again we see how a high proportion of learner errors occur with inflectional morphemes.

Sometimes less proficient ESL/EFL learners become confused by nouns that end in "s" but that are not plural such as *news* or *linguistics*. As we saw in Chapter 2, the "s" of these words is not a separate morpheme. Nouns ending in "s" can also modify other nouns as in *news program* or *linguistics program*.

## *Participial Adjectives*

Look at the following poems. All the words in bold are another special type of adjective, called participial adjectives.

My world is made of things I like:
**creeping** bugs,
**wiggling** worms,
**leaping** frogs,
**drifting** seashells,

**shifting** stones,
**singing** birds,
**swimming** fish,
**dancing** butterflies,
**growing** fruit,
**falling** leaves,
**blooming** flowers,
**shining** sun,
**splashing** rain,
**glittering** stars,
**fluttering** moths,
and **glowing** moon.
Thank you world for everything.
[Ehlert, L. (2002). *In my world.* New York: Harcourt. No page numbers.]

Participial adjectives are adjectives that end in *–ing* or *–ed* (or *–en* in some instances). If you look at the selection above, you see many examples of adjectives ending in *–ing*. These are adjectives that are derived from verbs but that are functioning as adjectives.

### *How can we distinguish participial adjectives?*

Sometimes participial adjectives are mistakenly identified as verbs because of the *–ed* and *–ing* inflectional endings. These are the inflections used for past tense verbs and for present participle of progressive verb phrases (See Chapters 5 & 6). However, we know that in Sentences (21) and (22) below, *annoyed* and *irritating* are participial adjectives for several reasons.

(21) The *annoyed* bird squawked.
(22) There was an *irritating* quietness to the landscape.

First, an important structural clue is the sentence position of *annoyed* and *irritating*. Remember that word order is very important in English. Both words come before a noun, the most common position for adjectives.

Second, the *–ing* form, in order to be considered a verb must be part of a verb phrase. That is, a verb phrase with *–ing* must include any tense of the helping verb *be* and the present participle *–ing* attached to the main verb, as in *I am going* or *She is walking* (See Chapters 5 & 6).

A simple way to test whether or not an *-ing* or *–ed* word is an adjective as opposed to a verb is to use *very* before it:

| The "very" Test | |
|---|---|
| | → addition of **very** before participial adjective |
| (23) The *rushed* publication resulted in numerous errors. | (23a) The **very** *rushed* publication resulted in numerous errors. |
| (24) The text supplied *confusing* explanations for the problems. | (24a) The text supplied **very** *confusing* explanations for the problems. |

Because we can take our original Sentences (23) and (24), and add *very* before *rushed* and *confusing* as in (23a) and (24a), we know these are participial adjectives.

Now look at Sentences (25) and (26). If we try to add *very* before *resulted* or *supplying*, the sentences become very strange to the ears of native speakers or highly proficient non-native speakers:

*(25) The ambitious project **very** *resulted* in errors.
*(26) The text is **very** *supplying* confusing explanations for the problems.

While inserting *very* is a good clue that native speakers and proficient ESL/EFL learners can use, it does not always work. If you refer back to the selection at the beginning of this section, for instance, you will see that inserting *very* works with some of the *–ing* participial adjectives, but not with all of them:

My world is made of things I like:
**very** creeping bugs,
**very** wiggling worms,
**very** leaping frogs,
**very** drifting seashells,
**very** shifting stones,

The insertion of *very* before these participial adjectives sounds strange.

When you do Discovery 8, think about whether or not you can insert *very* and about the sentence position of the words you are trying to identify as participial adjectives. The answers are in the Answer Key.

**Discovery Activity 8: Participial Adjectives**

Look at the following teacher-written paragraphs.

1. Underline the participial adjectives.
2. Discuss what clues you used to identify the participial adjectives.

Jackie McKenzie, a researcher in archeology, is sitting at her desk with potted plants on the windowsill and describes her life as an archeologist:

"The life of a field anthropologist can be difficult. You may spend hours at a gritty, sweltering excavation; you may be screening soil samples for hours, even days with few results. But on the other hand you may encounter exciting finds that may revolutionize traditional scenarios."

In her forthcoming book, Dr. McKenzie describes some of the revolutionizing finds of the twentieth century and their impact on the field of archeology. She notes, for instance, that prolonged droughts did not necessarily drive inhabitants off settled areas, but that warfare and social breakdowns played larger roles in the abandonment of certain settlements."

## Do ESL/EFL students find the participial adjectives confusing?

### ▶ Learner difficulties

Learners, as well as some native speakers, often have difficulty recognizing participial adjectives as adjectives rather than as part of verb phrases. They may confuse an *–ing*, which is part of a verb phrase, with the *–ing* of a participial adjective:

> (27) The team *is winning* the game.
> (28) My team is the *winning* team.

In Sentence (27) *winning* is part of the verb phrase *is winning*. This sentence contrasts with Sentence (28) where *winning* is a participial adjective modifying the noun *team*.

#### -ing versus –ed

Another difficulty ESL/EFL learners have with participial adjectives is distinguishing between those that have contrasting *–ing* and *–ed* forms. It is often difficult for learners to remember and correctly use contrasting participial adjectives.

Contrasting participial adjectives are generally derived from verbs that have to do with emotion or mental states. We use the *–ed* participial form when we describe something that **was done by someone or something else**. Consider the sentence:

> (29) The girl is bored.

In Sentence (29), the subject noun phrase is *The girl*. This subject is not the one doing the action or the activity resulting in the state of boredom. It is something or someone else who is causing the boredom of *the girl*.

Grammar books often suggest that in many cases, the *–ed* form is related to what we call the passive voice (see Chapter 8). This means we can think of Sentence (29) as:

> (29a) The girl is bored by the book.

However, while this will work with some of the *–ed* adjectives, like so many other things we have looked at, it doesn't hold true in all instances. For example:

> (30) He's interested in science.

In Sentence (30) there is no "by" phrase that could relate this sentence to the passive voice.

The *–ing* participial form, in contrast to the *–ed,* is used when the **subject is the one doing an action or activity that affects others.** Consider the sentence:

(31) *The girl is boring the rest of the class.*

In Sentence (31), we understand that *The girl* is the one doing an action or activity affecting the state of others.

Not all verbs have contrasting *–ed* and *–ing* forms. For the most part, those that have this contrast are verbs of emotion, such as the verbs listed in the chart below.

| Common Verbs of Emotion | | | |
|---|---|---|---|
| amuse | concern | embarrass | frighten |
| interest | annoy | satisfy | please |
| love | bore | disappoint | comfort |
| surprise | terrify | worry | excite |

Finally, low level ESL/EFL learners sometimes become confused when they encounter words that contain *–ing* where it is part of the actual word and not an inflectional *–ing* ending. Such words include *bring, icing, everything, nothing, pudding,* and *wedding,* among others.

This concludes our examination of adjectives and we now move on to Section 2 to investigate adverbs.

## Section 2: Adverbs

### *Isn't an adverb a word that ends in –ly and something that describes a verb?*

The traditional definition of an adverb usually defines adverbs as words that generally end in *–ly* and that describe verbs. However, there are many other adverbs that do not end in *–ly* and that describe adjectives or other adverbs.

The adverb class is sometimes called the "trash can" class because grammarians have traditionally placed many words that fit nowhere else into this category. Adverbs can describe just about any part of a sentence or clause. Consequently, there are many subclasses of the adverb class, upon which not all grammarians agree.

Adverbs that take the derivational *–ly* ending comprise the largest subclass of adverbs. These adverbs are the easiest to identify and understand. These *–ly* adverbs are generally considered prototypical adverbs. Since these adverbs generally modify verbs, they have strong lexical meaning. They are often referred to as *descriptive* or *manner adverbs* because they answer the question "how" or "in what manner" the verb of the sentence does something:

(32) He responded angrily to their accusations.

> **Question:** How did he respond to their accusations?
> **Answer:** He responded *angrily* to their accusations.

(33) She answered the question correctly.

> **Question:** How did she answer the question?
>
> **Answer:** She answered the question *correctly*.

Many of these –*ly* adverbs are derived from adjectives:[1]

| Adjective + ly → Adverb | |
|---|---|
| sudden | sudden**ly** |
| soft | soft**ly** |
| beautiful | beautiful**ly** |
| gracious | gracious**ly** |
| frequent | frequent**ly** |

Unlike nouns and adjectives, the position of these adverbs is flexible. Manner (–*ly*) adverbs can occur in initial or final sentence position, or before or after the verb. In verb phrases, these adverbs can occur between the auxiliary verb (helping verb) and the main verb. Generally, the sentence position of an adverb depends on what the speaker wants to stress or emphasize.

### *What do you mean by "what the speaker wants to stress or emphasize?"*

Up until now we have emphasized repeatedly how important word order is in English. Because adverb position, unlike other parts of speech, is not as fixed, speakers can give different nuances of meaning to what they want to say by changing the sentence position of the adverb.

Look at the following examples. As you read each example, think about what difference the speaker is conveying.

> (34a) **Softly**, she called to the children.
> (34b) She called to the children **softly**.
> (34c) She **softly** called to the children.
> (34d) She called **softly** to the children.
> (34e) She was **softly** calling to the children.

In each sentence, the adverb *softly* has a different sentence position and is modifying something different. You may want to compare your thoughts with classmates or friends to see if they have similar interpretations.

### *Are all words that end in –ly adverbs?*

Although not all words that end in –*ly* are adverbs, most are. There are words that end in –*ly* and that are adjectives. These include such common adjectives as *friendly, lively,* and *lovely*. English also has some nouns and verbs that end in –*ly*, such as *assembly, jelly, supply,* and *rely*. These are not as difficult for ESL/EFL learners as distinguishing between –*ly* adverbs and -*ly* adjectives.

---

[1] See Appendix C for spelling changes after adding –*ly*.

***Is there anything to help me distinguish between -ly adverbs and –ly adjectives?***

There is a rule of thumb that you can use to help you distinguish between –*ly* adjectives and adverbs.

- If a word ends in –*ly* and you remove this ending and discover a noun, then the –*ly* word is an adjective.
- If the word ends in –*ly* and you remove this ending and discover an adjective, then the –*ly* word is an adverb.

| Adjective → Noun | |
| --- | --- |
| heavenly | heaven |
| wifely | wife |

| Adverb → Adjective | |
| --- | --- |
| quietly | quiet |
| sweetly | sweet |

As always, there are some exceptions to this rule of thumb. The word *lowly* is an adjective, but when you remove the –*ly*, the word *low* is also an adjective. Nevertheless, this rule of thumb is useful in most instances and can help identify the word class membership of a particular word.

See how well you do in distinguishing between adjectives and adverbs in Discovery Activity 9. You can check your answers in a dictionary.

---

**Discovery Activity 9: Adverb or Adjective?**

Look at words in the box below.

1. On a separate sheet of paper, write each word without the –*ly* ending.
2. Decide if the remaining word is an adjective or a noun.

   - If it is a noun, then the original word ending in –*ly* is an adjective.
   - If it is an adjective, then the original word ending in –*ly* is an adverb.

3. On your paper, make two columns. Label one column **Adjective** and the other column **Adverb.**

   - Categorize the original word with its -*ly* ending under either the **Adjective** or **Adverb** column.

*Example:*

heavenly → heaven = a noun; thus heavenly = adjective
heavenly    fully princely    richly nightly scholarly    sincerely
   brightly    newly yearly masterly    beastly nicely remarkably

| **Adjective** | **Adverb** |
| --- | --- |
| heavenly | |

## Different Subclasses of Adverbs

*In addition to the –ly or manner adverbs, what are some of the other subclasses of adverbs?*

Other commonly accepted subclasses of adverbs are frequency, and time and place adverbs. The subclasses are determined by the meaning and/or function of the different adverbs in sentences and in discourse.

## *Frequency Adverbs*

Another readily identifiable subclass of adverbs is that of *frequency*. These adverbs describe "how often" an action takes place and some of these also end in *–ly*. One of these frequency adverbs consists of two words, *hardly ever*.

| Common Adverbs of Frequency | | |
|---|---|---|
| always | generally | usually |
| frequently | often | sometimes |
| occasionally | hardly ever | rarely |
| seldom | never | |

*Are these frequency adverbs easy for ESL/EFL learners?*

▶ *Learner difficulties*

Of the frequency adverbs, the one adverb learners have the most difficulty with is *hardly ever*. First, it consists of two words, *hardly + ever*. Second, for many learners the phrase itself does not make sense. Many confuse the *ever* in *hardly ever* with another use of *ever* meaning *continuously,* as in the sentence *I have lived in this house ever since I was ten.*

Low proficiency ESL/EFL learners usually require practice in learning the use and the placement of frequency adverbs within the sentence. Because of the semantic meaning of these adverbs, they are often used with the simple present or simple past tenses (See Chapter 6). The most common sentence position of frequency adverbs is before the verb they are modifying, except the verb *be*. Whenever the verb *be* occurs, the frequency adverb follows.

| Common Sentence Position of Frequency Adverbs | |
|---|---|
| (35) Curtis **generally** *comes* on time. | before the main verb |
| (36) Julie *is* **seldom** late. | after the verb *be* |

Although the chart illustrates the most common sentence position of frequency adverbs, as we observed previously, their sentence position can vary, depending on the speaker's intent. We can change Sentence (35) to *Generally*

*Curtis comes on time*, for instance, particularly if we want to emphasize a contrast: *Generally Curtis comes on time, but today he's late.*

Discover Activity 10 asks you to identify all the frequency adverbs. Check your answers with a classmate or friend. If you are unsure, check a dictionary.

---

**Discovery Activity 10: Frequency Adverbs**

Look at the following paragraph.

1. Underline the frequency adverbs.

Brianna generally starts her mornings with a cup of coffee. She always has a splash of milk and one teaspoon of sugar in her coffee. Depending on her mood, she sometimes eats a slice of toast with a little jam or a bowl of cereal. On days when she is in a hurry, she frequently skips breakfast. Once she is at work, she is often too busy to eat anything until lunchtime. She rarely misses lunch because she is hardly ever home before 6:30 p.m. She occasionally stops at a restaurant on her way home from work, but she usually prefers to wait until she gets home to eat. She is hardly ever ready for bed before midnight.

---

Let's now look at another subclass of adverbs, those of time and place.

## *Time and Place Adverbs*

Time and place adverbs include both single words and phrases. **Time adverbs** refer to the time at which something occurred. This time reference can be:

- **definite** (e.g. *yesterday, today, tomorrow, last week, next month, a year ago*) or
- **indefinite** (e.g. *now, then, soon, just, before, still, already, next*).

Some of the time adverbs can also function as nouns:

| Different Functions of Time Adverbs | |
|---|---|
| (37a) I rode my bike **yesterday** | |
| (37b) I'll ride my bike **tomorrow**. | yesterday, tomorrow = adverbs of time |
| (38a) **Yesterday** was a sunny day. | Yesterday = noun, subject of the verb *was* |
| (38b) **Tomorrow** will be a sunny day | Tomorrow = noun, subject of the verb *will be* |

**Adverbs of place** refer to location, direction, or position as in *here, there, backwards*. They answer the question *where*. Many common adverbs of place also function as prepositions.

## *The "Other" Adverbs*

Most grammarians agree on the different subclasses of adverbs that we have considered up to this point. For the remaining categories, there is less general agreement. Both the labels and the number of subclasses vary among grammar texts because there are different ways of interpreting the functions and uses of these adverbs.

The subclasses discussed here should provide you with a general feel for and understanding of these adverbs, which are more difficult to classify than manner, frequency, or time and place adverbs. These are also the adverbs ESL/EFL learners have more trouble with in terms of understanding the nuances of meaning they can convey.

### Degree Adverbs

Adverbs that alter the tone or force of an adjective or adverb are called *degree adverbs*. Degree adverbs are generally divided into two categories, *intensifiers* and *downtoners*.

**Intensifiers** are adverbs such as *very* or *extremely*, which strengthen or intensify the meaning of adjectives or another adverb. When they modify adjectives, they are used with gradable adjectives that can take the comparative and superlative forms (*-er, -est* or *more, the most*). Intensifiers normally precede the adjective or adverb they are modifying.

> (39) Jan writes *extremely* well.
> (40) Jan is *very* busy.

In Sentence (39), the intensifier *extremely* modifies the adjective *well* and serve to emphasize how well the subject (Jan) writes. In Sentence (40), *very* modifies the adjective *busy* and stresses how busy Jan is.

**Downtoners** are adverbs, which decrease or lessen the tone of adjectives or another adverb.

> (41) Hannah read the book *fairly* quickly.
> (42) The ending is *somewhat* sad.

In Sentence (41), *fairly* is modifying the adverb *quickly* and serves to diminish or downplay the force of the adjective *quickly*. In Sentence (42), the downtoner *somewhat* is modifying the adjective *sad* and lessening the degree or intensity of this adjective. Like intensifiers, downtoners modify gradable adjectives and normally precede the adjective or adverb they are modifying.

To illustrate the nuance of meaning conveyed by degree adverbs, add the adverb *extremely* into the following sentence:

(43) Janet has written an interesting paper.

Now take the same sentence and substitute the adverb *somewhat* for *extremely*. What has happened to the meaning of the sentence with each change?

## Attitude Adverbs

Attitude adverbs are those adverbs that convey the attitude or opinion of the speaker. These adverbs generally modify a sentence. Words such as *frankly, unfortunately, obviously,* and *surprisingly* are some examples of attitude adverbs. Some grammarians also place adverbs that are related to possibility into this category based on the notion that such adverbs convey the speaker's attitude regarding the degree of truth or probability of an action or event. Such adverbs include *probably, perhaps, of course, maybe,* and *possibly.*

### Discovery Activity 11: Attitude Adverbs

One of the most famous movie lines is Rhett Butler's last line in *Gone With the Wind* when Rhett tells Scarlett:[2]

"Frankly, my dear, I don't give a damn."

At the time the movie was released in 1939, the U.S. government exercised strict censorship rules on swearing. The producer of the film, David Selznick, was given the choice of paying a $5,000 fine or changing the script to:

"Frankly, my dear, I just don't care."

Selznick chose to pay the fine.

1. Consider how deleting *frankly* might have altered the impact of the ending.
   "My dear, I don't give a damn."
   *or*
   "I just don't care."
2. Why do you think the director chose to pay the fine rather than omit the interjection *damn*?
3. Note that *just* is another adverb. What do you think the inclusion of this intensifier brings to the sentence?
4. What conclusions might you draw about the use of *frankly, just,* and *damn* in an utterance such as this?

---

[2] If you are unfamiliar with *Gone With the Wind*, you can view a clip of this scene at: http://www.destinationhollywood.com/movies/gonewiththewind/famouslines_content.shtml.

## *Discussion: Discovery Activity 11*

In Rhett's utterance, both *frankly* and *damn* serve to underscore Rhett's disgust with Scarlett. *Frankly* is an attitude adverb, *damn* an interjection, both of which work in tandem to convey forcefully the depth of Rhett's feelings. *Frankly* is accepted in standard speech, while *damn* is less so, although its strength of meaning has decreased in the decades since *Gone with the Wind* first appeared.

When the movie was originally released in 1939, the public use of *damn* was startling in an era of strict censorship rules on swearing, its use evoked a strong emotional impact in earlier audience. Even today, with modern viewers accustomed to flagrant taboo language, the use of choice of *damn* evokes a stronger emotional reaction than the blander *I just don't care*, even though it includes the intensifier, *just*. Eliminating *frankly* and/or *just* in either version above, whether with or without *damn* also lessens the emotional impact of the utterance.

### Focus Adverbs

Focus adverbs serve to draw attention to a sentence element, or to add to or to restrict another adverb or another construction in the sentence.

| Common Focus Adverbs | |
| --- | --- |
| **function** | **adverb** |
| draw attention to | especially, specifically, particularly, even |
| add, restrict | too, also; just, merely, only |

The sentence position of most focus adverbs is flexible, but we generally place them before that which they are modifying. Different sentence position may change the meaning of the sentence. Try the next Discovery Activity to see how changing the position of a focus adverb draws your attention to different parts of the sentence.

### Discovery Activity 12: Focus Adverbs

1. Look at the following groups of sentences.
2. Discuss how the change in sentence position of the italicized focus adverb affects the meaning of the sentence.

### Group 1

(1a) Lauren *especially* wants to attend this dance.
(1b) *Especially* Lauren wants to attend this dance.
(1c) Lauren wants to attend *especially* this dance.

**Group 2**

(2a)  *Only* you can use your skills to fix the problem.
(2b)  You can use *only* your skills to fix the problem.
(2c)  You have the skills to fix *only* the problem.

## *Discussion: Discovery Activity 12*

In both Group 1 and Group 2, changing the position of the italicized adverb draws our attention to a different part of the sentence.

- In (1a) *especially* focuses our attention on the verb wants.
- In (1b) on the person *Lauren* (versus some other person).
- In (1c) on the noun phrase *this dance* (as opposed to another dance).
- In (2a) *only* focuses our attention on the person *you* (versus some other person).
- In (2b) on the noun phrase *your skills* (as opposed to something else).
- In (2) on the noun phrase *the problem* (as opposed to something else).

Other interpretations are possible, particularly in spoken English where intonation and word or phrase stress combine with focus adverb sentence position to convey different meanings.

### *Do ESL/EFL learners find these "other" subcategories of adverbs difficult?*

▶ *Learner difficulties*

For learners of English, degree, attitude, and focus adverbs are more difficult to learn than other adverbs. They are often used to communicate subtle shades of meaning as you saw in Sentence (43) and in some of the Discovery Activities. These subtle shades of meaning are part of what we call a speaker's *pragmatic knowledge*. Pragmatic knowledge includes, among other things, knowing how to make the appropriate word choices in a particular situation.

Since context and shared knowledge are essential to understanding these subtleties in meaning, exposure to and discussion of authentic excerpts with these types of adverbs can help ESL/EFL learners at higher levels of proficiency understand the gradations of meaning and intent speakers or writers are conveying.

# Summary

| Adjectives | Adverbs |
|---|---|
| • describe nouns | • describe everything else |
| • comprise a large, open class with one main subcategory, participial adjectives. | • comprise a large open class with many subcategories |
| • can be identified on the basis of morphological, semantic, and syntactic clues | • are generally identified on the basis of morphological and semantic clues |
| • have three sentence positions: pronominal (before a noun), postnominal (after a noun) or after a linking verb. | • have variable sentence position |
|   • postnominal is infrequent and is possible only for a few adjectives | |
| • Most adjectives can be in either prenominal or predicate position; some can be in only one or the other position. | |

## Summary Chart: Adverbs

| Types of adverbs | Examples |
|---|---|
| **frequency** | always, often, generally, usually, frequently, hardly ever |
| **time** | |
| • **definite** | yesterday, tomorrow, today, last week, last month, a year ago, the day after tomorrow |
| • **indefinite** | soon, recently, then, now, then, just, before, still, already, next, nowadays, immediately, yet, since, for |
| **direction** | here there up down everywhere anywhere around outside inside indoors back nearby far ahead uphill sideways home<br>Often combined with prepositions to make adverbial phrases:<br>down here, down there, up here, up there; over here, over there<br>words that end in –ward(s ) |
| **movement** | backward(s) forward(s) northward(s) onward(s)<br>**Note:** *towards* is not an adverb, but a preposition. |
| **compass points** | north, south, east, west |
| **place** | upstairs, downstairs, forward, backward, here, there |

## Summary Chart: Adverbs

| Types of adverbs | Examples |
|---|---|
| **degree** | |
| • **intensifiers** | very, extremely, totally, completely, really, particularly especially |
| • **downtoners** | fairly, somewhat, rather, quite, slightly, almost |
| **attitude** | frankly, unfortunately, obviously, surprisingly |
| **possibility** | maybe, possibly, perhaps, of course |
| **focus** | especially, specifically, particularly, even<br>Add or restrict: too, also, just, merely, only |

## Practice Activities

### *Activity 1: Identifying Adjectives*

1. Look at the excerpts.
2. Underline the adjectives you find in each sentence.

**A.**

"The disguise is impeccable," says the Master dryly. "I'd never have known you but for your dulcet tone."
  [Maguire, G. (1999). *Confessions of an ugly stepsister* (p. 43). New York: Harper-Collins.]

**B.**

(Etienne-Maurice) Falconet saw [art]) as a product of his personal vision that would establish his artistic, intellectual and even moral superiority over his contemporaries and the great figures of the past. His statue of Peter (the Great) surpassed earlier efforts in its realism and psychological intensity.
  [Gibson. E. (2002. December 18). Long and bumpy ride to greatness. *Wall Street Journal*. p. D6].

**C.**

Caspar is here to learn the trade of drafting, but he's a hopeless fool ... He will canter into a low lintel one day and brain himself ... He is bereft of any real talent, or ... my current rival ... would have taken him in. Casper is almost as useless as you girls. This should make you feel in good company.
  [Maguire, G. (1999). *Confessions of an ugly stepsister* (p. 43). New York: Harper-Collins.]

### *Activity 2 (optional additional practice): Identifying Adjectives and Adverbs*

1. Read the excerpts.
2. Underline the adjectives and adverbs.
3. Discuss the clues that helped you identify each adjective (e.g. derivational morpheme, sentence position, semantic meaning).

**A.**

In one classic skit from a 1970 episode of *Monty Python's Flying Circus,* a waitress rattles off the contents of a menu in which all the items contain Spam. As she does this, she is repeatedly drowned out by a table of helmeted Vikings who sing, "Spam, Spam, Spam, Spam! Lovely Spam! Wonderful Spam!" For the techies, that perfectly captured the essence of relentless, annoying, repetitious, unwanted electronic solicitation.
  [Swidey. N. (2003. October 5). Spambusters. *Boston Globe*, p. 12].

**B.**

By the early thirties, art dealers were dropping by more and more frequently. Large empty patches appeared on the walls. Pieces of antique furniture were carried out of the house.

Even the worn banners and rusty swords our fierce ancestors had wrested from the hated
Turks were sold at auction.
[di Robilant, A. (2003). *A venetian affair* (p. 3). New York: Alfred A. Knopf].


## *Activity 3: Participial Adjectives: -ing versus -ed Adjectives*

A. Read the following sentences. Consider the difference in meaning in each
 pair.
B. How can you explain the differences in each pair?

(1a) The annoyed neighbors moved away.
(1b) The annoying neighbors moved away.

(2a) The worried mother looked for her children.
(2b) The worrying mother looked for her children.

(3a) The amusing boy has many friends.
(3b) The amused boy has many friends.

(4a) The intriguing detective was last seen at a bar.
(4b) The intrigued detective was last seen at a bar.


## *Activity 4: Making Correct Choices: -ing versus -ed Adjectives*

Read the samples below, which were produced by ESL learners.

a) Underline the incorrect uses of participial adjectives.
b) Why do you think learners make these mistakes?
c) What suggestion(s) could you offer learners to help them avoid such
 mistakes?

1. The news puzzled the charmed girl I met last night.
2. The test results were disappointed to me but I was cheered up by the news that I
 could earn extra points on the next project.
3. Their loved mother comforted the frightening children.
4. My disappointed children complained to their surprising father.
5. My friend John is a talented athlete who is interesting in soccer and
 basketball.


## *Activity 5: -ing and -ed Adjectives (optional additional practice)*

Look at the following excerpts.

1. Underline all the adjectives.
2. Which ones are participial adjectives?

**A.**

Laurence Canter leans forward, scrunches up his sunburned nose, and says with a smile, "I don't know – do I seem that evil to you?" But in 1994, Canter was the most loathed and feared man on the Internet. Laurence Canter is the father of modern spam.

[Swidey, N. (2003, October 5). Spambusters. *Boston Globe*, p. 12].

**B.**

Marylin's designs on Rex's fortune crumble when during the trial Miles introduces as star witness Heinz, the Baron Krauss von Espy (Jonathan Hadary), a mincing, irritable, dog-toting concierge.

[Morris, W. (2003, 10 October). 'Coens' 'cruelty' has comedic court appeal (review of the motion picture *intolerable* Cruelty) (dir. Joel Coen). *Boston Globe*, p. E1].

## Activity 6: Nouns Functioning as Adjectives

1. Underline the adjectives.
2. Circle the nouns functioning as adjectives.

**A.**

Elizabeth gathered up all the allowance she had been saving and hurried to the pet store. She bought three large fish tanks and hauled them home.

[Robinson, R. (2005). *Faucet fish*. New York: Dutton Children's Books. Picture Book, No page numbers.)

**B.**

[The letters] were not the usual household inventories that occasionally surfaced, like time-worn family flotsam . . . We pried them open one by one and soon realized there were inti-mate love letters that dated back to the 1750s.

[di Robilant, A. (2003). *A venetian affair* (p. 4). New York: Alfred A. Knopf.]

**C.**

Miss G. called on Susan, and Susan walked to the front of the room with poster board under her arm. When she placed it on the blackboard tray, I could see that there were photographs of fire fighters glued all over it.

[deGroet, D. (1994). *Annie Pitts, swamp monster* (p. 57). New York: Simon & Schuster.

## Activity 8 (optional additional practice): Finding Nouns Functioning as Adjectives

1. Find an article in a newspaper, magazine, or another place.
2. Underline all the nouns you find that are functioning as adjectives.
3. Circle the nouns these nouns are modifying.

## *Activity 9: Frequency Adverbs*

Frequency adverbs refer to how often an action occurs. These adverbs can be placed on a scale or range from 100% to 0%, like the one below.

1. Consider how often each frequency adverb in the box refers to an action taking place.
2. Rank each frequency adverb from the box below on the left side of the scale and add a percentage to the right side of the scale.

   • You may do this with a partner or individually.

> sometimes usually rarely often seldom frequently occasionally

3. As a class, discuss whether or not everyone's placement of the frequency adverbs agrees.
4. As a class, discuss how you could help learners of English practice the meaning of the frequency adverbs by using such a scale.

## *Activity 10: Error Analysis*

The following excerpts were written by learners of English. There are errors in adjective, and adverb use and form.

1. Underline **each adjective and adverb** error you find. **Ignore any other errors**.
2. For each error:

    (a) correct the error
    (b) discuss why the writer may have made the error.

*Example:*
People, have you ever thought that pandas are very endangered animals? Pandas are very interested animals.

> Pandas are very *interested* animals. → interesting
> The writer has confused the *–ing* and *–ed* participial adjective forms.

> People, have you ever thought that giant pandas are the more endangered animals? → the most endangered
> The writer has confused the forms *more* and *the most*.

**A.**

The giant pandas are more cute than a bear. They are more cuddly than a cat. And they are more big than a tiger. Giant pandas are not loved animals. They are unfriendly to each other. Some people burn the woods to make houses, so giant pandas' territories are getting more small.

**B.**

For many centuries, they treated women unequal, due to their more weak physical body structure. It took women a long time to gain their rights to work, but social convention sort of holds women back from being more successfully than men. The worse problem facing women is discrimination. Basically, people just don't believe women can be successfully as men. Also, women often get paid lesser than men although they have the same qualifications. So they can work more than men but their pay is more cheaper and they have to work more harder to make as much money the men.

## *Activity 11: Finding Adjectives and Adverbs*

1. Read the excerpt
2. Find all the adjectives and adverbs, including any nouns functioning as adjectives.

- If you are unsure if a word is an adjective or an adverb, try using one of the test frames discussed in the chapter.
- Check a dictionary for words you aren't sure of.

> "I feel like a bird with jeweled wings when I dance," she said ... "yes, surely this twirling, flying dance is for a girl like me."
>     [Raczek, L. (1999). *Rainy's powwow*. Flagstaff, AZ: Rising Moon. Picture Book, No page numbers].

## Activity 12: Finding Adjectives and Adverbs (optional additional practice; more advanced)

1. Read the newspaper excerpt.
2. Find all the adjectives and adverbs, including any nouns functioning as adjectives.

- If you are unsure if a word is an adjective or an adverb, try using one of the test frames discussed in the chapter.
- Check a dictionary for words you aren't sure of.

### A.

Did you stay within your budget for holiday spending? so, pat yourself on the back for a job well done. But if you spent money you did not have, I have a suggestion for next year: Start saving now.

### B.

The best way to handle expenditures with budget-busting potential is to plan for them in advance. After all, it's a pretty safe bet that Christmas is coming again next year.

### C.

You probably know that you need to save for retirement as well as for tuition for any future college students in your family. But many people overlook the importance of saving for shorter-term goals, such as vacation, the down payment on a car or holiday spending.

### D.

The best way to do that is through automatic savings plans such as payroll deduction and automated transfers from a checking account.

### E.

Many credit unions make the process easy with a version of the Old "Christmas club" account, now more commonly titled a holiday club account.

**F.**

The concept is simple: Save a set amount each payday and take out the accumulated pro-
ceeds when the holiday spending seasons rolls around. To get started, you simply decide
how much you want to save, then divide it by the number of weeks or paydays left before
you will withdraw the money.

[Huntley, H. (2003, 12 December). Next year, be ready to spend freely. *St. Petersburg
Times*, pp. D1, D4].

# Answer Key: Chapter 4 Discovery Activities

## *Discussion: Discovery Activity 3*

### *Excerpt A*

- adjectives: *delicious, creamy*

### *Excerpt B*
adjectives: *little, empty, small, old*

### *Excerpt C*

- adjectives: *giant, big*

## *Discussion: Discovery Activity 5*

(a) The *new* students had *excellent* scores on the tests.
    *New* modifies *students; excellent* modifies *scores*.

- -*ent* at the end of a word often indicates membership in the adjective class.
  Other adjectives ending in –*ent* include *prudent* or *absorbent*.
- When teaching –*ent* as an indicator of adjective class membership, it is impor-
  tant to point out that many words that end in –*ent* are not adjectives.
  - *Accident* and *basement* are nouns that also end in –*en*.
  - The irregular past tense of the verb *lend* is *lent*.

(b) Some of the concerns we had were *important*.

- *Important* follows *be*, modifying the noun phrase *some of the concerns*.
  - -*ant* at the end of a word often indicates membership in the adjective class.
    Other adjectives ending in –*ant* include *hesitant* or *significant*.

(c) Some parents are *unhappy* with the *current* changes in the curriculum.

- *Unhappy* comes after the verb *be*, modifying the noun phrase *many parents*.
  See Example 2 for discussion of –*y*.
- *Current* modifies *changes*. See (a) for discussion of –*ent*.

(d) Although their home is *humble*, they are *content* to live as they do.

- *Humble* comes after the verb *be*
  ○ modifies the noun phrase *their house.*
- *Content* comes after the verb *be* modifying the noun *they.* See (a) for discussion of *–ent.*

(e) The *cold, snowy* weather over the *long* weekend kept many people at home and resulted in *slow* sales for retailers.

- *Cold* and *snowy* both modify weather;
- *long* modifies *weekend;*
- *slow* modifies *sales.*

(f) When the viewers saw the movie, they were *ecstatic* over the *ambitious* plot and the *stupendous special* effects.

- *Ecstatic* comes after the verb *be* and modifies the noun *they.*
- *Ambitious* modifies *plot.*
- *Stupendous* and *special* both modify *effects.*
- The endings *–ic, –ous*, and *–ial* generally indicate membership in the adjective class.
  ○ Other adjectives with these endings include *nomadic, pragmatic, hectic; outrageous, fabulous, sagacious;* and *official, martial, social.*

## Discussion: Discovery Activity 6

(a) Do you own any *light cotton* dresses?
(b) The pirates' *swift* ship outran the *ponderous* tanker.
(c) Her *elderly* mother received a box of *expensive Swiss* chocolates for her birthday.
(d) Mr. Branch was a *little squat* man with *bushy black* hair.
(e) Rapunzel's *long golden* hair was wrapped in a *priceless silk* scarf.
(f) The flower consists of *delicate* blossoms on a slender *green* stalk with *broad rectangular* leaves.
(g) The *busy young* architect displayed his plans on a *drawing* board.

## Discussion: Discovery Activity 7

The following nouns are functioning as adjectives: *baseball, tree, pajama, fish, school*

| general description | size | shape | color | place of origin | material | use |
|---|---|---|---|---|---|---|
| | large | | spotted light | | | |
| elderly | | | | | cotton | |
| swift | | | | | | |
| ponderous | | | | | | |
| expensive | | | | Swiss | | |
| | little | squat | | | | |
| | | bushy | black | | | |
| | long | | golden | | | |
| priceless | | | | | silk | |
| delicate | | | green | | | |
| | | broad | | | | |
| | | rectangular | | | | |
| busy | | | | | | |
| young | | | | | | |
| | | | | | drawing | |

## Discussion: Discovery Activity 8

- participial adjectives: *potted, sweltering, exciting, forthcoming, revolutionizing, prolonged*, and *settled*.
- verb phrases: *is sitting* and *may be screening*.
- *played* is the past tense form of the verb *play* and not a participial adjective.

# Chapter 5
# Introduction to Verbs and Verb Phrases

## The Heart of the Sentence

## Introduction

In this chapter we investigate verbs. The chapter is divided into four sections, each one of which looks at a different aspect of verbs: Section 1 discusses how to identify verbs. Section 2 explores two main categories of verbs, main verbs and auxiliary verbs. The next section examines two types of main verbs, transitive and intransitive. Section 4 considers infinitives and gerunds, and the last section delves into a special type of verb, phrasal verbs.

We often think of the verb as being the "heart" of the sentence because it is the verb that provides the central meaning to a sentence. Verbs express what the subject does or describe something about the state or condition of the subject. This, however, is only the beginning. Verbs are complex elements that not only provide crucial sentence meaning, but that also provide support for other verbs, determine what kinds of sentence elements can come after them, combine with prepositions and adverbs to make special, idiomatic verbs known as phrasal verbs, and show time references, the topic of Chapter 6.

## Section 1: Identifying Verbs

*What makes a verb a verb?*

In the same way we did with nouns, adjectives, and adverbs, we can identify verbs on the basis of semantic, structural, and morphological clues. As we have noted previously, semantic and morphological clues are not as powerful as structural clues in identifying word class membership since in English form is not equal to function.

## Semantic Clues

Earlier we said that a verb tells us something the subject does or something about the subject's state of being. You will notice that this semantic definition is broader than the traditional definition of verbs, which are usually defined as being action words, such as *jump, walk,* and *recognize.* While explaining what a verb is or does is useful in introducing verbs to learners, semantic clues only provide limited information in identifying words as verbs, especially for ESL/EFL learners.

## Morphological Clues

### *Derivational*

In Chapter 2, we reviewed how derivational endings of verbs can indicate class membership. Common verb suffixes of the verb class include *–ate, -fy, and -ize,* as in *create, classify,* and *realize.*

### *Inflectional*

To some extent, verbs can be distinguished from other parts of speech on the basis of morphological characteristics in that they inflect for present and past time. As we observed in Chapter 2, although English is a language that does not show much inflection in verb forms, it does have some.

| Subject | Verb + Inflection | Function |
|---------|-------------------|----------|
| he, she, it | walk**s**, laugh**s**, call**s**, | present tense, 3rd person singular *–s* |
| he, she, it, I, you, he, she, it, we, they | walk**ed**, laugh**ed**, call**ed**, | past tense regular verbs, all persons |

- In present tense, third person singular (*he, she, it*) English verbs require an *–s* ending. This is the only inflection in present tense, except for the verb *be.*
- In past tense, all regular verbs take an *–ed* ending.

  - Irregular verbs follow different patterns, e.g. *drink, drank; sleep, slept,* but still indicate past tense by having a different form from the present tense.
  - Even irregular verbs such as *cut* that do not change their form have an irregular past tense form in that there is no third person singular *–s* inflection.

***How is the verb* be *different from other verbs in terms of inflections?***

The verb *be* is the only verb in English that has more than one inflectional form in present and past tense. In present tense *be* has three forms: *am, are,* and *is.* In past tense *be* has two forms, *was* and *were.*

## Structural Clues

The sentence position of the verb, like most sentence elements in English, is highly fixed. In affirmative sentences, the verb comes after the subject:

(1) *The boy* **laughed** at the joke.
(2) One dark and dreadful night, *Jack's mother* **sent** him to market to sell the cow.
   [Cecil, R. (2004). *One dark and dreadful night.* New York: Henry Holt. No page number.]

Even when the sentence is a long, complex one with more than one verb, we still find a verb after a subject:

(3) *The hapless child* **went** into the Woods of Woe, where *the dark*[1] **grew** darker, and *the trees* **grew** more twisted, and *all the sharp pointy things* **grew** sharper and pointier.
   [Cecil, R. (2004). *One dark and dreadful night.* New York: Henry Holt. No page numbers.]

If you examine Sentences (1), (2), and (3) again, you will notice that each verb is a single word. Many verbs, however, consist of more than one part:

(4) Hunky **was watching** the game furtively from the sidewalk on the other side of the chain-link fence.
   [Langton, J. (2000). *The Time Bike* (p. 65). New York: HarperTrophy.]
(5) The designers **have put** the finishing touches on their outfits. Everyone in Toenail **has bought** a ticket to the event.
   [McMullan, K. (2005). *Beware! It's Friday the 13.* (Dragon Slayers' Academy 13) (p. 30). New York: Grosset & Dunlap.]

### *Why do you say that Sentences (4) and (5) have two parts to the verb?*

The answer to this question has to do with our next section, the difference between main verbs and auxiliary verbs. Main verbs are verbs that do not have any "helping" or auxiliary verbs. Auxiliary verbs are verbs that have to accompany or "help" another verb. The fact that some verbs need auxiliary verbs is difficult for learners of English because they need to remember that a sentence needs at least two verbs: the main verb and the helping or auxiliary verb. In this chapter and in Chapter 6, we will be looking at the different auxiliary verbs and their functions.

---

[1] *dark* is functioning here as a noun, as we discussed in Chapter 3.

## Section 2: Main Verbs versus Auxiliary Verbs

Verbs are generally divided into two major categories: main verbs and auxiliary verbs. Main verbs are verbs that can stand alone and that do not need to be accompanied by any other verb. Main verbs also contribute the key semantic meaning in any verb phrase.

> (6) I **walk** to school.
> (7) Jenny **walks** to school.
> (8) She **walked** to school yesterday.

In Sentence (6), the main verb is *walk*. In Sentence (7), the main verb is also *walk*, but this time it has the third person present tense –*s* inflectional ending.

In Sentence (3), the main verb is still *walk*, but this time it has the past tense –*ed* inflectional ending, which all regular past tense verbs in English take. None of these three sentences has an auxiliary verb. There is only the main verb *walk*.

Other types of sentences need auxiliary verbs. Auxiliary verbs accompany main verbs. They are only there to "help" the main verb in some way and they have no semantic meaning. Different auxiliary verbs have different functions. For example, auxiliary verbs can support the negative as in Sentence (9) below.

> (9) I **do not** (or **don't**) **w**alk to school.

In Sentence (9), we have to include the auxiliary *do* before *not* and the main verb to make a negative sentence in present tense. This is a grammatical requirement in standard English. We cannot say:

> *(9a) I **not walk** to school.

Before we continue on with our exploration of the difference between main verbs and auxiliary verbs, review your knowledge of main verbs by completing Discovery Activity 1. If you feel confident in your ability to identify main verbs, continue on to the following section. The answers to this Discovery Activity are at the end of the chapter in the Answer Key.

---

**Discovery Activity 1: Identifying Main Verbs**

Look at the excerpt.

1. Underline the main verbs.

**A.**

> The elephant's trunk is both a hand and a nose ... Elephants also use their trunks to communicate in a kind of sign language. A young elephant sucks its trunk the way babies suck their thumbs.

[Schwartz, A. (2005). *Elephants can paint too*. New York: Simon & Schuster. No page numbers.]

**B.**

She grabbed Claudius by the collar and looked out through the curtain. Light from the kitchen fell on the stoop. Joey Chavez stood there. She jerked the door open. Claudius wriggled free from Annie's clutches. He sniffed Joey's jeans and wagged his tail.
[Campbell, A. (2002). *Wolf tracks* (p. 72). New York: Signet.]

We now continue with our examination of the three primary auxiliary verbs in English.

## The Primary Auxiliary Verbs *Have, Be, Do*

As you will recall, auxiliary or helping verbs accompany main verbs. They have no meaning on their own and they do not contribute semantic or content meaning to the sentence but grammatical meaning. By grammatical meaning, we mean that auxiliaries tell us something about the verb phrase, such as time reference.

There are three primary auxiliary verbs in English: *have, be,* and *do*. They are often confused with their counterparts, the three main verbs, *have, be,* and *do*. Although these auxiliary and main verbs look alike, they have completely different meanings and uses.

Compare the main and auxiliary uses of the three verbs in Discovery Activity 2.

**Discovery Activity 2: *have, be, do***

Look at the following sentences.

a. Explain the meaning of *have, be,* and *do* in Column A.
b. Compare these verbs with those in Column B and explain how they are different from the verbs in Column A.

| A. | B. |
|---|---|
| (1) I have a cat. | (1) I have always liked cats. |
| (2) I had a cat for many years. | (2) I had liked cats for a long time. |
| (3) Jo is a teacher. | (3) Jo is teaching now. |
| (4) Jo was a teacher. | (4) Jo was teaching when the bell rang. |
| (5) Emily does her homework carefully. | (5) Emily does not like homework. |
| (6) Emily did her homework yesterday. | (6) Emily did not like her homework. |

## *Discussion: Discovery Activity 2*

In this discussion, you may see terms that are unfamiliar to you. Don't worry if you don't understand all the terms. Most of these have to do with tense and aspect, discussed in Chapter 6. The important point to take away from this activity is the ability to distinguish between main verbs and auxiliary verbs.

### Column A

- *Be, have,* and *do* are main verbs. They are main verbs because they contain lexical or content information.
- In Sentences (A1) and (A2), *have* refers to possession, present tense and past tense respectively.
- In Sentences (A3) and (A4), *be* is telling us something about Jo. (A3) is present time, third person singular and (A4) is past time, third person singular.
- In Sentences (A5) and (A6), a synonym for *do* is "perform" or "execute." In (A5), *do* is in the present tense third person singular form *does*. In (A6), *do* is in the past verb tense, *did*.

### Column B

Remember, you will find a complete discussion of the different verb tenses in Chapter 6. This is intended only as an introduction.

- *Have, be,* and *do* are functioning as auxiliary verbs. *Have* and *do* indicate time references; *do* supports present and past tense negation, and question formation.
- In Sentence (B1), *have* is part of the verb phrase *have liked*. The main verb is *liked*. It is carrying the *–ed* past participle inflection of the present perfect tense.
- Sentence (B2) *had* is part of the verb phrase, *had liked*. In this sentence, *had + liked* compose the verb tense called the past perfect.
- In both (B1) and (B2), *have* carries no semantic meaning. The auxiliary *have* indicates time; it shows whether something is present or past and combines with a participle form of the main verb to form a verb phrase that shows time and aspect.
- In Sentences (B3) and (B4), *be* is part of the verb phrase. The main verb in both sentences is *teaching*. This teaching is the present participle inflection.
- Sentence (B3) is a present progressive verb phrase, which is composed of the present tense form of the auxiliary verb *be* (is) + the main verb in present participle form, *teaching*.
- Sentence (B4) is a past progressive verb phrase, composed of the past tense form of the auxiliary verb *be* (was) + the main verb in present participle form, *teaching*.

In American English, all present tense verbs except *be* require the use of the *do* auxiliary to form negative statements in simple present and simple past.

- Sentences (B5) and (B6) use the *do* auxiliary to form negative statements in simple present and simple past respectively. The main verb in each of these two sentences is *like*.

  - The main verb does not change its form when the *do* auxiliary is present because *do* carries the time inflection (present or past).
  - In the case of the simple present, also inflections for third person singular (*does*).

This activity should have helped clarify for you the differences between the main verbs *have, be,* and *do,* and their auxiliary counterparts. Keep in mind that any difficulties you may have had in distinguishing these verbs will be similar to those faced by ESL/EFL learners.

Discovery Activity 3 focuses on helping you practice the different functions of *be* and *have*. These two differ from *do* in that when *be* and *have* function as auxiliary verbs, they work together with a main verb to tell us something about the time reference of the main verb.

---

### Discovery Activity 3: Introduction to Identifying the Different Functions of *be* and *have*

Look at the following excerpts.

1. Underline all the uses of *be* and *have*.
2. Explain each use of *be* and *have*. Is it the main verb *be* or *have*, or the auxiliary *be* or *have*?

*Example*:
Gina *is* late.

- main verb is the third person singular form of the verb *be*, "is".
- used to describe something about Gina.

**A.**

"How much is it worth? I asked him...
"That says 1851," he said. "Certain years are worth more...
I explained I was carrying it around for a good luck piece...
We were walking down the corridor now but I wasn't really walking. I was floating.
"I'm rich," I yelled. "I got nine more just like this at home."
... Mr. Snowden set his books down on the low brick ledge that coursed the side entrance. Because it was hot he took off his coat, opened his white short-sleeved shirt and loosened his tie. His arms were thick and heavy.... He had big hands with very thick fingers.
[Platt, K. (1966). *Sinbad and Me* (pp. 86–87) New York: Tempo Books.]

\* set, took off, opened, loosened,

**B.**

"Mr. Dickinson, if you believe that all that has fallen upon us is merely talk, I have no response. There is no hope of avoiding a war, sir, because the war has already begun. Your king and his army have seen to that.

[Shaara, J. (2001). *Rise to Rebellion* (p. 366). New York: Ballantine.]

## *Discussion: Discovery Activity 3*

### Excerpt A

- *be* functioning as an auxiliary verb in the verb phrases: *was carrying, were walking, wasn't... walking, was floating.*
- *be* functioning as the main verb in: *How much is ..., Certain years are ..., I'm rich ..., it was hot ... His arms were ... He had big ...*

### Excerpt B

- *have* functioning as an auxiliary in the verb phrases: *has fallen, has ... begun,* and *have seen.*
- *have* functioning as the main verb in the sentence *I have no response.*
- *be* and *have* functioning as the main verb in *... is merely talk ..., There is no hope ...*

### *Does* do *as an auxiliary function just like* be *and* have?

Although *do, be,* and *have* are all auxiliary verbs, the *do* auxiliary has a different function from that of the *have* and *be* auxiliaries. As you saw in Discovery Activity 3, *have* and *be* show time information. These two auxiliaries combine with main verbs to form verb phrases that convey time information:

| | |
|---|---|
| (10) The girls **are** *walking* to school. | **present** progressive |
| (10a) The girls **were** *walking* to school. | **past** progressive |
| (11) The girls **have** *walked* to school. | **present** perfect |
| (11a) The girls **had** *walked* to school. | **past** perfect |

You may not be familiar with the labels for the tenses in Sentences (10/10a) and (11/11a), but you will notice the different time conveyed by the auxiliary.

## *Do* as a Verb Helper

The *do* auxiliary is used to form questions and negatives in simple present and simple past tense of all verbs except *be*. Unlike the auxiliaries *be* and *have, do* does not provide time information. It simply helps the verb by being there in questions or negative statements, which is why grammar books often refer to *do* to as a "filler" verb. We will discuss *do* in more detail when we look at simple present and simple past in Chapter 6.

*Can you explain how* **do** *works with verbs?*

| *Do* in Simple Present | |
| --- | --- |
| (12) He walks to school. | *walk* + *-s* |
| (13) He **does** not walk to school. | *do* + *-s*, no *–s* on *walk* |
| (14) **Does** he walk to school? | |

Like its main verb counterpart, the auxiliary *do* has different inflections. When the *do* auxiliary is in a sentence, the main verb loses any inflections it may have, *do* is inflected instead. As we saw in Chapter 2, only the third person singular, *he, she,* or *it* takes an inflectional ending in simple present tense and only in affirmative statements. When the verb in simple present tense is used in a question or negative statement, the *–s* inflection is dropped from the main verb and is attached to the auxiliary *do*, as in Sentences (13) and (14). The main verb keeps its base form with no *–s* ending.

| *Did* in Simple Past | |
| --- | --- |
| (15) He walk**ed** to school. | *walk* + *-ed* |
| (16) He **did** not walk to school. | *did*, no *-ed* on *walk* |
| (17) **Did** he walk to school? | |

As you will remember, there is only one past tense inflectional ending for regular verbs, *-ed*. When we use a past tense verb in a question or negative statement, we drop the *–ed* inflection from the main verb and attach it to the auxiliary *do* (with a spelling change), as in Sentences (16) and (17). The main verb keeps its base form with no *–ed* ending. Irregular verbs change back to the base form with the addition of the *do* auxiliary, e.g. *Did you drive* or *I didn't come.*

Now that you have a general sense of how *do* functions as an auxiliary verb, let us explore more thoroughly what it means to say *do* functions as a filler or support verb. Look at the chart below and compare how questions are formed with *have, be* and *do*. As you examine the chart, think about why *do* is often called a "filler verb."

| | | | aux | main verb | |
| --- | --- | --- | --- | --- | --- |
| (18) | | Jane | is | walking. | |
| (19) | | Jane | has | walked. | |
| | | | | | statement |
| (20) | | Jane | | walks. | |
| (21) | | Jane | | walked | |
| | aux | | | | |
| (22) | Is | Jane | | walking? | |
| (23) | Has | Jane | | walked? | |
| | | | | | question |
| (24) | Does | Jane | | walk? | |
| (25) | Did | Jane | | walk? | |

What you will notice is that Sentences (18) and (19) are composed of an auxiliary + main verb. To make these into questions, we simply move the verb to before the subject noun phrase, as in Sentences (22) and (23).

Sentences (20) and (21), in contrast, do not have an auxiliary verb, only a main verb. Therefore, to make these sentences into questions, we need to add something to the position before the noun phrase. This "something" is the auxiliary *do*, which functions to "fill" the auxiliary slot before the noun phrase in a question.

The next chart illustrates the filler function of *do* in negatives:

|       |      | aux  |     | main verb |                      |
|-------|------|------|-----|-----------|----------------------|
| (26)  | Jane | is   | not | walking.  |                      |
| (27)  | Jane | has  | not | walked.   |                      |
|       |      |      |     |           | negative statement   |
| (28)  | Jane | does | not | walks.    |                      |
| (29)  | Jane | did  | not | walked    |                      |

Again we observe that in sentences where the verb phrase is composed of an auxiliary + main verb, *not* simply follows the auxiliary, as in Sentences (26) and (27). When there is no auxiliary present, we have to add *do* before *not,* as in Sentences (28) and (29).

In summary, if there is already an auxiliary verb present, we do not need to add another auxiliary. Simple present and simple past are called simple tenses because they are not composed of an auxiliary + main verb. However, English requires that

- all yes/no questions begin with an auxiliary.
- the negative *not* follow the auxiliary (and can attach to the auxiliary in contracted forms).

Therefore, for the simple present and the simple past we must insert the *do* auxiliary, but we do not insert an auxiliary for any verb that already has an auxiliary, as in our previous examples, Sentences (26) and (27).

The next Discovery Activity gives you the opportunity to see how skilled you are in identifying the different functions of *do*. As you complete the activity, think about which uses of *do* ESL/EFL learners might find confusing and how you might explain *do* to them. You will find the answers to Discovery Activity 4 at the end of the chapter in the Answer Key.

**Discovery Activity 4: Identifying the different functions of *do***

Look at the following excerpts.

1. Underline all the uses of *do*.
2. Label each use of *do*. Is it the main verb *do* or the auxiliary *do*?

*Example*:

She *didn't* want help. She *did* her homework by herself.

two uses of *do*:

- *did* + not; *do* is the auxiliary for a negative past tense statement.
- *do* main verb, past tense

**A.**

"She was a big part of this studio's reputation, since this is where she started and did a lot of coaching."

"As good as he was to her, she was rude to him."

"People don't usually commit murder simply because someone was rude, Jane," Shannon said.

[Graham, H. (2004). *Dead on the dance floor* (p. 87). New York: Mira.]

**B.**

"Did you run a charter service in Virginia, too?"

"What?" He frowned. "Oh, yeah. I love boats. . . . Do you like the water?"

"Sure."

"Do you fish? Dive?"

"I fished when I was a kid. And I did some diving in the middle of the state when I was a teenager. I did a few of those dives where you go in with the manatees."

"You didn't like it?"

"I loved it."

"But you don't dive anymore?"

She shrugged. "I don't think I do anything anymore. I've gotten too involved with work."

[Graham, H. (2004). *Dead on the dance floor* (p. 102). New York: Mira.]

## What kinds of difficulties do ESL/EFL learners have with the do auxiliary?

▶ *Learner difficulties*

Using the *do* auxiliary requires mastery of several different features. ESL/EFL learners must learn to place correctly the auxiliary, and correctly inflect *do* and not inflect the main verb. Because there are various steps to remember in using *do*, ESL/EFL learners frequently have difficulty forming questions and negatives in simple present and simple past.

One of the common problems learners confront is remembering to use the *do* auxiliary in negative statements. Learners frequently use *not* alone with the verb as in:

*\*I not go*
    *or*
*\*She not walked*

Depending upon their native language, some ESL/EFL learners may use *no* before the verb:

>   **I no go*
>     *or*
>   **She no walked.*

Learners may also invert the subject and verb to form a question where *do* is necessary:

>   **Want you to go home?*
>     *or*
>   **Like they this restaurant?*

Another difficulty for ESL/EFL learners is remembering to use the correct simple present tense form of the auxiliary, *do* or *does*, in negative statements and questions. Learners may produce such sentences as:

>   **My brother don't help me much.*
>     *or*
>   **Her baby don't cry all the time.*

When ESL/EFL learners make errors such as, *She live here,* native speakers tend to recognize this as a learner error and will generally ignore it. In case of using *don't* instead of *doesn't*, however, the use of *don't* is a non-standard, stigmatized form in English. This *don't* is frequently characterized as a form used by speakers who are less educated, less intelligent, and so on. It is therefore important that ESL/EFL learners learn to use *doesn't* correctly to avoid negative stereotyping based on their use of this stigmatized grammatical form.

A further problem for ESL/EFL learners is that they may forget to leave the main verb in its base form. They may add the *–s* third person singular inflectional ending onto both the *do* auxiliary and the main verb, producing such sentences as:

>   **He does not (doesn't) goes*
>     *or*
>   **Does he goes?*

Here, learners are adding the *–s* inflection to both *do* and the main verb. Similarly, ESL/EFL learners may also create past sentences and questions such as:

>   **Did she came?*
>     *or*
>   **She didn't drove me*

In these sentences, ESL/EFL learners are using *did* + the irregular past form instead of the base form of the verb.

***What are all the problems learners have with the auxiliary verb* do?**

| Summary: Common Learner Errors with *do* | |
| --- | --- |
| *Why you walk every day? <br> *I not walk every day. <br> *He no want to walk. <br> *Why you not come? | no *do* auxiliary |
| *Why does she walks every day? <br> *She does not walks everyday. <br> *He does no want to walk. <br> *They did no(t) wanted to walk. <br> *Why did you came late? | *do* auxiliary + inflection on main verb |

We end our exploration of the auxiliary verbs for now and turn to a discussion of two major types of main verbs, transitive and intransitive. We will return to auxiliary verbs again in later chapters.

## Section 3: Transitive and Intransitive Verbs

***What are transitive and intransitive verbs?***

## Transitive Verbs

Main verbs can be classified into transitive or intransitive verbs. Transitive verbs are verbs that must be followed by an *object*. The grammatical term *object* means a noun, pronoun or noun phrase that receives the action of the verb. Compare the following sentences:

| Group A | Group B |
| --- | --- |
| * I mailed. | I mailed a letter. |
| *Jane copied. | Jane copied the sentence. |
| *The boys took. | The boys took a bus. |
| *We bought. | We bought a new car. |

All the sentences in Group A are ungrammatical because the sentences are incomplete. Even if we add an adverb, e.g. *I mailed quickly* or *We bought suddenly,* the sentences in Group A remain incomplete. This is because the verbs in Group are transitive and must be followed by an object, as in Group B.

## Intransitive Verbs

Intransitive verbs, in contrast do not need to be followed by an object. Intransitive verbs can form a sentence with just a subject:

(30) The baby slept.

Or an intransitive verb can be followed by something else that is not an object, such as an adverb.

(30a) The baby slept quietly.

## Distinguishing the Object of a Transitive Verb

*How can I tell what the object of a transitive verb is?*

The object of a transitive verb can often be determined by asking a *what* or *who* question. Take the sentences below and practice making *what* questions to find the object of the verb.

(31) Pam reads books.
(32) Mary and I drive vans.
(33) You mailed packages and letters.

You should have come up with questions like these:

| *what* question | answer= object |
|---|---|
| (31a) What does Pam read? | books |
| (32a) What do Mary and I drive? | vans |
| (33a) What did you mail? | packages and letters |

Discovery Activity 5 will give you practice in identifying transitive verbs and their objects, using authentic excerpts. When you have completed this activity, compare your answers to those in the Answer Key at the end of the chapter.

**Discovery Activity 5: Transitive Verbs**

Look at the following sentences.

1. Find and underline the transitive verbs.

   - If you aren't sure, ask yourself a *what* or *who* question to find the object and help you identify the transitive verb.

*Example:*
When they *remodeled* their house, they *added* a second story.
*What questions:*

- What did they remodel? (their house)
- What did they add? (a second story)

(a) He washed the dishes and polished all the silverware.
   [Asch, F. (1993). *Moondance.* New York: Scholastic. No page numbers.]
(b) A stiff breeze started up and blew us into the air. Ahead, we saw a big blue circle.
   [Cole, J. (1999). *The magic school bus explores the senses* (p. 12). New York: Scholastic.]
(b) The woman sat down. She carefully put her red leather bag on the seat to her left.
   [Adler, D. (1999). *Cam Jansen and the barking treasure mystery* (p. 13). *New York:* Penguin.]
(c) I'll tell jokes. And I don't even need the speaker box.
   [Adler, D. (1999). *Cam Jansen and the barking treasure mystery* (p. 54). New York: Penguin.]

### Can the object of a transitive verb consist of more than one word?

In Discovery Activity 6, there are several examples of objects with more than one word. In (b), for instance, the object of *saw* is *big blue circle.* In (c) the object of *put* is *red leather bag.* As you see, the object can be a noun phrase consisting of several words. Let's consider this some more by exploring what we can do with our earlier sentence:

| subject | verb | object |
|---------|------|--------|
| (31) Pam | reads | books |

Sentence (31) consists of a subject + verb + direct object. We can expand the object as follows:

| subject | verb | object noun phrase |
|---------|------|--------------------|
| Pam | reads | best-selling books. |
| | | the hottest best-selling books. |
| | | the hottest best-selling paperback books. |
| | | the newest, hottest, best-selling paperback books. |
| | | the newest, funniest, hottest, best-selling paperback books. |

In each of the expanded sentences, we have added more words to make a longer direct object noun phrases. Yet, regardless of the length of the object, in all the sentences above the direct object can be replaced by the object pronoun *them*. All the different sentences become the identical sentence, *Pam reads them*. You can use such object pronoun substitution as a clue for identifying which words make up the object noun phrase.

## Di-transitive Verbs (transitive verbs with more than one object)

### Can transitive verbs take more than one object?

Some transitive verbs can take more than one object. These verbs are often called **di-transitive verbs**. When there are two objects, one is called the **direct object** and the other is called the **indirect object**. The direct object is the person or thing that receives the action of the verb, as in Sentence (34).

(34) Jan hit **the ball**.

In this sentence, the direct object is *the ball* because it receives the action described by the verb *hit*. Compare Sentence (34) with Sentence (35):

(35) Jan hit **the ball** *to the pitcher*.

In Sentence (35), the verb *hit* has two objects. There is both a direct object (*the ball*) and an indirect object (*to the pitcher*). We can describe an indirect object as the person or thing that is secondarily affected by the action of the verb.

When the indirect object follows the direct object, it is usually preceded by *to* as in Sentence (35). Sometimes the indirect object is preceded by *for*, as in *Rick opened the box for me*. This *to* or *for* can help identify the indirect object in a sentence.

| subject | verb | direct object | indirect object w/*to* |
|---|---|---|---|
| (36) Pam | reads | books | to children. |
| (37) Mary and I | give | money | to our children. |
| (38) You | mailed | packages and letters | to the soldier. |

Sometimes, speakers place the indirect object before the direct object. In this case, we drop *to* or *for* before the indirect object.

| subject | verb | indirect object without *to* | direct object |
|---|---|---|---|
| (36a) Pam | reads | children | books. |
| (37a) Mary and I | give | our children | money. |
| (38a) You | mailed | the soldier | packages and letters. |

The structural clue *to* or *for* only indicates an indirect object when the indirect object follows the direct object. When the indirect object precedes the direct object, we cannot use "to" or "for" as a clue. In such instances, we must rely upon word order and semantic meaning to understand which noun phrase is the indirect object and which is the direct object.

### *Is this all I need to teach my students about di-transitive verbs?*

There is one more important aspect that we need to examine. All the sentences we have looked at up to now in discussing di-transitive verbs have had object *noun phrases* and not object *pronouns*. Examine the following chart. As you do, think about word order, and the direct and indirect object pronouns.

|  |  | direct object | indirect object | direct object | indirect object |
|---|---|---|---|---|---|
| (39) Liz | passed | a note |  |  | to her friends. |
| (39a) Liz | passed |  | her friends | a note |  |
| (39b) Liz | passed | **it** |  |  | **to them** |

In Sentences (39) and (39a), we see the two options we have in ordering the direct and indirect objects when they are noun phrases. Sentence (39b) illustrates how when the object noun phrases become pronouns, the generally preferred option is the **direct** object pronoun **followed by** the **indirect** object pronoun.

### *Do ESL/EFL learners find the different word order of direct and indirect objects confusing?*

▶ *Learner difficulties*

Less proficient ESL/EFL learners often have difficulty with verbs that take both a direct and an indirect object. They need practice in remembering the correct order of objects, particularly when the objects occur in pronoun form. ESL/EFL learners may confuse which pronoun takes which position and produce sentences such as:

(40) *Lynn gave *it them*.
       *or*
(41) *Lynn gave *to them it*.

The importance of word order in English must be continually emphasized with learners of English who may speak languages where word order is not as important. While they can use sentence position and other clues in identifying direct versus indirect objects, they must also have a grasp of correct English word is in order to understand.

Discovery Activity 6 is designed to help you review di-transitive verbs and pronouns. This will help prepare you for the more difficult excerpts in Discovery

Activity 7. Be sure to check your answers, which you can find in the Answer Key at the end of the chapter, before you move on to Discovery Activity 7.

**Discovery Activity 6: Di-transitive Verbs and Pronouns**

**Part I**

1. Label each direct object as **DO**.
2. Label each indirect object as **IO**.

    a) The college gave the outstanding student an award.
    b) The mother baked a chocolate cake for her daughter.
    c) The player passed the football to his teammate.
    d) The teacher is going to read her young students a different book.
    e) The committee granted the applicant an extension.
    f) The mother cut the food for the toddler.

**Part II**

3. On a separate sheet of paper, go back to the sentences above and change the objects you identified to pronouns. You may have to change the word order in some of the sentences.

Now try Discovery Activity 7 and see how well you can distinguish the direct versus indirect objects. You will probably find this Discovery Activity more challenging than the previous one.

**Discovery Activity 7: Transitive Verbs**

Look at the excerpts.

1. Underline the transitive verbs.
2. Label each direct object as **DO**.
3. Label each indirect object as **IO**.

**A.**

Just then the door opened . . .
"I asked my old friend Captain Gil to send me tickets. We're going today. . . .
"Yay!" Ralphie yelled. . . " I've always wanted to see a real live whale. . .
"We might see a blue whale," Ms. Frizzle said. "I can't promise."
    [Moore, E. (2000). *The wild whale watch* (*magic school bus chapter book #3*) (pp. 1–2). New York: Scholastic.]

**B.**

> Koko and Yum Yum were a pair of purebred Siamese... Koko was the communicator
> of the family. He ordered the meals, greeted the guests, told them when to go home
> and always, always, spoke his mind...
>
> [Jackson Braun, L. (2004). *The cat who talked Turkey* (p. 9). New York: G.P.
> Putman's Sons.]

**C.**

> [Polly Duncan] would be flying home the next morning. Qwilleran said he would
> pick her up at the airport and asked if she was bringing him something...
> "Yes, and you'll love it!"
>
> [Jackson Braun, L. (2004). *The cat who talked Turkey* (p. 10). New York: G.P.
> Putman's Sons.]

**D.**

> ... When they arrived at the door of suite 400, Edythe gave him her keys. He
> unlocked it and pushed the door gently open. She walked in, and her knees buckled.
> Qwilleran caught her.
>
> [Jackson Braun, L. (2004). *The cat who talked Turkey* (p. 165). New York: G.P.
> Putman's Sons.]

## Intransitive Verbs and Complements

You may have had some difficulties in completing Discovery Activity 7. The activity
included both transitive and intransitive verbs, some of which are followed by words
that are not objects. We previously observed that although intransitive verbs do not
take objects, they can be followed by other sentence elements as in these sentences
from earlier in this section:

   (30) The baby slept.
   (31) The baby slept quietly.

If something follows an intransitive verb, such as *quietly,* it is generally called a
*complement.* We use the term *complement* to refer to words and phrases that follow
verbs but that are not objects because they do not receive the action of the verb. A
complement can be a single word or a phrase. In Excerpt C, for instance, you saw
the sentence:

   *[Polly Duncan] would be flying home the next morning.*

In this sentence, there are several words after the verb phrase *would be flying.*
These words do not function as objects of the verb. We cannot make a *who* or *what*
question for the phrase, *home the next morning*, which tells us that these words
are sentence complements. Additional examples of complements are shown in the
following chart:

| Intransitive Verbs | | |
|---|---|---|
| subject | verb | complement |
| Alina | is | my best friend. |
| Pete and I | live | in the corner house. |
| You | are feeling | sick from the heat. |
| They | are | friends forever. |

As you see, we find different types of complements after intransitive verbs. These include:

- a noun (*friend*), or noun phrase (*my friends*)
- a prepositional phrase (*in the corner house*)
- an adjective (*sick*), or adjective phrase (*very sick*)
- an adverb (*here*) or an adverb phrase (*here on Main Street*).

Discovery Activity 8 is designed to help you practice distinguish intransitive verbs and their complements. You will find the answers at the end of the chapter in the Answer Key.

**Discovery Activity 8: Intransitive Verbs**

Look at the excerpt.

1. Underline the intransitive verbs.
2. If the verb has a complement, circle it.

**A.**

It's opening day, and the owners give speeches while the office staff listen... Horray!
[Tarsky, S. (1997). *The busy building book.* New York: G.P. Putnam's Sons. Picture Book, No page numbers.]

**B.**

All was ready... Qwilleran had showered and shaved and trimmed his moustache...
Playing the genial host, Qwilleran stepped forward...
"Mr. Hedges, I presume."
"Hodges," the guest corrected him.
[Jackson Braun, L. (2004). *The cat who talked Turkey* (p. 63). New York: G.P. Putman's Sons.]

**C.**

... the land unfolds in a gigantic plateau... To the south of the Great Basin, deserts sprawl across the Intermountain regions... At the eastern edge of the Intermountain region, the elevation soars upward into the Rocky Mountains.
[Ritchie, R., & Broussard, A. (1999). *American history: The early years to 1877* (p. 23). New York: Glencoe.]

## Verbs that are Both Transitive and Intransitive

*Are all main verbs either transitive or intransitive? For example, what about a verb such as "eat?" Can't it be both transitive and intransitive?*

Some verbs are both transitive and intransitive, depending on how they are used, as we saw in Discovery Activity 8, Excerpt B. Take another example. In response to the question, "What are you doing?" we can say, "We're eating." In this case *eat* is being used intransitively. Even if we add a phrase after the verb, such as *in the dining room*, it is still intransitive. The phrase *in the dining room* is a complement not an object.

However, if someone asks us, "What are you eating?" we respond by using *eat* in its transitive sense, "We're eating **spaghetti**" or "We're eating **a large gooey chocolate brownie**." In the first sentence, **spaghetti** is the object. In the second sentence, **a large gooey chocolate brownie** is the object.

Discovery Activity 9 allows you to see explicitly the difference between related transitive and intransitive verbs. After you have discussed your responses with those of your classmates, compare them to the answers in the Answer Key at the end of the chapter.

### Discovery Activity 9: Related Meanings of Transitive and Intransitive Verbs

Discuss the different meanings of the verbs in Column A versus Column B

| A | B |
| --- | --- |
| Alan teaches. | Alan teaches math. |
| Sandra drives. | Sandra drives a BMW. |
| Carson smokes. | Carson smokes cigars. |
| Alexa reads. | Alexa reads novels. |

## Linking Verbs

Linking verbs are a subcategory of verbs. They can be both transitive and intransitive. They are called linking verbs because in their intransitive sense they "link" the subject noun phrase with something after the verb. Most linking verbs are related to our senses, e.g. *smell, hear,* or *feel*. As you examine the chart below, think about how the verbs differ in their intransitive and transitive use.

| A. Intransitive | B. Transitive |
| --- | --- |
| The rose smelled nice. | I smelled the rose. |
| The soup tasted salty. | The chef tasted the soup. |
| He didn't hear well. | He didn't hear the bell. |

When you look at these sentences, you will notice that in Column A, the verb is followed by an adjective, which describes something about the subject. Thus we see how the verb "links" the subject and the adjective. Contrast this with Column B, where the same verbs are followed by objects.

| Common Linking Verbs | | | | | | | |
|---|---|---|---|---|---|---|---|
| appear | be | become | continue | feel | grow | hear | look |
| | remain | sound | seem | stay | smell | taste | |

In addition to objects and complements, other types of structures can follow nouns, including the topic of the next section, infinitives and gerunds.

## Section 4: Verbs Followed by Infinitives and Gerunds

*Why can we say, "I want to see a movie" but not "I want seeing a movie?" Or "I enjoy seeing a movie" but not "I enjoy to see a movie?"*

The answer to this question lies in the main verb. As we will see in the following section, certain verbs are followed by the "to" infinitive form of the verb. Others are followed by the *–ing* form of a verb.

Many verbs are followed by *infinitive verbs*. Infinitive verbs have this label because they are verbs that:

- do not show time (or "tense")
- do not have a subject and
- are preceded by "to" as in *I want* **to go**.

Other verbs are followed by the *–ing* form of a verb as in *I enjoy* **seeing** *movies*. This *–ing* inflection is often called a *gerund*. A gerund is not a verb, but is derived from a verb. Remainder that form is not equal to function.

In Chapter 2 and earlier in this chapter, we observed that the *–ing* functioning as the present participle of main verbs in progressive verb phrases, something which we will explore more in Chapter 6. In Chapter 4 we observed that the *–ing* forms participial adjectives, such as *the moving van*. In this chapter we are introducing the concept of the *–ing* inflection as a gerund, which we will expand upon in Chapter 12. For now it is enough to know that some verbs are followed by an *–ing* form of a verb.

Certain verbs take infinitives and other verbs take gerunds, and some verbs take both. Sometimes, when a verb can be followed by either an infinitive or the gerund, there may be a difference in meaning.

Consider the following pairs of sentences Discover Activity 10 and see if you can explain the differences in meaning.

**Discovery Activity 10: Infinitive versus Gerund**

1. Compare the sentences in Column A with those in Column B and explain the differences in meaning between the two columns.

| A. Verb + Infinitive | B. Verb + Gerund |
| --- | --- |
| (42a) I attempted to solve the problem. | (42b) I attempted solving the problem. |
| (43a) She remembered to write me. | (43b) She remembered writing me. |
| (44a) He stopped to smoke. | (44b) He stopped smoking last year. |

## Discussion: Discovery Activity 10

(42a) describes a mental effort with a hoped-for conclusion

(42b) describes a process engaged in, but not completed successfully.

(43a) describes a particular action

(43b) describes a mental process or state.

(44a) describes a single event

(44b) describes a habit

You may or may not have had difficulty in choosing whether to use the infinitive versus the gerund. You may have had no difficulty choosing which form and greater difficulty explaining the difference in meaning.

Native speakers and highly proficient non-native speakers know which verb takes which form and for which meaning when there is a choice, but this is something ESL/EFL learners, on the other hand, need to learn. They often find it helpful to have a list of the most common verbs followed by the gerund, since far more verbs are followed by the infinitive than by the gerund.

| Common Verbs followed by Gerunds | | | |
| --- | --- | --- | --- |
| acknowledge | discuss | miss | regret |
| admit | enjoy | omit | remember |
| appreciate | finish | postpone | resist |
| avoid | keep | practice | resume |
| consider | imagine | put | risk |
| contemplate | include | quit | suggest |
| deny | mind | recall | tolerate |
| delay | mention | recommend | understand |

This list is not an exhaustive list, but does show some of the most common verbs that are followed by gerunds. See Appendix E for a more complete list of verbs and other expressions followed by gerunds.

See how easily you recognize gerunds by completing the next Discovery Activity. Check your answers with those in the Answer Key at the end of the chapter.

**Discovery Activity 11: Finding Gerunds**

Look at the following excerpts.

1. Circle all the gerunds you find.

**A.**

> "Can I do anything?" Nicky asked.
> "No." Anna kept breathing, counting, feeling the pulse.
> [Barr, N. (2004). *High country* (p. 40). New York: G.P. Putnam's Sons.]

**B.**

> I was wondering what it was like upstairs, when Mr. Newbury said in a high voice,
> "Well speak up, lad. Are you considering lodging her or did you have other busi-
> ness?"
> [Platt, K. (1966). *Sinbad and me* (p. 90). New York: Tempo Books.]

**C.**

> Somewhere in that second day's night of reflection, Galileo stopped writing so that
> the conversation among the *Dialogue's* three characters hung suspended for sev-
> eral years while their author continued thinking through the intricate proofs to be
> presented...
> [Sobel, D. (2004). *Galileo's daughter* (p. 156). New York: Penguin Books.]

**D.**

> By the time Galileo finished writing his book about the world systems, just as
> December 1629 drew to a close, he had established a new closeness with his daugh-
> ter.
> [Sobel, D. (2004). *Galileo's daughter* (p. 187). New York: Penguin Books.]

*Do ESL/EFL learners have trouble deciding whether to use a gerund or infinitive?*

▶ *Learner difficulties*

ESL/EFL learners do confuse which verbs take gerunds and which take infinitives:

> *I finished **to do** my homework.

At times ESL/EFL learners may combine the "to" and the *–ing:*

> *I finished to doing my homework.

When ESL/EFL learners confuse the gerund and infinitive, it is an error that frequently catches native speakers' attention. However, this type of error rarely interferes with comprehension.

## Verb/Gerund Variations

### *Verb + Preposition + Gerund*

*If a verb takes a gerund, does the gerund always come immediately after the verb?*

Some verbs require a certain preposition after them. After this preposition, a gerund will follow and not an infinitive:

> (45) He thought *about leaving* early.

Gerunds coming after prepositions are considered objects of that preposition.

### *Verb + Object + Preposition + Gerund*

Other verbs may take an object between the verb and preposition + gerund, e.g.:

> (46) The police suspected **the tall young man** *of robbing* the bank.

*or*

> (47) The police suspected **him** *of robbing* the bank.

While these may seem somewhat obscure points to native speakers, they are constructions that more advanced ESL/EFL learners need to become familiar with.

See if you can identify the prepositions followed by gerunds in Discovery Activity 12. The answers are in the Answer Key.

### Discovery Activity 12: Verb + Preposition + Gerund

Look at the following excerpts

1. Circle all the verbs + prepositions + gerunds you find.

**A.**

> [Mrs. Glenn] was firmly resolved on carrying him back to Switzerland for another winter, no matter how much he objected.
> [Wharton, E. Her Son. (1990/1933), In A. Brookner (Ed.), *The stories of edith wharton* (p. 232). New York: Carroll & Graf.]

**B.**

> Where male antifeminists balked at sharing their prerogatives, females feared losing the few they had.
>    [Burrows, E. & Wallace, M. (1999). *Gotham: A history of New York City to 1898* (p. 819). New York: Oxford University Press.]

**C.**

> "Your voice is delightful," my father answered, but I cannot refrain from pointing out that this part of the cycle carries little conviction.
>    [Graves, R. (1982/1955). *Homer's Daughter* (p. 63). Chicago, IL: Academy Press.]

**D.**

> I'm not out to hurt people, but I don't believe in walking on eggshells.
>    [Brown, L. (2006, June/July). *Cosmo girl* (p. 101).]

English has other additional gerund constructions, which we will leave until Chapter 12. We turn now to the last topic in this chapter, phrasal verbs, a special type of verb.

## Section 5: Phrasal Verbs

*In the sentence "I need to pick up my mail," is the verb "pick" + a preposition?*

"Pick up" is an example of a verb that consists of more than one word. There are many verbs in English like this. Prepositions and adverbs combine with a main verb to form a new verb with a different meaning. Verbs that consist of more than one word have different labels, including *multiword verbs, two- and three-word verbs* or *phrasal verbs*. We will refer to them here as phrasal verbs. A phrasal verb can have one, two, or even three prepositions/adverbs. Phrasal verbs are among the most difficult structures to teach and learn.

*How can a preposition or adverb be part of a verb?*

In a phrasal verb, the preposition or adverb no longer has a literal meaning. The preposition or adverb following the verb is a part of the verb itself and gives it an idiomatic meaning. This is a concept that is difficult for native speakers and ESL/EFL learners alike, although for different reasons. Native speakers are generally unaware that there is such a category as phrasal verbs. ESL/EFL learners have difficulty learning and remembering the many verb + preposition/adverb combinations.

In order to clarify what a phrasal verb is, consider the chart below, where merely changing or adding a preposition changes the meaning of the verb *take*.

| verb | example | meaning |
|------|---------|---------|
| take | They *take* the train to work. | use something to get somewhere |
| take **off** | The plane *takes off* at 9. | leaves |
| take **off on** | Her husband *took off on* her. | deserted |
| take **in** | They *took in* the stray dog. | allowed in, adopted |
| take **over** | The army *took over* the building. | took control of, occupied |
| take **after** | She *takes after* her father. | resembles |

Although the verb in each of the sentences is the same, *take*, changing the preposition/adverb changes the meaning of the verb. Because the preposition/adverb is integral to the meaning of each of these verbs and cannot be left out without changing meaning, the preposition/adverb is functioning as part of the verb itself.[2]

## Phrasal Verbs versus Verb + Preposition/Adverb

*How can I tell the difference again between a verb + preposition/adverb and a phrasal verb?*

It is not always easy to distinguish between these, which is one of the reasons that make phrasal verbs so difficult for ESL/EFL learners. Let's start by looking at the following pairs of sentences and comparing their meanings.

| A. verb + preposition/adverb | B. phrasal verb |
|------------------------------|-----------------|
| (48a) I ran up the hill. | (48b) I ran up a bill at the store. |
| (49a) She turned down Main Street. | (49b) She turned down the promotion. |

In Sentence (48a), *up* is an adverb. It is indicating movement from a lower point to a higher point. In Sentence (49a), *down* is an adverb referring to movement along a course or path.

In Sentences (48b) and (49b), on the other hand, the adverb following the verb is part of the verb. Neither *up* nor *down* refers to direction. Both words have combined with the verb to form a new phrasal verb with an idiomatic meaning:

- In Sentence (48b), *ran up* means to charge a large amount of money or to create a lot of debt.
- In Sentence (49b), *turned down* means to refuse.

---

[2] Many grammar books refer to a preposition or adverb that belongs to the verb as a *particle*. The term *particle* specifically refers to prepositions and adverbs that have combined with verbs to make new verbs and have thus lost their prepositional or adverbial function.

Look at the following two charts. Think about what the meanings of the phrasal verbs are. Consider the function of the prepositions/adverbs and think about our discussion above. Why are these phrasal verbs and not verbs + prepositions/adverbs?

| Chart I: Phrasal Verb with 1 Preposition/Adverb | |
|---|---|
| take **out** | Alyce *took out* a new life insurance policy. |
| point **out** | Ben *pointed out* all the sights in the city. |
| take **off** | The plane *takes off* at 9. |
| bring **up** | Josh always *brings up* interesting questions. |
| **Chart II: Phrasal Verb with 2 Prepositions/Adverbs** | |
| keep **up on** | Bianca likes to *keep up on* new fashions. |
| catch **up on** | Rex *caught up on* the news when he got home. |
| cut **down on** | Dieters *cut down on* calories. |
| get **away from** | We need to *get away from* the stress. |

These two charts highlight what makes phrasal verbs special: They are verbs that consist of a verb + at least one preposition/adverb and that have a unique, idiomatic meaning not obvious by looking at the separate parts.

***But what if I'm still unclear if it's a phrasal verb or not?***

## Testing for Phrasal Verbs

It can be difficult to distinguish phrasal verbs from verbs + prepositions/adverbs. There are some ways to "test" for phrasal verbs. These tests are generally more useful for native English speakers, who can rely upon native speaker intuition, than for learners of English.

### Adverb Insertion

One way to test for a phrasal verb is adverb insertion. Only when a preposition/adverb is **not** part of a phrasal verb, can we insert an adverb between the main verb and the following preposition or adverb.

| Verb + Preposition/Adverb | | | | |
|---|---|---|---|---|
| | verb | adverb | prep/adverb | complement |
| (50) We | turned | quickly | **off** | the road. |
| (51) The rain | ran | slowly | **down** | the roof. |

Sentences (50) and (51)) allow for adverb insertion because *off* and *down* are not part of the verb. *Off* and *down* are indicating direction. Compare these sentences with Sentences (52) and (53):

| **Phrasal Verb** | | | | |
| --- | --- | --- | --- | --- |
| | **verb** | **adverb** | **prep/adverb** | **complement** |
| (52) *We | turned | quickly | **off** | the lights. |
| (53) *The car | ran | slowly | **down** | the squirrel. |

Sentences (52) and (53) are grammatically incorrect. Because they are phrasal verbs, we cannot insert an adverb. The combination of *turn + off* and *run + down* creates verbs with idiomatic meanings different from Sentences (50) and (51). *Off* and *down* are integral parts of the verb. They do not indicate direction and have lost their literal meaning.

## Substitution

Another test that works for determining phrasal verbs in many, although not in all cases, is substituting another verb for what looks like a phrasal verb. Usually there is a single verb synonym, often less colloquial, for a phrasal verb. For example, parents *bring up* (phrasal) or *raise* their children, and John can *fix up* (phrasal) or *repair* the old car.

See how well you do in finding the phrasal verbs in Discovery Activity 13. Use any of the tests we have discussed to help you if you are not sure whether or not an underlined phrase is a phrasal verb or not. When you have finished, go to the Answer Key at the end of the chapter and check your work.

### Discover Activity 13: Testing for Phrasal Verbs

Look at the following excerpts and the italicized words.

1. Using any of the tests above, determine if the italicized words are phrasal verbs or not.

**A.**

It was spring vacation, and we *were hanging out* because we didn't know what else to do. The night before, I *stayed up* till midnight, *working on* my scary story about the Blob Monster. I want to be a writer when I *grow up*. I write scary stores all the time.

[Stine, R.L. (1997). *Goosebumps: The blob that ate everything* (p. 7). New York: Scholastic.]

**B.**

[Mom and Dad] love crossword puzzles. I'm not sure why. Both of them are terrible spellers... Lots of times, they *end up* fighting about how to spell a word. Usually, they *give up* and *rip the puzzle to pieces.*

[Stine, R. L. (1997). *Goosebumps: The blob that ate Everything* (p. 28). New York: Scholastic.]

**C.**

I *burst into* the classroom, eager to tell my spy story, but class had already started. Another spelling bee. I *went down* on the first round with a hoot from Howard... I *struggled with* the class through sentence diagrams, the Revolutionary War, and some word problems involving fractions and percentages.

[Nolan, P. (2000). *The spy who came in from the sea* (p. 36). Sarasota, FL: Pineapple Press.]

**D.**

Wiflaf turned to see Mordred *standing on* the castle steps. He was *decked out* like a king—in a purple cape trimmed in gold braid.

[McMullan, K. (2005). *Beware! It's Friday the 13.* (Dragon Slayers' Academy 13) (p. 10). New York: Grosset & Dunlap.]

## Types of Phrasal Verbs

*Is there more than one type of phrasal verb?*

While all phrasal verbs have the same structure (verb + preposition/adverb), there are different patterns the phrasal verbs follow. The phrasal verbs are generally classified into four types:

- intransitive and inseparable
- transitive and inseparable
- transitive and separable
- transitive with inseparable preposition/adverbs.

*Why do we need to know the different types of phrasal verbs?*

The different types of phrasal verbs function differently grammatically, as we will explore shortly. While this is part of the innate knowledge of a native speaker, ESL/EFL learners need to learn the different patterns.

## Intransitive Inseparable

| Intransitive Inseparable Phrasal Verbs | |
|---|---|
| verb + preposition/adverb, no complement | verb + preposition/adverb + complement |
| (54) Anita *works out*. | (54a) Alison *works out* **three times a week**. |
| (55) Marc *passed away*. | (55a) He *passed away* **after a long illness**. |

Specific characteristics:

- Like all intransitive verbs, these phrasal verbs cannot take an object although they can take complements.
- They are *inseparable* because we cannot put anything between the verb and its preposition/adverb. If there is a complement, it follows the phrasal verb.

## Transitive Inseparable

| Transitive Inseparable Phrasal Verbs | |
|---|---|
| verb + preposition/adverb + object noun phrase | verb + preposition/adverb + pronoun |
| (56a) Alison *ran into* **Jack** at the store yesterday. | (56b) She also *ran into* **him** last week. |
| (57a) John and Julie often *drop in on* **Steven and Brittany**. | (57b) John and Julie often *drop in on* **them**. |

Specific characteristics:

- Like any transitive verbs, these phrasal verbs take objects.
- The object must come directly after the entire phrasal verb. We cannot put the object between the verb and preposition/adverb.

## Transitive Separable

This next group is more difficult for ESL/EFL learners **because noun phrase objects** after the phrasal verbs have *variable* sentence position, but **object pronouns do not**. Compare Charts A and B:

Chart A

| Transitive Separable Phrasal Verbs | |
|---|---|
|  | type of noun phrase and sentence position |
| (58) Jeremy *filled* an application *out*. | short noun phrase between the *verb + preposition* |
| (59) Jeremy *filled out* an application. | noun phrase after the *verb + preposition* |
| (60) Jeremy *filled* it *out*. | object pronoun between the *verb + preposition* |

**Chart B**

**Transitive Separable Phrasal Verbs**

|  | type of noun phrase and sentence position |
|---|---|
| (61) Jeremy *filled out* an application to graduate school. | long noun phrase after the *verb + preposition*; generally does not come between the *verb + preposition* |
| (62) Jeremy *filled* it *out*. | object pronoun between *verb + preposition* |

In Chart A, in Sentences (58) and (59), the noun phrase *an application* is a short noun phrase and can come between or after the verb + preposition/adverb. In Chart B, in Sentence (61), the noun phrase, *an application to graduate school*, is long; thus, we prefer to place it after the verb + preposition/adverb.

In Sentences (60) and (62), we have substituted an object pronoun, *it,* for the noun phrase, *an application to graduate school.* Whenever an object pronoun is used, it **must** come between the verb and the preposition/adverb.

Specific characteristics:

- Like all transitive verbs, these phrasal verbs take objects.
- If the object is a noun phrase, it can come either *between* the verb + preposition/adverb or *after* the verb + preposition/adverb.
- If the noun phrase is long, it will generally come after the verb + preposition/adverb.
- If the object is in *object pronoun form*, it **must** come between the verb and preposition/adverb.

## *Transitive Inseparable with 2 Prepositions/Adverbs*

**Transitive Inseparable w/2 Prepositions/Adverbs Phrasal Verbs**

| verb + 2 preposition/adverbs + object | type of object |
|---|---|
| (63) It is important to *stand up for* **your beliefs**. | noun phrase |
| (64) After the contract was signed, one of the partners *backed out of* **it**. | pronoun |

Specific characteristics:

- These phrasal verbs are composed of verb + **two** prepositions/adverbs.
- The object must follow both preposition/adverbs even when the object is a pronoun.[3]

In Discovery Activity 15, you have the opportunity to practice recognizing phrasal verbs. You may find this activity difficult, but keep in mind that accurately recognizing phrasal verbs versus verbs + prepositions/adverbs is not easy and takes practice. The answers are in the Answer Key at the end of the chapter.

---

[3] Some grammar books classify this type of phrasal verb as phrasal-prepositional verbs.

**Discovery Activity 14: Phrasal Verbs**

1. Look at the following excerpts.
2. Underline the phrasal verbs. If the phrasal verb is transitive, circle the object.
3. Decide if the transitive phrasal verbs are separable or inseparable.

**A.**

When Shannon Dunn needs a break from snowboarding, she doesn't exactly turn into a couch potato. Far from it... she packs up her surfboard and hits the beach... On quieter days, she settles for golf or tennis...

[Layden, J. (2001). *To the extreme* (p. 30). New York: Scholastic.]

**B.**

"Why did you leave it home?"
"Because I didn't plan on using it here, that's why... "
"But, Brenda, that doesn't make any sense. Suppose you did come home, and then you came back again... "

[Roth, P. (1969/1959). *Goodbye, Columbus* (p. 93). New York: Bantam.]

**C.**

All [Frank] expects Mary to do is what he's doing—going on as if nothing had happened, holding no grudges, not bringing up the hateful things that were said in anger... He cannot be expected to read her mind! This isn't the first time he's run into this problem with Mary, but he has never... [known] what the cues are that it's coming... ; he's willing to go as far as he has to to make that unambiguously clear to her, so she'll cut it out.

[Elgin, S. (1993). *Genderspeak: Men, women, and the gentle art of verbal self-defense* (p. 238). New York: John Wiley.]

*What makes phrasal verbs difficult for ESL/EFL learners?*

▶ *Learner difficulties*

Phrasal verbs are difficult for ESL/EFL learners for several reasons. First, the meaning of a phrasal verb is generally idiomatic. The meaning is not clear from the verb or the preposition/adverb. This means that learners must learn each phrasal verb individually, and like any verb in English, phrasal verbs can have multiple idiomatic meanings.

Second, different preposition/adverbs combine with a verb to form verbs with different meanings. It is not always clear to learners which preposition/adverb to use for a specific meaning.

Another difficulty is producing correct structures with phrasal verbs that are transitive and separable when the object is a pronoun. ESL/EFL learners must remember that the object must come between the verb and preposition/adverb. This pattern is not easy for learners to remember.

Given the large number of phrasal verbs, the idiomatic meanings, and the different structural patterns the phrasal verbs follow, the single best way for anyone to confirm whether or not a verb is a phrasal verb or not is to use a dictionary geared to learners of English. Dictionaries such as the *Cambridge International Dictionary of Phrasal Verbs* or the *Longman Dictionary of American English* are extremely useful, and are available in print and online versions.

## Summary

**There are main verbs and auxiliary verbs**

| Main verbs | Auxiliary verbs |
|---|---|
| • have lexical meaning; add content to a sentence | • have no lexical meaning; only grammatical function |
| • infinite number | • "help" main verbs |
| • may be followed by only a gerund (-*ing*) or an infinitive (to + verb), or by either | • are only 3 in number: *have, be, do.* |
| | • are followed by some form of main verb |

*Auxiliary Rule for Negative Statements and Questions*

- *For* **negative** *statements*

  ○ *if there is an auxiliary verb, place* not *after the auxiliary verb*
  ○ if there is no auxiliary verb, insert the *do* auxiliary and add *not.*

- *For* **questions**

  ○ *if there is an auxiliary verb, invert the subject and the auxiliary verb*
  if there is no auxiliary verb, insert the *do* auxiliary before the subject and keep the main verb in its simple or base form.

**Principal Parts of Regular Verbs**

| Present | Past | Past Participle | Present Participle |
|---|---|---|---|
| walk, walks | walk**ed** | walk**ed** | walk**ing** |

## The Different Types of Main Verbs

### Transitive verbs

- require at least one object

  - Maria hit *the ball*.

### Intransitive verbs

- take no objects, only complements if anything

  - Maria lives in Cincinnati.

### Certain main verbs are followed by

- "to" infinitive only

  - Maria wants *to go*.

- gerund only

  - Maria enjoys *dancing*.

- either gerund or "to" infinitive

  - Maria likes *to dance*.
  - Maria likes *dancing*.

### Phrasal verbs

- Consist of a main verb + preposition/adverb

  - The baby *kicked up* a fuss.
  - Maria *turned down* the volume.

- The preposition/adverb is integral to the meaning of the verb; removing or changing the preposition/adverb changes the meaning of the verb.

- Prepositions/adverbs that are part of phrasal verbs are often called *particles*. This helps us distinguish between prepositions & adverbs when used as such versus when these words become part of verb phrasal verbs and lose their original function and meaning.

---

### Examples of Common Phrasal Verbs

| | |
|---|---|
| **about** | come about, see about, throw about |
| **at** | come at, get at, go at |
| **away** | drive away, get away, peel away |
| **back** | keep back, give back, take back, |
| **down** | break down, knock down, wind down |
| **for** | fall for, head for, make for |
| **in** | drop in, check in, fill in, phase in |
| **into** | crowd into, make into, talk into |
| **of** | know of, hear of, strip of |

**Examples of Common Phrasal Verbs**

| | |
|---|---|
| **off** | hold off, put off, write off |
| **on** | egg on, keep on, log on, pick on |
| **out** | cut out, drop out, find out, rule out |
| **over** | blow over, get over, take over |
| **through** | pull through, sit through, talk through |
| **to** | gear to, resort to, stoop to |
| **up** | draw up, give up, talk up, stock up |
| **with** | bear with, finish with, go with |

## Practice Activities

### Activity 1: be, have, do

1. Underline all the instances of *be, have* and *do* you find.
2. Decide whether *be, have* and *do* are being used as main verbs or auxiliary verbs.

- If the verb is being used as an auxiliary, explain its function in the sentence.

*Example:*

"*Did* you see the license plate this time?" Stephen asked. He *was* anxious; the thieves who stole the car *were* probably responsible for the earlier attack on Mrs. Cahan.

- *did*: auxiliary verb necessary to form a past tense question
- main verb: *see*. The main verb does not carry tense in a question because the tense is carried by the auxiliary.
- In the second sentence, two examples of main verb *be*:

  - *was*: referring to a past tense third person singular subject "he."
  - *were*: referring to past tense third person plural subject, "thieves."

**A.**

"Obviously, water doesn't flow backward... "Why don't you tell the truth? The stuff is coming from that damn storage dump... I was saying it back in seventy and I'll say it now: Allowing that PCB dump was a big mistake.
[Spencer-Fleming, J. (2003). *A fountain filled with blood* (p. 6). New York: Thomas Dunne Books.]

**B.**

"Paul," Clare said, "it's time. The pilot's going to warm up the engines now.".. Paul stepped forward. "Did I ask you about taking care of the dogs?"
[Spencer-Fleming, J. (2003). *A fountain filled with blood* (p. 15). New York: Thomas Dunne Books.]

## C.

The bride and bridegroom do not have any etiquette problems that Miss Manners knows of, other than the ones you may cause... Miss Manners congratulates you, both on your daughter and on your realization that parenthood does funny things to objectivity. It also does things to one's schedule. It is up to the parents to make the necessary compromises without passing the burden on to others. Babies do not belong at wedding receptions... Champagne is not good for them, and it does them no good to catch the bouquet.

[Martin, J. (1989). *Miss manners guide for the turn-of-the millennium* (pp. 228–229). New York: Pharos Books.]

## *Activity 2:* **be**

The verb *be* is the most common English verb.

1. Choose a paragraph of at least 10 lines in a newspaper, magazine or book.
2. Circle all the instance of the verb *be*.
3. Count how many instances of the verb *be* you find.
4. Identify which ones are auxiliary uses of *be* and which ones are main uses.
5. Discuss how you could use an activity such as this for learners of English.

## *Activity 3: Transitive and Intransitive Verbs*

1. Read the following excerpts.
2. Label the transitive verbs with a **T**.
3. Label the intransitive verbs with an **I**.
4. For transitive verbs, underline the object phrase following the verb.

*Example:*

$$T$$

In 1568, Waldkirch commissioned... *Tobias Stimmer*... [He]

$$T$$

surrounded *the building's asymmetrical windows* with friezes... Mythological and

$$I$$

allegorical themes were characteristic of... the sixteenth century. [Hein, L. (2004). Switzerland's painted ladies. *German Life,* April/May, 21.]

### A.

These athletes [Tony Hawk and Mat Hoffman] have fan clubs and Web sites. They compete for prize money... They even land lucrative endorsement contracts. Surprised? Pick up a magazine and flip to the back cover... The men and women featured in this book are some of the top performers... They are properly prepared.

[Layden, J. (2001). *To the extreme* (pp. 4–7). New York: Scholastic.]

### B

If every picture tells a story, then Switzerland's painted façades hold a treasure trove of tales. More than just pretty painted ladies, the buildings are links to the country's folklore and history... Both towns brim with Renaissance and medieval houses... Many of the houses' paintings celebrated knightly virtues and victories. Figures with lion and snake symbols represent strength and intelligence... Maidens, horses, armored soldiers, and mythic beasts dance across the façade...

[Hein, L. (2004). Switzerland's painted ladies. *German Life,* April/May, p. 21.]

## *Activity 4: Gerunds and Infinitives*

1. Look at the following excerpts.
2. Circle the gerunds and infinitives.
3. Underline the verb that is followed by a gerund or an infinitive.

**A**

As the United States tried to stay neutral during Washington's second term, relations with France grew worse... The XYZ affair forced President Adams to seriously consider asking Congress to declare war on France...

[Ritchie R., & Broussard A. (1999). *American history: The early years to 1877* (p. 345). New York: Glencoe.]

**B.**

Historic Speedwell in Morristown is the scene of one of the most important American achievements. It was here that Samuel Morse and Alfred Vail spent years perfecting the electromagnetic telegraph...

[Hudson, B. (1998). *New Jersey day trips: A guide to outings in New Jersey, New York, Pennsylvania & Delaware* (8th ed., p. 47). Green Village, NJ: Woodmont Press,.]

**C.**

Dear Miss Manners:

A few months ago, I got a job at a wonderful company. I admire the pleasant group of people with whom I work, people who would never consider hurting others under normal circumstances. However, I have just discovered that every year, the members of my company go on a retreat where they are required to discuss what they really think about one another... How can I handle this horrible situation and avoid hurting others or getting my feelings hurt?

[Martin, J. (1989). *Miss manners guide for the turn-of-the millennium* (pp. 128–129). New York: Pharos Books.]

## *Activity 5: Phrasal Verbs*

1. Look at the following excerpts.
2. Underline the phrasal verbs.
3. Discuss how you identified them.

**A.**

Infections caused by viruses, fungi and other assorted critters never respond to antibiotics. As special drugs are developed for them, new foes such as bird flu crop up.

[Simon, H. (2006, December 11). Old bugs learn some new tricks. *Newsweek,* p. 74.]

**B.**

Many aspects of the new, improved China will be up for the world's inspection during the Olympic Games.

> [Fallows, J. (2006, December). Postcards from tomorrow square. *The Atlantic Monthly*, p. 106.]

**C.**

I had one little glimpse of another thing. . . It was just what I needed, in order to carry out my project of escape. . . you get my idea; you see what a stunning dramatic surprise I would wind up with at the palace. It was all feasible, if I could only get hold of a slender piece of iron which I could shape into a lock-pick.

> [Twain, M. (1972, edition). A Connecticut Yankee in King Arthur's Court. In *The Family Mark Twain* (vol. 2), (p. 841). New York: Harper & Row.]

**D.**

"Well, we should be getting back, I guess?" Nancy said. . . There's just something about MLA, I think. Everybody goes into a kind of bizarre state. It brings out the worst in people."

"Could it bring out murder?". . .

"Well, you know, there *is* a person I would just love to see done away with," she told him crisply. . . It's a certain 'Sharon'. . . And the reason I'm almost sure to do her in—Nancy was looking straight at Boaz—has to do with the conniving she did to get her son hired at Boston. . . I was with Ruth last year when she ran into this Sharon jerk."

> [Jones, D. H. H. (1993). *Murder at the MLA* (pp. 132–133). Athens, GA: University of Georgia Press.]

## Activity 6: Error Analysis A: Do and Gerunds/Infinitives

The following excerpts were written by ESL learners. There are different types of errors because these are samples taken from actual students. However, **only pay attention to** the errors relating to:

- the *do* auxiliary and
- verbs requiring gerunds or infinitives

1. Underline each auxiliary and verb + gerund/infinitive error you find. **Ignore any other errors.**
2. For each error:

   a. correct the error
   b. discuss why the writer may have made the error. Remember to ignore any other errors.

**A.**

While we chat with others, we usually use our own nicknames. They are not real names and we no like to becoming known; that's why many anonymous crimes happen. For example, a man could to chat with a girl while he thinks bad thing and he might to suggest to meet her outside.

**B.**

"Snow White" or "Cinderella" is one of the most popular fiction stories for children. Why most people know these stories? The answer is these stories warn children what things are dangerous or should be to avoided. In "Snow White" the princess ate an apple that she got from stranger. This story means that you should avoid to talk or get something, especially food, from stranger.

**C.**

I believe that people study at college or university to expanding their knowledge, to obtaining a better job, and to networking with people of same area of interest. In college or university you don't not pick your classmate, but you pick class. You will be able to finding people who are also interested in the same area like you have; therefore, you will be able to expanding your network.

**D.**

The king is not a fair person. He don't want the princess marry with the young man, so he fails following the law. The princess didn't want to saw her lover's death by the tiger. She already had lost him so she pointed out to him the wrong door because she doesn't wanted his happiness with the lady.


## Answer Key: Chapter 5 Discovery Activities

### *Discussion: Discovery Activity 1*

*Excerpt A*

- *is (be, irregular)*
- *sucks* (present tense *–s* third person singular inflection),
- *use, suck* (present tense)

*Excerpt B*

- regular past tense verbs: *grabbed, looked, jerked, wriggled, sniffed, wagged*
- irregular past tense verbs *fell (fall), stood (stand.)* (See Appendix B).


### *Discussion: Discovery Activity 4*

*Excerpt A*
*did:*

- main verb in past tense
- describes the action of coaching. *Don't* is the present auxiliary *do* with the negative *not*. The *do + not* accompany the main verb *commit* to make the sentence negative.

*Excerpt B*

- first three uses of *do* are as an auxiliary verb to form questions, one in past tense and two in present tense: *Did you run...* , *Do you like...* , *Do you fish?*
- three instances of *do* as an auxiliary with *not*: *didn't like* (past), and *don't dive, don't think* (present).
- three instance of *do* as a main verb: *did some diving, did a few of those dives, do anything.*
- In one sentence we see both functions of *do*: *do* as an auxiliary verb to form a negative statement and do as the main verb denoting an action: *I don't think I do anything anymore.*

## Discussion: Discovery Activity 5

- Transitive verbs: *wash, polish, blow, see, follow, put, tell, need*
- Intransitive verbs: *started up, smiled, sat*

## Discussion: Discovery Activity 6

### Part I

- Direct objects: *an award, a chocolate cake, the football, a different books, an extension, the food*
- Indirect objects: *the outstanding student, her daughter, his teammate, her young students, the applicant, the toddler.*

### Part II

a. The college gave it to him/her.
b. The mother baked it for her.
c. The player passed it to him.
d. The teacher is going to read it to them.
e. The committee granted it to him/her.
f. The mother cut it for him/her.

## Discussion: Discovery Activity 7

*Excerpt A*

- direct objects: *old friend Captain Gill, tickets, a real live whale, a blue whale.*

- one indirect object, *me*.

  o We could change the sentence to... *to send tickets **to me.***

*Excerpt B*

- the direct objects: *the meals, the guests, them, his mind.*
- no indirect objects

*Excerpt C*

- direct objects: *her, something, it.*
- one indirect object, *him.*

  o We could change the sentence to... *if she was bringing something **for him.***

*Excerpt D*

- direct objects: *her keys, it, the door, her.*
- one indirect object, *him.*

  o We could change the sentence to... *Edythe gave her keys **to him**.*

## Discussion: Discovery Activity 8

*Excerpt A*

- intransitive verbs: *is, listen*

*Excerpt B*

- intransitive verbs: *was, showered, shaved, stepped, presume*

  o *was* is a main verb, not an auxiliary.
  o *stepped* is followed by an adverb complement, *forward.*
  o *shave* is both intransitive and transitive verb. In Excerpt B it is used intransitively. *Shave* can also be used transitively, as in *The barber shaved Qwilleran.*

*Excerpt C*

- intransitive verbs: *unfolds, sprawl, soars.* All of them are followed by complements.

## Discussion: Discovery Activity 9

The verbs in Column A express a general fact or truth, while the verbs in Column B describe something specific about this general fact or truth. The direct object after the verb limits or restricts the verb to describe a particular type of action.

- *Alan teaches* refers to his profession, while *Alan teaches math* specifies what he teaches.
- *Sandra drives* is a statement of an action she is capable of performing, while *Sandra drives a BMW* tells us what kind of car she drives.
- *Carson smokes* tells us about his habit in general, while *Carson smokes cigars* specifies which tobacco product he smokes.
- *Alexa reads* tells us about her ability, while *Alexa reads novels* describes what type of book she reads.

## Discussion: Discovery Activity 11

*Excerpt A*

- *kept*, the irregular past form of *keep*, is followed by three gerunds: *breathing, counting,* and *feeling*.

*Excerpt B*

- *are considering* is a present progressive verb phrase; *considering* is a present participle. The gerund *lodging* follows this verb phrase.

  ○ Learners may find examples such as this one confusing. Both the present participle and the gerund have an *-ing* inflection, but the grammatical function of this inflection is different. Learners need to be able to distinguish the present participle part of the verb phrase from the gerund.

*Excerpt C*

- *stopped writing, continued thinking*

*Excerpt D*

- *finished writing*

## Discussion: Discovery Activity 12

In Excerpts A, B, C, and D we see one example each of a verb + preposition + gerund:

- A. *resolved on carrying*
- B. *balked at sharing* in
- C. *refrain from pointing out*
- D. *believe in walking*

Note that in Excerpt B *feared losing* is an example of a verb + gerund.

## *Discussion: Discovery Activity 13*

*Excerpt A*

- *hang out, stay up, work on, grow up.*

*Excerpt B*

- *end up, give up.*

*Excerpt C*

- *deck out.*

## *Discussion: Discovery Activity 14*

*Excerpt A* phrasal verbs, all transitive

- *turn into + a couch potato*
- *packs up + her surfboard*

  ○ this is also the only one that is separable: *She packs* it *up.*

- *settles for + golf or tennis.*

*Excerpt B* phrasal verbs, both intransitive

- *plan on +* gerund *using*
- *came back,* the irregular past tense of *come back*

*Excerpt C*

- *(he's) going on,* intransitive
- *(he's) bringing up + the hateful things,* transitive and separable

  ○ *He's bringing them up.*

- *run into + this problem,* transitive, inseparable

  ○ *He's running into it.*

- *cut (it) out,* transitive verb, separable

*Excerpt D*

- *went down*

# Chapter 6
# Time, Tense, and Aspect of Verbs

## Introduction

In the previous chapter, we began our observation of verbs as a class. In this chapter we will be examining how English verbs function to express the time of an event (tense) and information regarding the duration or completion of an event (aspect). The chapter is divided into four sections. Section I reviews verb inflections one more time and introduces the concept of time, tense, and aspect. Sections 2 through 5 delve into the different English verb tenses: Section 2 looks at the present; Section 3 the past; Section 4 the future; and Section 5 the perfect.

You may recall our discussion in Chapter 1 of how early English grammarians attempted to impose Latin and Greek grammatical concepts and terminology onto English, and how these are often inadequate for describing the structure of English. This is particularly true in the case of verbs because English is a language that does not inflect to show tense to the degree that Latin, Greek and most other European languages do. Traditional descriptions of English verb tenses are often unsatisfactory, complicated, and confusing. This chapter attempts to present clearly the essentials of English verbs and time reference in view of what ESL/EFL learners need to know when learning English.

## Section 1: Verbs and Inflections

We have examined verb inflections at various times in the text. Each time we have emphasized that in English form is not equal to function. We have also observed repeatedly that although English has only eight inflections, these inflections cause many of the difficulties ESL/EFL learners encounter. The following chart summarizes again the inflections for English verbs.

A. DeCapua, *Grammar for Teachers,*
© Springer 2008

| English Verb Inflections | | | |
|---|---|---|---|
| he, she, it | | walks | **present third person singular** |
| I, you, we, they, he, she, it | | walked | **past –ed** |
| I, you, we, they | have | walked | **past participle** |
| he, she, it | has | | |
| I, | am | walking | **present participle** |
| you, we, they | are | | |
| he, she, it | is | | |

### Are you saying that these inflections show all the verb tenses?

As you look at this chart, you may be thinking to yourself that there is something missing. Surely these few inflections in the list cannot be all the possible time references in English! This is certainly true, which leads us to a key point of this chapter: Verbs show little inflection in English, but there are many ways to show time references. Most commonly, verbs combine with the auxiliaries *have* and *be* to show what is known as *aspect*.

## Time, Tense, and Aspect

### What does aspect mean? Why can't we just say tense?

### Aspect

In English, the grammatical labels *past* and *present* do not necessarily correspond to time in the real world, but rather to grammatical features of the verbs. Events often do not fit neatly into categories of past, present, and future time. English uses a variety of structures to express different time references.

One important structure that functions together with tense is *aspect*. Aspect is a grammatical category that indicates temporal features such as duration, frequency, and completion. Aspect is indicated by complex tenses that are composed of an auxiliary verb + a main verb.

There are two different aspects in English: the progressive and the perfect. In the previous chapter in our discussion of the auxiliary verbs *have* and *be*, we saw how these two auxiliaries help main verbs. When *be* combines with main verbs, the verb phrase shows the *progressive* aspect.[1]

We use the label *progressive* because the verb phrase describes the ongoing nature of an event or action. A progressive verb phrase consists of the auxiliary *be* in either present or past tense + the present participle of the main verb.

| Progressive Aspect | | | |
|---|---|---|---|
| subject | auxiliary *be* | present participle (verb+ *-ing*) | time reference |
| John | is | walking. | present |
| John | was | walking. | past |

---

[1] Some grammar texts use the term *continuous* rather than progressive.

When *have* combines with a main verb, the verb phrase shows the *perfect* aspect. The perfect aspect describes the relationship between an earlier event or action with a later event or action. A perfect verb phrases consists of the auxiliary *have* in either present or past tense + the past participle of the main verb.

| Perfect Aspect | | | |
|---|---|---|---|
| subject | auxiliary *have* | past participle (verb + -*ed*) | time reference |
| John | has | walked. | present |
| John | had | walked. | past |
| John | had | written | past, irregular[2] |

Because the regular past tense –*ed* and the past participle –*ed* inflections look identical, some grammar books refer to the past participle inflection as the –*en* inflection to differentiate it from the past inflection. This reference is derived from the fact that a number of common irregular words take an –*en* inflection on the past participle, e.g. *eaten, driven,* and *written*.

Try the next three Discovery Activities and see how much you already know about time, tense, and aspect. Be sure to check your answers after you complete each Discovery Activity in the Answer Key at the end of the chapter before you move on to the next Discovery Activity. This will help you if you are having problems with any of the activities.

## Discovery Activity 1: Time 1

1. Look at the following pairs of sentences.
2. All the sentences refer to the present, but have different time references. Try to explain the differences.

**A.**
The children walk to school.
The dog barks.
She is sick.

**B.**
The children are walking to school.
The dog is barking.
*She is being sick.

## Discovery Activity 2: Time 2

1. Look at the following pairs of sentences.
2. All the sentences refer to the past, but have different time references. Try to explain the differences.

**C.**
The children walked to school.
The dog barked.
She was sick.

**D.**
The children were walking to school.
The dog was barking.
*She was being sick.

---

[2] There are numerous irregular past participles. See Appendix B.

**Discovery Activity 3: Time 3**

1. Look at the following pairs of sentences.
2. All the sentences refer to the past again, but have different time references. Try to explain the differences.

**E.**
The children walked to school.
The dog barked.
She was sick.

**F.**
The children have walked to school.
The dog has barked.
She had been sick.

Now that you have a general idea of time, tense, and aspect, we will explore the different verb tenses of English and the different ways English refers to time and aspect.

## Section 2: Present

### *Simple Present*

The first thought many people have when seeing the phrase *simple present tense* is that this refers to something taking place now. Yet, as illustrated by the sentences in Discovery Activity 1: Time 1, present time generally does not refer to events taking place now. Instead, the label "present time" refers to general habits, customs, characteristics, or truths. If speakers wish to refer to an action occurring at the moment of speaking, they use the *present progressive*. An important exception to this is the *narrative* present, e.g. when a speaker describes in narrative form a series of events such as in a play-by-play account of a baseball game.

The simple present tense consists of the main verb in its simple form, except in third person singular when the *–s* inflection is added to the main verb. You will recall from Chapter 5 that for questions and negatives in the simple present and past we need to add the *do* auxiliary. As we observed in that chapter, the *do* auxiliary is a filler verb. It must be there to fulfill a grammatical requirement of English, but has no semantic meaning. The sentence types in present tense are summarized in the chart below.

| Sentence Types: Simple Present Tense | | | | | |
|---|---|---|---|---|---|
| auxiliary | subject | auxiliary + | not | verb | sentence type |
| | Sue | | | walks. | **affirmative** |
| | We | | | walk. | |
| | Sue | **does** not | | walk. | **negative** |
| | We | **do** not | | walk. | |
| **Does** | Sue | | | walk? | **question** |
| **Do** | we | | | | |

## *Uses of Simple Present*

### *What can I tell my students about when to use the simple present tense?*

The simple present is frequently explained as describing *timeless* time, i.e. time reference that has no terminal points, time that can include the past, present, and future. Often frequency adverbs, such as we saw in Chapter 4, are used in conjunction with the simple present to express the frequency of an event or action:

(1) Maggie and Katie *always* drink coffee at breakfast.
(2) I *never* take the bus home.
(3) George *usually* calls before he comes.

For general guidelines, the simple present is used to:

| | |
|---|---|
| • describe repeated actions, customs, or habits | (4) Ned *leaves* for school at 8:00. |
| | (5) Blair and Jamie *work* at a bank |
| • describe general truths or facts | (6) The sun *rises* in the east. |
| | (7) The president and his family *live* in the White House. |
| • describe certain characteristics, mental states, emotions, and senses. | (8) Gina *is* thin. |
| | (9) The sky *looks* gray. |
| | (10) Good teachers *understand* their students' needs. |
| | (11) Max *loves* pizza. |
| | (12) Helen *seems* happy. |
| | (13) A baby's skin *feels* smooth. |
| ○ *feel, smell, taste* used intransitively, with the idea of using one of the "five senses" | (14) The soup *smells* delicious. |
| | (15) The noodles *taste* salty. |
| | (16) The audience *hears* the orchestra tuning up. |
| ○ *hear, see* used transitively with the idea of using one of the "five senses"[3] | (17) The worshippers believe God *sees* everything. |
| • narrate stories and events | (18) "And the batter hits the ball into the outfield for another home run for the Yankees." |
| | (19) "She gets up, turns on the oven, leaves the room, and the next thing you know, there's smoke coming out of the kitchen." |
| • summarize stories, articles | (20) The president addresses the soldiers and asks for their continued support in the fight against terrorism. |
| | (21) The reviewer argues that the conclusions presented by the researchers are erroneous. |

---

[3] These are the linking verbs, introduced in Chapter 5. *Feel, smell, taste, hear,* and *see* are also called verbs of perception, or sensory verbs.

▶ *Learner difficulties*

> A common problem among ESL/EFL students is using simple present tense
> when referring to something happening now when native speakers would pre-
> fer the present progressive.
> More significantly for ESL/EFL learners are problems using the *do* auxiliary
> correctly, an issue that we explored in the previous chapter. To recap briefly,
> learners frequently forget to insert *do* in questions and negatives, and/or to
> inflect *do* and the main verb correctly.

*If the present tense doesn't refer to something happening now, which tense does
refer to current events or happenings?*

## Present Progressive

As we noted earlier, the progressive aspect shows the ongoing nature of an event.
Progressive verbs are composite verbs. We call them composite verbs because they
have more than one part. All progressive verbs require *be* + present participle. This
means that we need the *be* auxiliary in the appropriate tense plus the present participle of the main verb. The present participle is the main verb with the *–ing* inflection
attached to it. The auxiliary tells us the time and the present participle indicates the
aspect, or the duration of an event or action.

The *present progressive* describes events occurring now, at the moment of speaking. Because it describes present time, the auxiliary verb *be* must be in present form:
*am, is,* or *are.*

As you learned in Chapter 5, when an auxiliary verb is already part of the verb
phrase, there is no need to add *do* for questions or negatives. Instead, all you need
to do is invert the subject and the verb for questions. For negatives, simply place *not*
after the auxiliary. The sentence types are summarized below.

| | | Sentence Types: Present Progressive | | | |
|---|---|---|---|---|---|
| **auxiliary** | **subject** | **auxiliary** | **+ not** | **present participle** | **sentence type** |
| | Jenny | is | | leaving. | **affirmative** |
| | Jenny | is | **not** | leaving. | **negative** |
| **Is** | Jenny | | | leaving? | **question** |

*Don't we sometimes use the present progressive to refer to events that take place
over a relatively long period of time?*

The concept of *now* is subjective in the mind of the speaker. Generally, when teaching the present progressive to beginning learners of English, teachers emphasize the
aspect *now* or *at this moment.* However, as learners become more proficient, it is
necessary for them to be exposed to more subjective uses of now reflecting longer

periods of time, yet still temporary and contrasting with the timeless sense of the simple present. For example, consider these sentences:

(22) He is studying at Cornell University.
(23) They are living in Europe.

*He is studying at Cornell University* can refer to a time period of four years and *They are living in Europe* can refer to a decade. So while these are current events in the mind of the speaker, they are not "current" or "now" in the sense often conveyed by ESL/EFL grammar texts.

In summary, the present progressive is used to describe temporary events and actions that have a beginning and an end. Although this time period may be relatively long, the key point is that it is temporary and limited. By using the progressive aspect, speakers emphasize the duration of an event or action, whether this duration is momentary, short or relatively long.

### What is difficult about the present progressive for ESL/EFL learners?

#### ► Learner difficulties

A key difficulty with composite verbs such as the present progressive is remembering both parts of the verb phrase: *be* and the present participle. ESL/EFL learners often forget the *be* auxiliary in attempting to form the present progressive and will produce incomplete verb phrases such as:

  * We **going** home.
  * I **e-mailing** you about my problem.

If you are not confident that you can clearly identify the present progressive, you will find it helpful to complete Discovery Activity 4. Note that many of the examples use the contracted forms of *be,* which we saw in a previous chapter. The answers to Discovery Activity 4 are in the Answer Key at the end of the chapter.

#### Discovery Activity 4: Present Progressive

Look at the excerpts.

1. Une verbs derline all thin present progressive. Be sure to underline all parts of the verb phrase.

**A.**

What are they doing?' '. . . They're putting down their names,' the Gryphon whispered in reply, 'for fear they should forget them before the end of the trial.'
[Carroll, L. (1865/1996). *Alice's adventures in wonderland.* Available online at http://www.literature.org/authors/carroll-lewis/alices-adventures-in-wonderland/]

**B.**

Dean asked Leach, "Chief, how come everybody's hanging around in the
barracks?"...
Leach grinned broadly at him. "Well, Dean, nobody's doing any work because this
is Saturday. We're all on liberty."
   [Sherman, D., & Cragg, D. (1997). *Starfist: First to fight. Book I* (pp. 117–118).
New York: DelRey.]

**C.**

"I'm taking a few days off, to see an old friend who's dying of cancer," said Joe
Burner. "I have at this date twenty-seven friends who are dying of cancer."
   [Cheever, J. (1959). *The wapshot scandal* (p. 188). New York: Harper & Row.]

The next Discovery Activity provides you with the opportunity to see how the simple present tense is used for something occurring now. The purpose of this activity is to help you in clarifying your thinking so that you can better explain to your ESL/EFL learners situations when we use the simple present and not the present progressive for something taking place now. Compare your responses to those in the Answer Key at the end of the chapter.

**Discovery Activity 5: Simple Present, not Present Progressive**

**Part A**

Look at Excerpt A.

1. Underline the verbs in present tense.
2. In Excerpt A, *now* occurs with the simple present tense.

   • Explain why the simple present tense is used together with *now*, even
     though *now* is generally associated with the present progressive.

**A.**

You *now* face a new world, a world of change. The thrust into outer space of the
satellite spheres and missiles marks a beginning of another epoch in the long story
of mankind... We deal *now*, not with things of this world alone, but with the...
unfathomed mysteries of the universe.
   [MacArthur, D. (1962, May 12). General Douglas MacArthur reminds west point
cadets of duty, honor, Country. In W. Safire (Ed.), *Lend me your ears: Great speeches
in history* (rev. ed., p. 72). New York: Norton.]

**Part B**

1. Look at Excerpt B.
2. In Excerpt B, simple present tense is used for actions happening at the
   moment.
3. Explain why the simple present tense is used in this excerpt instead of
   present progressive.

**B.**

I run into Jane on the street. We speak of a woman we both know whose voice is routinely suicidal. Jane tells me the woman called her the other day at seven ayem.

[Gornick, V. (1996). Approaching eye level. In P. Lopate (Ed.), *Writing New York: A Literary Anthology* (p. 137). New York: The Library of America.]

### Can we use all verbs in the present progressive?

Some verbs are not usually used in the present progressive. These are usually non-action verbs, called *stative* verbs (think "state" as in "state of mind") because they describe:

- mental states
- attitudes
- perceptions
- emotions
- existence

These verbs are used in the present tense, even when describing something taking place now. The following chart lists some of the more common stative verbs.

| Common Stative Verbs | | | | | |
|---|---|---|---|---|---|
| believe | hear | know | please | see | think |
| feel | (dis)like | love | prefer | smell | understand |
| hate | guess | mean | recognize | suppose | want |
| have | imagine | need | remember | taste | wish |

### Are these verbs difficult for ESL/EFL learners?

▶ *Learner difficulties*

For one, ESL/EFL learners sometimes forget which verbs are generally not used in the progressive form and may therefore use these verbs incorrectly:

* I'm preferring to go home now.
* She's not believing me.

An additional area of confusion for ESL/EFL learners lies in the different meanings certain stative verbs have when they are used in the simple present versus when they are used in the present progressive. Some stative verbs have different, often idiomatic meanings, when they are used in the present progressive.

Consider for instance, the common greeting card line, *I'm thinking of you* versus the general statement, *I think he's right*. In the first instance, the use of the present progressive form emphasizes that you are keeping that person in your thoughts at this time; in the second instance, you are stating a belief.

The next Discovery Activity focuses on distinguishing the meaning of some of the stative verbs when used in the present tense and when used in the present progressive. The answers are in the Answer Key.

**Discovery Activity 6: Simple Present, Present Progressive and Change in Meaning**

1. Look at the following pairs of sentences and explain the differences in meaning.

| Column A | Column B |
|---|---|
| a. A rose smells sweet. | a. The children are smelling the rose. |
| b. The noodles taste salty. | b. The chef is tasting the noodles. |
| c. I see without glasses. | c. They are seeing their father this weekend. |
| d. What do you think of Brad Pitt? | d. I'm thinking of going to Moscow. |
| e. Joe is a bad boy. | e. Joe's being a bad boy. |
| f. Connor has a girlfriend. | f. Scott is having a sandwich. |

## Section 3: Past

### Simple Past

The simple past is used to describe completed past actions or events. As you know, there is only one past inflection for all regular past tense verbs, the –ed added to the verb. There are many irregular past tense forms, including some of the most common verbs used in English, such as *went, had, was* and *were, wrote, ate, drank,* etc. There are also spelling changes for some verbs, such as *carry* and *carried* or *rob* and *robbed*. There is a complete list of these in Appendix B.

To form questions and negatives, simple past tense verbs, like present tense ones, require the *do* auxiliary, as we saw in Chapter 5. Since we are using *do* with simple past, *do* changes to *did*. Remember also that the main verb remains in its simple or base form, with no –ed attached.

The different sentence types in simple past are summarized below.

| Sentence Types: Simple Past Tense | | | | |
|---|---|---|---|---|
| auxiliary | subject | auxiliary + not | verb | sentence type |
| | Sue | | walked. | affirmative |
| | Sue | did not | walk. | negative |
| Did | Sue | | walk? | question |

*Do ESL/EFL learners have problems in simple past with the do auxiliary?*

► *Learner difficulties*

ESL/EFL learners have the same problems using the *do* auxiliary in the simple past that they do in using it with the simple present. These problems include:

- forgetting to insert *did* for questions and negative statements.

  *They **no wanted** her help.

- using *did* together with the *–ed* inflection or the irregular form of the verb, rather than leaving the main verb in its base form.

  *She **didn't liked** that story.
  *Did he **went** home already?

  At times learners use *do* instead of *did*

  *They **don't** want to come last night.

## Pronunciation of *–ed*

*If all regular past tense verbs take the same –ed inflection, why does the ending sound different? We say **walked** with a "t" sound but **called** with a "d" sound.*

Although there is only one past tense inflection for regular verbs, there is a difference in pronunciation when the *–ed* inflection is added. The change in pronunciation depends on what **sound** the verb ends in. The different pronunciations of *–ed* are not reflected in written English. The chart shows the different pronunciations of the *–ed* inflection.

| Pronunciation of *–ed* | | |
|---|---|---|
| Verbs that end in the sounds *p, k, f, s, sh, ch* | *t* sound | helped, baked, coughed missed, washed, pitched |
| Verbs that end in the sounds *d* or *t* | *id* sound extra syllable added | wanted, needed |
| All other verb **sound endings** (*b, g, v, z, zh, th, j, m, n, ng, l, r*, or a vowel sound) | *d* sound | robbed, dragged, shaved, garaged, breathed, raged, blamed, ruined, pinged, called, ordered, played |

It is important to emphasize with ESL/EFL learners that the pronunciation of *–ed* depends on the final **sound** of a verb, and **not the spelling** of the verb. The verb *cough*, for instance, is not spelled with an *f*, but has an *f* sound; the verb *fix* is written with an *x*, but has a final *s* sound. Both *cough* and *fix*, therefore, take the *t* pronunciation of the *–ed* past tense inflection.

Discovery Activity 7 provides practice both in identifying past tense verb and in recognizing the different pronunciation patterns of *–ed*. You may need to refer back to the chart above to help you remember the pronunciation rules.

**Discovery Activity 7: Past Tense Identification and Pronunciation**

Look at the following excerpts.

## Part I

1. Underline the past tense verbs. There are regular and irregular verbs.
2. For the irregular verbs you underlined, write the base form above it.

**A.**

> Gently, I tugged at the knot, pulling it carefully apart... Her shiny brown hair was thick, but the brush glided down... Her shoulders relaxed, and then she sighed deeply.
>
> [Shapiro, R. (2004). *Miriam the medium* (p. 81). New York: Simon & Shuster.]

**B.**

> He ran across the lawn and leaped over the three white wood steps. His heel struck the slate floor of the porch. He skidded but righted himself without having to grab the railing. He looked back at Danny and Encyclopedia and grinned cockily.
> When he got no answer to the doorbell, Bugs walked a step to the window that faced onto the porch. He rapped on the glass.
>
> [Sobol, D. (1996). *Encyclopedia brown finds the clues* (p. 19). New York: BantamSkylark.]

**C.**

> When Mrs. Frederick C. Little's second son arrived, everybody noticed that he was not much bigger than a mouse. The truth of the matter was, the baby looked very much like a mouse in every way ... Mr. and Mrs. Little named him Stuart, and Mr. Little made him a tiny bed out of four clothespins and a cigarette box.... Every morning before Stuart dressed, Mrs. Little went into his room and weighed him on a small scale.
>
> [White, E. B. (1945). *Stuart little* (pp. 1–2). New York: HarperCollins.]

## Part II

3. On a separate sheet of paper, list the verbs you underlined and label their pronunciation. Explain the pronunciation rule for each labeled verb.
4. Check your answers with those in the Answer Key at the end of the chapter.

   • If you made any mistakes, review the *–ed* pronunciation rules above.

*Example:*

> My sister *watched* me.
>
> watched → pronounced with a "*t*" sound because the base verb ends in the *ch* sound.

*Do ESL/EFL learners have problems remembering the different pronunciation patterns?*

▶ *Learner difficulties*

> ESL/EFL learners often have difficulty in remembering whether the *–ed* should be pronounced with a *t* or a *d* sound and whether the extra syllable needs to be added in spoken English. Since the differences are not reflected in written English, oral practice is an important means for helping students master the different pronunciations of *-ed*.
>
> In addition, since there are many different irregular past tense forms, learners need extensive opportunities, both oral and written, for practicing these forms. There are spelling changes for many of the regular verbs, which learners also need to become familiar with and practice (see Appendix B).

### Are there other past verb tenses?

In addition to the simple past, English has the past progressive, which you were briefly introduced to earlier in the text.

## Past Progressive

The past progressive describes ongoing events or actions in the past. Like the present progressive, the past progressive is a composite verb consisting of the auxiliary *be* plus the present participle of the main verb. The auxiliary *be* indicates time (past) and the present participle the ongoing nature (aspect) of the event or action.

Since the past progressive is a composite verb with an auxiliary, we form questions by simply inverting the subject and auxiliary. To make a sentence in the present progressive negative, we place the *not* after the auxiliary. The sentence types are summarized below.

| Sentence types: Past Progressive | | | | | |
| --- | --- | --- | --- | --- | --- |
| auxiliary | subject | auxiliary | + not | present participle | sentence type |
| | Sue | was | | walk**ing.** | **affirmative** |
| | We | were | | | |
| | Sue | was | **not** | walk**ing.** | **negative** |
| | We | were | | | |
| **Was** | Sue | | | walk**ing?** | **question** |
| **Were** | we | | | | |

### When do we use the past progressive?

For general guidelines, we use the past progressive for:

| | |
|---|---|
| • an event or action that was happening when another event or action interrupted it | (24) She *was driving* home when the rain started.<br>(25) My computer crashed while I *was e-mailing* you. |
| • emphasizing the ongoing nature of an event or action in the past | (26) She *was working* all morning.<br>(27) It *was raining* the whole night. |
| • an event or action that was already happening at a particular time in the past | (28) Nathan *was studying* at midnight. |

Sentence (24) uses *when* before the clause containing the simple past verb phrase *rain* to indicate an action that interrupted another one, *was driving*. In Sentence (25) *while* introduces the ongoing action *was e-mailing* that was interrupted by *crashed*. In Sentence (28), the use of the present progressive *was studying* underscores the fact that Nathan was studying before, at, and probably after, midnight.

### Why do we often use the past progressive + the simple past together?

The past progressive is often used together with the simple past to contrast two actions or events. The past progressive emphasizes the ongoing nature of the one event or action. The simple past emphasizes the single occurrence of the other.

When both the past progressive and simple past occur in a sentence, the order in which the two verb phrases occurs can vary. *When* and *while* are used in such sentences. *When* is used with the simple past and *while* is used with the past progressive.

| | past progressive | | simple past |
|---|---|---|---|
| | We were eating | **when** | Joyce called. |
| **While** | we were eating, | | Joyce called. |

The order of these sentences can be changed to:

| | simple past | | past progressive |
|---|---|---|---|
| **When** | Joyce called, | | we were eating. |
| | Joyce called | **while** | we were eating. |

### I often hear people using **when** and not **while** before the past progressive. Is that wrong?

According to the rules of prescriptive grammar, *while* must occur before the past progressive and *when* before the simple past. Native speakers, however, will commonly substitute *when* for *while* before the past progressive.

ESL/EFL learners need to be aware of the usage rule, particularly for situations requiring formal writing, but they should also be aware that this rule is often ignored, particularly in casual writing and speech.

The next Discovery Activity provides practice in recognizing the past progressive and the simple past. If you are confident in your knowledge of these two verb tenses, you may wish to skip this activity. The answers are at the end in the Answer Key.

**Discovery Activity 8: Past Progressive and Simple Past**

1. Look at the excerpts.
2. Underline the past progressive verb phrases and label them PProg.
3. Underline the simple past verb phrases and label them SP.
4. Explain the time represented by each of the past progressive verb phrases.

*Example:*

         SP                  SP

When he *entered* the room, he *didn't see* anyone at first, but then he

   SP          PProg

*noticed* that I *was sitting* in the corner with Cecily and James.

*Was sitting* describes an action that was happening when something else
(*he noticed*) occurred.

**A.**

... I remember the time last fall we were playing kickball. We were losing, like, nine
to nothing. We scored a bunch of runs in the last inning. And you kicked a grand slam
to win it, ten-nine.
[Fletcher, R. (1998). *Flying solo* (p. 101). New York: Yearling.]

**B.**

... I saw Cara and Rory in my mind. I knew Cara was sitting on her bed and Rory
in the rocking chair. He was leaning forward, his elbows at his knees. He looked
in control. I blinked away the vision. I didn't want to interfere... I had to sing "The
Star-Spangled Banner" in my head... By the time I reached "The rocket's red glare,"
Cara was screaming, "I hate my life! I can't live like this!" As I ran to the steps, Rory
was coming down.
[Shapiro, R. (2004). *Miriam the medium* (p. 139). New York: Simon & Schuster.]

In the next section we will be exploring how we talk about future time in English.
Unlike the simple past and simple present, English does not have a verb that inflects
for future time. In our discussion of the future, you will see how English uses different structures to refer to future time.

## Section 4: Future

Some languages have no future tense and rely on different means such as time
expressions (e.g. *tomorrow*) to express future events. Other languages have specific inflectional endings attached to the verbs to express future tense. English is a
language that relies on a variety of structures to express future time.

These different structures, all of which have different nuances of meaning, are
often confusing to ESL/EFL learners. There are rules to guide learners in their
choice of structures, but it is important to stress that these rules are not absolute

rules. Rather, they are general guidelines of use, depending upon the meaning the speaker wants to convey. Learning the different structures for expressing future time is not as difficult for ESL/EFL learners as is mastering which structure to use in which context.

### *How is the future usually expressed in English?*

The most common ways to refer to future time in English are *will* and *be going to*. Neither construction is a simple tense. *Will* is an auxiliary verb, which must be followed by a main verb in its base form:

(28) We **will** *study*.

There are no inflections on either *will* or the main verb.

Another very common way to refer to the future is the structure *be going to*.

(29) They **are going to** *come*.

Although *will* and *be going to* are similar in meaning, they are not identical and cannot always be used interchangeably.

## *Will*[4]

This future structure is the one traditionally referred to as the English future tense. In reality, it is somewhat less commonly used than *be going to*+ verb.

Because *will* is an auxiliary verb, similar to *be* in the present progressive and past progressive tenses we have explored so far, you know that you can:

- ask questions by inverting *will* and the subject.
- form negative statements by placing *not* after *will*.

There is one minor change to be aware of: When *will* and *not* are contracted, the form changes to *won't*.

| Sentence Types: *Will* and the Future | | | | | |
|---|---|---|---|---|---|
| auxiliary | subject | auxiliary | + not | verb | sentence type |
| | Sue | will | | walk | **affirmative** |
| | Sue | will | **not** | walk | **negative** |
| **Will** | Sue | | | walk? | **question** |

### *Do we ever use* **shall** *to refer to the future?*

ESL/EFL learners who have had some exposure to British English will have learned that *shall* is the preferred form for *I* and *we*. In American English, however, *shall* is used primarily in questions requiring agreement or permission, such as *Shall we*

---

[4] The future auxiliary *will* is different from the main verb *will* meaning bequeath, as in *She willed her estate to her grandchildren.*

go? *Shall I turn off the lights*, or found in legal terminology with the meaning of obligation or duty.

### What are the rules for using will?

For general guidelines, we primarily use *will* to:

| Will | |
|---|---|
| • refer to planned future events, arrangements, schedules | (30) Nordstrom's *will begin* holiday shopping hours tomorrow. |
| | (31) A formal dinner *will conclude* the meeting. |
| | (32) Northbound trains *will depart* at 10 minutes past the hour. |
| • make predictions that are not completely certain or definite | (33) Gas prices *will drop* soon. |
| | (34) The center of the hurricane *will continue* to gain strength. |
| • express immediate decisions or intention | (35) Neil: "I forgot my wallet." Bart: "I'*ll get* the check." Jack: "And then I'*ll take* you home to get it." |
| • make a promise | (36) We'*ll review* the material again before the test. |
| | (37) I'*ll invite* them over next week. |

At this juncture, we turn to the other future construction, *be going to*.

## Be Going To

While some grammar texts focus on *will* as the future tense in English, the default future form is *be going to*. This construction is the most commonly used future form. We only use *will* under the relatively limited circumstances listed above.

*Be going to* is generally considered a "fixed" structure with a particular meaning; however, some texts for learners of English describe *be going to* as the present continuous form of *go* plus the "to infinitive" of the verb.[5]

Since *be* is an auxiliary verb in *be going to*, we follow our first auxiliary rule in forming negative statements and questions.

| | Sentence Types: *Be Going To* | | | | | |
|---|---|---|---|---|---|---|
| auxiliary | subject | auxiliary | + not | | | sentence type |
| | Sue | is | | going to | walk. | **affirmative** |
| | Sue | is | **not** | going to | walk | **negative** |
| **Is** | Sue | | | going to | walk? | **question** |

---

[5] The term *infinitive* in English is used to describe "to + verb" when the *to* is part of the verb phrase and not a preposition.

### *What are the rules for using* be going to?

For general guidelines, *be going to* is primarily used to:

| Be Going To | |
| --- | --- |
| • predict an event, happening, action<br>• express a prior plan, that is, something speakers intend to do in some future time that they planned or decided to do previously. | (38) It*'s going to rain* tomorrow.<br>(39) Mr. Jones is tired of all the cold weather in New York. He*'s going to retire* to Florida next year. |

Note that in Sentence (38), *It will rain* could be substituted for *It's going to rain.* Either *will* or *be going to* can be used to make a prediction that is true or that is likely to happen in the future. In Sentence (39), on the other hand, only *He's going to retire* can be used.

When we refer to a prior plan or intention about a future event, we do not use *will,* but *be going to.* As you see, the distinctions between *will* and *be going to* are not exact, but only approximate guidelines to help ESL/EFL students understand and use the two structures.

This next Discovery Activity will provide you with more insights into the use *will* and *be going to.* When you have completed both Parts A and B of this Discovery Activity, turn to the back of the chapter to check your answers.

### Discovery Activity 9: Will versus Be Going To

### Part A

1. Look at Excerpts A and B.
2. Try substituting *be going to* for *will.*

   • Is the meaning the same? Why or why not?

**A.**

> "Sir, under the constitution of our Confederation, you have the right to a fair and speedy trial. As the supreme judicial power in this quadrant of Human Space, I guarantee you will get one. It will be over and sentence passed before your company even knows you've been charged. The Fleet Judge will assist you in finding counsel..."
>
> [Sherman, D., & Cragg, D. (1997). *Starfist: First to fight. Book I* (p. 149). New York: DelRey.]

**B.**

> "You will have a substitute teacher tomorrow," Mrs. North told her third-grade class...
>
> "I will be gone for one week," said Mrs. North. "I won't be back until next Thursday..."

"I will leave detailed instructions for the substitute," she warned. "And if any of you misbehave, I will know about it. . . "

[Sachar, L. (1994). *Marvin redpost: Alone in his teacher's house* (pp. 1–2). New York: Random House.]

## Part B

4. Look at Excerpts C and D.
5. Try substituting *will* for *be going to.*

## C.

"I have to meet Mrs. North in the parking lot. She**'s going to** drive me in her car. . . " "She**'s going to** pay me to take care of her dog while she's away [said Marvin]."

[Sachar, L. (1994). *Marvin redpost: Alone in his teacher's house* (p. 5). New York: Random House.]

## D.

The sea thundered loudly, and a large wave rose up like a hand. It seemed to grab the tiny boat and hurl it right at the shore. Right at the jagged rocks. "Oh, no! Galen**'s going to** hit the rocks! He**'s going to** crash!"

[Abbott, T. (2000). *The secrets of droon: Quest for the queen* (p. 12). New York: Scholastic.]

### *Do ESL/EFL learners have trouble remembering which future construction to use?*

▶ *Learner difficulties*

There are several difficulties ESL/EFL learners have with the future constructions. First, when referring to a prior plan or intention about a future event, native speakers use *be going to,* as in Sentence (39). When referring to a person's willingness to do something in the future, native speakers use *will.* When one future structure is substituted for the other, a different meaning may be conveyed, as shown below.

| Meaning: willingness | Meaning: this is my plan or intent |
|---|---|
| Abbey: We need more milk. | Abbey: We need more milk. |
| Nancy: I'll get it. | Nancy: I'm going to get it |

Although native speakers generally have no difficulty understanding the future meaning learners are trying to convey, they may be struck by the "oddness" of the use of one construction over the other in a particular context.

Another difficulty for learners of English is remembering to include all parts of the future with the *be going to* verb phrase. They may leave out the *be* auxiliary and produce such sentences as:

*I *going* to write him.

Finally, ESL/EFL learners also sometimes add "to" after *will* rather than using just the main verb alone as in:

*They will *to* change the law.

## Present Progressive for the Future

### Are there any other ways to express future time?

English also uses the present progressive to express future time. We frequently use the present progressive with a time expression to indicate close future time, especially with verbs of direction or motion.

| Present Progressive for Future | | |
|---|---|---|
| Subject | Present Progressive | Time Expression |
| The plane | is leaving | tonight at 8:00. |
| We | are coming | tomorrow. |
| The movie | is starting | next Wednesday. |
| Her mother | is visiting | next week. |

There is still yet another future structure, the future progressive.

## Future Progressive

The future progressive consists of *will* + *be* + the present participle. Although the future progressive is not used nearly as often as *will* or *be going to*, ESL/EFL learners need to be aware of this tense and its use.

We use the future progressive to:

| The Future Progressive | |
|---|---|
| • emphasize the ongoing nature of an event or action in the future. | (40) We *will be working* on this project for a long time. |
| • indicate the duration of a future event or action at a future point in time. | (41) The children *will be sleeping* by 10 p.m. |
| • emphasize closeness to present time, especially when used together with *soon*. | (42) Vacation *will be starting* soon. |
| • indicate a good guess or a supposition regarding an upcoming event or action. | (43) If we don't get back to work soon, *they'l be docking* our pay again. |

*What happens to our auxiliary rule for questions and negatives when there is more than one auxiliary?*

You will notice that the future progressive has two auxiliaries: *will* and *be*. Earlier we said that whenever there is an auxiliary, this auxiliary takes the initial position in questions:

(44)
We *are* sleeping            → **Are** we sleeping?
He *will* leave soon         → **Will** he leave soon?

We now have to refine our rule to state that whenever there is more than one auxiliary verb present, **only the first auxiliary** is moved to the initial position:

(45) The children **will** *be* sleeping by 10.→ **Will** the children *be* sleeping by 10?

We also said previously that in forming a negative statement, we place *not* after the auxiliary (or attach it if it is a contraction). We now need to refine our rule to state that when there is more than one auxiliary, *not* comes after the **first** auxiliary (or attaches to it if it is a contraction).

## First Auxiliary Rule for Negative Statements and Questions

- For **negative** statements
  - if there is more than one auxiliary verb, place *not* after the **first** auxiliary verb
  - if there is no auxiliary verb, insert the *do* auxiliary and add *not*.
- For **questions**
  - if there is one or more auxiliary verb, invert the **first** auxiliary verb and the subject
  - if there is no auxiliary verb, insert the *do* auxiliary before the subject and keep the main verb in its simple or base form.

In the next section, we will be examining the perfect tenses, all of which have at least one auxiliary, *have*. All questions and negatives in the perfect tenses will follow the rules we have just refined.

The tenses we have discussed up to this point refer to times and aspects that can be relatively easily explained. The next section looks at the perfect tenses. Because perfect tenses refer to less specific times than the tenses we have explored up to now, they are often referred to as indefinite tenses. These indefinite tenses are also more difficult for many ESL/EFL learners to understand and master.

# Section 5: Perfect

## *Present Perfect*

You will recall that the present perfect consists of the auxiliary verb *have* + past participle of the main verb. Regular past participles are the same as the past tense of the verb, e.g. *walked, camped, loaned*, etc. Irregular past participles have various forms (See Appendix B). To form negative statements and questions, we follow our first auxiliary rule.

|  | | | | | |
|---|---|---|---|---|---|
| **Sentence Types: Present Perfect** | | | | | |
| **auxiliary** | **subject** | **auxiliary** | **+ not** | **past participle** | **sentence type** |
| | Sue | has | | walk**ed.** | affirmative |
| | Sue | has | not | walk**ed.** | negative |
| **Has** | Sue | | | walk**ed?** | question |

### Use of the Present Perfect

#### *When do we use the present perfect?*

Traditionally, the present perfect is described as referring to indefinite time, that is, to events or actions that start in the past and extend into the present and even possibly into the future. The present perfect is generally presented in contrast to the simple past, which describes events that are over and completed.

ESL/EFL learners are also told that the present perfect tense is difficult because there is much variation as to when it is used. However, learners will have fewer problems if we regard the present perfect as occurring in two primary ways: **stable** and **variable** (Marshall, 1989). By stable usage, we mean that there are two instances when the present perfect is always used.

Stable Time

The present perfect is used to express *continuative* or *durative* time, that is, to describe an event or action that occurs over a period of time. This is stable time. The present perfect often co-occurs with such expressions of time as **for** and **since**.

> (44) I *have lived* here **for** ten years.
> (45) She *has studied* English **since** 2003.

Because the present perfect is also used to express *repeated* time, that is, an event or action that occurs more than once, that is repeated. Frequency or time expressions often co-occur with this use of the present perfect.

> (46) Andy *has* always *lived* in New York.
> (47) That's my favorite movie. I *have seen* it at least 20 times.
> (48) Florida *has had* numerous hurricanes.

- In Sentences (46), the speaker is telling us about the repetition of the event by using the frequency adverb *always.*
- In Sentence (47), the speaker is indicating the repeated nature of the action by including *at least 20 times.*
- In Sentence (48), the speaker uses *numerous* to give us a sense of the repetition of the event and the frequency.

Variable Time

The present perfect is also used for what is commonly called *indefinite* time. Here the present perfect is used to describe events or actions that ended in the recent past but *without a specific time marker* to indicate when they ended or occurred. The time is unspecified. Because native speakers alternate between using simple past and present perfect to describe such events with little or no change in meaning, this use of the present perfect is *variable.* Choice of one tense over another when referring to one event or action occurring in the recent past is dependent on context, the region of the United States, and the individual.

(49a) Cleo just took her exams.
(49b) Cleo has just taken her exams

(50a) Ethan already took his exams.
(50b) Ethan has already taken his exams.

Both sets of Sentences (49) and (50) include the time adverbs *just* and *already.* The time indicated by these adverbs, unlike an adverb such as *always,* does not specify anything about when or how often these actions or events occurred.

Note also that unlike *for* and *since, just* and *already* can occur with either the past tense or the present perfect. Although *yet* and *already* are often taught together with the present perfect, ESL/EFL learners need to be aware that these adverbs can occur with the simple past, depending upon the context and intent of the speaker.

Discovery Activity 10 is designed to help you identify the present perfect. If you do not need to practice this, move on to the next section. The answers are in the Answer Key.

## Discovery Activity 10: Identifying the Present Perfect

1. Look at the excerpts.
2. Underline the present perfect verb phrases.

**A.**

"An armed man need not fight. I haven't drawn my gun for more years than I can remember."
"Come to think about it, I haven't pulled mine in four years or more."
[Heinlein, R. (1942/1997). *Beyond this horizon* (p. 276). New York: ROC Books.]

**B.**

The evidence provided by radioactive dating, along with observations of long-term geological processes, has enabled geologists to compile a remarkably accurate history of life on our planet. Using these data, scientists have determined that the Earth is about 4.5 billion years old. By combining radioactive dating, relative dating, and observations of important events in the history of life on Earth, scientists have divided the 4.5 billion years into larger units called eras... Unlike the periods of time we use daily, the components of geological time do not have standard lengths.

[Miller, K., & Levine, J. (2000). *Biology* (p. 276). Upper Saddle River, NJ: Prentice-Hall.]

**C.**

Researchers have documented many cases of evolution in action, some of which involve organisms that have devastating effects on the lives of humans... Certain insect pests have evolved resistance even to the very latest pesticides.

[Miller, K., & Levine, J. (2000). *Biology* (p. 303). Upper Saddle River, NJ: Prentice-Hall.]

*Is the present perfect difficult for ESL/EFL learners?*

▶ *Learner difficulties*

The present perfect requires extensive practice in authentic contexts since learners of English often have difficulty using this tense correctly. In many cases, they will substitute the simple past, the simple present, or the present progressive for the present perfect. This arises in part because these other three tenses seem more "logical" to them in terms of time progression and sequence.

Alternatively, ESL/EFL learners may overuse present perfect, often because they associate certain expressions such as *for, since, just, already,* and *How long...?* with the present perfect.

**For versus Since**

Another area of confusion for learners of English is the use of *for* and *since*. They need to learn and have opportunities to practice that:

| for | since |
|---|---|
| • precedes **a length** of time: ten years, two months, five days, a long time, and so on. | • precedes **a point** in time: 2003, last month, Saturday, 8 p.m., and so on. |
| • tells how long an event or action has continued up to the present. | • tells when the event or action began. |

> Finally, the subject pronouns, *he, she,* and *it,* when contracted with the auxiliary *has* may be confused by ESL/EFL learners with the contracted auxiliary *is.* Both *has* and *is,* when contracted, are written as *'s* :
>
> | | |
> |---|---|
> | He's come. | He *has* come. |
> | He's here. | He *is* here |

In spoken English both *has* and *is* are reduced to a "*z*" sound and sound the same. ESL/EFL learners confuse these two forms more in spoken English than in written English because of the need to process input more quickly. In addition, because in spoken English the *'s* contraction is a reduced sound, it does not receive any stress in speech, thus learners may not hear even and be aware of the *'s.*

### Does the auxiliary **have** *only contract with subject pronouns?*

Noun phrases are often contracted in spoken English (*My friend's eaten; the dogs've jumped*), but less so in written English. When such contractions are found in written English, they are generally used in dialogues.

Because the sounds of the contractions are reduced, learners of English may not always recognize these auxiliary forms in spoken English. They need oral practice in learning to distinguish these contractions in the spoken language.

## Past Perfect

### What is the past perfect and when do we use it?

The past perfect consists of the past form of the auxiliary verb *have, had,* and the past participle of the main verb. The past perfect tense indicates an event or action completed prior to another point of time in the past. Since *had* is an auxiliary verb, it follows our first auxiliary rule in forming negative statements and questions.

| Sentence Types: Past Perfect | | | | | |
|---|---|---|---|---|---|
| auxiliary | subject | auxiliary | + not | past participle | sentence type |
| | Sue | had | | walked | affirmative |
| | Sue | had | not | walked | negative |
| Had | Sue | | | walked? | question |

### Past Perfect versus Simple Past

The past perfect is generally used in conjunction with a past tense verb phrase.

(51) We carefully *walked* through the dirt that *had accumulated* on the floors.
(52) It *had stopped* raining, so we didn't take our umbrellas.

In Sentences (51) and (52), the past perfect occurs together with the simple past in order to clarify which action happened first. Both actions took place in the past, but one occurred before the other:

- In Sentence (51), *we walked* occurred after *the dirt that had accumulated.*
- In Sentence (52), *we didn't take our umbrellas*, took place after *It had stopped raining.*

You will note that even though the clause order is different in Sentences (51) and (52), the sequence of events is still clear because the past perfect indicates which action took place first, while the simple past indicates the later action.

### Do speakers always use the past perfect to indicate the earlier action or event?

When time sequence is not important, speakers may substitute simple past for past perfect:

(53a) She *had called* before I left.
(53b) She called before I left.

Sentences (53a) and (53b) differ from Sentences (51) and (52) in that (53a) and (53b) include the word *before*. This word by itself indicates which action was the first past action. The use of the past perfect is not required in order to establish the sequence of events. Both (53a) and (53b) are acceptable English sentences conveying the same information. When *before* and *after* occur, speakers commonly choose to use simple past to refer to both past actions since the sequence of events is clearly established by these time adverbs. Some native speakers rarely use the past perfect, especially in casual spoken and written English and use the past tense only, relying on the surrounding context to make the meaning clear.

Discovery Activity 11 asks you to identify the past perfect verb phrases. As you do this activity, think about the time reference of the different verb phrases. After you have finished, check your responses with those in the Answer Key.

### Discovery Activity 11: Identifying the Past Perfect

1. Look at the excerpts.
2. Underline the past perfect verb phrases.

**A.**

> Forty-eight thousand dollars was still a lot of money. More than he'd ever had in his life. And since he had never intended to split it with Earl, it was all his. But his bad luck hadn't stopped there. Earlier today, he had learned through Rose's cousin in Toledo that Arturo Garcia had showed up at her house, put a knife to her throat

> and demanded to know where Ian was. Marie, who was afraid of her own shadow, had claimed to have had no choice but to tell him the truth.
>     [Heggan, C. (2003). *Deadly Intent* (p. 95). Ontario, Canada: Mira.]

**B.**

> Her rounds finished, Abbie returned to the kitchen, feeling much more relaxed than she had been twenty minutes earlier. Agonizing over a man who had apparently vanished from sight was stupid and nerve-racking. Whoever had attacked her was gone, and so was Ian.
>     [Heggan, C. (2003). *Deadly intent* (p. 164). Ontario, Canada: Mira.]

### *Are there any other perfect tenses?*

There are several more perfect tenses that we will look at now. These tend to occur less frequently than other tenses, particularly the last three in this section.

## *Future Perfect*

The future perfect consists of two auxiliaries, *will* and *have,* plus the past participle of the main verb. Based on our first auxiliary rule, we know that questions are formed by inverting the first auxiliary, *will* and the subject. The negative is formed by placing *not* after *will.*

| Future Perfect | | | | | | |
|---|---|---|---|---|---|---|
| auxiliary | subject | auxiliary | + not | auxiliary | past participle | sentence type |
|  | Sue | will |  | have | walked. | **affirmative** |
|  | Sue | will | **not** | have | walked. | **negative** |
| **Will** | Sue |  |  | have | walked? | **question** |

The future perfect is used to refer to events or actions in the future that will take place before another future point in time. *By* or *before* phrases are often found with the future perfect. The future perfect is not a very commonly used tense, but ESL/EFL learners still need to become familiar with this structure.

Discovery Activity 12 asks you to find the future perfect verb phrases and discuss it in conjunction with the other verb tenses in the excerpt. Answers are in the Answer Key.

---

**Discovery Activity 12: Identifying the Future Perfect**

Look at the excerpt.

1. Underline the future perfect verb phrase.
2. Discuss how the other verb tenses in the excerpt function together to describe the events or actions.

> On the way down over coffee and Krispy Kremes, Parks went over the attack plan:
> "We're going to send one of the trucks down to the house after we disguise it as a
> county survey vehicle... Some of our men will be inside the truck. The others will
> have surrounded the place and set up a perimeter ... with any luck no shots are fired,
> and we all go home happy and alive."
> [Baldicci, D. (2004). *Split second* (p. 326). NY: Warner.]

## *Present Perfect Progressive, Past Perfect Progressive, Future Perfect Progressive*

We will discuss these three verb forms together because they occur relatively
infrequently. Since they are less common verb forms and ESL/EFL learners will
have less exposure to them, they may have difficulty remembering and recognizing
their uses. All three tenses form questions and negatives according to the first
auxiliary rule. Recall also from our earlier discussion of the present progressive that
certain verbs are generally not used in progressive sense.

### Present Perfect Progressive

The present perfect progressive consists of **three** parts: *have* + *been* + present
participle of the main verb. The present perfect progressive is used to stress the
ongoing nature or duration of an event or action that is indefinite with no specific
beginning or end. It is also used to indicate an event or action that began in the
past and continues into the present and possibly the future. Our earlier discussion of
stable and variable time in conjunction with the present perfect also applies to the
present perfect progressive.

Often the present perfect and present perfect progressive are interchangeable.
When speakers wish to emphasize that an event or action is repeated or ongoing and
not short- term, they will use the present perfect progressive.

(54) We have been living here for 15 years.
(55) We have lived here for 15 years.

Sentences (54) and (55) are not significantly different in terms of their meaning.
Sentence (54), however, emphasizes the length of the event somewhat more than
Sentence (55). In other instances the difference may be more significant.

### Past Perfect Progressive

The past perfect progressive also consists of **three** parts: *had* + *been* + present
participle of the main verb. Like the present perfect progressive, it is used to stress
the ongoing nature or duration of an event or action.

(56) I *had been living* in the house for many years when I decided to move to
something smaller.

## Future Perfect Progressive

The future perfect progressive consists of **four** parts: *will* + *have* + *been* + present participle of the main verb. Like the present perfect progressive and the past perfect progressive, the future perfect progressive is used to stress the ongoing nature or duration of an event or action. The future perfect progressive is often used with expressions that begin with *for*.

(57) By the time Kirsten finishes her dissertation, she *will have been working* on it **for seven years**.

The following Discovery Activity provides practice in recognizing different perfect progressive tenses. If you feel confident in your ability to recognize these tenses, you may wish to do only some, not all, of the excerpts. Be sure to check your answers in the Answer Key.

### Discovery Activity 13: Identifying Perfect Progressive Tenses

1. Look at the excerpts.
2. Underline the present perfect progressive, and past perfect progressive verb phrases. Label each verb tense.

**A.**

When Skelton had had a good sleep, a bath, and a read, he went out on to the veranda. Mrs. Grange came up to him. It looked as though she had been waiting.
   [Maugham, W. S. (1977). Flotsam and jetsam. In *W.S. Maugham: Sixty-five short stories* (p. 308). New York: Heinemann.]

**B.**

"I could see Ritter like I said, and there was the man behind him, real close."
"Secret Service. Agent Sean King."
Baldwin stared hard at her. "That's right. You say that like you know the man."
"Never met him. But I've been doing a lot of research."
   [Baldicci, D. (2004). *Split second* (p. 80). New York: Warner.]

**C.**

The paper said that Lord Mountdrago had been waiting in a Tube station, standing on the edge of the platform, and as the train came in was seen to fall on the rail. . . . The paper went on to say that Lord Mountdrago had been suffering for some weeks from the effects of overwork, but had felt it impossible to absent himself while the foreign situation demanded his unremitting attention.
   [Maugham, W. S. (1977). Lord mountdrago. In *W.S. Maugham: Sixty-five short stories* (p. 359) New York: Heinemann.]

**D.**

"When I found out it was once owned by the United States Army, I started wondering why Scott might want to own a spread like that. He'd been living in Montana for a while, real militia person, I guess, so why the move? Well, I've been pouring over maps, blueprints and diagrams, and I found out the damn property has an underground bunker built into a hillside."

[Baldicci, D. (2004). *Split second* (pp. 322–323). New York: Warner.]

*Can you summarize what ESL/EFL learners find difficult about the verb tenses in English?*

► *Learner difficulties*

The difficulties ESL/EFL learners with English verb tenses have fall into two types: structural problems and semantic problems. You will notice that the list is much shorter under "semantic problems," but keep in mind that choosing the correct verb tense is as important as knowing how to form a correct structure.

| Structural problems | Semantic problems |
|---|---|
| • remembering the few but necessary English inflections<br><br>*They **color** a picture yesterday.<br>* She **like** reading. | • choosing the correct form. The descriptions or guidelines of use do not reveal the nuances of meaning; there are often subtle differences when choosing between related verb tenses, e.g. *will* versus. *be going to*; *simple past* versus *present perfect* |
| • inserting the *do* auxiliary when necessary **and** remembering the appropriate inflections<br>*He no go home.<br>*Did he went home? | *I **worked** here since 2002. |

| Structural problems | Semantic problems |
|---|---|
| • remembering all the elements of composite verbs, e.g. the present progressive has **2** elements; the present perfect progressive has **3** elements; the future perfect progressive **4**.<br>*We **going** to the movies. | |

## Summary

The chart below is a good way to help conceptualize the 12 verb tenses. Note that these 12 so-called tenses are actually **12 combinations of time + aspect**.

Summary Chart: Time + Aspect

| ASPECT | Simple<br>*No auxiliary* | Perfect<br>*1 primary auxiliary +<br>main verb* | Progressive *1*<br>*primary auxiliary +<br>main verb* | Perfect Progressive *2*<br>*primary auxiliaries<br>+ main verb* |
|---|---|---|---|---|
| | 0<br>(no aspect) | *have* + -past participle<br>(V+ *-ed*) | *be* + present participle<br>(V+ *-ing*) | *have + been +* present participle<br>(V+ *-ing*) |
| **TIME** | | | | |
| Present | call / calls<br>eat / eats | *has/have* called | *am/is/are* calling | *have/has been* calling |
| Past | called | *had* called | *was/were* calling | *had been* calling |
| Future* | will call | *will have* called | *will be* calling | *will have been* calling |

* Note that future with *will* follows a different pattern across the chart. *Will* is a special type of auxiliary verb, called modal, that combines with *have* and *be* to form the different tenses.

### First Auxiliary Rule for Negative Statements and Questions

• For negative statements
  ○ if there is one or more auxiliary verb, place *not* after the **first** auxiliary verb
  ○ if there is no auxiliary verb, insert the *do* auxiliary and add *not*.

- For questions
  - if there is more than one auxiliary verb, invert the **first** auxiliary verb and the subject
  - if there is no auxiliary verb, insert the *do* auxiliary before the subject and keep the main verb in its simple or base form.

## Practice Activities

### *Activity 1: The Parts of the English Verb*

A. Complete the table below to help you clarify your understanding of English verb forms.

| base verb | 3rd person singular | past | present participle | past participle | total number of forms |
|---|---|---|---|---|---|
| walk | walks | walked | walking | walked | 4 |
| sing | | | singing | | |
| clean | | | | cleaned | |
| make | makes | | | | |
| eat | | | eating | | |
| ride | rides | rode | riding | ridden | 5 |
| write | | | | written | |
| speak | speaks | | | | |
| study | | studied | | | |
| Teach | | | teaching | | |
| paint | | painted | | | |
| cut | cuts | | | | |
| learn | | | | learned | |
| love | loves | | | | |
| bring | | | bringing | | |
| speak | | | | spoken | |
| buy | | bought | | | |

B. Now do the same for the verb be. When you finish the charts, you will see that *be* has more forms than any other English verb.

| base verb | present (I, you/we/they, he/her/it) | past | present participle | past participle | total number of forms |
|---|---|---|---|---|---|
| be | | | | | |

## Activity 2: Verb Tense Practice

### A. Regular Verb

Take the phrase *Chloe paint* and on a separate sheet of paper, create a sentence for each of the following tenses. You may need to add words (e.g. a time expression or another clause) to make a comprehensible sentence.

1. present
2. past
3. future
4. present progressive
5. past progressive
6. future progressive
7. present perfect
8. past perfect
9. future perfect
10. present perfect progressive
11. past perfect progressive
12. future perfect progressive

### B. Irregular Verb

Take the phrase *Chloe drives a car* and on a separate sheet of paper, create a sentence for each of the following verb tenses. You may need to add words (e.g. a time expression or another clause) to make a comprehensible sentence.

13. present
14. past
15. future
16. present progressive
17. past progressive
18. future progressive
19. present perfect
20. past perfect
21. future perfect
22. present perfect progressive
23. past perfect progressive
24. future perfect progressive

## Activity 3: Distinguishing Between Participial Adjectives and the Present Participle in Verb Phrases

1. Underline all the participial adjectives.
2. Label them PartAdj

3. Underline the present and past progressive verb phrases.
4. Label the present participle PresPart

*Example:*

**PartAdj        PresPart**

The *crying* baby *was lying* in its crib.

> [W]hen ABC newsman Sam Donaldson stands up on the White House lawn. . . on display
> is the fading glory of the well-coiffed balding man.
>     "Twenty years ago, of the guys who were balding, I'd say 50 percent combed over," says
> Sal Cecala. . .
>     "My advice," Mr. Henson says, "to guys like me who are losing a little: Wash it, blow it
> dry. Use a fine-tooth comb and comb it and wrap it around. . . "
>     Though on the trailing end of fashion, the comb-over remains unbeatable in its
> versatility. . . "I'm covering nine miles of scalp with six miles of hair," boasts late-night
> television host Tom Snyder. . .
>         [Bailey, J. (2004). Domes of resistance. In K. Wells (Ed.), *Floating off the page: The
> best stories from the wall street journal's "middle column"* (pp. 61–63). New York: Simon
> & Schuster.]

## Activity 4: Identifying Auxiliary Verbs (optional additional practice)

1. Find the verbs in the following excerpt and underline them. Be sure to underline
   the entire verb. (You can ignore the verb *said*, which appears repeatedly.)
2. Label the auxiliary verbs Aux
3. Label the main verb V
4. Identify the tense of the verb.

*Example:*

**Aux V                          Aux V                     Aux Aux V**

Jane *was drinking* tea because she *didn't want* coffee. She *had been drinking* water
earlier.

>     was drinking—past progressive
>     didn't want— past, negative
>     had been drinking—past perfect progressive

> Snooping had rewarded him well. . . . He wasn't snooping, however, when he came into the
> Brown Detective Agency. He was drooping.
>     "I nearly had it all," he moaned and sagged against the wall. . . .
>     He whipped out a piece of cloth. The colors had run together, making one large red
> smear. . . .
>     "I'll bet Pete first made a copy of the map. . . ." said Winslow angrily. "After he brought
> me home, he probably returned to the islands."

"He won't find anything there but a sunburn," said Encyclopedia. He pointed to a tiny black smudge on the back of the map....

"It was writing," replied Encyclopedia. "It said 'New York World's Fair....'"

[Winslow's] face lit up. "Peter's off digging for treasure—he thinks....!"

"We don't know that Pete ruined your map on purpose," Encyclopedia said.

"I'll hire you," said Winslow....

Encyclopedia agreed, and two hours later the boys were heading toward the islands in a skiff....

"Pete will be digging by a group of three coconut trees," said Winslow...

[Sobol, D. (1970). *Encyclopedia Brown saves the day* (pp. 57–60). New York: Bantam.]

## Activity 5: Analyzing Verb Tenses

1. Look at the verbs in bold.
2. Label each verb tense.
3. Discuss why each tense is used.

When [Eric] **woke up**, light **was streaking** across his face.... [The planet's] sun **crossed** over the mouth of the pit.

"Holy crow!" he cried. "I**'ve been** here all night. Oh, man!"...

Eric **felt** a sharp pain in his stomach.... It **had been** a day since he**'d eaten**. His stomach **was** empty... He **felt** something round and hard under his foot. It **was** one of those smelly fruits he**'d found** in the garden....

"No way!" he cried. "I**'m not going to** eat it...."

But he couldn't stop himself.

The fruit **tasted** sweet! It **was** delicious.

"This **is** the most delicious food I**'ve ever eaten**!" he cried." I**'ve never tasted** anything so—"

"Please keep it down," whispered a voice...

"You**'re talking** too much," said another voice.

"... how can I understand you?" Eric asked.

"The tangfruit.:... Its taste **is** magic... "

"You **are now speaking** our language. The effect **will wear off**, of course... "

[Abbot, T. (2001). *The secrets of droon: The hawk bandits of tarkoom* (p. 27). New York: Scholastic.]

## Activity 6: Choosing Verb Tenses

In the following excerpt some of the verbs are given only in their base form.

1. Write the verb tense you feel fits best here.
2. Compare your answers with others in the class.

• Explain why you chose the tenses you did, e.g. what sentence clues did you use to help you make your choice?

When Mendanbar (**1. get back**) to the castle, the first person he (**2. see**) was Willin, standing in the doorway looking relieved. By the time Mendanbar (**3. get**) within earshot, however, the elf's expression (**4. change**) to a ferocious scowl.

"I (**5. be**) happy to see that Your Majesty (**6. return**) safely," Willin said stiffly. "I (**7. be**) about to send a party to search for you. . . ."

"What's happened?"

"Your Majesty (**8. have**) an unexpected visitor." He paused. "At least, I (**9. presume**) he (**10. be**) unexpected. . . ."

"Who is it?" Mendanbar asked. "Not another complaint from the Darkmorning Elves, I (**11. hope**)? If it (**12. be**), you can tell them I (**13. see, not**) them. I (**14. have**) enough of their whining and I've got more important things to attend to right now."

"No," Willin said. "It (**15. be**) Zemanar, the Head Wizard of the Society of Wizards."

"Oh, lord," Mendanbar said. He (**16. meet**) the Head Wizard once before, at his coronation three years earlier, and he (**17. not, like**) the man much then. . . .

"How long (**18. he, wait**)? What (**19. he, want**)?"

"He only has only been here for a few minutes," Willin reassured him. . . .

"As I (**20. recall**), he (**21.have got**) an exaggerated idea of his own importance. . . . Oh (**22. not, worry**), I (**23. not, say**) anything improper when I (**24. talk**) to him. Where (**25. he, be**)?"

[Wrede, P. (1991). *Searching for dragons: The enchanted forest chronicles book II* (pp. 42–44). New York: Scholastic.]

## Activity 7: Finding and Analyzing Verb Tenses (optional additional practice)

1.  Look at the following excerpts.
2.  Underline the verbs and identify their tense.

**A.**

She and Adam broke off their engagement, she's not even speaking with Paris anymore, and she's being hounded by the tabloids who love to talk about the protrusion of her collarbone.

**B.**

But rather than walking around feeling wounded, Nicole has become stronger in the past year.

**C.**

"I've been trying to focus on always taking a step forward and trying to do the right thing."
[Baer, D. (2006, June/July). *Cosmo girl*, p. 131.]

## Activity 8: Error Analysis

The following excerpts were written by ESL and EFL learners. There are errors in verb forms and tense.

1.  Underline each verb form and tense error you find. **Ignore all other errors.**
2.  Correct the error (remember, **focus *only* on verb tense errors**.

*   Explain the problem; for example, the writer should have used tense X and not tense Y because. . .

**A.**

Rabbit's name is Len. Her nose and mouth is red. Her eyes are orange. She like carrots. She is not like onions.

**B.**

My sister mess up my room. My sister write on my work. She rip my folder.

**C.**

I had felt the freedom from the army three months ago before my mind began to bothers me about no work. I made my appointment with the boss of the jewelry shop and on an early Monday morning I go to meet my future place. There were ten workers and the boss who were wore warm smiles.

**D.**

Dear Mayor,

I just heard you thinking about different ways to solve the traffic problem. People drive cars and they got late to work because they have only one road. For example, in front of my building, people working construction and people has to go around to come to the highway. If there is more roads, then people comes different ways and don't got late to work. If our city has many different ways to go, then people won't accidents. Therefore I think improving the streets and highways will to solve the traffic problem that we have.

**E.**

Today, we are living in Global Village. The Global Village means the world become smaller, like a small town. I think internet, TV, movies is making world be a Global Village. By using the internet, we can chat with many different people and I am downloading whatever I want and I am send message using e-mail. By watching TV, we will hear about world news so we know what happen in this world now. We can learn about other cultures. In my case, I learn about many cultures through TV programs.

**F.**

I am wishing you Happy Holidays. When Christmas is coming, I am becoming a child again. I am wanting to believe in Santa Claus because it makes the magic of Christmas.

## Activity 9: Reviewing Tense and Aspect (optional additional review and practice)

1. When do we use present tense in English?
   - How are simple statements formed?
   - How are questions formed?
   - How is the negative formed?
   - Are the rules governing statement, question, and negative formation prescriptive grammar rules or fundamental rules of English? Explain your choice.

2. What is the present progressive?

   - How does this contrast with simple present? i.e. what is the general rule governing the use of present progressive?
   - What exceptions are there? Are these exceptions rule-governed? Explain your reasoning.
   - How are questions formed?
   - How is the negative formed?
   - Are there any verbs not generally used in the progressive? If so, which ones?

3. When do we use simple past?

   - How are simple statements formed?
   - How are questions formed?
   - How is the negative formed?
   - Are the rules governing statement, question, and negative formation prescriptive grammar rules or fundamental rules of English? Explain your choice.

4. What is the present perfect?

   - What do we mean when we say *stable* and *variable* time?
   - How does the present perfect contrast with simple present, present progressive and simple past?
   - How are simple statements formed?
   - How are questions formed?
   - How is the negative formed?

5. Why do we say that English does not have a future tense?

   - Explain how English expresses future time and the different meanings associated with the different possibilities for expressing future time.

## Answer Key: Chapter 6 Discovery Activities

### *Discussion: Discovery Activity 1*

*Column A*

- The sentences refer to facts, truths or characteristics.
- They are in present tense.

*Column B*

- The sentences refer to actions that are occurring now or at the moment of speaking.
- They are in the present progressive. This verb tense is composed of the auxiliary verb *be* + present participle.
- The auxiliary *be* is inflected for tense and works together with the present participle to form indicate time (present) and aspect (ongoing).

- The last sentence *She is being sick* is not a grammatical English sentence here because *be* used to describe a characteristic or fact cannot used in this form.[6]

## Discussion: Discovery Activity 2

*Column C*

- The sentences are in the past tense. They refer to actions that are completed.

*Column D*

- The sentences are in the past progressive. This verb tense is composed of the auxiliary verb *be* + the present participle. The participle form in Column D is identical to the one used in the sentences in Column B, Discovery Activity 1, but the time reference has changed because the auxiliary *be* is now inflected for past tense.
- The meaning, use, and function of the past progressive is also different from the present progressive, which we will discuss in greater detail later in this chapter.

## Discussion: Discovery Activity 3

*Column E*

- The sentences are the same sentence as those in Column C, Discovery Activity 2. They are in the simple past.

*Column F*

- These sentences are in the present perfect. This verb tense is composed of the auxiliary *have* + the past participle. The auxiliary *have* is inflected for tense and works together with the past participle to form verb phrases that indicate time (past) and aspect (completion).

## Discussion: Discovery Activity 4

*Excerpt A*

- Question: *What are they doing?*
  - ○ Because it is a question, the auxiliary *be* inverts with the subject pronoun *they*, which is followed by the present participle *doing*.

---

[6] There is an idiomatic use of *be* + *being* +*sick* which means vomiting, but this is different from the general meaning where *be* + *sick* refers to a person's health.

- *They're putting down*
  ○ Note that *put down* is a phrasal verb.

*Excerpt B*

- *everybody's hanging around*; contracted form of *everybody is hanging around*.
  ○ Note that *hanging around* is another phrasal verb.
  ○ *How come* is an informal, primarily spoken form meaning *why*. Unlike *why* and other –*wh*-question words, *how come* does not take question word order after it.
- *nobody's doing*, contracted form of *is doing*

*Excerpt D*

- *I'm taking*
- *who's dying*, contracted form of *is dying*
- *are dying*

## Discussion: Discovery Activity 5

In Excerpt A, the simple present tense co-occurs with the use of *now* because the speaker is making statements of fact or truth. Even though the speaker uses the word *now*, he is not in fact referring to the occurrence of a specific event or action.

In Excerpt B, the use of simple present is used to narrate events in the story. It is a rhetorical device that gives readers a sense of participating in or being a part of a story as it takes place. The tone of the narration would change significantly if the author used present progressive in place of simple present.

## Discussion: Discovery Activity 6

- Sentences Aa and Ab: *smell* and *taste* are used intransitively and are followed by adjectives.
  ○ Both *smell* and *taste* refer to the characteristic of the subject noun phrase, *a rose* and *the noodles* respectively.
- Sentences Ba and Bb: *smell* and *taste* are being used transitively and are referring to actions (*are smelling, is tasting*).
- SentenceAc: refers to a fact
- Sentence Bc: a more idiomatic use of the verb *see*, referring to an impending action.[7]
- SentenceAd: asks about a fact or opinion

[7] There is an even more idiomatic use of *see* in present progressive, e.g. Miles is seeing Kim. In this case *is seeing* refers to dating.

- Sentence Bd: referring to an action occurring now.
- Sentence Ae: describing something about Joe's personality
- Sentence Be: referring to a behavior taking place now.
- Sentence Af: *has* refers to possession.
- Sentence Bf: a more idiomatic use of *have,* namely to eat.

## *Discussion: Discovery Activity 7*

| Excerpt A | |
| --- | --- |
| tugged | pronounced with the *d* sound |
| was | irregular past tense form of *be* |
| glided | ends in a *d* sound; pronounced *id* |
| relaxed | pronounced with the *t* sound |
| sighed | pronounced with the *d* sound |

| Excerpt B | |
| --- | --- |
| ran | irregular past tense form of *run* |
| leaped | ends in a *p* sound; pronounced with the *t* sound |
| struck | irregular past tense form of *strike* |
| skidded | ends in a *d* sound; pronounced *id* |
| righted | ends in the *t* sound; pronounced *id* |
| looked | ends in a *k* sound, pronounced with the *t* sound |
| grinned | ends in an *n* sound, pronounced with the *d* sound |
| got | irregular past tense form of *get* |
| walked | ends in a *k* sound, pronounced with the *t* sound |
| faced | ends in an *s* sound, pronounced with the *t* sound |
| rapped | ends in *p* sound; pronounced with the *t* sound |

| Excerpt C | |
| --- | --- |
| arrived | ends in an *v* sound, pronounced with the *d* sound |
| noticed | ends in an *s* sound, pronounced with the *t* sound |
| was | irregular past tense form of *be* |
| was | irregular past tense form of *be* |
| looked | ends in a *k* sound, pronounced with the *t* sound |
| named | ends in an *m* sound, pronounced with the *d* sound |
| made | irregular past tense form of *make* |
| dressed | ends in an *s* sound, pronounced with the *t* sound |

(continued)

| Excerpt C | |
|---|---|
| went | irregular past tense form of *go* |
| weighed | ends in a vowel sound, pronounced with the *d* sound |

## Discussion: Discovery Activity 8

| Excerpt A | |
|---|---|
| *past progressive* | *simple past* |
| were playing | scored |
| were losing | kicked |

- In Excerpt A, the two examples of past progressive are used to stress the ongoing nature of the event. The two examples of simple past are used to indicate single actions.

| Excerpt B | | |
|---|---|---|
| *past progressive* | *simple past* | |
| was sitting | saw | didn't want |
| was leaning | knew | had to |
| was screaming | looked | reached |
| was coming down | blinked | ran |

- In Excerpt B, the past progressive *was sitting* and *was leaning* are used to stress the ongoing nature of the event.
- The past progressive *was leaning* and *was screaming* are used to emphasize that these actions were occurring as something else happened, *reached* and *ran* respectively.
- The verb *know* is an example of a stative verb that is generally not used in a progressive tense.
- The other past tense verbs in this excerpt refer to single actions or events.

## Discussion: Discovery Activity 9

*Excerpt A*

- The use of *will* rather than *be going to* stresses the promise, or guarantee, that the events described will happen.
- Substituting *be going to* instead of *will* conveys more the idea of fact rather than a promise.

*Excerpt B*

- *be going to* can be substituted for *will* in the first four sentences with no change in meaning because all the sentences refer to a prediction about a future event.
- In the last sentence of the excerpt, *will* conveys a sense of promise or threat, which cannot be conveyed by *be going to*.

*Excerpt C*

- The use of *be going to* conveys the idea of a prior plan about future events that the speaker (Marvin) is recounting to someone else. The use of *will* would not work here.

*Excerpt D*

- *will* can be substituted for *be going to* with no change in meaning because all the sentences refer to a prediction about a future event.


## Discussion: Discovery Activity 10

*Excerpt A*

- two examples of the present perfect, *haven't drawn* and *haven't pulled.*
  - Both are negative verb phrases where the *not* is contracted with the auxiliary *have.*
  - The past participle *drawn* is the irregular past participle of the verb *draw*, and the past participle *pulled* is the regular past participle of *pull.*

*Excerpt B*

  - The first present perfect verb phrase is *has enabled.*
- The subject of *has enabled* is "The evidence provided by radioactive dating."
- The next examples of the present perfect are *have determined* and *have divided.*
  - In each sentence the subject of the verb phrase is "scientists."
- In the final sentence of this excerpt we see *do not have.* This is not the present perfect, but the negative present tense of the verb *have* in the sense of "possession."

*Excerpt C*

- The first sentence has the present perfect *have documented.*
- the second part of the sentence may be confusing where we see "have devastating." This is the use of the main verb *have* in the sense of "cause." *Devastating* is functioning as a participial adjective describing *effects* (See Chapter 4).
- In the last sentence we see the present perfect *have evolved.*

## Discussion: Discovery Activity 11

*Excerpt A*

- *he'd* ever *had* (contraction)
- *had* never *intended.*
  - ○ Both of these examples have a frequency adverb placed between the auxiliary *had* and the past participle of the main verb.
- *hadn't stopped* (negative contraction)
- *had learned* and *had showed up.*
  - ○ Note that *show up* is a phrasal verb. See Chapter 5.
- *had claimed*
  - ○ Note: *to have had* is a perfect infinitive, which we discuss in Chapter 12.

*Excerpt B*

- *had been*
- *had* apparently *vanished* (adverb *apparently* placed between the auxiliary and the past participle)
- *had attacked*


## Discussion: Discovery Activity 12

The excerpt begins with the simple past (*went over*) to introduce the events described by a character named Parks.
  - ○ *went over* is a phrasal verb (see Chapter 5).

- Parks begin his narration with the *be + going to* future (*we're going to send*).
- The next sentence has the future, *will be.*
- We see the future perfect in the next sentence, *will have surrounded* to refer to an action occurring after another action in the future (*will be inside*).
- The rest of the excerpt is present tense narrative.


## Discussion: Discovery Activity 13

*Excerpt A*

- past perfect progressive: *had been waiting.*
  - ○ No substitution of another verb tense possible

*Excerpt B*

- present perfect progressive: *I've been doing.*
  - ○ In this context it would be possible to substitute the simple past, *I did*, without a significant change in meaning.

*Excerpt C*

- two past perfect progressive forms, *had been waiting* and *had been suffering*.
  - It would be possible to substitute the past perfect (*had waited, had suffered*), but the length or duration of the action would no longer be emphasized.

*Excerpt D*

- past perfect progressive form, *He'd been living*
- present perfect progressive form, *I've been pouring*.

In either case the non-progressive form could be substituted (*he'd lived, he poured*).

# Reference

Marshall, H. (1989). Language variation and the ESL classroom. In M. R. Eisenstein (Ed.), The dynamic interlanguage: Empirical studies in second language variation (pp. 297–313). New York: Plenum.

# Chapter 7
# Modal Auxiliary Verbs and Related Structures

## Introduction

In Chapter 5 we introduced the concept of auxiliary verbs and examined the three primary auxiliary verbs, *be, have,* and *do.* Chapter 6 explored how *be* and *have* act as helping verbs in forming different verb tenses, and how *do* acts as a helping verb to form questions and negatives in present and past tense. This chapter examines another type of auxiliary verb, the modal auxiliaries, which are referred to as *modal auxiliary verbs,* or *modal auxiliaries*, or simply *modals.* Included in this examination are related structures. The chapter is divided into three sections: The first section examines modals; the second focuses on one particular modal with many uses, *would,* and the last section discusses what is commonly referred to as "the conditional."

> ...I told you what I think **should** happen vis-à-vis teaching grammar in the public school. It goes without saying that teachers **must** be taught how to carry out such a program. The design of a specific program is beyond the scope of this book—not that I **couldn't** do it, mind you...
>
> [Bruder, M. N. (2000). *The grammar lady: How to mind your grammar in print and in person* (p. 148). New York: Barnes & Noble.]

In the excerpt above, the verbs in bold are modal auxiliaries (hereafter referred simply as "modals"). These modals affect the meaning of the main verb in many different ways. Modals are used to make requests, ask for permission, offer suggestions, give advice, make logical deductions, and to fulfill many other social functions.

## The "Pure" Modals

In this chapter we examine the following "pure" modals:

| should | must | can | could | would | may | might | will |
|--------|------|-----|-------|-------|-----|-------|------|

These modals are often referred to as "pure" modals because they consist of only one word and form. Other constructions can function similarly, but are not considered "pure" modals. For example, *ought to* is very similar in meaning to *should*, but

212 7 Modal Auxiliary Verbs and Related Structures

is not considered a "pure" modal because it consists of two words (*ought + to*); instead it is referred as a "semi-modal." In addition, for some of the modals there are related structures that convey similar meanings. As we will see in our exploration of the "pure" modals, there are various structures that are generally discussed together with these modals because they are closely related in meaning and/or structure.

The modals and related structures are some of the most difficult for ESL/EFL learners to master because of their varied meanings and uses. To help learners understand and use the modals, semi-modals, and related structures, it is important that teachers themselves are clearly aware of the different meanings these can convey and how these meanings may change according to context.

*How do the modal auxiliaries differ from the primary auxiliaries?*

## Modal Auxiliaries versus Primary Auxiliaries

Like the three primary auxiliary verbs, the modals must accompany a main verb. Unlike the primary auxiliary verbs we have examined, thus for the modal auxiliaries *should, must, can, could, would, may, might, will,* and *would* do not change form or inflect for tense or person. They have only one form that does not change, although, for instance, *can* changes to the past form *could*. However, as we will see, this change in form is only when *can* is used in the sense of "ability."

A significant difference between the primary auxiliaries and the modal auxiliaries is that the primary auxiliaries add grammatical information. You will recall, for instance, that *was* or *were* together with a present participle indicates a past ongoing action or event. The past form of *be* tells us time and the *–ing* tells us that something is continuous. Modals, on the other hand, do not give us grammatical information. Instead, they convey semantic and what we call *pragmatic* information. If, for example, someone asks you,

(1) Could you pass the salt, please?

how, in your mind, does this differ from

(2) Pass the salt, please.

Chances are, you will have noted something along the line that Sentence (1) is more polite and less direct or abrupt than Sentence (2). Why is this so? The answer lies in the choice of the modal *could + you* versus the imperative or command form *Pass*. We can say that in Sentence (1) the speaker conveys a different intended meaning by using *could you* pass rather than *pass*. This difference in speaker intent is what we mean by *pragmatic* information.

Thus, modal auxiliaries, unlike the primary auxiliaries, are used to suggest possibility, grant permission, make deductions, judgments, and assessments, indicate obligation, necessity and ability, advise, and express speakers' attitudes.

The modals differ from the primary auxiliaries in other ways. The modals do not always have parallel meanings either for negation or tense. By this we mean that the meaning of a modal can change when it is used with *not*. What exactly this means will become clearer as we delve into the different modals.

The meaning of a modal may also change with a different time reference. While the modals themselves do not inflect for tense, they can have different time references. For these different time references, we use the primary auxiliaries:

   (3) I **should** *be doing* my homework.

In Sentence (3), the modal *should* is followed by the auxiliary *be* + present participle. In this sentence, *should* is conveying semantic and pragmatic information. *Be doing* is conveying what action *should* is referring to and the time reference. We can think of (3) as:

   (3a) I am not doing my homework at this time.
   (3b) I am supposed to be doing my homework now.
   (3c) A strong suggestion for me is to do my homework now.

As you see from these sentences, *should be doing* is conveying a great deal of information that is not necessarily immediately obvious to ESL/EFL learners.

To clarify the use of these modals, we will examine them based on their semantic meaning. We will also explore semi-modals and structures with related semantic meanings and/or function where appropriate.


# Section 1: The Modal Auxiliaries

## *Modal Meaning: Ability*

| *can* *could* |
| --- |

One of the first modals introduced to learners of English is *can* in the sense of expressing either present or future ability and its past tense counterpart *could*. This is the only pure modal that inflects for tense when it is used to convey the meaning of ability.

Since *can* and *could* are modal auxiliaries, we follow our first auxiliary rule introduced previously. We make negative statements by adding *not* after *can/could*, and form questions by inverting the subject and *can/could*.

The negative of *can* and *could* is parallel in meaning to affirmative statements with *can* and *could*. In other words, when *can* and *could* are used with *not*, they mean the opposite of what they mean in affirmative statements. As we will observe later, this is sometimes not the case with other modals where adding *not* to a modal may give it an entirely different meaning.

*Do these sentences mean the same thing:* "I can go" *and* "I'm able to go?"

| Related Structure: *Be able to* |

*Be able to* is a non-modal counterpart of *can/could* in the sense of "ability." *Be able to* is not considered a modal because *be* inflects for person and tense. At lower levels of proficiency, ESL/EFL students are generally taught that *can/could* and *be able to* are identical in meaning. However, although these structures are often interchangeable, there are some differences in use.

### Can/could versus be able to

*How do I explain the difference between* can/could *and* be able to?

| can/could OR *be able to* | ONLY *be able to* |
|---|---|
| (4) She could read at an early age. | (6) She was able to get us tickets |
| (5) She was able to read at an early age. | yesterday for the concert. |
| *general ability* | *single action or event* |

Both can/could and *be able to* are interchangeable when we refer to a general ability, as in Sentences (4) and (5). When we refer to a single action or event, we use only *be able to*, as in Sentence (6). We do not say

*(7) She could get us tickets yesterday for the concert.

### ► *Learner difficulties*

> As learners of English become more proficient, they are generally introduced to the concept that *can* and *be able to* are not identical in all cases. Nevertheless, even at higher levels of proficiency learners may confuse the use of *can/could* and *be able to*, as in Sentence (7).

Try Discovery Activity 1 to see how well you do in finding *can/could* and *be able to*. If you confident in your knowledge of these two structures, you may choose to continue on without completing this activity. The answers are at the end of the chapter in the section labeled "Answer Key."

### Discovery Activity 1: can, could, be able to

Look at the excerpts.

1. Underline the verb phrases containing *can, could, be able to*. Be sure to underline the entire verb phrase, not just the modal.
2. Decide whether or not another one of the verbs above could be substituted.

**A.**

> I went a couple miles out of my way, but I was able to reach Pancek's house without running into Morelli.
>
> [Evanovich, J. (2004). *Ten big ones* (p.146). New York: St. Martin's Press.]

**B.**

> "Elsie... had a bit of honest money of her own, so she gave us all the slip and got away to London... It was only after her marriage to this Englishman that I was able to find out where she was... I lived in that farm, where I had a room down below, and could get in and out every night and no one the wise."
>
> [Doyle, S. C. (1959). The adventure of the dancing men. In G. Bennet (Ed.), *Great tales of action and adventure* (pp. 150–151). New York: Dell.]

## *Modal Meaning: Permission and Polite Requests*

### *Is it* "May I leave?" *or* "Can I leave?"

| may    can    could    would |
|---|

There are three modals that are used in asking for permission, *may, could,* and *can.* Of the three, *may* is the most formal and, among traditional prescriptive grammarians, is considered the correct form to use when asking for permission. From this traditional point of view, *can* refers to ability rather than permission; thus, only *may* should be used when asking for permission and not *can.* Nevertheless, *can* has increasingly become the preferred form over *may.*

### *How do I explain the difference between* "Could you help me" *and* "Can you help me ?" *And what about* "Would you help me?"

In spoken English, *can* is more commonly used, especially between people who know each other. *Could* and *would* are considered identical in terms of politeness, but *can* is considered somewhat less polite.

*May, could, can,* and *would* all refer to present or future time when used to ask for permission or to make a polite request. Note that *may* is only used with "I" or "we." You will also notice that these polite requests all follow our first auxiliary rule where we invert the subject and verb to form a question.

Although earlier we discussed *could* as being the past form of *can,* this is only true when it is used in the sense of ability. When *could* is used in asking for permission or in making a request, it is a polite form and not considered a past form. Often *could* and *would* used in the sense of permission or request are referred to as conditional forms or polite forms.

| May, Can, Could, Would | | |
|---|---|---|
| May I leave, please? | | |
| Could I leave, please? | **permission** | **Present** |
| Can I leave, please? | | **or** |
| Could you pass the salt, please? | | |
| Can you pass the salt, please? | | **Future Time** |
| Would you pass the salt, please? | **polite request** | |

## ▶ *Learner difficulties*

It is frequently difficult for ESL/EFL learners to make the distinctions in use among the different modals. A common problem among learners of English is the overuse of *can* in making requests. In many situations, native speakers find *could* or *would* to be less abrupt and more appropriate than *can*.

## *Modal Meaning: Possibility or Probability*

| *may     might     could     must* |

Speakers use these modals to indicate their level of certainty about something. These modal meanings range from slight possibility (*may, might, could*) to a high degree of certainty (*must*). A good way to help learners visualize the difference in probability reflected by these modals is to use a scale:

| **Present Situation:** | **Speaker A** Brian is always in class, but he's not here today. |
|---|---|
| **low certainty** ↓ | **Speaker B** He *may be* sick. OR He *might be* sick. OR He *could be* sick. |
| **high certainty** | **Speaker C** He *must be* sick. |
| **Future Situation:** | **Speaker A** It's the end of October, but it's going to be a beautiful sunny and warm weekend. |
| **low certainty** ↓ | **Speaker B** We may drive to the country. OR We might drive to the country. OR We could drive to the country.* |
| **high certainty (logical deduction)** | **Speaker C** It must be an Indian summer. |
| | *The context will usually indicate whether the speaker means possibility or ability; however, the distinction between the two meanings is not always clear-cut. |

The use of *must* to indicate degree of probability is often discussed in terms of a **logical deduction**. The speaker is making an inference with a high degree of certainty about a situation or event.

## Possibility or Probability and Past Time

### *What about referring to past situations?*

In referring to **past possibility**, *may, might, could,* and *must* are followed by *have* + the past participle of the main verb. This is the same way the present perfect is formed, but with a modal verb, there is no "perfect" meaning.

| Past Situation | Speaker A<br>Brian is always in class, but he didn't come yesterday. |
|---|---|
| low certainty | Speaker B<br>He *may have been* sick. OR<br>He *might have been* sick.  OR<br>He *could have been* sick. |
| high certainty<br>(logical deduction) | Speaker C<br>He *must have been* sick. |

When *may* and *might* are used with *not*, they mean negative possibility:

(8) Alex *may be* sick.      He *may **not** come* to school.

(9) Alex *might be* sick.      He *might **not** come* to school.

### *What about* **must not have?**

When *not* is added to *must have*, where *have* is an auxiliary verb and referring to past time, it implies a negative logical deduction. *Must not have* also has another meaning, which we explore later.

(10) Jack didn't pass the course. He **must not have studied.**

### *Does* **could not** *refer to negative past possibility?*

When *not* is added to *could, could not* refers to lack of possibility. It often includes an element of surprise or disbelief or something contrary to fact. When there is this element of surprise or disbelief, *couldn't* generally receives stress in the sentence.

| | |
|---|---|
| (11) He couldn't come because he was sick. | **lack of ability** |
| (12) He couldn't be sick! I just saw him. | **negative possibility** |

Although you may think this next Discovery Activity somewhat long, you will see that each excerpt has different modals. Be sure you can find and explain all of modals before going on to the next section. For this Discovery Activity, the discussion follows the excerpts.

---

**Discovery Activity 2: may, might, might have, can, could, could have**

Look at the excerpts.

1. Underline the modal verb phrase. Be sure to underline the entire verb phrase, not just the modal.
2. Explain the meaning and time reference of the modal verb phrase, i.e. is it possibility, ability, or a logical deduction; is it past or present time?

**A.**

Before your next long run, you might fuel up by toasting a few frozen waffles. You might also pack an energy bar if you're going especially far. Along with all those energizing carbs, you figure you'll consume several grams of fat. But with all the calories you burn during your workout, there's nothing wrong with a few grams of fat, right?... That depends...

[Fuel. (2005, January), *Runner's World,* p. 47.]

**B.**

These hieroglyphics have evidently a meaning. If it is a purely arbitrary one, it may be impossible for us to solve it... This particular sample is so short that I can do nothing and the facts which you brought me are so indefinite that we have no basis for an investigation...

[Doyle, S. C. (1959). The adventure of the dancing men. In G. Bennet (Ed.), *Great tales of action and adventure* (p. 124). New York: Dell.]

**C.**

He introduced himself as Inspector Martin, of the Norfolk Constabulary, and he was considerably astonished when he heard the name of my companion.

"Why, Mr. Holmes, the crime was only committed at three this morning. How could you hear of it in London and get to the spot as soon as I?"

"I anticipated it. I came in the hope of preventing it."

"Then you must have important evidence, of which we are ignorant..."

Holmes sat in a great, old-fashioned chair, his inexorable eyes gleaming out of his haggard face. I could read in them a set purpose to devote is life to this quest..."

[Doyle, S. C. (1959). The adventure of the dancing men. In G. Bennet (Ed.), *Great tales of action and adventure* (pp. 137–138). New York: Dell.]

**D.**

Of course, the uptick in productivity growth might have been just another bubble. With the end of the bull market and the economic expansion of the 1990s, the end of the productivity miracle may be near as well.

[Gerseman, O. (2004). *Cowboy capitalism* (pp. 34–35). Washington, DC: Cato Institute.]

**E.**

> "No one remembers seeing him at the briefing," Collins continued, "but he could have been listening outside of the tent."
>   [Brockmann, S. (2004). *Hot target* (p. 11). New York: Ballantine.]

## Discussion: Discovery Activity 2

*Excerpt A*

- two uses of the modal *might* to indicate future possibility: *might fuel up* and *might (also) pack*

  - *May* could be substituted here with no change in meaning.

*Excerpt B*

- *may be*: indicates present/future possibility.
- *can do* indicates present ability.

  - *Be able to* can be substituted without a change in meaning.

*Excerpt C*

- two uses of the past *could* to indicate ability: *could (you) hear* and *could read*.

  - *Be able to* could be substituted for both of these modal verb phrases.

- strong probability or logical deduction: *must have*.

  - The *have* is the main verb *have* meaning possession and referring to present time.

*Excerpt D*

- past possibility: *might have been*

  - In this instance *have* is part of the modal verb phrase that refers to past time.
  - *May have been* could be substituted for this verb phrase with no change in meaning.

- future possibility: *may be*

  - *might be* could be substituted with no change in meaning.

*Excerpt E*

- past possibility: *could have been listening*.

  - The reference is to past possibility, not ability. This is an example of the past progressive: *could + have + been +* present participle.

○ In this instance the modal verb phrase is in the progressive form, stressing the ongoing nature of the action.

*At the end of Excerpt D, we saw a sentence that ended with:... the productivity miracle may be near as well. Do ESL/EFL learners confuse* **may be** *and* **maybe?**

► *Learner difficulties*

---

A common problem, even among more advanced learners of English, is distinguishing between *may + be* and *maybe*. While both express possibility, *maybe* is an adverb. *May + be* is the modal *may* and the simple form of the main verb *be*. Because *may + be* and *maybe* belong to different word classes, they function differently in sentences. Since *maybe* is an adverb, it comes before a subject and verb (*we + will + go*). *May be* is the verb phrase of the sentence and follows the subject (*we*).

(13) *Maybe* we'll go to the beach tomorrow.
(14) We *may be* at the beach tomorrow.

In spoken English, there is also a difference in pronunciation. The adverb *maybe* is pronounced together as one word, with stress upon the first syllable, *may*. In the verb phrase *may + be*, the modal *may* receives stress and is spoken as a separate word unit from *be*.

---

## Modal and Related Structures Meaning: Necessity or Obligation

| | |
|---|---|
| Jason: | "I **have to go**." |
| Graduate Advisor: | "Before you leave this office, you **must complete** this form." You've got to listen to me about this. You don't want to lose your fellowship." |

| must |

Another use of *must* in addition to that of logical deduction, is to express **necessity** and **obligation**. When *must* is used in this meaning, there are two related structures that convey this same meaning. All three structures express necessity, but only *must* is a modal.

*Must* expresses necessity in present and future. There is **no past form** of *must* in the sense of necessity. We use *had to* when referring to past necessity, as in the excerpt above and in Sentence (18) below. There is also no negative form for this meaning of *must*. In other words, adding *not* does not convey lack of necessity or obligation. Must not is a logical deduction or high probability, as we discussed previously. Moreover, must not can be used to convey the meaning of prohibition, which we will investigate shortly.

---

### Related Structures: have to    have got to

---

*Have to* and *have got to* are idiomatic structures that express necessity. They are not modals but convey the same or similar meaning as *must* in the sense of necessity or obligation:

- In *have to* and *have got,* "have" is a main verb. Both *have to* and *have got to* inflect for person. We form questions by inserting the *do* auxiliary in simple present and simple past.
- We form the negative of *have to* by using the *do* auxiliary and *not,* as in Sentence (19). In Standard American English we do not use *don't have got to,* although it is found in some dialects.
- *Have got to* is used only in the present and future, is generally a spoken, informal form, and usually contracts, as in Sentence (17) below.
- *Have to* is used in any tense and generally does not contract.

### Must versus Have To

| Necessity: Must, Have To | | | |
|---|---|---|---|
| | **Meaning** | **Structure** | **Time** |
| (15) She *must pay* her bills. | | modal | |
| (16) She *has to pay* her bills. | **necessity** | *have to*, no contraction possible | present/ future |
| (17) She*'s got to pay* her bills. | | *have got to*, contraction possible | |
| (18) She *had to pay* her bills | | *have to* | past |
| (19) She *doesn't have to pay* her bills | **lack of necessity** | *have to* + present *do* auxiliary | present |
| (20) She *didn't have to pay* her bills. | | *have to* + past *do auxiliary* | past |

### Are must and have to interchangeable?

In general, *must* is considered stronger than *have to*. Grammar books often attempt to distinguish between the two by citing the difference as "external" versus "internal obligations." External obligation refers to regulations, conventions, conditions, rules, laws, etc. imposed by someone or something. Internal obligation refers to something imposed by speakers themselves:

| (21) Drivers **must obey** traffic laws. | external |
| (22) I **have to** get my oil changed. | internal |

In reality, this distinction is not always maintained, particularly in spoken American English. In spoken English, speakers will generally use *have to* or *have got to* more frequently than *must*, even when there are external obligations.

Only *must* and *have to* are used in questions, although in informal spoken English speakers will ask questions, such as *You gotta go right now?* relying upon intonation to convey the question. For questions, *must* inverts with the subject, and *have to* uses the *do* auxiliary, in accordance with our first auxiliary rule.

Speakers may use additional greater stress on *have* in the verb phrase *have to*, or *got* in the verb phrase *have got to* in order to emphasize the importance or necessity of a particular action.

       /

(23) You've **got** to get a new car.

    /

(24) I **have** to get a new car.

**When we speak, we don't usually enunciate the "have" in have to and have got to, do we?**

In spoken English *have to* is often reduced to *hafta*. *Has to* often sounds like *hasta*. *Have got to* is often reduced to *gotta* and in dialogues may be written as such to reflect the spoken form.

Since *have to* and *have got to* are very reduced in spoken speech, ESL/EFL learners may have difficulty recognizing and understanding these forms. Inexperienced native speakers and ESL/EFL students exposed to informal English frequently need to be taught that *gotta* is actually the spoken form of *have got to* and to avoid writing *gotta* in place of *have got to*.

**Don't we sometimes use should when we mean obligation?**

| **Related Modal:** *should* |

In certain contexts *should* conveys the notion of necessity or obligation. It is usually substituted for *must* to soften a demand or requirement but as with *must*, there is no choice involved.

(24) All submissions to the *Quarterly* **should conform** to the requirements of the *Publication Manual of the American Psychological Association*. . . Authors of full-length articles. . . **should include** two copies of a very brief biographical statement. . .

    [General Submission Guidelines. (2002). *TESOL Quarterly, 36*, 128.]

## Modal Meaning: Prohibition

| *must not* |
|:---:|

*Must not* can mean something is prohibited. In American English *must not* to mean prohibition is considered formal and often the meaning of prohibition is conveyed via other sentence structures.

| Prohibition | |
|---|---|
| (25) You *must not* drink and drive. | **must + not** |
| (26) Drinking and driving is against the law. | **alternatives** |
| (27) No drinking and driving. | |
| (28) Drinking and driving is illegal. | |

*Must not* meaning logical deduction or inference versus *must not* meaning prohibition is differentiated based on the context in which the modal verb phrase occurs. To help clarify the meaning of *must not* versus *must, have to,* and *have got to,* consider the chart below. This chart summarizes the different uses of *must not, must, have to,* and *have got to,* and their related meanings.

Remember that "related" does not mean "identical," and that the use of each structure does differ. Keep in mind also that adding *not* **significantly alters** the meaning of *must.* Note also that this chart does not include other meanings and forms of *must.*

### Comparison of **must, must not, have to, have got to**

| must, must not, have to, have got to | | | |
|---|---|---|---|
| | **Meaning** | **Tense** | **Form** |
| We *must obey* the law.<br>We *have to obey* the law.<br>We*'ve got to obey* the law. | necessity | present | statement |
| *Must we obey* the law?<br>*Do we have to obey* the law? | | | question |
| They *must not open* that door.<br>They *do not have to* come. | prohibition<br>lack of necessity | | negative statement<br>statement |
| We *had to come.*<br>We *didn't have to come.* | necessity<br>lack of necessity | past | statement<br>negative statement |

The next Discovery Activity provides practice in identifying and ascertaining the meaning of *must, must have, have to,* and *have got to.* After you have completed the activity, check your answers with those in the Answer Key.

**Discovery Activity 3: must, must have, have to, have got to**

Look at the excerpts.

1. Underline the modal verb phrase. Be sure to underline the entire verb phrase, not just the modal.
2. Explain the meaning of the modal verb phrase, e.g. is it necessity or logical deduction?

**A.**

Mack had the *Atlantic Ranger's* engine running and was perched on the bench in front of the wheel, putting on his shoes. He must have sprinted barefoot to reach the water before Anna.
[Barr, N. (2003). *Flashback* (p. 42). New York: G.P. Putnam's Sons.]

**B.**

He seemed to think for a second. "Strange, but I haven't lied about anything." He looked puzzled. "It's been a long time since that was true."
"My condolences," I said.
He frowned at me. "What?"
"It must be difficult never being able to tell the truth. I know I'd find it exhausting."
[Hamilton, L. K. (2003). *Cerulean sins* (p. 5). New York: Berkely Books.]

**C.**

Until this was over, or until she convinced HeartBeat that the threat wasn't real, she was going to have to stay in J. Mercedes Chadwick mode around the clock... Right now she even had to stay in character here, in her upstairs private office... Jane had to take Robins' advice and turn this fiasco into free publicity for *American Hero*.
[Brockmann, S. (2004). *Hot target* (p. 36). New York: Ballantine.]

**D.**

A third-party in *loco parentis* applying on behalf of a minor under the age of 14 must submit a notarized written statement or affidavit from both parents or guardians authorizing a third-party to apply for a passport. When the statement or affidavit is from only one parent/guardian, the third-party must present evidence of sole custody of the authorizing parent/guardian.
[http://travel.state.gov/passport/get/minors/minors_834.html. Retrieved 01/02/05]

**E.**

"I had my ear pierced," Ethan said tightly. "It's no big deal."
"It must have been a big deal because you did it seven times," said my mother.
[Heller, J. (2003). *Lucky stars* (p. 17). New York: St. Martin's Press.]

**F.**

"Does that mean that you're not coming over to my place for cider and doughnuts?"...

"No, Mrs. Zimmerman... but right now I've got to go up to my room and finish one of John L. Stoddard's books. I've gotten to the exciting part..."

[Bellairs, J. (1993). *The house with a clock in its walls* (p. 71). New York: Puffin.]

## Modal and Related Structure Meaning: Advice or Suggestion

| should    ought to |

Dear Miss Manners:

My daughter will be meeting the secretary of defense and possibly the president of the United States in September. She will be with her fiance, who is receiving an ROTC Air Force honor. How **should** she address each if introduced to them?

[Miss Manners. (2006, September 6), Widow's Pique. *Washington Post*, p. C10. Accessed online 9/25/2006 at http://www.washingtonpost.com/wp-dyn/content/article/2006/09/05/AR2006090501101.html].

*Should* and *ought to* both express advisability or suggestion and the two are interchangeable in meaning. Some grammarians consider only *should* a pure modal and argue that *ought to* be classified as a related structure. Regardless of how they are classified, *should* and *ought to* are closely related semantically and generally taught together in ESL/EFL texts. *Ought to* occurs less frequently in American English than *should*, although there are regional variations.

Questions and negatives with *should* and *ought to* follow the first auxiliary rule. However, in American English, *not* is rarely used with *ought to*, nor is *ought to* generally used in questions.

### ▶ *Learner difficulties*

In spoken speech, *ought to* is generally reduced and sounds like *outta* or *oughta*, and may be written as such in dialogues to reflect spoken speech. In its reduced form *ought to* (*outta/oughta*) can be considered more informal than *should*.

(29) Tiller clutched Sairy's arm as they followed Dallas. Florida trailed them, kicking at rocks and tree trunks as she went. "Oughta just run away right now," Florida mumbled. "Oughta just bury us alive."

[Creech, S. (2002). *Ruby holler* (p. 84). New York: HarperCollins.]

### Related Structure: Had Better

*Had better* is an idiomatic, fixed form. In American English *had better* is considered somewhat stronger than *should* and *ought to*. It implies very strong advice, a warning, a threat, or the expectation that the action will occur.

Although *had better* looks like a past tense form, it is used only for present and future time reference. Since *had better* is a fixed structure, *not* comes after both words.

▶ *Learner difficulties*

In spoken English, the *had* in *had better* is often contracted and reduced, which makes it difficult for learners of English to distinguish.

(30) You'*d better* come now.
(31) You'*d better **not*** be late.

Furthermore, speakers often drop the *had* altogether in spoken English.

(32) Oh! You better watch out,
You better not cry,
You better not pout,
I'm telling you why:
Santa Claus is coming to town! (refrain from the Christmas song, *Santa Claus is Coming to Town*)

Discovery Activity 4 asks you to identify *should, ought to, had better*. If you do well on the first two or three excerpts, you may not need to do the rest. Note that the last excerpt is long, but provides an interesting contrast in the use of two of the modal verb phrases. The answers are available in the Answer Key.

### Discovery Activity 4: should, ought to, had better

Look at the excerpts.

1. Underline the modal verb phrase. Be sure to underline the entire verb phrase, not just the modal.

**A.**

[Tiller] eyed the dark storm clouds in the distance. "We'd better get that tent up or we're going to get soaked tonight," Tiller said.
[Creech, S. (2002). *Ruby holler* (pp. 207–208). New York: Harper Collins.]

**B.**

"You know I'm hypoglycemic. The doctor says I shouldn't go more than two hours without eating."
[Grafton, S. (2004). *R is for ricochet* (p. 51). New York: G.P. Putnam's Sons.]

**C.**

"...If you give me some basic supplies, I'm sure I can build some glasses myself."
"No, no," the foreman said, his surgical mask curling into a frown. "You'd better leave optometry to the experts."
[Snicket, L. (2000). *The miserable mill* (p. 101). New York: HarperCollins.]

**D.**

"...I designed that game myself, Pete....It's strictly for suckers..."
"But look—I've figured out a way to beat it. I thought you ought to know."
[Heinlein, R. (1942/1997). *Beyond this horizon* (p. 39). New York: Penguin.]

**E.**

A central element of any program to develop the private sector is that the government should transfer commercial activities now carried out by state-owned enterprises or government agencies to the private sector... The vast literature on privatization gives little guidance to countries on what the objectives ought to be. However, it is recognized that countries should specify their objectives and then design a privatization program to achieve those objectives.
[Anderson, R. (2004). *Just get out of the way: How government can help business in poor countries* (pp. 87–88). Washington, DC: Cato Institute.]

## *Modal Meaning: Expectation*

"I can go and nose around, see if I can pick up any sense of what kind of security they have... It **shouldn't** take long.
[Smith, T. (2006). *Slim to none* (p. 96). Ontario Canada: Mira.]

### *The* shouldn't *in this excerpt doesn't mean "advice" or "suggestion," does it?*

### Should, Ought to

*Should/ought to* also carry the meaning of expectation or a high degree of certainty, similar to *must* in the sense of logical deduction. The degree of certainty is not, however, as strong as with *must*. In American English, *ought to* is not used as often as *should* in this sense, although there are regional variations.

(33) It's late. Helen *should be* here by now.
(34) You *ought to receive* your paycheck by the first of the month.

When adding *not*, the meaning is simply negative without a change in meaning or use, as we can see in the excerpt above.

## *Modal Meaning: Unfulfilled Expectation, Mistake*

### *Does* should have + past participle *mean advice or suggestion?*

> I knew what was happening. I **should have** done something. . .
> I **shouldn't have** let it go on so long.
>   [Shayne, M. (1993). *Reckless angel* (p. 15). New York: Silhouette.]

| *should have    ought to have* |
|---|

*Should* and *ought to* can refer to past time by adding *have* + the past participle of the main verb. However, when ***should*** and ***ought to*** are used in **past** time reference, **the meaning** of these modals **is different** from their meaning than when used in present or future time reference.

*Should/ought to have* + past participle conveys the meaning of a comment on or evaluation of an action or event that was a mistake or that did not meet expectations. Depending on the context, *should/ought to have* + past participle may convey a reprimand or implied criticism.

The chart below summarizes the different uses of *should, ought to,* and *had better* and their related meanings. Remember again that "related" does not mean "identical," and that the use of each structure may differ in different contexts.

### *Comparison of* Should, Ought to, Had Better

| Should, Ought To and Had Better | | |
|---|---|---|
| **Affirmative** | **Meaning** | **Time** |
| She *should come* early. She *ought to come* early. | advice or suggestion | present/future |
| She *had better come* early. | strong advice or suggestion | present/future |
| It's late. She *should be* here by now. | expectation or high certainty | present/future |
| She *should have come* early. She *ought to have come* early. | unfulfilled expectation or reprimand; unheeded, ignored past advice | past |

Complete the Discovery Activity below, which contrasts *could, should,* and *should have.* This Discovery Activity should help clarify the meaning and use of these modals in your mind. You can find the answers to Discovery Activity 5 in the Answer Key.

**Discovery Activity 5: should, should have, could**

Look at the excerpts.

1. Underline the modal verb phrase. Be sure to underline the entire verb phrase, not just the modal.

2. Explain the meaning of the modal verb phrase, e.g. is it possibility, advice, or unfulfilled expectation/obligation?
3. Explain what time the modal verb phrase is referring to.

**A.**

"Threw my back out," he said by way of explanation. "I was moving boxes last week. I guess I should have done like Mother taught me and lifted with my knees."
    [Grafton, S. (2003). *Q is for quarry* (p. 29). New York: G.P. Putnam's Sons.]

**B.**

A few organizations are already acknowledging that the money currently pouring in for tsunami victims should be sufficient to meet their needs...One factor that should comfort donors: Many well-known international aid groups generally have high so-called efficiency ratings...
    [Silverman, R., & Bernstein, E. (2005, January 4). New challenge for aid groups: Lots of money. *Wall Street Journal*, D1.]

**C.**

"What you're saying is true and you're entirely correct. Grand should have come down here. She should have sent word, but I think she was afraid to face you.
    [Grafton, S. (2003). *Q is for quarry* (p. 149). New York: G.P. Putnam's Sons.]

**D.**

There's an art gallery across the court you really should see. You could talk to the owner about your work.
    [Grafton, S. (2004). *R is for ricochet* (p. 99). New York: G.P. Putnam's Sons.]

## Section 2: Would and the Conditional

### *The Many Uses of* Would

*Would* is a modal that has many different uses. For one, *would* + main verb can be used to express past custom or habit, that is, something that happened repeatedly in the past.

(35) Two years later, her grandfather had died of a sudden heart attack, but she **would** always **treasure** the solitary time she to got spend with him that summer...
    [Smith, T. (2006). *Slim to none* (p. 162). Ontario Canada: Mira.]

*Would* is also used to refer to the **future in the past.**

(36) Before he made any decisions, he **would make** a few more inquiries. Then, he **would consider** his options.
[Smith, T. (2006). *Slim to none* (p. 304). Ontario Canada: Mira.]

*Would* is used for future time reference when there is a sense of possibility or capability. It is generally regarded as a weaker alternative to *will* when used in this sense.

(37) The President is proposing a new bill that **would** significantly **change** Social Security.

*Would have* + past participle can also refer to past time in the sense of possibility or capability.

(38) In a calculated decision, she'd left her M-16 rifle back at the house with Nuñez, as well as the two-way radio that **would have allowed** her to communicate with him.
[Smith, T. (2006). *Slim to none* (p. 101). Ontario Canada: Mira.]

*Would* is also used to express wishes or conditions in present or future.

(39) I wish spring **would come** soon.

*Would have* + past participle is used to express wishes or conditions in the past.

(40) She wished her friends **would have written.**

## Would *and the* Conditional

*Would*, as used in Sentences (37)–(40), is commonly associated with what grammarians refer to as the *conditional*. In essence, the conditional means something that refers to a hypothetical state of affairs, which we introduce here and which we will discuss again in Chapter 9.

Violet... tried to imagine what Klaus **would have said** *if* he **had been** there, unhypnotized, in the library with his sisters.
[Snicket, L. (2000). *The miserable mill* (p. 14). New York: HarperCollins.]

*Would*, along with *could*, is used to indicate actions or events that are hypothetical or contrary to fact. The use of *would, could,* or *might* to speculate about events, talk about events or actions that did not occur or that are not true, is called the *conditional*.

Although conditional clauses will be examined in greater detail in Chapter 9, it is appropriate to introduce the conditional in this chapter on modals because of the use of *would, could,* and sometimes *might* in conditional clauses. These clauses are also referred to as hypothetical "if" clauses.

"If" Clauses

The conditional consists of two clauses: an "if" clause and a main clause. In the **present conditional**, the "if" clause consists of *if + simple past*. The main clause consists of *would/could/might* + simple verb. The **past conditional** consists of *if + past perfect*. The main clause consists of *would/could/might + have +* past participle, as in the excerpt introducing this section.

| | Conditional | |
|---|---|---|
| **"if" clause, initial position** | **main clause** | **time** |
| (41) **If** I *had* time, | I *would study* more. | present |
| (42) **If** she *had studied* more, | she *could have passed* the course. | past |

The order of the "if" clause and the main clause may vary without a change in meaning.

| **main clause** | **"if" clause, second position** |
|---|---|
| (41a) I *would study* more, | **if** I *had* time |
| (42a) She *could have passed* the course, | **if** she *had studied* more. |

In the main clause, speakers will use either *would, could,* or sometimes *might*. *Would* implies an intended or desired action or event; *could* and *might* imply a possibility or possible option. *Would* occurs more frequently than *could* or *might* in conditional sentences.

The conditional use of *would, could,* and *might* must be understood from their occurrence in discourse. Like all modals, *would* and *could/might* have different meanings and functions, depending on the structure of the sentence and the context in which they are used.

Discovery Activity 6 provides practice in identifying the different uses of *would*. You can find the answers in the Answer Key at the end of this chapter.

---

**Discovery Activity 6: Would**

Look at the excerpts.

1. Underline the *would* modal verb phrase. Be sure to underline the entire verb phrase, not just the modal.
2. Explain each meaning of *would*.

**A.**

When the three children lived in the Baudelaire home, there was a huge dictionary in their parents' library, and Klaus would often use it to help him with difficult books.
[Snicket, L. (2000). *The miserable mill* (p. 123). New York: HarperCollins.]

**B.**

"We don't have to go," Violet said. "We could run away..."
"...; Who would protect us from Count Olaf, if we were all by ourselves?"
[Snicket, L. (2000). *The miserable mill* (p. 151). New York: HarperCollins.]

**C.**

The bank officer would prepare the CTR as required and place a copy in the files,
only instead of shipping the original to the IRS, he'd run it though a shredder...
[Grafton, S. (2004). *R is for ricochet* (p. 90). New York: G.P. Putnam's Sons.]

**D.**

"...If I'd suspected who he was at Baskul, of course, I'd have tried to get in touch
with Delhi about him—it would have been merely a public duty.
[Hilton, J. (1933/1971). *Lost horizon* (p. 118). New York: Pocket Books.]

## Modals and ESL/EFL Learners

The modal auxiliary verbs present a number of problems for learners of English,
some of which we have touched upon in *Learner difficulties*. Since the modals
represent many difficulties for ESL/EFL learners, we discuss these difficulties in
greater detail here.

Some of these problems have to do with the form of the modals, particularly
at lower levels of proficiency. ESL/EFL learners may try to add *to* + verb after a
modal:

*We must to go.
*We will can go.

Or, they may string more than one modal together:

*We should being go.

Or, they may inflect the main verb:

*We could went early.

Another difficulty for learners is that *would* is often reduced in spoken English
making it hard to identify and distinguish. In written informal English, *would* is
frequently written as a contraction *'d* and learners may confuse this with the past
perfect *'d* as in Discovery Activity 5, Excerpt D and in the following table.

| | |
|---|---|
| (43) He**'d** visit us if he had time. | conditional *would* |
| (44) Roy said he**'d** visited us before. | past perfect, auxiliary *had* |

## Modal Meaning and Use

*What do ESL/EFL learners find the hardest about modals?*

▶ *Learner difficulties*

The greatest difficulty for ESL/EFL learners lies in the meanings and uses of the modals. Because the modals have more than one meaning or function, as well as many nuances of meaning, even advanced ESL/EFL learners often have difficulty both in understanding intended meanings and in choosing the correct modal auxiliary in the correct form to express what they actually mean. This is compounded by the fact that the modals have social pragmatic functions related to politeness and status, which are not always easy for learners to distinguish and use.

In addition, it is sometimes very difficult to isolate the exact meaning of a modal, as for example:

*I should tell my husband first.*

Does *should* in this sentence indicate obligation or advisability? Although context will help to clarify the meaning of a modal, the line between meanings may be fuzzy.

Use and choice of modals also vary somewhat regionally across the United States. In some areas, for instance, *ought to* occurs more frequently than in others.[1]

Furthermore, ESL/EFL learners often find it difficult to remember the changes in meaning and use when certain modals are used in affirmative versus negative statements. They may question, for instance, why English uses both *must* and *have to* for present and future necessity but only *had to* for past necessity:

(45) You **must** fill out this form.

*or*

(46) You **have to** fill out this form

but only:

(47) You **had to** fill out this form.

Likewise, ESL/EFL learners have trouble when a modal changes its meaning when the time reference changes. Some modals, such as *should* and *must*, mean something different when used for present versus past time reference. Learners may have trouble with the notion that *should* means a suggestion or advice when in a sentence such as:

---

[1] In addition, in some parts of the southern United States it is not unusual to string together *might could*, e.g., We might could help you with that. However, unlike choosing between *ought to* and *should*, this use of *might could* is not generally considered Standard American English.

(48) You should do your homework.

but a reprimand when in:

(49) You should have done your homework.

## Modals and Pronunciation

*Do ESL/EFL learners have trouble with accurately hearing the modals in spoken English?*

▶ *Learner difficulties*

As we saw earlier in our exploration of the different modals, they are frequently usually pronounced in a reduced form; therefore, learners may have difficulties in hearing and identifying them. Remember that by "reduced" we mean that a word does not receive stress in a sentence.

For example, in the sentence, *I can pick up the kids from school for you,* learners may not hear the *can* in the sentence because this word does not receive stress. They may then misinterpret the statement as: *I pick up the kids from school for you*—a sentence that by its structure conveys a statement of fact.

When *should, would,* and *could* are followed by *have* + past participle, the *have* is frequently reduced to sounding like "of". Both inexperienced native speakers of English and learners of English need practice in identifying this reduced *have* as "have" and not "of."

In sum, ESL/EFL learners have various issues in mastering the modals. These can be divided into two types: structural and semantic/pragmatic. Structural difficulties refer to difficulties in form, e.g. using "to" + verb infinitive after a modal rather than the simple or base verb. Semantic and pragmatic difficulties refer to choosing the appropriate modal for a given situations.

Given the many difficulties learners have in recognizing, understanding, and producing appropriate modals, semi-modals, and related structures, it is essential that learners have numerous opportunities to practice identifying meaning and use of modals in a variety of contexts, both written and oral.

# Summary

## Modal Auxiliaries

- The class called modal auxiliaries consists of a number of words that are considered "pure" modals and other related structures.

- The modal auxiliaries are characterized by:

  - multiple of meanings
  - lack of guarantee that there are parallel meanings between

    - their affirmative and negative forms
    - past and present forms

  - lack of inflections, including tense, except for *could* in the sense of ability.

    - past time reference conveyed by the use of *modal* + *have* + past participle

- There are a variety of related structures,

  - some of which inflect for person and tense.
  - some are used only in certain time references.
  - some are more informal than their modal counterpart(s).

- *Would* and *could* are both modals and conditional forms.

  - As conditionals, they form "if" clauses
  - "if" clauses refer to something hypothetical, unreal, contrary-to-fact, or untrue.

| The Two Types of Auxiliary Verbs | |
|---|---|
| **Primary** | **Modal** |
| be, have, do | will, would, must, ought to, can, could may, might |

| Primary Auxiliary Verbs versus Modal Auxiliary Verbs | | |
|---|---|---|
| **type** | | **explanation** |
| primary auxiliary verb | I *am* running. | *am* = primary auxiliary, part of the progressive aspect, *be* + present participle |
| modal auxiliary verb | I *can* run. | *can* = modal auxiliary, conveying the semantic meaning of *ability* |
| primary auxiliary verb | I *have* run. | *have* = primary auxiliary, part of the present perfect aspect, *have* + present participle |
| modal auxiliary | I *should* have run yesterday, but I didn't. | *should* = modal auxiliary, conveying the semantic meaning of something not done. *should* + *have* + *run* conveys a past meaning. |

## Modals and Related Structures

| | |
|---|---|
| can, could<br>*related structure:* be able to | **ability**<br>Jane can drive.<br>Jane is able to drive.<br>Jane could drive when she was sixteen. |
| can, may | **permission**<br>You can go.<br>You may go. |
| can, could, would | **polite request**<br>Can you pass the salt?<br>Could you pass the salt?<br>Would you pass the salt? |
| may, might, could | **possibility, probability**<br>We may go to Venice next year.<br>We might go to Venice next year.<br>We could go to Venice some time. |
| must | **logical deduction**<br>The doorbell is ringing. It must be Tanya. |
| must<br>*related structures:* have to, have got to | **necessity, obligation**<br>You must have a license to drive.<br>You have to have a license to drive.<br>You have got to have a license to drive. |
| must not | **prohibition**<br>You must not drive without a license. |
| should, ought to<br>*related structure:* had better | **advice, suggestion**<br>You should listen to your mother.<br>You ought to listen to your mother.<br>You had better listen to your mother. |
| should have, ought to have | **unfilled expectation, mistake**<br>You're late.<br>You should have left earlier.<br>You ought to have left earlier. |
| will<br>*related structure:* be going to | **future**<br>You will take the required test.<br>You are going to take the required test. |
| would | **possibility, capability, wish, conditional**<br>Adam would leave if he could. |
| would | **past custom, habit**<br>She would always drive to work. |
| would have | **wish, conditional, hypothetical, past**<br>Taylor wishes she would have studied more. |

**Note:** This list is intended as a general summary only. It does not necessarily include all the modals in all their possible meanings or communicative functions.

# Practice Activities

## *Activity 1: Polite Requests*

1. Soften the following commands by using different modals. You can do this orally or write your responses on a separate sheet of paper.
2. Discuss how the different modals change the intensity or directness of the command.
3. Would you add any other word(s)? Why or why not?

*Example*:
Help me do my homework.
Could you help me do my homework?
a. Get me a pen!
b. Stop talking!
c. Come on time!
d. Lend me your notes!

## *Activity 2: Semantic Meanings*

(a) Look at the following groups of sentences.
(b) Explain the differences in meaning between the sentences in each group.

(1a) I should talk to the teacher about my grade.
(1b) I should have talked to the teacher about my grade.
(1c) I shouldn't have forgotten to talk to the teacher about my grade.

(2a) Jean must have the receipt.
(2b) Jean must have lost the receipt.

(3a) Jason could help you with your homework.
(3b) Jason could have helped you with your homework.

(4a) Jin can speak English.
(4b) Jin couldn't speak English until he was a teenager.

(5a) You had better get your license renewed soon.
(5b) You should get your license renewed.

(6a) I was able to study abroad in college.
(6b) I could have studied abroad in college.
(6c) I should have studied abroad.

## *Activity 3:* Can *and* May

1. Read the following excerpt.
2. Discuss what the author is trying to convey by using *may* versus *can*.

...for years and years Danny has been begging his father to let him run the locomotive some night. For years and years, his father has been saying no. Then, finally, the night comes. "Can I run the engine tonight, Daddy?" asks Danny, who is too young to know about "can" and "may."

[Kaufman, G. (1957/2001). Annoy Kaufman, Inc. In D. Remnick & H. Finder (Eds.), *Fierce pajamas: An anthology of humor writing from the New Yorker* (p. 294). New York: Random House.]

## Activity 4: Mixed Modals, Semi-modals, and Related Structures

1. Read the following excerpts.
2. Identify the modal verb phrases.
3. Explain the meaning and function of each modal verb phrase.

**A.**

Should I tell Reba what was going on or should I not? More important, should I bring her father into the loop?...if I told her about Beck and Onni, what would she do? She was going to crash and burn. And if I *didn't* tell her and she somehow got wind of it...much crashing and burning would ensue anyway...

[Grafton, S. (2004). *R is for ricochet* (p. 104). New York: G.P. Putnam's Sons.]

**B.**

I told her to take her time thinking about the situation before she decided what to do. Vince Turner might be in a hurry, but he was asking a lot and, one way or the other, she'd better be convinced.

[Grafton, S. (2004). *R is for ricochet* (p. 138). New York: G.P. Putnam's Sons.]

**C.**

Kiloran knew that frightened whispers in Cavasar were spreading the story of Josarian's death. That was as it should be. He held the city now. Nothing could threaten that... Sileria's ancient capital must be brought to its knees.

(Resnick, L. (2004). *The white dragon: In fire forged, part one* (pp. 318–319). New York: Tor.]

**D.**

"You should have kept your court date," I said to Cantell. "You might have only gotten community service."
"I didn't have anything to wear," she wailed. "Look at me. I'm a house! Nothing fits..."
"You're not as big as me," Lula said... "You just gotta know how to shop. We should go out shopping together someday."

[Evanovich, J. (2004). *The big ones* (p. 18). New York: St. Martin's Press.]

**E.**

She felt saddened by the air of defeat which seemed to descend upon her assistant whenever the conversation turned to her personal circumstances. There was no real need for Mma. Makutsi to feel like this. She might have had difficulties in her life until now—certainly one should not underestimate what it must be like to grow up in Bobonong, that rather dry and distant place from where Mma. had come...

[McCall Smith, A. (2002). *The Kalahari typing school for men* (p. 14). New York: Pantheon Books.]

**F.**

"I suppose we should have told you were going—"

"—out in the woods," Florida said... "We probably should have told you."

"No call to do that," Sairy said... "Kids ought to have a little choice, that's what I think. They ought to be able to do stuff without someone watching over their shoulders every minute."

[Creech, S. (2002). *Ruby holler* (p. 153). New York: HarperCollins.]

## Activity 5: Finding and Analyzing Modals, Semi-Modals and Related Structures (optional additional practice)

1. Find 2–3 excerpts from any printed source with examples of the modals and semi-modals discussed in this chapter.
2. Identify each modal and semi-modal verb phrase and consider the meaning of each.
3. Make photocopies of your excerpts for each member of your class and bring these copies to class.
4. Form small groups of 4–6 participants.
5. In your small group distribute among yourselves the copies that the members of your group prepared.
6. After each participant has received a copy of each excerpt from the other member's of the group, work individually, examine these excerpts and:

- identify the modals and semi-modals
- consider the meaning of each

When everyone in the group has had a chance to finish, together as a group:

- Discuss whether you all identified the same structures. If there is disagreement, consider why.
- Compare the meanings each member suggested for the modals and semi-modals. If there is disagreement, consider why.

## Activity 6: Would, Could, Might

1. Underline the different modal verb phrases with *would, could* and *might*. Be sure to underline the entire verb phrase and not just the modal.
2. Explain the different meanings and uses of these three modals in this excerpt.
3. There is also the idiomatic structure *used to* in this excerpt. Could you substitute *would* here and keep the same meaning?

Mr. Preble was a plump middle-aged lawyer... He used to kid with his stenographer about running away with him. "Let's run away together," he would say... "All righty," she would say.

One rainy Monday afternoon, Mr. Preble was more serious about it than usual...

"My wife would be glad to get rid of me," he said.

"Would she give you a divorce?" asked the stenographer.

"I don't suppose so," he said.

"You'd have to get rid of your wife," she said.

Mr. Preble was unusually silent at dinner that night. About half an hour after coffee, he spoke,...

"Let's go down in the cellar," Mr. Preble said to his wife.

"What for?" she said... "We never did go down in the cellar that I remember..."

"Supposing I said it meant a whole lot to me," began Mr. Preble... "We could pick up pieces of coal... We might get up some kind of a game with pieces of coal."

[Thurber, J. (1935/2001). Mr. Preble gets rid of his wife. In D. Remnick & H. Finder (Eds.), *Fierce pajamas: An anthology of humor writing from the New Yorker* (pp. 133-134). New York: Random House.]

## *Activity 7: Error Analysis*

The following excerpts were written by ESL/EFL learners. There are errors in modal verb choices and forms. Since these are authentic excerpts, there are other errors in addition. However, **ignore any other errors.**

1) Underline each error in modal verb phrase form and choice you find. Remember to **focus *only* on modal errors**.
2) For each error in modal choice:

- Discuss which modal the writer probably intended
- Provide the correct modal verb phrase and discuss why the learner may have made the error.

**A.**

I can swim very good. My brother cans swim very good too. We learn to can swim together. My uncle can swims very good. He teaches us to can swim.

**B.**

If I were a giant, I will be bored. Because I think I can't to do anything! I can't to study because books can to be small and I can't to see. Because I'm too big I can't to do anything!

**C.**

Some students want to spend most of their time for academic study in high school. I think that students need to study different things. I support that all students should taking art and music class. If school has art or music class for everybody, students will can learn those skills easier than outside school. Schools might to provide students with good instruction, art materials, or music instruments. I think that schools should be give the opportunity to each student to study both academic subjects and art and music. I would rather students should be playing and creating than studying all the time, and there might be became good life experience.

**D.**

If I win the lottery, I would can give my parents new house. They will be very happy if I gave them big new house with beautiful garden. If I had much money, I would could do much travel. If I had time, I would may go around the world. I could study anywhere. If I went to France, I would can learn French very well.

**E.**

When I graduated I was hoping that I could became a business lawyer. After seven years as business lawyer, I would decided that I would became a real estate person.

**F.**

When I was five, I started going to school and I was responsible to get ready by myself. With the time, I was getting more responsibilities. I began a part-time work before and after school. In the morning, I was working with my mother at home. She sold sweet rolls to the stores and I must help her. I must to put the sweet rolls in groups of five, and then, I put them into a plastic bag, and I must go to the stores that had already submitted their orders and delivered to them. Later when I was a student, I had a part-time job as a secretary. I must got at the office at 7:00 p.m.

**G.**

Can women successfully combine family and career? Everything must changed in this world. What are the roles of man and woman in family? What is the goal of woman's life? What can to make her happy and successful? When I begin to think about this I feel that nowadays woman should do many things. She is responsible for everything including children, husband, job, money.

## Answer Key: Chapter 7 Discovery Activities

### Discussion: Activity 1

*Excerpt A*

- The narrator is referring to a single past ability by using *I was able to reach* and only this structure can be used.

*Excerpt B*

- the narrator uses both *I was able to find out* and *could get in/out*.
  - The first structure refers to a single past ability and only this structure can be used.
  - The second structure refers to a repeated or general past ability. Although *be able to* could be substituted, it sounds awkward and wordy in this particular context.

## Discussion: Activity 3

*Excerpt A*

- *must have sprinted*: logical deduction or high probability in the past

*Excerpt B*

- *must be*: logical deduction or high probability in the present.

*Excerpt C*

- three examples of the use of *have to* in the sense of necessity.

  - The first is a past reference to future time in the past, *was going to have to*.
  - The second two examples are simple past, *had to stay* and *had to take*.

*Excerpt D*

- illustrates the use of *must* to refer to requirements or laws in the present, *must submit* and *must present*.

*Excerpt E*

- *must* together with *have* + *been* refers to a logical deduction or strong probability about an event or action in the past.

  - the only past form of *must* referring to necessity is *had to* as illustrated above in Excerpt C.

*Excerpt F*

- *have got to* in the second sentence, *I've got to go*.

  - ESL/EFL learners might confuse this structure with that in the last sentence, *I've gotten*. Although the two structures look similar, the *I've gotten* is the present perfect form of *get* in the sense of "reach."

## Discussion: Activity 4

*Excerpt A*

- Tiller uses *had better* followed by the transitive separable phrasal verb *get up*. *We'd better get that tent up* stresses the advisability of the action Tiller is proposing.

*Excerpt B*

- the speaker uses *shouldn't go* in present time to describe his doctor's advice.

*Excerpt C*

- strong advice: *had better*

*Excerpt D*

- present suggestion: *ought to know*

*Excerpt E*

- three instances of advice or suggestion, *should transfer, ought to be* and *should specify*

## Discussion: Discovery Activity 5

*Excerpt A*

- *should have done*: unheeded, ignored past advice.

*Excerpt B*

- *should be* and *should comfort*: strong present possibility or expectation.

*Excerpt C*

- *should have come down* and *should have sent*: unfulfilled past obligations.

*Excerpt D*

- *should see:* future suggestion
- *could talk*: future possibility

## Discussion: Discovery Activity 6

*Excerpt A*

- *would use*: habitual or repeated action in the past.

*Excerpt B*

- *would protect*: hypothetical question *Who would protect us?*

*Excerpt C*

- two instances of *would* to describe a repeated or habitual action, one of which is contracted: *would prepare, he'd run*

*Excerpt D*

- two examples of *'d* as a contraction:
  - *I'd suspected*: contraction of the past perfect form *I had suspected*
  - *I'd have tried*: contraction of *I would have tried* and referring to something contrary-to-fact in the past

  Because the contracted form *I'd* is identical in both instances, ESL/EFL learners have difficulty distinguishing between the two forms.
- *would have been*: past possibility

# Chapter 8
# Basic Sentence Patterns and Major Variations

## Introduction

This chapter reviews sentence constituents and basic sentences, and then investigates variations of basic sentences. The chapter is divided into four sections.
Section 1 reviews basic sentences. The next section explores different types of
questions; the third considers passive constructions, and Section 3 looks at sentence
substitutions.

In Chapter 1, Practice Activity 2 asked you to create as many original sentences
as possible using these nonsense words:

mishiffen a drinking keg gwisers some were stoshly frionized

The purpose of the activity was twofold. It reinforced the idea that derivational morphemes provide clues to word class in English. It also illustrated the fixed nature
of word order in English. Although there were many possible sentences you could
create, the number of total possible sentences, about 28, was constrained by the
word order of English. The sentence parts and the way they combine create basic
sentences, as in:

Some mishiffen gwisers were stoshly drinking a frionized keg.
or
Stoshly frionized, some gwisers were a mishiffen drinking keg.

The sentence parts are sentence constituents, which you as a native or highly proficient non-native speaker of English recognize intuitively, even though the words
themselves are generally nonsense words. Take another example:

friends the exuberantly walked two to their large house happy

The way you choose to combine these words again reveals some of the basic
constituents of sentences. Constituents are the basic units of a sentence, including

noun, adjective, adverb, prepositional, and verb phrases. Sentence constituents are combined in meaningful ways to form sentences. You probably wrote:

(1) *The two exuberantly happy friends walked to their large house.*

What you wrote is a basic sentence consisting of noun phrase, verb phrase and prepositional phrase.

Let us now review sentence constituents, which you are already familiar with from other chapters.

## Section 1: Types of Sentence Constituents

### *Noun Phrases and Prepositional Phrases*

In its most basic form, a noun phrase consists of just one word, a noun. Noun phrases, however, often consist of more than just one word: a noun and another element or elements. As we saw in Chapter 3, the elements that can occur in a noun phrase include determiners, modifiers, and prepositional phrases. Determiners include articles, quantifiers, numbers, possessive adjectives, and demonstrative adjectives:

| Noun phrase | | |
|---|---|---|
| **determiner** | **noun (headword)** | **type of determiner** |
| a/the | boy | article |
| some | friends | quantifier |
| two | bicycles | number |
| her | coat | possessive adjective |
| this | car | demonstrative adjective |

Grammar books often refer to the main word in a noun phrase as the *headword*. The headword of the noun phrase may be modified by any number of modifiers. Modifiers include determiners, other nouns, adjectives, and adverb-adjective combinations:

| **modifier** | **noun (headword)** | **type of modifier** |
|---|---|---|
| smart | girls | adjective |
| quickly finished | homework | adverb + adjective |
| brick | wall | noun |

Noun phrases can also include prepositional phrases. Prepositional phrases are units of words that begin with a preposition and include a noun phrase:

| Prepositional Phrase | |
|---|---|
| **preposition** | **noun phrase** |
| in | the bedroom |
| by | some scattered rocks |
| from | that new reporter |
| under | her oak desk |

## Verb Phrases

As you will recall from Chapters 5 and 6, a verb phrase can consist of a single verb, a phrasal verb, auxiliary verbs + a main verb. Some grammarians expand the definition of verb phrase to include, a main verb + "to" infinitive or a main verb + gerund. Other grammarians include verbs, auxiliaries, complements, and other modifiers in their definition of a verb phrase. We will restrict our definition of a verb phrase to a verb and any auxiliaries.

| Verb Phrase | | |
|---|---|---|
| | **Type** | **Tense** |
| walked | single verb | past |
| picked up | phrasal verb | past |
| is driving | *be* auxiliary + main verb in present participle form | present progressive |
| has been driving | *have* + *been* + main verb in present participle form | present perfect progressive |
| will have been driving | *will* + *have* + *been* + main verb in present participle form | future perfect progressive |
| should visit | modal auxiliary + main verb | present/future |
| wants to go | main verb + *to* infinitive | present |
| likes driving | main verb + gerund | present |

Verb phrases also include the negative *not*, e.g. *did not work* or *is not driving.* Some grammar books also consider adverbs that occur within a verb phrase part of the verb phrase, e.g. *has **already** been driving*; generally, however, only the actual verbs are considered to constitute a verb phrase.

See how well you know the different types of phrases by doing Discovery Activity 1. Keep in mind that a phrase consists of one or more words. You can find the answers to this Discovery Activity at the end of the chapter in the section labeled Answer Key.

**Discovery Activity 1: Identifying Noun Phrases, Prepositional Phrases and Verb Phrases**

1. On a separate sheet of paper, make a chart with three columns. Label one column *noun phrase*, the second *verb phrase*, and the last one *prepositional phrase.*

2. In each of the excerpts, find the noun phrases, verb phrases, and prepositional phrases and enter them into your chart as in the example below.

*Example:*

| **Noun phrase** | **Verb Phrase** | **Prepositional Phrase** |
|---|---|---|
| Scuffy | sailed | into a big city |

**A.**

... Scuffy sailed into a big city... Horses stamped and truck motors roared, streetcars
clanged and people shouted.
   [Crampton, G. (1955/1946). *Scuffy the tugboat and his adventures down the
river.* New York: Little Golden Books. No page numbers.]

**B.**

Felix stopped walking. He had a gift.... Mr. Nubble frowned.... "You're stepping
on my house!" Felix jumped off the hose...
   [Buller, J., & Schade, S. (1996). *Felix and the 400 frogs* (pp. 6–8). New York:
Random House.]

**C.**

She waved toward the pond. Four hundred frogs' heads poked out of the water...
   [Buller, J., & Schade, S. (1996). *Felix and the 400 frogs* (pp. 15–16). New York:
Random House.]

## *Adjective and Adverb Phrases*

Adjective phrases include one or more adjectives. An adjective can follow one or
more adverbs to form an adjective phrase.

| | | |
|---|---|---|
| | tall, young, unhappy | 3 adjectives |
| **Adjective phrase** | exuberantly happy | adverb + adjective |
| | very cold, wet | adverb + 2 adjectives |

Adverb phrases include one more adverbs. Adverbs, as we observed in Chapter 4,
can modify verbs, adjectives, adverbs, or just about anything in a sentence.

| | | |
|---|---|---|
| **Adverb phrase** | carefully | adverb |
| | quite readily | 2 adverbs |

Using our nonsense sentences, we noted earlier in this chapter that sentence
constituents, or phrases combine in fixed ways to form basic sentences. Although
the words in each type of phrase can change, the order in which the sentence

constituents are placed is fixed. Only adverb phrases can be placed in different parts of a sentence. The following sentence is composed of phrases that we have seen in the sample charts. See if you can separate the sentences into the different phrases and identify the type of phrase each one is. The answer is in the Answer Key.

(2) The smart boy very carefully picked up some scattered rocks by the river.

If you can do this successfully, you have a clear understanding of sentence constituents and basic sentence patterns of English, and are ready to explore variations on the basic sentence.

We now turn to examining sentences that are still composed of these sentence constituents, but that are no longer basic sentences. We will look at three categories of variations on basic sentences: Section 2: Questions; Section 3: The Passive, and Section 4: Substitution.

## Section 2: Questions

### *Yes/No Questions*

In English, there are two basic types of questions, *yes, no* questions and *wh-questions*. The first group, *yes-no* questions, refers to questions which can be answered with either a "yes" or a "no." Yes/no questions follow our first auxiliary rule.

#### *Do ESL/EFL learners have trouble forming yes/no questions?*

ESl/EFL learners find yes/no question formation easier for some verb tenses than for others. Try the following Discovery Activity to see if you can discover which ones are generally easier for them to learn and why.

---

**Discovery Activity 2: Yes/No Questions**

Look at the following sentences.

1. Try to explain how each question is formed.
2. Which questions do you think are most difficult for ESL/EFL learners? Why?

*Example*

Are you happy?
The subject *(you)* and the verb *(be)* are inverted. *Be* is the main verb.

1. Is she coming?
2. Was she waiting for me?
3. Have you seen the new movie with Tom Hanks?

---

4. Had he been working hard?
5. Does she travel a lot?
6. Did you call home last night?
7. Can you see me?

## Discussion: Discovery Activity 2

| | |
|---|---|
| 1. **Is** she coming? | Subject-verb inversion: *be* is the first auxiliary |
| 2. **Was** she waiting for me? | |
| 3. **Have** you seen the new movie with Tom Hanks? | Subject-verb inversion: *have* is the first auxiliary |
| 4. **Had** he been working hard | |
| 5. **Can** you see me? | subject-verb inversion: *can* is a modal auxiliary |
| 6. **Does** she travel a lot? | Insertion of *do* auxiliary: *Do* must be inserted in the appropriate tense; main verb remains in its base form (no inflection) |
| 7. **Did** you call home last night | |

When you look at the questions, you will notice that Sentences (1–5) follow our first auxiliary rule: Whenever there is one or more auxiliary in a verb phrase, the first auxiliary moves to initial position when forming a question.

Sentences (6) and (7) follow the corollary to this pattern that we have discussed repeatedly: Whenever there is no auxiliary present, an auxiliary must be inserted. As we saw in Chapters 5 and 6, simple present and simple past have no auxiliary; therefore, we must use *do/does* or *did*. In addition, the main verb retains it base form. This means that it does not take the third person present tense –*s* inflection (*she travels*), nor the past tense –*ed* inflection (*you called*).

The exception to this is the verb *be*, as we see in the Discovery Activity example sentence. *Be*, whether functioning as a main verb or an auxiliary, always inverts with the subject in questions.

Remember that the *do* auxiliary insertion and the corresponding forms are more difficult for ESL/EFL learners than inverting the first auxiliary and the subject.

### Negative Yes/No Questions

*Yes/no* questions can also be negative. Often such questions imply an element of surprise, disbelief, or disdain because the speaker has a different expectation in mind.

(3) **Aren't** you happy?     (You should be happy; you have a good life.)
(4) **Isn't** she coming?     (She said she was.)
(5) **Didn't** you drive?     (You always drive.)

We will now look at a second type of questions, *wh- questions*, and how they are formed.

## Wh-Questions

The second group of question types are questions formed with a question word, such as *who, what, when, where,* or *how.* These question words are also referred to as interrogative words.

Look at the *wh*-questions in Discovery 3. See if you can come up with the rules of *wh*-question formation. You can find the answers to this activity in the Answer Key at the end of the chapter. Be sure you try all of the sentences in Discovery Activity before you check your answers. You may find parts of this Discovery Activity difficult to explain, which will be the same areas of difficulty for ESL/EFL learners.

### Discovery Activity 3: Wh-Questions

Look at the following sentences.

1. Try to explain how each *wh*-question is formed.
2. Which *wh*-questions do you think are most difficult for ESL/EFL learners? Why?

*Example*

When is he coming?
The *wh*-question word is in initial position. Then the subject and verb are inverted according to the first auxiliary rule.

1. Where was he going?
2. Why has she called so often?
3. When is the party?
4. When did she call?
5. Who wrote that book?
6. Who did you call last night?
7. Who are you calling now?
8. What did you read last summer?
9. What author do you like the best?

### *How can I explain* **wh-question formation to my students?**

Question words follow our auxiliary rule **if** the question word is asking for information about the **subject** of the verb. To review, our auxiliary rule states that:

- if there is an auxiliary in the verb phrase, the question word is then followed by subject-verb inversion. If there is more than one auxiliary, only the **first** auxiliary changes places with the subject.

- if the main verb is *be*, it inverts with the subject.
- if the main verb is in simple present or simple past tense, we must insert the *do* auxiliary and leave the main verb in its base form.

***Why did we sometimes ignore this rule in some of the questions we formed in Discovery Activity 3?***

### *Who* and *What*

Two of our question words, *who* and *what*, differ somewhat as you saw in Sentences (6)–(9) in the previous Discovery Activity. The question words *who* and *what* can ask for information about the **subject** of the verb **or** the **object** of the verb:

- When *who* or *what* asks for the **subject**, there is no change in word order, and we do not need to add the *do* auxiliary to simple present and simple past tense verb.
- When *who* or *what* asks for the **object**, the word order changes and we need to follow our first auxiliary rule.

Look at the charts and see if you can determine whether *who* and *what* are asking for information about the subject of the verb or the object of the verb. Note also what happens with respect to auxiliaries. Compare these examples with Sentences (6)–(9) in Discovery Activity 3.

| Asking for the *Subject* of the Verb | | | | | |
|---|---|---|---|---|---|
| **Question** | | | **Answer** | | |
| **wh-word** | **verb** | **complement** | **subject** | **verb** | **complement** |
| Who | called | last night? | Sam | called | last night. |
| What | is | your name? | My name | is | Brandon. |

| Asking for the *Object* of the Verb | | | | | |
|---|---|---|---|---|---|
| **Question** | | | | **Answer** | |
| **wh-word** | **auxiliary** | **subject** | **main verb** | **subject** | **verb** | **object** |
| Who | is | Ryan | calling? | Ryan | is calling | Marty. |
| What | did | Kate | read? | Kate | read | a newspaper. |

### *Is there another way to explain wh-question formation?*

Another way to visualize *wh-question* formation is to think about adding *who, what, when, where, why* or *how* to a simple question. If the *wh-question* word does not change the meaning of the basic question, it is asking for information about the object of the sentence.

| Basic Question with *be* Auxiliary *Is she driving?* | | |
|---|---|---|
| **Question word** | | **Possible response** |
| Who (m) | | She's driving Kevin. |
| What | | She's driving a Honda. |
| Which car | | She's driving the Honda Civic. |
| Whose car | is she driving? | She's driving my sister's car. |
| When | | She's driving tonight. |
| Where | | She's driving in New York. |
| Why | | She's driving because there is no bus. |
| How | | She's driving fast. |

| Basic Question with *do* Auxiliary *Did he drive?* | | |
|---|---|---|
| **Question word** | | **Possible response** |
| *Who (m)* | | He drove his mother. |
| What | | He drove a convertible. |
| Which (car) | | He drove the red one. |
| Whose car | did he drive? | He drove Nancy's car. |
| When | | He drove yesterday. |
| Where | | He drove on the highway. |
| Why | | He drove because he was in a hurry. |
| How | | He drove carefully. |

Preparing simplified versions of such charts can be helpful to ESL/EFL learners who are having difficulties with correctly forming *wh*-questions.

### *Who* versus *Whom*

#### *Is it* who *or* whom?

In formal prescriptive English, the question word *who* has two forms, *who* and *whom*. *Who* is used when asking for the subject and *whom* for the object. In modern English, *who* is replacing *whom* in all but the most formal situations.

| | | |
|---|---|---|
| (6) *Who(m)* did you see? | I saw *Leon*. | **Leon = object** |
| (7) *Who* called you? | *Dana* called me. | **Dana = subject** |

### *How Much* versus *How Many*

#### *What about* how many *and* how much?

*How* combines with *much* and *many* to ask questions about quantity. Remember in Chapter 3 we discussed count and noncount nouns. The choice between *much* and *many* depends on whether the noun to which *how* is referring is noncount (Sentence 8) or plural count (Sentence 9).

(8) How *much* change do you have?
(9) How *many* oranges are you buying?

For an unknown quantity, we use *how much*:

(10) How *much* is that doggie in the window?

*How* often combines with adjectives and adverbs to ask about descriptions and characteristics:

(11) How *big* is her new house?
(12) How *often* does the supervisor visit?

This next Discovery Activity provides practice in identifying different types of questions and in examining word order. The answers are in the Answer Key.

---

**Discovery Activity 4: Identifying Questions**

Look at the following excerpts.

1. Underline the questions.
2. Decide whether they are *yes/no* or *wh-questions*.
3. Describe the word order in each question you have identified. For example, is there subject-verb inversion? Is there a *do* auxiliary? If yes, why?

**A.**

Pepito was afraid of heights. So when it was time to leave the nest, he decided that he would go his own way . . . until he came to a river.
"Can you swim?" asked the fish. . . He was making real progress. But then he came to a busy road.
"Why don't you fly over?" asked the gopher.
"I'm afraid of heights," said Pepito. . . Finally, he saw his brothers' and sisters' new tree. . . "Pepito!" they cheered. "How did you get here?"
   [Beck, S. (2001). *Pepito the brave*. New York: Dutton Children's Books, No page numbers.]

**B.**

"I have a question," Violet said, although the truth of the matter is she had many questions. . . . "How can you force small children to work in a lumbermill?" was one of them. "How can you treat us so horridly, after all we've been through?" was another... But none of these seemed like questions that were proper to ask ... So Violet ... asked, "What is your name?"

[Snicket, L. (2000). *A series of unfortunate events, book 4: The miserable mill* (pp. 55–56). New York: HarperCollins.]

### C.

"Alice darlin'," said Uncle Harold, "do you think you could entertain your grandfather while we pack up the wedding presents... ?"

"Sure," I said ... I walked over to where Grandpa McKinley sat...

"What was your first car, Grandpa?"...

"I had a 1927 Model T Roadster," he said...

"What did the car have?" I asked...

Two days later ... we got word that Uncle Charlie had died of a heart attack on his honeymoon...

"Can honeymoons kill you?" I asked Dad.

"Usually they make you feel better, not worse," said Dad.

"Did you and Mom have a honeymoon?" I wanted to know...

[Naylor, P.(2002). *Starting with alice* (pp. 84–86). New York: Atheneum.]

*What are some of the problems ESL/EFL learners have with wh-questions?*

▶ *Learner difficulties*

In Discover Activity 3, you observed some of the problems ESL/EFL learners have with forming *wh-* questions. To review, ESL/EFL learners sometimes confuse the use of *what* and *who* in subject position, and insert the *do* auxiliary inappropriately or leave it out:

(13) Kelly came last night.

*Who *did come* last night?
*Who *did came* last night?

(14) I had a 1975 Beetle Volkswagen.

*What the car have?
*What car I have?

ESL/EFL learners sometimes also have difficulty with subject / verb inversion and the *wh-question* words:

*(15) When the car is coming?
*(16) Where you have been?

We turn now to examine another variation on the basic sentence, the *passive*.

## Section 3: Passive

Many grammar books discuss the active or passive use of a verb as *voice*. Active voice refers to sentences where the "doer" or the "agent" is the grammatical subject and the "receiver" of the action is the grammatical object.

Only transitive verbs, that is verbs that can take an object (See Chapter 5), can be found in the passive. This is because the **subject** of a sentence in *passive* voice is the original **object** of the verb in *active* voice.

### How do we form the passive?

The passive consists of *be* + main *verb* in the past participle form. The verb *be* can occur in any tense, but the main verb is always in the past participle form.

|  | Active | |
| --- | --- | --- |
| **subject** | **verb** | **object** |
| (17) Leonardo DaVinci | **painted** | *the Mona Lisa.* |

Sentence (17) is an active sentence. The verb *painted* is a transitive verb in the past. The subject of (17) is "Leonardo DaVinci" and the object of *painted* is "*the Mona Lisa.*"

|  | Passive | |
| --- | --- | --- |
| **subject** | **verb** | *by* **phrase** |
| (17a) *The Mona Lisa* | was painted | by Leonardo DaVinci |

Sentence (17a) is a passive sentence. The former subject "Leonardo DaVinci" is now part of a "by phrase" at the end of the sentence. The former object "*the Mona Lisa*" is now the subject of the passive verb phrase *was painted*. Since the time reference is past, *be* must also be in past tense followed by the past participle form of the main verb, *painted*.

## The "by-phrase"

### Do we always include a "by-phrase" in a passive sentence?

Many passive sentences include what is called a "by-phrase." The "by phrase" is the doer or agent of the verb in the original or active form of the passive sentence.

(18) *Romeo and Juliet* was written by Shakespeare.

Because Sentence (18) is written in the passive, the reader's attention is focused on the play, *Romeo and Juliet* rather than on the playwright, *Shakespeare*. The "by-phrase" is included because the name of the playwright is significant information.

Many passive sentences do not include a "by phrase." The "by phrase" is not included when the agent or doer is not important or anyone specific.

## The Passive and Tense

### Can we use the passive in every tense?

We can use the passive in every tense. The sentences in the following chart illustrate the passive in a variety of tenses. You will note that not all tenses are included, just enough to give you a sense of how the passive is formed in different tenses. The "by phrase" is not used in these examples because the doer is not significant.

| The Active and the Passive: Selected Tenses | | |
|---|---|---|
| (19) People **design** new computer games. | New computer games **are designed**. | **Present** *am, is, are* + past participle |
| (20) People **are designing** new computer games. | New computer games **are being designed** | **Present Progressive** *am, is, are* + *being* + past participle |
| (21) People **designed** new computer games. | New computer games **were designed**. | **Simple Past** *was, were* + past participle |
| (22) People **were designing** new computer games. | New computer games **were being designed.** | **Past Progressive** *was, were* + *being* + past participle |
| (23) People **have designed** new computer games. | New computer games **have been designed.** | **Present Perfect** *have/has been* + going to be participle |
| (24) People **had designed** new computer games. | New computer games **had been designed.** | **Past Perfect** *had* + *been* + past participle |
| (25) People **are going to** design new computer games. | New computer games **are going to be designed.** | **Future be going to** *am, is, are* + *going to be* + past participle |
| (26) People **will design** new computer games. | New computer games **will be designed.** | **Future *will*** *will* + *be* + past participle |
| (27) People **can design** new computer games. | New computer games **can be designed.** | **Modal Present/Future** *can* + *be* + past participle |
| (28) People **should have designed** new computer games. | New computer games **should have been designed.** | **Modal Past** *should* + *have* + *been* + past participle |

## The Passive versus the Active

### When do we use the passive voice instead of the active?

When the doer or agent is unimportant or self-evident, we prefer to use the passive. You will notice that the passive is more appropriate than the active in Sentences (19)–(28) because the object, *new computer games*, is more important than the doer, *people*. In these examples the "by phrase" has been omitted because "people" is very general, obvious, and inconsequential. In essence, the passive is used when we want to forefront or highlight the receiver, or when the doer is not important or unknown. The passive is often found in academic and science writing, as illustrated below. Can you identify the tense of each bolded passive verb phrase?

(29) But in addition to being fortunate in his adversaries, Washington **was blessed** with the personal qualities that counted most in a protracted war.

[Ellis, J. (2005, January). Washington takes charge. *Smithsonian*, 103.]

(30) So far the remains of sixty-five people **have been unearthed**. Many of the remains **were interred** as part of complex rituals. One headless man **had been laid** to rest on top of a pile of wild ox bones, while at least four children **were buried** with fox mandibles.

[Keys, D. (2003, November/December). *Archeology Today*, p. 10.]

In Sentence (29) *Washington was blessed* is not followed by a "by phrase" because the agent or doer is unknown. The sentence is an example of past passive. In Sentence (30) we see four examples of the passive:

- *have been unearthed*: the present perfect passive
- *had been laid*: the past perfect passive
- *were interred, were buried*: past passive

See if you can find all the passive verb phrases in Discovery Activity 5. Even if you are confident that you know and understand the passive, try at least Excerpt F. Check your answers with those in the Answer Key before moving on to the next section.

### Discovery Activity 5: Identifying the Passive

Look at the excerpts.

1. Underline the entire passive verb phrase.
2. Explain the tense of each passive verb phrase.

**A.**

Trevor Anderson has pored through twelfth-to-fourteenth-century documents to discover that ... [d]entures were fashioned from cow bones, teeth were whitened with a paste of sage and salt ...
[From the Trenches. (2005, January/February). *Archeology Today*, p. 13.]

**B.**

"I don't think he's a flight risk ... He can never be retried for the crime." "Pathetic," Julia muttered. "When this is all over, our illustrious district attorney should be recalled from office."
[Erickson, L. (2004). *Husband and Lover* (p. 96). New York: Berkley.]

## C.

Were the marines being sent as well as the grenadiers and light infantry companies? ... Other spies had been bringing news of the embarkation.... [Pitcairn] had been seen with a civilian cape wrapped about him heading for the Common.

[Forbes, E. (1971/1943). *Johnny tremain* (p. 217). New York: Yearling/ Doubleday.]

## D.

We know a great deal of the history of English because it has been written for about 1,000 years. Old English is scarcely recognizable as English... A line from *Beowulf* illustrates why Old English must be translated.

[Fromkin, V., Rodman, R., & Hyams, N. (2003). *An introduction to language.* (7th ed., (pp. 499–500)). Boston: Heinle.]

## E.

Edmond Casarella has developed an unusual color relief-print technique... Casarella makes a "rough" gouache sketch, which will continually be transformed through each step in the process. The sketch is then analyzed... One sheet of tracing paper is prepared for each block... When each block has been prepared, cutting can begin.

[Eichenberg, F. (1976). *The art of the print* (pp. 157–158). New York: Harry N. Abrams.]

## F.

Entering the room, I immediately sensed that something was wrong... Someone else's things were distributed around the head of the bed and the table. Somebody else's toilet articles... were in the bathroom. My first thoughts were, "What if I am discovered here?... Clearly they had moved somebody else into my room... I took the elevator to the lobby... At the desk I was told by the clerk... that indeed they had moved me. My particular room had been reserved in advance by somebody else. I was given the key to my new room and discovered that all my personal effects were distributed around the new room almost as though I had done it myself."

[Hall, E. T. (1981/1976). *Beyond culture* (pp. 58–59). New York: Anchor/ Doubleday.]

## *Is it hard for ESL/EFL learners to form passive verb phrases?*

### ▶ *Learner difficulties*

Because the passive always includes *be* inflected for the tense along with any necessary additional auxiliaries plus the main verb in past participle form, the verb phrase can be quite long and confusing for learners to identify and to remember. Recall that in our discussion of time, tense, and aspect in Chapter 6 we noted that any verb phrase that has more than one part to it causes difficulties for ESL/EFL learners. If you refer back to Sentences (19)–(28) in the previous chart, you will notice that the passive sentence in (28) has *four* parts to the verb phrase:

(28) New computer games **should have been designed.**

Sentence (25) has *five* parts to the verb phrase:

(25) New computer games **are going to be designed.**

Given the complexity of these verb phrases, you can see how ESL/EFL learners have trouble remembering to include all the various components with the appropriate inflections.

## Explaining Passive Formation

### How can I explain passive formation to my students?

In teaching the forms of the passive, grammar books for ESL/EFL learners generally introduce the forms by showing and practicing transformations of active sentences to passive ones:

(31) The best professor teaches graduate seminars.

   a. Move the object *graduate seminars* to the front of the sentence.
   b. Change the verb to *be (present)* + past participle → *are taught.*
   c. Be sure it agrees with the new subject, *seminars*, not with the old subject, *professor.*
   d. Add the "by phrase" to the end

    **a**       **b, c**    **d**
Graduate seminars are taught by the best professor.

In Sentence (31), the "by" phrase must be left in to give the sentence meaning, in contrast to Sentences (19–28) where the "by" phrase was best left out.

Discovery Activity 6 provides practice in forming the passive. If you are sure you can form any verb phrase in the passive and can identify the different parts of all the parts of the passive verb phrases for your students, you may choose to move on to the next section after completing one or two sentences and checking your answers in the Answer Key.

### Discovery Activity 6: Practice Forming the Passive

1. On a separate sheet of paper, change each active sentence to a passive sentence.

   • Decide whether or not to use the "by" phrase.

2. Label the tense of the verb phrase.

- Remember to keep the same tense.

*Example*

Security is checking the passengers.
The passengers *are being checked* (by security).

- *Are being checked* is the present progressive form of the passive voice.
- The verb *are* agrees with the subject *the passengers*.
- The "by" phrase can either be included or excluded. The lack of context does not suggest which form might be better.

1. Computer scientists will develop new computer chips.
2. The Internet has revolutionized communication.
3. The artist painted the portrait in the early 1800's.
4. People can buy the new product at any drugstore.
5. Everyone must obey helmet laws.
6. Researchers are going to test the new drug next year.
7. The insurgents blew up the bridge.

## Understanding Passive Use

### Is the passive always the opposite of the active?

Although the passive is frequently discussed as the counterpart of the active, this is not always true. The verb *have,* for instance, is a transitive verb that cannot be used in the passive, except in the stock (and archaic phrase) "A good time was had by all." ESL/EFL students often attempt to form the passive with *have,* forming sentences such as:

*(32) A good teacher *was had* by my friend.
*(33) A new car *will be had* by me next year.

There are also some passive forms that have no active equivalents, or that have different meanings when used in the passive versus the active.

(34a) Daniel married Miriam.
*(34b) Miriam was married by Daniel.
(34c) Miriam was married by her cousin, Daniel.

Sentence (34a) tells us that the man, Daniel, married the woman, Miriam. The passive sentence (34b) is not possible, **unless** the speaker is expressing a fact parallel to that of Sentence (35a), namely that "Daniel" and "her cousin" refer to a minister, rabbi, judge, or other man who performed the actual marriage ceremony for Miriam.

***I learned that writers should avoid using the passive. Is this true?***

Grammar and style books caution both native and non-native speakers of English from overusing the passive and rightly so. It is better in many cases to be more direct; active sentences are often less pompous and wordy sounding.

However, there are times when it is important to use the passive, particularly when the receiver or agent is unknown, unimportant, or unspecific, or when the reader's attention should be focused on the receiver or agent rather than the "true" subject. We have seen various examples in this section where using the passive was the more appropriate choice.

## *Get*

### Is **get** *a kind of passive?*

The passive can also be formed with the verb *get*. This form is generally more informal than passives formed with *be*. It is often used when there is no agent or doer. Passive *get* is also labeled as "causative" because verb expresses the idea that someone or something is "caused" to receive the action of the main verb.

(35a) The thief **got** *caught* robbing the house.
(35b) The thief **was** *caught* robbing the house.

(36a) The land *will* **get** *destroyed*.
(36b) The land *will* **be** *destroyed*.

*Get* can also combine with an adjective or past participle to mean *become*, as in *get well, get rich, get lucky* or *get bored, get annoyed, get tired*. Most grammarians consider these forms a type of passive because there is some assumption that there is an underlying agent or thing bringing about this condition, state, or event.

Passive *get* should not be confused with the form *have got*. As discussed in Chapter 7, *have got* is an idiomatic structure that can have the meaning of *have to* or *have*.

Let us turn now to the last variation of the basic sentence we will be exploring, *substitution*.

## Section 4: Substitution

## *Do*

### *What do you mean by* **substitution?**

Substitution refers to words English speakers use to replace longer utterances. A common type of substitution is the use of auxiliaries to refer to verb phrases and their complements that have already been mentioned. When substitution occurs, the entire sentence is shortened.

> (37) Lois: Did you read the assigned pages?
>      Allie: Yes, I *did*.

The question and response in Sentence (37) are in simple past tense. As you know, the main verb requires the auxiliary *do* for questions and negatives in this tense. When we want to substitute the verb phrase in simple present or simple past, we also use the *do* auxiliary. In Sentence (37), *did* stands in or substitutes for the verb *read* and complement, the object noun phrase *the assigned pages*.

> (38) Lois: Have you read the assigned pages?
>      Allie: Yes, I *have*.

## Substitution and First Auxiliary Rule

*What do we do for substitution when the main verb is not in simple present or simple past?*

In Sentence (38), *have* is an auxiliary verb. Since *have* already is an auxiliary verb, it can substitute for the rest of the sentence. We can now expand our first auxiliary rule to apply to substitution:

- When the verb phrase contains one or more auxiliaries, the first auxiliary can substitute for the rest of the verb phrase and complement.
- When the verb *be* is present, either as a main verb or auxiliary, it can substitute for the rest of the verb phrase.

> (39) Is Jackie always late?
>      Yes, she is.

## Substitution and Inversion

Substitution does not only occur in answers to questions. It also occurs in other sentences. Can you explain these examples?

> (40) Allie always reads her assignments. Lois *does*, too
> (41) Pete works harder than Alex *does*.

- In Sentence (40), *does* substitutes for *reads + her assignments*, and the word *too* is added to show the sameness of the action or event described by the verb.
- In Sentence (41), *does* substitutes for *works + harder than*.

**So**

Now look at Sentence (42). Can you explain what happened here?

   (42) Kim should always read her assignments and so *should* Frank.

- In Sentence (42), *should* is part of the verb phrase *should read* and since *should* is an auxiliary, it can substitute for the previously mentioned verb phrase + complement. *So* used in this type of substitution **requires the inversion** of the subject and the auxiliary.

**Neither, Either**

Another example of this inversion occurs after *neither:*

   (43) Sam isn't coming and *neither* is Lillian.

*Either* is semantically similar to *neither*, but differs structurally. First, when *either* is present, the verb must be negated with *not* if the intent is to convey a negative meaning. *Neither*, in contrast is already negative and therefore the verb is always in the affirmative. Second, there is no word order inversion with *either* the way there is with *neither*. Compare Sentence (43) above and Sentence (44) below:

   (44) Craig isn't listening and Paul is*n't either*.

*Is substitution confusing to ESL/EFL learners?*

► *Learner difficulties*

Using substitution correctly requires much practice. ESL/EFL learners need to remember which auxiliary to use. They often forget to use the *do* auxiliary and will use only the main verb:
   (45) Lois: Did you read the assigned pages?

      * Allie: Yes, I *read*.

   Learners of English also often forget to change word order after *so* and *neither*:
   (46) Laurie: Jason has never come on time.

      * Doug: *Neither Albert has.*

Although less proficient ESL/EFL learners are often asked to answer to questions in complete sentences in classroom practice, in authentic language, repeating the entire verb or verb phrase is awkward and wordy, and does not reflect the way native speakers actually use the language. Native speakers use substitution regularly in responding to questions. Thus, learners should have practice in using the different substitution forms.

Discovery Activity 5 provides practice in identifying substitutions. Try at least two excerpts before you move on to the next section. The answers are in the Answer Key.

## Discovery Activity 7: Substitution

Look at the excerpts.

1. Underline the substitutions.
2. Explain the substitution you underlined.

*Example*

> "You're drenched."
> "And *so are you.*"
>   [Seth, V. (1993). *A suitable boy* (p. 453). New York: Harper Collins.]

- *So* substitutes for *drenched*, which is functioning as a participial adjective such as we saw in Chapter 4.
- *are you* is an example of inversion after *so*.

**A.**

> He asked me, "Do you think your mother helps him by buttering his rolls?" ...
> "In fact, yes, I think she does."
>   [Maclean, N. (1976). *A river runs through it* (p. 84). Chicago: University of Chicago Press.]

**B.**

> "You think he's here, on Eelong?" Boon asked.
> "Yes, I do," was my answer... I don't know what Seegen told you, but... Saint Dane is a killer..."
> "Let him try!" Boon shouted with defiance. "I'm not afraid and neither is Seegen."
>   [MacHale, D. J. (2004). *Pendragon, book five: Black water* (pp. 57–58). New York: Aladdin Paperbacks.]

**C.**

> "Where's Varun?"
> "I don't know," said Meenakshi. "He hasn't returned and he hasn't called. I don't think he has, anyway"...
> "I've been dreaming about you," lied Meenakshi.
> "You have?" asked Arun...
>   [Seth, V. (1993). *A suitable boy* (p. 489). New York: HarperCollins.]

**D.**

I said, "Paul, I'm sorry. I wish I knew how I could have stayed away from this guy."
"You couldn't," he said...
[Maclean, N. (1976). *A river runs through it* (p. 68). Chicago: University of Chicago Press.]

## One

### *Is* one *a substitution form?*

*One* is another form that can substitute for other elements in a sentence to avoid repetition. *One* is sometimes referred to as a *pro-form* because it acts like a pronoun.

*One* when it substitutes for other sentence elements, should not be confused with the number *one*. When *one* functions as a substitute, it is substituting for phrases with a count noun. The plural form *ones* substitutes for phrases containing plural count nouns.

(47) Maggie prefers teaching a small class, but I like teaching a large *one.*
(48) Leslie likes big cars, but she has always driven compact *ones.*

In Sentence (47), *one* replaces *teaching a small class*, contains the singular count noun, *class*. In Sentence (48), *ones* replaces *big cars*, a plural count noun.

An additional clue in spoken English is stress. When speakers refer to the numeral *one*, this word is stressed. The pro-form, on the other hand, is never stressed.

(49) Do you have any books for me? I have *one.* (stressed)
(50) Can you lend me a pencil? I need *one* for this test. (unstressed)

There is still another *one*, the indefinite pronoun used when speakers wish to refer to an unnamed and/or unspecific person. This *one* is sometimes referred as the generic "one."

(51) *One* should be skeptical of such results.

This next Discovery Activity is designed to help you become familiar with the different uses of *one*. You will find the answers in the Answer Key.

### Discovery Activity 8: Identifying the Uses of *one* (s)

Look at the excerpts.

1. Find all the uses of *one* and underline them.
2. Decide if *one* is the numeral or a substitution form.

- If *one* is functioning as a substitute, identify what elements the sentence each use of *one* is replacing.

**A.**

"Where were you?"
"Here. And after it shut we went over to that other café..."
"The Café Suizo."
"That's it... I think it's a better café than this one."
[Hemingway, E. (1976/1976). *The sun also rises* (p. 100). New York: Charles Scribner's Sons.]

**B.**

"I'd best stop on here, though. I've not much more time to fish."
"You want those big ones in Irati."
[Hemingway, E. (1976/1976). *The sun also rises* (p. 127). New York: Charles Scribner's Sons.]

**C.**

Most dog books fall roughly into two types: the ones that focus on training, and the ones that tell dog stories.
[Blumber, B., & Coppinger, R. (2005, February). Review: Can dogs think? *Natural History, 114*(1), 48.]

## Summary

| The Basic Sentence Constituents | |
| --- | --- |
| **noun phrases** | *the black book* |
| **prepositional phrases** | *on the dock* |
| **verb phrases** | *have gone, is walking* |
| **adjective phrases** | *big heavy* |
| **adverb phrases** | *very happy* |

| Parts of a Noun Phrase | |
|---|---|
| **noun (also called head noun)** | *dog* |
| **determiners** | |
|     ●  **articles** | |
|        ○ **definite** | *the dog* |
|        ○ **indefinite** | *a dog* |
|     ●  **demonstratives** | *this dog, these dogs* |
| | *that dog, those dogs* |
|     ●  **possessive adjectives** | *my dog, your dog, his dog, her dog, its dog,* |
| | *our dog, their dog* |
|     ●  **quantifiers** | *some dogs, many dogs, a lot of dogs, a few dogs* |

| Functions of a Noun Phrase | |
|---|---|
| **subject** | *The book* is black. |
| **object** | Jess likes *books.* |
| **complement** | This is a *best-selling book.* |
| **object of the preposition** | Jack wants to buy *some new books.* |

| Parts of a Verb Phrase | |
|---|---|
| verb | The girls *dance.* |
| | Maggie *danced.* |
| ●  negative | |
|   ○ do/does/did + *not* + base verb | The girls *do not* dance. |
|     (simple present, simple past) | Kelly *did not dance* at yesterday's performance. |
|   ○ *be* as main verb + *not* | This *is not* a good idea. |
| *be* or *have* auxiliary + (*not*) + (adverb) + main verb in present or past participle form | The child *is often dancing.* The child *has often danced* this routine. The boys *are not coming* today. Jake *had not seen* the movie before. |
| *have* auxiliary + (*not*) + (adverb) + *been* + main verb in present participle form | The company *has often been dancing* for weeks. The company *had often been dancing* for weeks before opening night. The children *have not been eating* enough fruit. The students *had not been studying* until the test. |
| modal auxiliary (*not*) + (adverb) + base verb | Kathy *should eat* more fish. Taxis *should not charge* extra for additional passengers. |
| modal auxiliary + (*not*) + *have* + (adverb) + main verb in past participle form | The children *must have forgotten* the time. She *must not have remembered* his birthday. |

---

## The Basic Sentence Is

---

- noun phrase + verb phrase

  *Cats sleep.*

  - Optional constituents are prepositional phrases, adjective phrases, and adverb phrases.

  *Some fat cats walk very quietly up the stairs.*

---

### Basic Sentences can be Combined with Conjunctions

Cats sleep a lot. Birds sing a lot.

- *Cats sleep a lot and birds sing a lot.*

Dog bark. Cats meow.

- *Dogs bark but cats meow.*

---

### Variations on the Basic Sentence: Questions, Passive, Substitution

---

## Questions

---

- **yes/no**

  ○ subject/verb inversion when there is one or more modal or the verb *be*

  ○ insertion of *do* auxiliary for simple present and simple past

- ***wh*-questions**

  ○ subject/verb inversion when there is one or more modal or the verb *be*

  ○ insertion of *do* auxiliary for simple present and simple past

  ○ *what* and *who* can ask for both subject and objects, and will have different structures accordingly.

  ○ Use *who, what, when, where, why, how, which*

---

---

## Passive

---

- consists of *be* (in any tense) +past participle
- used when the agent or doer is unimportant or unspecified.
- may or may not have a "by phrase."

---

---

## Substitution

---

**In responding to a question**

the *do* auxiliary, the first auxiliary and certain words (e.g. *so, neither*) can substitute for the verb phrase and parts of a sentence.

---

| Substitution and Expansion of the First Auxiliary Rule |
| --- |
| • When the verb phrase contains one or more auxiliaries, the first auxiliary can substitute for the entire verb phrase and remaining sentence. |
| • When the verb *be* is present, either as a main verb or auxiliary, it can substitute for the entire verb phrase and complement. |

## Practice Activities

### *Activity 1: Generating Phrases*

On a separate sheet of paper, write phrases according to the patterns. Label the type of phrase you have created.
*Example:*

> article + noun *the car, noun phrase*

1. number + adjective + noun
2. quantifier + adjective + noun
3. adverb + adjective
4. adjective + adjective
5. adverb + adjective + noun
6. preposition + determiner + noun
7. possessive adjective + adverb + adjective + noun

### *Activity 2: Identifying Verb Phrases*

1. Choose an excerpt from a newspaper, magazine, or book.
2. Underline all the verb phrases.
3. Label the tense of each verb phrase.
4. Circle any adverbs that occur within any of the verb phrases.

### *Activity 3: Question Formation*

1. Complete the following dialogues by adding questions in the blanks.
2. Compare your dialogues with your classmates. Were they identical? Which elements were the same? Which ones differed? Why?

**A.**
Jerry: _____?
Lilly: No, not usually. _____ ?
Jerry: I have, but not this week. _____?
Lilly: Maybe tomorrow.

**B.**

Sara: _____?

Wes: Only on Mondays. _____?

**C.**

Karen: In Toronto. _____?

Joe: Because we wanted to. _____?

**D.**

Chelsea: _____?

Donna: Sure, I'd love to.

Chelsea: _____next weekend?

Donna: Great!

## Optional Follow Up

After you have completed the dialogues and discussed these with your classmates, talk about:

- how you could use such dialogues with ESL/EFL students.
- what aspects of question formation learners need to be aware of.

## Activity 4: Identifying Questions

- The selections are long, so you may choose to do only A or B.
  - If, however, you find you are having problems identifying questions, you may want to complete both A and B.

1. Examine the following two selections from actual interviews.
2. Underline all the *yes/no* and *wh*-questions.
3. Explain the structure of the different questions. For example, does the question follow the first auxiliary rule? What tense is the question in?

**A.**

*What is the secret of Harry Potter?*

JKR: I don't know. That's the question I get asked most of all, I think and it's really hard for me to say because as far as I am concerned, this was my private little world...

*Why did He-Who-Can-Not-Be-Named, Voldemort, if I can get away, Voldemort, why did he do it?*

JKR: Well, that's a really key question and I can't answer it because you will find that out over the course of the 7 book series...

*Where did you come by the sort of — there is a code — a sort of a DNA pattern to these stories? Again, the boy who grows up, a foundling, so to speak, in somebody else's cupboard. He's treated very badly by this other boy in the house. Where does this start? I don't want to say formula, but where did the idea, the posture of these stories begin in your own head?*

JKR: The funny thing is that Harry came into my head almost completely formed...

*What about the names themselves? Muggles, to begin, but the whole catalog of wizards, Albus Dumbledore, Voldemort, Hagrid.*

JKR: I'm big on names. I like names, generally. You have to be really careful giving me your name if it's an unusual one because you will turn up in Book 6...

*I was going to say, are you a Hermione?*

JKR: Yeah... Hermione is a caricature of what I was when I was 11, a real exaggeration, out in depth.

*Are you sticking with that outline of the 7?*

JKR: Yeah, but each time I hit a new book, I will find that there's other stuff I want to do...

*Why 7 and what is the contour that you want to complete?*

JKR: Well 7 is for several reasons, but I suppose the main one, I was 7 years at my secondary school. That's kind of standard in England...

*How are you going to protect him on the silver screen?*

JKR: Warner Brothers are giving me a lot of input, I feel. I can't lie to you, I am nervous about it...

   [Rowling, J.K. (1999, October 12). *The connection* (WBUR Radio). Interview transcript. Accio Quote! Retrieved February 6, 2005 from http://www.accio-quote.org/articles/1999/1099-connectiontransc.html].

**B.**

*How long have you been writing?*
Well, I've been writing since I was sixteen...

*What is your favorite book that you've written?*

I guess that would be my first published book, *Space Station Seventh Grade*.

*What inspired you to write* Maniac Magee?

Actually, there was no particular inspiration...

*Will Maniac Magee appear in another book?*

I don't have any plans for a sequel...

*How many books have you written?*

At last count, I've written twenty books, but only sixteen are published...

*Have any of your books ever been turned down by a publisher?...*

My first four books were never published...

*What was your first book, and how long did it take you to write it?*

Let's see – it took about six months to write...

*What college did you go to? What did you major in?*

I went to Gettysburg College... I majored in English...

*Did you think you would win one of the Newbery Medals?*

No, I can't say that I expected it...

*Where is the one place you want to go the most?*

I guess I've already been to the place on the top of my list – that was Egypt...

*Did you ever know someone like Maniac Magee?*

... Basically he's a patchwork of memories and imagination.

*What are some of the new books you're working on?*

I'm not working on anything right now – I've given myself a sabbatical...

*Did you ever run away from home and if you did, where did you go?*

No, I'm afraid I wasn't the type to run away...

*What is your favorite food?*

Chocolate almond ice cream...

*Were you raised by a black family like the kid in* Maniac Magee?

No, but I did play with a lot of African-American kids, and that was part of my inspiration for the theme of the book...

*Besides yourself, who is your favorite author?*

My favorite author now is Eileen Spinelli, who happens to live in my house here. She's my wife...

*Have you ever wanted to change your career?*

Not lately... When I was the age of most of my readers I wanted to be a baseball player.

*Are you going to write any more books in the School Daze series?*

No, I think the School Daze series is over now...
[Spinelli, J. (no date). Interview transcript. *Scholastic.* Accessed on line February 6, 2005 from http://content.scholastic.com/ browse/collateral.jsp?id=370&FullBreadCrumb=%3Ca+href%3D%22%2Fbr owse%2Fsearch. jsp%3Fquery%3DJerry+Spinelli++interview%26c1%3DCONTENT30%26c2%3Dfalse%22 3EAll+Results+%3C%2Fa%3E].

## *Activity 5: Practice in Changing Sentences from Active to Passive*

On a separate sheet of paper, change the following sentences from active to passive. Be careful to keep the same tense. Evaluate whether or not to include a "by" phrase.

*Example:*

> People are finding many artifacts. *Many artifacts are being found.* The "by phrase" is not necessary here.

1. Archeologist reconstruct the past.
2. Everyone followed the directions.

3. The company is going to fire some of the employees.
4. The police have apprehended the stalker.
5. You can find the answers in the back of the text.
6. The management will return unauthorized checks.
7. The painter is painting our house.
8. Someone had accused the man of stalking when someone else found exonerating evidence.
9. The high voter turnout encouraged all the political parties.

## Activity 6: Finding Different Uses of the Passive (optional additional practice)

1. Find excerpts that include the passive in at least two types of writing from the following list:

   - textbook
   - popular novel
   - science magazine
   - newspaper
   - popular magazine
   - recipe

2. Make photocopies for your classmates.

*Before class:*

3. Underline all examples of the passive verb phrases on your copy only.
4. Underline any examples of the passive "by" phrases on your copy only.
5. Explain which tense each passive verb phrase is in.

*In class, break into groups of 2–3*

6. Share your excerpts.
7. Compare your results with those of the other members of your group.

## Activity 7: Error Analysis 1

The following questions were overheard in an ESL classroom. The students are from a variety of language backgrounds.

- What mistakes do you find?
- What do you think these learners need to practice?

   1. How you close the window?
   2. What you mean by this?
   3. Why teacher say that?
   4. Who his listening teacher?

5. When she gave back the homework?
6. Which part you come from?
7. When he hurted himself?
8. What made her gave up?
9. Where you come from part of USA?
10. Who your mother like best?
11. What that word *sparkle*?
12. Where we at?
13. Why he do that?
14. Which book she want?

## *Activity 8: Error Analysis 2*

The following excerpts were written by ESL students.

1. Identify the problems you see in the use of **the passive only.**
2. Explain what each problem is.
3. Suggest a correction for each problem you have identified.
4. **Ignore other errors.**

### A.

I recommend you try a dish called "degue." It is a kind of drink that is had by people in my country for breakfast, lunch, or dinner. There is couscous and chocolate. In addition, only the eggs yolk is added. Water is also added. It is always made by women.

### B.

When people buy something, some people is influenced advertisements. Others are decided by themselves in the store. But some people could not be decided without advertisements and buy unnecessary things. As for me, advertisements have useful information for buying, and should not be required for me to buy because I can make my own decision.

### C.

During vacation, I went to New York City. I like New York City very much. But, I don't like the hotel. The hotel was expensive, but not good. I bitted. There was lice, little animals living in your hair.

### D.

I love New York and Xmas. Especially, in Xmas season, trees is decorated in many lights.

### E.

Every person was being a baby when they were just born. They grow and they've been learned and experienced language by their mothers and fathers.

# Answer Key: Chapter 8 Discovery Activities

## *Discussion: Discovery Activity 1*

| Noun phrase | Verb Phrase | Prepositional Phrase |
|---|---|---|
| Scuffy | sailed | into a big city |
| Horses | stamped | |
| truck motors | roared | |
| streetcars | clanged | |
| people | shouted | |
| Felix | stopped | |
| He | had | |
| Mr. Nubble | frowned | |
| You | 're stepping | on my house |
| Felix | jumped | off the hose |
| She | waved | toward the pond |
| Four hundred frogs' heads | poked out (phrasal verb) | of the water |

## *Discussion: Sentence Problem*

(2) The smart boy very carefully picked up some scattered rocks by the river.

| | |
|---|---|
| The smart boy | noun phrase |
| very carefully | adverb phrase |
| picked up | verb phrase (past, phrasal) |
| some scattered rocks | object noun phrase |
| by the river | prepositional phrase |

## *Discussion: Discovery Activity 3*

| | In every question, the wh-question word is in initial position, then: |
|---|---|
| 1. **Where was** he going? | the subject and *be* auxiliary are inverted according to our auxiliary rule. |
| 2. **Why has** she called so often? | the subject and *have* auxiliary are inverted according to our auxiliary rule. |
| 3. **When is** the party? | the subject and verb are inverted because the main verb is *be*. |
| 4. **When did** she call? | the *do* auxiliary must be inserted according to our auxiliary rule. |
| 5. **Who wrote** that book? | the verb follows in the appropriate tense because *who* is asking for the subject of the verb. |
| 6. **Who did** you call last night? | *did is* inserted because *who* is asking for the object of the verb and the verb is in simple past. |
| 7. **Who are** you calling now? | the subject and verb are inverted according to our auxiliary rule. *Who* is asking for the object of the verb[1]. |
| 8. **What did** you read last summer? | *did* must be inserted because *what* is asking for the object of the verb and the verb is in simple past. |
| 9. **What** author **do** you like the best? | The subject, followed by an auxiliary verb, unless the main verb is *be* because *what* is asking for the subject of the verb. |

---

[1] In formal prescriptive grammar *whom* is the correct form for Sentences 6 and 7.

## *Discussion: Discovery Activity 4*

*Excerpt A*

- *Can you swim:* yes/no question using the auxiliary modal *can* and requiring only subject-verb inversion to form the question
- *Why don't you fly: wh*-question with insertion of *do* auxiliary because time is simple present
- *How did you get here? wh*-question with insertion of *do* auxiliary because time is simple past

*Excerpt B*

- *How can you force* and *How can you treat: wh*-question with the modal *can*, which inverts with the subject of the sentence
- *What is your name: wh*-question with *be* as a main verb. It is asking for the subject of the verb phrase, so regular sentence word order is kept

*Excerpt C*

- *Do you think:* yes-no question with insertion of *do* auxiliary because time is simple present
- *What was your first car: wh*-question with *be* as a main verb. It is asking for the subject of the verb phrase, so regular sentence word order is kept.
- *What did the car have: wh*-question with insertion of *do* auxiliary because time is simple present. It is asking for the object of the verb phrase, so we need question word order.
- *Can honeymoons kill you:* yes-no question. The auxiliary modal *can* inverts with the subject.
- *Did you and mom:* yes-no question with insertion of *do* auxiliary because time is simple past.

## *Discussion: Discovery Activity 5*

*Excerpt A*

- *dentures were fashioned, teeth were whitened*: past passive

*Excerpt B*

- *can (never) be retried, should be recalled:* present passive with modals.

*Excerpt C*

- *Were the marines being sent*: question, passive past progressive
  - Since *were* is the first auxiliary, it is inverted with the subject, *the marines,* to form the question.
- *had been seen*: past perfect passive

*Excerpt D*

- *has been written:* present perfect passive
- *must be translated:* modal present passive

*Excerpt E*

- *will (continually) be transformed:* future passive
- *is analyzed* and *is prepared:* present passive
- *has been prepared:* present perfect passive

*Excerpt F*

- *were distributed:* past passive
- *am discovered:* present passive
- *was told:* past passive
- *had been reserved:* past perfect passive
- *was given* and *were distributed*: past passive

## Discussion: Discovery Activity 6

1. New computer chips will be developed.

   - "by computer scientists" is unnecessary.
   - Future passive

2. Communication has been revolutionized by the Internet.

   - In this sentence, "by the Internet" is important to the meaning of the sentence.
   - present perfect passive

3. The portrait was painted in the early 1800's.

   - "by the artist" is unnecessary.
   - past passive

4. The new product can be bought at any drugstore.

   - "by people phrase" is unnecessary.
   - modal present passive

5. Helmet laws must be obeyed by everyone..

   - "by everyone" is optional and used only if there is an emphasis on everyone versus, for example, children under the age of sixteen.
   - modal present passive

6. The new drug is going to be tested next year.

   - "by researchers phrase" is unnecessary.
   - future passive with *going to*

7. The bridge was blown up by insurgents.

- In this sentence, "by insurgents" is important to the meaning of the sentence.
- past passive

## Discussion: Discovery Activity 7

*Excerpt A*

- *does* substitutes for *helps him by buttering his roles.*
  - ○ Because *helps* is in simple present, third person singular, the *do* auxiliary acts as the substitute verb form.

*Excerpt B*

- *do* substitutes for *think he's here.*
  - ○ Because *think* is simple tense, the *do* auxiliary acts as the substitute verb form.
- *neither is* substitutes for *Seegan is not afraid.*
  - ○ *Neither*, like *so*, requires subject – verb inversion after it.

*Excerpt C*

- *has* substitutes for *hasn't returned and hasn't called.*
  - ○ The negative is expressed in the first part of the clause *I don't think.*
- *have* substitutes for *have been dreaming.*

*Excerpt D*

- *couldn't* substitutes for *couldn't have stayed away from this guy.*

## Discussion: Discovery Activity 8

*Excerpt A*

- *one* replaces *Café Suizo.*

*Excerpt B*

- *ones* replaces *fish*, implied in the dialogue.
  - ○ Although *fish* is generally a non-count noun, we use *ones* rather than *one* when we are referring to more than one individual fish.

*Excerpt C*

- *the ones that focus* and *the ones that tell* : both substituting for *types of dog books.*

# Chapter 9
# Compound Sentences and Introduction to Complex Sentences: Adverbial Clauses

## Introduction

In the previous chapter, Chapter 8, we reviewed the constituents of basic sentences and examined some common variations of the basic sentence. In the next three chapters, we will examine expanded sentences. In this chapter, we will start by considering compound clauses and then begin our investigation into complex sentences, where we will focuses on adverbial clauses. In Chapters 10 and 11, we will investigate two other types of complex sentences, relative clauses and noun clauses.

There are three parts to Chapter 9. Section 1 considers compound sentences coordinators, and transition words. Section 2 delves into the various types of adverbial clauses, and Section 3 examines reduced adverbial clauses.

### How can we define a sentence?

A sentence consists of one or more clauses. A clause is the smallest syntactic unit that has meaning. This is a complicated way of saying that a clause is a sentence that can stand alone. Minimally, a sentence consists of one clause.

### What is a clause?

As we observed in Chapter 8, a clause minimally consists of two constituents, a noun phrase and a verb phrase, and, as you will recall, a phrase is a word (*child; meow*) or group of words (*the angry child; is loudly meowing*) that functions as a unit within a sentence.

## Clauses versus Phrases

### How does a clause differ from a phrase?

A phrase differs from a clause in that a phrase does not generally occur independently. A phrase cannot form a sentence by itself.

A. DeCapua, *Grammar for Teachers,*
© Springer 2008

| noun phrase + verb phrase = sentence | |
|---|---|
| The cat | is meowing. |
| The angry dogs | have been barking. |
| Alyssa and her new friend | will be coming. |

Most English sentences, even basic sentences, consist of more than a noun phrase and verb phrase. In Chapter 5, for instance, we discussed how certain verbs are transitive and therefore require an object:

| Jack **threw** *the ball.* | **transitive verb + direct object** |
|---|---|
| Jack **threw** *the ball to me.* | **transitive verb + direct object + indirect object** |

We also saw how many verbs do not require an object, but a complement.

| Jack **walked** downstairs. | **intransitive verb + adverbial complement** |
|---|---|

### *Are these sentences still basic sentences?*

All of the examples above are still simple sentences. The examples can also be labeled declarative sentences. Let us now expand our simple sentences by exploring compound sentences.

## Section 1: Compound Sentences

### *What is a compound sentence?*

## Coordinators

When two sentences are combined with *and, but, or, yet,* or *for,* they are called compound or coordinate sentences. Each part is a complete clause that can stand on its own. The words that join two equal clauses are called *coordinating conjunctions* or simply *coordinators.*

The coordinator *and* is the most commonly used coordinator to combine compound sentences, followed by *but* and *or.* Less common is *yet,* followed by *for.* *Yet* and *for* are generally considered more formal than the other three coordinating conjunctions, *and, but, or.*

In compound sentences, identical phrases that have the same function can be combined:

(1a) Boys *read* books and girls *read* books.
(1b) *Boys and girls read* books.

In Sentence (1a) *boys* and *girls* are both subject noun phrases and *read* is the same verb. To avoid repetition, we can reduce the sentence to a single noun phrase by conjoining the two subject noun phrases with *and*, as in Sentence (1b).

We can also substitute a pronoun for a noun phrase that has the same function in different parts of a compound sentence:

| Main Clause | | | Main Clause | | |
|---|---|---|---|---|---|
| (2a) Barry likes chocolate | | and | *Barry* often buys *chocolate.* | | |
| **NP** | **NP** | | **NP** | | **NP** |
| (2b) Barry likes chocolate | | and | *he* | often buys | *it.* |
| **NP** | **NP** | | **pronoun** | | **pronoun** |

Because *Barry* and *chocolate* are identical in both main clauses Sentence (2a), in Sentence (2b) we can substitute the pronouns **he** for *Barry* and **it** for *chocolate*.

Look at the excerpt below and see how well you can identify and explain the different parts of the compound sentences.

(3)  Was Tarby kidding, or was he trying to deny to himself that he had seen what he really had seen? Lewis didn't know, and he didn't care.
   [Bellairs, J. (1973). *The house with a clock in its walls* (p. 89). New York: Puffin.]

First, we see two compound questions conjoined with the coordinator *or*. You may have found this a little tricky because these are compound questions rather than statements, which we have discussed until now. Nevertheless, you can see how compounding also applies to questions.

The second sentence in this excerpt uses *and* to conjoin the two main clauses. In addition, you will notice that *Tarby* and *Lewis* are replaced in their second mention by the pronoun *he*.

Discovery Activity 1 reviews compound sentences. If you have no difficulties with the first two excerpts, move ahead to the next section after you have checked your answers in the Answer Key.

---

**Discovery Activity 1: Compound Sentences**

Look at the following excerpts.

1.  Circle the coordinate conjunction
2.  Underline each main clause.

*Example:*

*She rode a bike*, but *he drove a car.*

**A.**

Mowgli walked on, for he was feeling hungry. . .
[Kipling, R. (1961/1894). *The jungle books* (p. 56). New York: Signet Classics.
Also available on line at: http://www.gutenberg.org/files/236/236-h/236-h.htm]

**B.**

"Keep him!" she gasped. "He came naked, by night, alone and very hungry; yet he
was not afraid.
[Kipling, R. (1961/1894). *The jungle books* (p. 16). New York: Signet Classics.
Also available on line at: http://www.gutenberg.org/files/236/236-h/236-h.htm]

**C.**

The rescuer tries to coax [the baby koala] from the tree, but he scampers past her and
takes off running.
[Musgrave, R. (2005, March). *National Geographic Kids*, p. 16.]

**D.**

Then they sleep. . . , and weave little baskets of dried grass and put grasshoppers in
them, or catch two praying mantises and make them fight, or string a necklace of red
and black jungle nuts, or watch a lizard basking on a rock, or a snake hunting a frog
near the wallows.
[Kipling, R. (1961/1894). *The jungle books* (p. 62). New York: Signet Classics.
Also available on line at: http://www.gutenberg.org/files/236/236-h/236-h.htm]

### *Do ESL/EFL learners have many difficulties with compound sentences?*

▶ *Learner difficulties*

Because *for* and *yet* have other sentence functions, less proficient ESL/EFL
learners are occasionally confused when these words are used as coordinators.
They must learn to distinguish between *for* as a preposition and *yet* as an
adverb from their coordinating conjunction counterparts.

|  | Function |
| --- | --- |
| (4) She came *for* me. | preposition |
| (5) She came *for* we had invited her. | coordinator |
| (6) We haven't eaten *yet*. | adverb |
| (7) He had eaten, *yet* he was still hungry. | coordinator |

# Transition Words or Phrases

*Is there any other way to connect main clauses?*

Main clauses may also be connected by *conjunctive adverbs* or *transition words* as they are often referred to in writing or composition textbooks. Different transition words express different types of relationships between one main clause and another one.

The meaning of the relationship between the two main clauses depends upon the meaning of the transition word or phrase, as you can see in the following chart. Specific transition words and phrases may be classified in the same category; however, they are not always interchangeable due to subtleties in meaning.

| Meaning | Common Transition Words/Phrases |
|---|---|
| contrast | however, nevertheless, nonetheless, still, yet, in fact, in contrast, on the contrary, on the other hand |
| addition | furthermore, further, moreover, in addition, additionally, likewise, similarly, also |
| result | therefore, consequently, accordingly, thus, hence, as a result, then |
| time sequence | then, afterward, meanwhile |
| condition | otherwise |

*Why use the term* transition words *rather than* conjunctive adverbs?

As you examine the chart, you will notice that there are phrases consisting of two or three words rather than single words. These phrases are technically not conjunctive adverbs, but, based on their meanings and use, they are often classed together with the conjunctive adverbs in many grammar and writing texts.

The term *transition words* more clearly conveys the idea of the role of these types of words, both conjunctive adverbs and these related phrases, in sentences. We will use the terms *transition word* to refer to the actual adverbs themselves and *transition phrases* to refer to groups of words that establish these similar types of sentence relationships.

## Sentence Position and Punctuation

*Is the sentence position for transition words and phrases fixed the way it is for coordinators such as "and?"*

Transition words and phrases can occur in three positions: at the beginning, in the middle, or at the end of a main clause. The punctuation of the transition words and phrases differs according to their position.

| Position and Punctuation of Transition words | | |
|---|---|---|
| Main clause 1 | Main clause 2 | Clause position |
| Voting ended at 9 pm; | *however*, the election results were not announced until the next day. | initial |
| Voting ended at 9 pm. | *However*, the election results were not announced until the next day. | |
| Voting ended at 9 pm. | The election results, *however*, were not announced until the next day. | middle |
| Voting ended at 9 pm. | The election results were not announced until the next day, *however*. | final |

To summarize, when transition words or phrases occur

- at the beginning of an main clause, they may be preceded by either a period or semi-colon, as illustrated in the first two sentences of the chart.
- in the middle of an main clause, they are generally offset by commas.
- at the end of an main clause, they are generally preceded by a period.

### *Why have I seen different punctuation used with transition words and phrases?*

There are stylistic variations to these general guidelines. More detailed guidelines to punctuation of transition words can be found in any stylebook. It should be noted that first, there is not complete agreement among the different stylebooks as to punctuation of the transition words and phrases in different instances; and that second, these guidelines have changed over the years.

ESL/EFL learners should be encouraged to follow the basic punctuation guidelines in their textbook. As learners become more proficient writers, they can be introduced to stylistic variations.

### *Do speakers use many transition words and phrases in every day English?*

Most transition words and phrases are found more commonly in formal written English rather than in casual written or spoken English. Therefore, you will see that the next Discovery Activity contains somewhat long excerpts taken from academic writing: history books, a linguistics text, and a philosophy book.

See how well you do in identifying and understanding the use of transition words and phrases. If this is an area you are strong in, you may want to try just Excerpt C or D before going on to the next section. Be sure to check your answers in the Answer Key at the end of the chapter.

## Discovery Activity 2: Identifying and Using Transition Words and Phrases

Look at the following excerpts.

1. Underline the transition words.
2. Explain the meaning of each one.

**A.**

> Because the raw data have no secure place in this tradition, they tend to be left out, and ... streamlined case reports have tended to take the place of the original data ... As a result, the path from observation to theory can never be retraced; thus we have no way to confirm or disconfirm an observation, much less combine old observations in a new formulation.
>
> [Spence, D. (1982). *Narrative truth and historical truth: Meaning and interpretation in psychoanalysis* (p. 23). New York: Norton.]

**B.**

> Discrete boundaries between dialects are often difficult to determine, since dialects share many features with one another. In addition, even the smallest dialect areas are characterized by incredible heterogeneity. Speakers use different language forms ... based not only on where they live but also on such factors as their social class, their ethnicity, their gender, and even whether or not they view the home region as a good place to live. Further, different dialect boundaries may emerge depending on which level of language we choose to focus on...
>
> [Wofram, W., & Shilling-Estes, N. (1998). *American english: Dialects and variation* (p. 91). Malden, MA: Blackwell.]

**C.**

> ... there does not seem to have been the same readiness to abandon children in public places among the poorest families in Holland as elsewhere in Europe. In Paris, for example, upwards of three hundred children were found abandoned in the 1670s, whereas the figure for Amsterdam, half as big a city, for 1700 was around twenty... The same pattern, moreover, seems to hold true for infanticide figures. Both phenomena of relative benevolence may owe something to the more stable position of working families and their domestic budgets in the Republic, to the apparent ability ... of the Dutch population to stabilize its own growth and hold mean household size at the lowest in Western Europe ... Nonetheless, it seems equally likely that the disparity with other European urban experiences owed something to cultural aversion to child exposure and abandonment.
>
> [Schama, S. (1987). *The embarrassment of riches: An interpretation of Dutch culture in the golden age* (pp. 522–523). Berkeley, CA: University of California Press.]

**D.**

> Broad's analogy brings out the point that there are two quite different ways in which one thing can causally affect the movement of another. Either it can cause it to change its speed ... or it can causally affect the direction in which the object moves ... But

after something hits the weight and begins its movement, where it goes depends upon the length of the string attached to it. Thus attaching strings of different length to the weight changes the course of the weight but in no way affects the overall amount of energy of the weight. According to this analogy we are to take the causal role of different mental events to be like the causal role of different lengths of string. There would, consequently, be different results in the brain. . .

[Cornman, J., & Lehrer, K. (1974). *Philosophical problems and arguments: An Introduction* (2nd ed., p. 257). New York: Macmillan.]

*What kinds of problems do ESL/EFL learners have with transition words and phrases?*

▶ *Learner difficulties*

Because most transition words and phrases occur primarily in formal written English, ESL/EFL learners frequently lack adequate exposure to the use and meanings of these words and phrases, a problem also faced by inexperienced native speakers. There are often subtle differences in the meanings of similarly categorized transition words and phrases; therefore, learners need practice in understanding and using the different transition words and phrases. This again is difficult given the relatively infrequent use of many of these transition words and phrases in spoken and informal written English. Repeated exposure and practice will help learners become more aware of the use and subtleties of meaning of the transition words.

At this juncture we have completed our review of compound sentences and begin our investigation into complex sentences.

## Section 2: Complex Sentences

Open just about any book, magazine, or newspaper and you will quickly notice that simple sentences and compound sentences are only a part of the picture. There are other important sentence types in English called *complex sentences*. Complex sentences are so labeled because they consist of a main clause and a subordinate clause.[1]

Unlike sentences with coordinating conjunctions, the two clauses in the sentence are not equal: One part, the subordinate clause, is dependent upon the other part, the main clause. We call clauses that need to be attached to another clause *subordinate* clauses.

---

[1] Some grammar books refer to main clauses as independent clauses and to subordinate clauses as dependent clauses.

Remember that we have defined a main clause as one that can stand alone as a complete sentence. A subordinate clause is generally introduced by a word, called a *subordinator* or *subordinating conjunction*. Contrast these sentences:

I walked home.
I walked home and I called my mother.
I walked home after I called my mother.

The first of these three sentences, *I walked home,* is a main clause and a sentence all by itself. It stands alone. The second sentence is what we saw previously in our discussion of compound sentences. It consists of two main clauses joined by the coordinating conjunction *and.*

The last sentence, *I walked home after I called my mother,* is an example of a complex sentence. The first part of the sentence, *I walked home,* is a main clause that can stand alone. The second part of the sentence, *after I called my mother,* cannot stand alone. It needs to be attached to an main clause. The word *after* is a subordinator. It has changed the main clause, *I called my mother,* into a subordinate clause, *after I called my mother.*

## Complex Sentences and Multiple Subordinate Clauses

### *Do complex sentences have just one subordinate clause?*

Complex sentences can have more than one subordinate clause:

| Main Clause | Subordinate Clause | Subordinate Clause |
|---|---|---|
| (8) I was watching the game | while they were talking to Jane | who lived nearby. |
| (9) Jack drove home | after the game | which they had lost. |

Visually, we can think of complex sentences as:

main clause
. . . . . . . . . . . . . . . . . . . . . . . . . .
              subordinate clause 1
              . . . . . . . . . . . . . . . . . . . . . . . . .
                            subordinate clause 2
                            . . . . . . . . . . . . . . . . . . . . . . .
                                    and so on. . .

## Subordinate Clauses and Word Order

*Can we change the order of the main clause and the subordinate clause?*

A feature of complex sentences is that in many instances, although not in all, the main clause and subordinate clause can reverse order without a change in meaning. The order of the subordinate clauses remains the same.

| Subordinate Clause | Subordinate Clause | Main Clause |
|---|---|---|
| (8a) While they were talking to Jane, | who lived nearby, | I was watching the game. |
| (9a) After they finished the game, | which they lost, | Jack drove home. |

In the first set of Sentence, (8) and (9), the main clause is in initial position. In the second set of Sentences, (8a) and (9a), the main clause is in final position. When the main clause is in final position, it is preceded by a comma.

## GLUE

Another useful way to envision main clauses, subordinate clauses and the use of subordinators is to think of subordinators as GLUE (Marshall 1982). If we think of two pieces of paper that we want to put together, they won't stick unless we use glue. In complex sentences, if we don't have grammatical GLUE to join two subject noun phrases and verb phrases, we don't have complete sentences.

| GLUE (subordinator) | subject noun phrase | verb phrase | complement |
|---|---|---|---|
| Because | it | was | late |
| After | I | called | my mother |

In the example above, we do not have a complete sentence because the number of GLUE words is exactly the same as the number of noun phrases and verb phrases, namely one.

In order to make a complete sentence, the number of GLUE words needs to be one *less* than the number of noun phrases + verb phrases. In other words, English sentences need **one more subject noun phrase than GLUE**:

| | | GLUE Word Between Clauses | | | |
|---|---|---|---|---|---|
| subject noun phrase | verb phrase | GLUE (subordinator) | subject noun phrase | verb phrase | complement |
| The boys | left | because | it | was raining | hard. |

In this example, we have a complete sentence because we have one GLUE word, *because,* and two noun phrases and verb phrases, *it was* and *we left*.

## Sentence Position

### Must the GLUE word come between two clauses?

An important element with GLUE words is that they do not always need to come between two clauses. As we saw in our initial discussion of complex sentences, the GLUE word + the main clause can begin the sentence.

| Glue Word in Initial Position | | | | | |
|---|---|---|---|---|---|
| GLUE (subordinator) | subject noun phrase | verb phrase | complement | subject noun phrase | verb phrase |
| Because | it | was raining | hard, | the boys | left. |

### What, in general, do ESL/EFL learns find difficult about adverbial clauses?

### ▶ Learner difficulties

Learners of English, in forming adverbial clauses may not use the correct number of GLUE words. For example, they may write fragments, or incomplete sentences, as in,

*Because I went.

Or, ESL/EFL learners may add too many GLUE words:

*Even though I study hard; however, I'm still getting low grades.

To help ESL/EFL learners, remind them that there **must always be one less GLUE word than noun phrase and verb phrase.** This holds true, regardless of the sentence position of the subordinate clause.

## Types of Complex Clauses

### Are there different types of complex clauses?

There are many types of adverbial clauses, but they all have something in common: They tell us something about the information in the main clause. Adverbial clauses are usually subcategorized according to type. Although some grammar books may vary slightly in their categorizations, the basic categories of adverbial clauses are: time, contrast, place, cause, result, purpose, conditional, and manner.

The type or category of an adverbial clause is determined by its subordinator. For example, the subordinators *after* and *when* introduce adverbial time clauses. The subordinators *since* or *because* introduce reason or cause clauses.

## Adverbial Clauses of Time

| Common Time Subordinators |
| --- |
| before    after    until    while    when    since    as |

These time subordinators indicate different time references or time sequence. When we are referring to future events, *before, after, until, while,* and *when* are followed by the simple present. We do not use *will* or *be going to* after these time subordinators, even when the sentence is referring to future time.

(10a) Before Bree *leaves,* she'll call you.
*(10b) Before Bree *will leave,* she'll call you.
*(10c) Before Bree *is going to leave,* she'll call you.

### When and While

In Chapter 6, we noted that in formal prescriptive grammar a distinction is made between the use of *when* and *while* in past time when two events or actions are described, one of which is interrupting the other event or action. As you will recall, *when* should be used with the simple past to refer to the single event or action that interrupts the ongoing event or action. *While,* when it refers to something in progress or ongoing, should be used with the past progressive form and not the simple past.

| | |
| --- | --- |
| Lynn called **while** we *were eating* | **while + past progressive** |
| **When** Lynn called, we *were eating.* | **when + simple past** |

As we observed in Chapter 6, however, native speakers do not always adhere to this rule and will frequently use *when* with the past progressive.

### Whenever

The subordinator *when* can also combine with *–ever* to refer to indefinite time.

(11) ***Whenever*** Lynn called, we were eating.

### Until

*Until* is often reduced to *till* in spoken and informal written English.

(12a) We can't leave *until* her mother comes.
(12b) We can't leave *till* her mother comes.
(12c) We can't leave *'til* her mother comes.

Different writers will use either *till* or *'til* to reflect the shortened form. *Till* is considered a synonym of *until* by formal prescriptive grammarians, while *'til* is considered an incorrect written form.

## Sentence Position

Time clauses can occur in either initial or second position. When the time clause is in initial position, it is followed by a comma.

| Time clause in initial position | Time clause in second position |
|---|---|
| **While** we *were eating*, Lynn called | Lynn called **while** we *were eating*. |
| **Until** *her mother comes*, we can't leave | We can't leave **until** *her mother comes*. |

### What is hard about time clauses?

▶ *Learner difficulties*

One problematic area for ESL/EFL learners is remembering that future verb forms cannot follow time subordinators. Errors similar to our earlier Sentences (10b) and (10c), are common:

*(10b) Before Bree *will leave*, she'll call you.
*(10c) Before Bree *is going to leave*, she'll call you.

Adverbial clauses with *since* are also confusing for learners because *since* has two different meanings as a subordinate conjunction. It can refer to time or it can refer to reason:

|  | meaning |
|---|---|
| **Since** we moved to Florida, we've gone to the beach everyday. | **time** |
| **Since** the weather is warmer here, we moved to Florida. | **reason** |

Because *since* is also an adverb used to mark a specific point in time, ESL/EFL learners occasionally confuse this function of *since* with the adverbial subordinator *since*:

(13) I've lived here **since** 1995.
(14) Shame and disgust are enjoying their biggest legal comeback **since** colonial times.

[Braverman, A. (2005, February). Sign of the times. *University of Chicago Magazine*, 22].

In Sentences (13) and (14), *since* does not introduce an adverbial clause. In these examples, *since* indicates a particular point in time.

Another problematic subordinator for learners of English is *as* because it can express either a time or a reason relationship:

|  | meaning |
|---|---|
| **As** we entered the room, the noise died down. | **time** |
| **As** Katie hadn't done her homework, she didn't get an "A." | **reason** |

Although *as* introduces both subordinate clauses above, the meaning and function of *as* is different. We will shortly review the use of *as* to introduce an adverbial clause of reason.

See how well you can identify the adverbial time clauses in Discovery Activity 3. After you have completed all the excerpts, see if your answers are the same as those in the Answer Key at the end of the chapter.

**Discovery Activity 3: Identifying Adverbial Time Clauses**

Look at the following excerpts.

1. Circle the subordinators

- Each subordinator is the GLUE. Observe how in each sentence there is one more subject noun phrase than GLUE.

**A.**

This American had started from London when he was young, and he wanted to do the old town a good turn.
[Conan Doyle, A. (1983/1892). The Red-Headed League. *The original illustrated sherlock holmes* (p. 29). Secaucus, NJ: Castle. Also available on line at: http://www.gutenberg.org/files/2038/2038-h/2038-h.htm#The_Red_ Headed_League]

**B.**

Things were so simple at the start, before grammar came along and ruined things.
[Truss, L.( 2004). *Eats, shoots and leaves* (pp. 71–72). New York: Gotham Books.]

**C.**

As you read this, criminals ... are destroying portions of mankind's past... As you continue to read, other people across the globe are purchasing some of mankind's oldest and most exquisite creations...
[Vincent, S. (2005, April). Ancient treasures for sale. *Reason, 36*(11).]

> **D.**
>
> He sets up a bank account and feeds money in, transferring funds until he has what he needs. Then he can go on merrily cheating 'til someone's onto him.
> [Grafton, S. (2001). *P is for pearl* (p. 85). New York: Putnam.]

The next group of adverbial clauses we will discuss are those of contrast.

## Adverbial Clauses of Contrast

| Contrast Subordinators | | | Type |
|---|---|---|---|
| although | even though | though | **unexpected result** |
| while | whereas | inasmuch as | **direct opposition** |

Adverbial clauses of contrast are often subcategorized into two types: *unexpected result* and *direct opposition*.

### *Unexpected Result*

When *although, even though,* and *though* are used, the implication is one of unexpected result or of a contrast of ideas between the main clause and the subordinate clause. All three subordinators have the same meaning, but *though* is generally considered more informal than the other two.

(15a) *Although* it was raining, we took a walk.
(15b) *Even though* it was raining, we took a walk.
(15c) *Though* it was raining, we took a walk.

Subordinate clauses of contrast and main clauses can be reversed:

(16) We took a walk, *although* it was raining.

### *Direct Opposition*

*While, whereas,* and *inasmuch as* are used to convey the notion of direct opposition. The information in the subordinate clause is the direct opposite of the information in the main clause. *Whereas* and *inasmuch as* are generally found only in formal written English.

(17) "Life is one fool thing after another *whereas* love is two fool things after each other." (Oscar Wilde)

(18) "We are fast approaching the stage of the ultimate inversion: the stage where the government is free to do anything it pleases, *while* the citizens may act only by permission." (Ayn Rand)

▶ *Learner difficulties*

> ESL/EFL learners sometimes have a tendency to overuse *though* in more formal writing. *While* used in adverbial clauses of contrast is often confusing to learners of English because they more commonly associate *while* with time clauses.

## Adverbial Clauses of Place

| where |
| --- |

The most common subordinator for adverbial clauses of place is *where*. When speakers are referring to an indefinite place, *–ever* is attached to *where*. To refer to different kinds of places, *-where* can also be attached to other adverbs forming subordinators such as *anywhere, nowhere,* or *everywhere*:

(19) The lamb goes *where* Mary goes.
(19a) The lamb goes *everywhere* Mary goes.

Adverbial clauses introduced by *where* are often discussed together with relative clauses, clauses that modify, i.e. describe or expand a noun phrase in a sentence because *where* will often modify a noun. (See Chapter 10).

(20) The lamb follows Mary to the **school** *where* she goes.

Sentence (20) is a relative clause and not a subordinate clause because *where* modifies the noun phrase *the school*. We will explore these two functions of *where* in greater length in Chapter 10.

## Adverbial Clauses of Cause

| **Common Cause Subordinators** | | |
| --- | --- | --- |
| because | since | as |
| whereas | inasmuch as | |

Adverbial clauses of cause are also referred to as *reason* clauses because they explain the *why* of the main clause. In adverbial clauses of cause, *since* and *because* are synonymous. *As*, which we saw earlier as introducing adverbial clauses of time, can also introduce clauses of cause or reason.

Another commonly used structure, *now that*, is not a subordinator, but is often used to introduce adverbial cause clauses. This structure is used only for present and future events or actions, not past ones.

(21a) *Because* it's snowing, we'll stay home.
(21b) *Since* it's snowing, we'll stay home.
(21c) *As* it's snowing, we'll stay home.
(21d) *Now that* it's snowing, we'll stay home.

*Whereas* and *inasmuch as* are also subordinators indicating cause. *Whereas* and *inasmuch as* are generally used only in formal written English.

As you do Discovery Activity 4, think about the different excerpts. How do you think formal writing differs from casual writing or casual speech in terms of adverbial clauses? Do you think how formal a piece of writing is influences the number and type of clauses used?

## Discovery Activity 4: Identifying Adverbial Clauses of Contrast, Place, and Cause

Look at the excerpts.

1. Circle the subordinator
2. Underline the subordinate clause.

   - Each subordinator is the GLUE. Observe how in each sentence there is one more subject noun phrase than GLUE.

3. Label each type of adverbial clause.
4. Check your answers in the Answer Key at the end of this chapter.

**A.**

Nancy examined the leather sandals. "They are quite large," she said. "and Mr. Moto is a small man." "Let's ask Mr. Kikichi," George declared. "They might belong to him, even though he's not a tall person, either."
   [Keene, C. (1979). *Nancy drew: The thirteenth pearl* (p. 33). New York: Grosset & Dunlap.]

**B.**

In the United States ... people seem to assume that time is a given ... that it is the same wherever one goes in the world.
   [Hall, E. T. (1983). *The dance of life: The other dimension of time* (p. 134). New York: Anchor/Doubleday.]

**C.**

Publishers are not responsible for things getting lost in the mail, and although postal insurance may cover photocopying, it will not cover retyping...
[Luey, B. (1995). New York: Cambridge University Press (3rd ed), p. 61.]

**D.**

While some of the admiration expressed was undoubtedly for stoicism in the face of personal tragedy, most seem to have their places through their satellite position vis-à-vis a "worthy" man whose fame puts them in the limelight.
[Tuchman, G., Daniels, A. K., & Benet, J. (Eds.) (1978). Introduction: News-papers and their women's pages. *Hearth and home: Images of women in the mass media* (p. 148). New York: Oxford University Press.]

**E.**

Because relatives share genetic material, the benefits of group membership would be enhanced if the group were made up of kin... . To collect tissue samples for the genetic project, I return to the Pennsylvania woods in late summer... As we approach the boulder-strewn clearing, dozens of females and their babies are lying in huge piles at the base of a large rock... Since natural breaks in the woods are so important ... it is not uncommon to find several different snake species sharing basking ... sites.
[Clark, R. (2005, March). Social lives of rattlesnakes. *Natural History.*]

**F.**

Grandin argues that animals and autistic people are specialists, masters of individual skills and individual senses, whereas ordinary people are generalists.
[Klinkenborg, V. (2005, May). What do animals think? *Discovery*, 51.]

## Adverbial Clauses of Result

| | | |
|---|---|---|
| **such** + (adjective) + noun | + **that** |
| **so** + adjective or adverb | + **that** |
| **so** + many, few, much, little | + **that** |

Result clauses indicate the consequence or result of an action or event. *Such* and *so* must be followed by specific types of words or phrases as indicated in the box above. Here again we see the importance of ESL/EFL learners understanding the distinction between count and noncount nouns, discussed in Chapter 4.

- If the noun after *such* is a singular countable noun, *a* or *an* must precede this noun:

    (22) This is *such **a bad mistake** that* I don't know how to fix it.

- *Many* and *few* are followed by plural count nouns:

    (23) We have *so* **many friends** *that* we can't see everyone at once.
    (24) We have *so* **few quarters** *that* we can't fill the parking meter.

- *Much* and *little* are followed by noncount nouns.

    (25) We have *so* **much fun** *that* we never want to leave.
    (26) We have *so* **much information** *that* it's hard to digest it all.

### Do we always use **that** with **such** and **so**?

In spoken English and less formal written English, we often use *such* and *so* ... without the *that* before the adverbial clause:

    (22a) This is *such* a bad mistake I don't know how to fix it.
    (23a) We have *so* many friends we can't see everyone at once.
    (25a) We have *so* much fun we never want to leave.

Many native speakers, when dropping *that* as in Sentence (22a), will add a pause in speaking and a semi-colon or comma when writing before the adverbial clause:

    (22b) This is *such* a bad mistake; I don't know how to fix it.

### Can we switch the order of the result clause and the main clause?

Unlike the adverbial clauses we have discussed up to now, result clauses and main clauses cannot change order.

### What problems do ESL/EFL learners have with result clauses?

▶ *Learner difficulties*

ESL/EFL learners often have difficulty using the correct article and/or quantifier after *such* and *so* because they have to remember whether or not the noun is count or noncount. Furthermore, if the noun is a count noun, they need to be aware whether it is singular or plural.

Learners of English also become confused as to the meaning of *so* ... *that* clauses when *that* is omitted since *so* can have other meanings.

*Isn't there also another type of clause with* **so and that?**

## Adverbial Clause of Purpose

so that

An adverbial clause with *so that* indicates an intention or purpose. Unlike the *so. . . that* result clause, this *so that* is not separated.

*So that* conveys the idea that the action or event of the main clause deliberately resulted in the action or event in the subordinate clause.

(27) Peggy studied hard *so that* she would do well on the test.

*So that* is usually followed by *can* or *will* for present or future meaning and by *could* or *would* for past time reference. Like the result clauses we just discussed, a purpose clause and a main clause do not change order.

### *Do we always use* **that** *with* **so?**

As we saw with adverbial clauses of result, the *that* after *so* is often omitted, especially in casual speech and informal written English.

(27a) Peggy studied hard *so* she would do well on the test.

*Are clauses with so . . . that and so that confusing to ESL/EFL learners?*

▶ *Learner difficulties*

Learners of English often confuse *so that* purpose clauses with *so. . . that* result clauses. They must keep in mind both the different meanings and the different constructions used with each one.

| so that (purpose)    *versus* | so. . . that (result) |
|---|---|
| • When optional *that* is used with *so*, the two words are together and followed directly by the adverbial clause (Sentence 27).<br>• If *that* is not present, the adverbial clause immediately follows *so* (Sentence 27a). | • *So. . . that* has different constituents inserted between the *so* and the optional *that* (Sentences 22–26).<br>• The adverbial clause follows *that* if is present. If *that* is not present, the adverbial clause follows the sentence constituents after *so* (Sentences 22a, 23a, 25a). |

Another problem for learners of English is confusing *so* meaning *therefore* with the *so* of both result and purpose clauses, especially when *that* is omitted.

The next Discovery Activity will help you practice identifying result versus purpose clauses. The answers are in the Answer Key.

## Discovery Activity 5: Identifying Result and Purpose Clauses

Look at the following excerpts.

1. Circle the subordinator
2. Underline the subordinate result and purpose clauses.

   - Each subordinator is the GLUE. Observe how in each sentence there is one more subject noun phrase than GLUE.

3. Explain which type of subordinate clause each one is.

**A.**

... the little man was much more favourable to me than to any of the others, and he closed the door so that he might have a private word with me.

[Conan Doyle, A. (1983/1892). The Red-Headed League. *The original illustrated sherlock holmes* (p. 30). Secaucus, NJ: Castle. also available on line at: http://www.gutenberg.org/files/2038/2038-h/2038-h.htm#The_Red_Headed_League]

**B.**

Seidel's book succeeds with a simple and honorable premise. [JoeDiMaggio's fifty-six-game hitting] streak itself is such a good story, such an important event in our cultural history, that the day-by-day chronicle will shape a bare sequence into a wonderful drama...

[Gould, S. J. (2003). *Triumph and tragedy in mudville* (p. 178). New York: London.]

**C.**

She was never happy at home, Miss Alice wasn't, from the time that her father married again... As well as I could learn, Miss Alice had rights of her own by will, but she was so quiet and patient, she was, that she never said a word about them, but just left everything in Mr. Rucastle's hands... He wanted her to sign a paper so that whether she married or not, he could use her money.

[Conan Doyle, A. (1983/1892). The adventure of the copper beeches. *The original illustrated sherlock holmes* (p. 180). Secaucus, NJ: Castle. Also available on line at: http://www.gutenberg.org/dirs/etext99/advsh12h.htm#12]

**D.**

"I was so happy to have you helping with the horses," Ashleigh went on, "and so excited about your interest in the farm that I forgot your school responsibilities are just as important..."

> "I'll do better, Aunt Ashleigh, really," Melanie blurted. "I'll learn how to manage my time so I'll get all my homework done."
> [Campbell, J. (1999). *Thoroughbred: Dead heat* (p. 134). New York: Harper-Entertainment.]

We will now investigate adverbial clauses of condition, to which you were originally introduced in Chapter 7 in our examination of the uses of the modal auxiliary *would*. This chapter explores in greater depth the structure and use of these sentences, which refer to some type of possibility or reality.

## Adverbial Clauses of Condition

To review, conditional sentences consist of two parts. One clause is called the *if* class because it is introduced by or begins with the word *if*. The other clause is referred to as the *conditional clause* because this is the part of the sentence that refers to some type of possibility or reality.

There are two types of conditional clauses: (1) real or true and (2) unreal or contrary-to-fact clauses. Both types of conditional clauses are introduced by *if*.

*If* clauses, like many adverbial clauses we have already explored, can be reversed. The *if* clause can come in initial position and the main clause can come in second position:

| | |
|---|---|
| (28) **If** I *had* the time and money, I *would travel* more. | *If* **clause, initial position** |
| (28a) I *would travel* more, **if** I *had* the time and money. | *If* **clause, second position** |

The following chart illustrates the types and times of conditional sentences:

| Conditional Sentences | | | |
|---|---|---|---|
| *if* clause | conditional clause | type | Time |
| (29) *If* Marta *likes* the idea, | I *will present* it to everyone else. | real | present/future |
| (30) *If* Dino *paid* his bills, | he *wouldn't be* in trouble. | unreal | present |
| (31) *If* Jason *had called*, | Beth *would have been* happy. | unreal | past |

*What were the rules for forming the conditional for the different time references?*

## *Real Conditions*

To form **present or future** *real* conditions (Sentence 29):

- In the *if* clause, use a present tense verb.
- In the main clause, use either a present tense verb or *will* + a main verb.

## *Present Unreal Conditions*

To form **present** *unreal* sentences (Sentence 30):

- In the *if* clause, use a past form of the verb.
- In the main clause, use *would* + a main verb.

*Could* and *might* + a main verb can also occur in the main clause. *Could* and *might* change the meaning from contrary-to-fact or unreal to possibility, as we saw in Chapter 7.

## *Past Unreal Conditions*

To form past unreal sentences (Sentence 31):

- In the *if* clause, use the past perfect form of the main verb.
- In the main clause, use w*ould* + *have* + past participle.

*Could/might* + *have* + past participle *can* also occur in the main clause.

### *Are there any irregular conditional verbs?*

One verb, *be*, has the irregular form, *were*. According to formal prescriptive grammar, *were* must be used for first person and third person singular instead of *was*.

> (32)"Maybe *if I weren't* so repulsive-looking—maybe *if I were* pretty like you—"
> [L'Engle, M. (1976/1962). *A wrinkle in time* (p. 10). New York: Dell.]

This form, however, is being lost in modern English. Native speakers will commonly say and write *was* rather than *were* in present unreal clauses. This is true even in formal written English, especially in situations where the subject noun phrase is long and does not immediately precede *be,* as you can see in (33):

> (33)Tobacco prices would have been more stable and less subject to monopoly pricing if tobacco could have freely crossed national borders and **was** supplied from a wider geographical area.
> [Pecquet, G. (2003). British mercantilism and crop controls in the tobacco colonies: A study of rent-seeking costs. *The Cato Journal, 22,* 482.]

## Conditional Sentences Without "If"

### *Do we always use "if" in conditional clauses?*

Past unreal clauses are not always introduced by *if.* Sometimes speakers introduce the subordinate clause by inverting *had* (whether it is the main verb or the auxiliary) with the subject:

| Inverted Past Unreal Clauses | |
| --- | --- |
| (34) *Had* I the time and money, I *would travel* more | **present** <br> *had* = main verb |
| (35) *Had* I *had* the time and money, I *would have traveled* more. | **past** <br> *had* = auxiliary verb |

These past unreal clauses with inversion are less common than past unreal clauses introduced by *if*.


## Pronunciation of Modals in the Conditional

In spoken English the auxiliary *had* and the modals *would / could / might + have* are often contracted. We often see written versions of the contracted forms in dialogues to reflect spoken language.

> (36) You should**'ve** heard him before you showed. . . If *he'd had* a gun on him, *he'd have blown* his brains out.
>     [Grafton, S. (2003). *Q is for quarry* (p. 95). New York: G.P. Putnam's Sons.]

These contractions are not used in formal written English.

You may find Discovery Activity challenging. Do the best you can and be sure to check your answers in the Answer Key only after you have tried the activity.


### Discovery Activity 6: Recognizing Conditional Sentences

Look at the following excerpts.

1. Underline the conditional clauses.
2. Decide which type of conditional clause each one is, i.e. real or unreal.
3. Describe the time referred to in each conditional clause.

**A.**

> "Are you his attorney?"
> She almost smiled. "If I were, I wouldn't be telling you this. . .
>     [Lee, R. (2003). *Last Breath*. New York: Warner, p. 52].

**B.**

> "Have you done your homework, Meg?"
> "Not quite," Meg said. . .
> "Then I'm sure Calvin won't mind if you finish before dinner."

### C.

Had Bianca an adult eye, she might have guessed from its mismatched roofs and inconsistent architectural details that many owners had lived here before her family arrived...

[Maguire, G. (2003). *Mirror mirror: A novel* (p. 6). New York: HarperCollins Publishers.]

### D.

The extent to which we commend someone for operating a complex piece of equipment depends on the circumstances... If he is following oral instructions, if someone is "telling him what to do," we give him slightly more credit... If he is following written instructions, we give him additional credit for knowing how to read...

[Skinner, B.F. (1971). *Beyond freedom & dignity* (p. 44). New York: Bantam.]

### E.

If I wanted to get the kind of Level II quotes and market executions I was used to, I'd have to spend more money than I was currently willing to part with. I opted instead to use a reliable discount broker.

[Richards, L. (2004). *Mad monday* (pp. 59–60). Don Mills, Ontario, Canada: Mira.]

## Mixed Time

*Do speakers always make only one time reference in conditional clauses?*

Frequently the time reference in the *if* clause, and the time reference in the main clause are different. When the time reference in the two parts of the sentence is not the same, we call this *mixed time*. You can see examples of mixed time references in Sentences (37), (38), and (39).

In Sentence (37) the *if* clause refers to **conditional past** time using the past perfect verb tense. The main clause is *could + do* and refers to **present** possibility.

(37) If he'd cooked up a false identity, he could do as he pleased...
    [Grafton, S. (2001). *P is for pearl* (p. 101). New York: Putnam.]

In Sentence (38) the *if* clause refers to **conditional past** time using the past perfect verb tense, just as in (37). The main clause, however, is the **simple past** and refers to a truth or fact.

(38) If Dow had been taken ill, if he'd been injured or killed in a fatal accident, I had no way to know...
    [Grafton, S. (2001). *P is for pearl* (p. 100). New York: Putnam.]

You can see a similar situation in Sentence (38). Here the first part of the sentence is what we call contrary-to-fact and has the conditional verb phrase, *would have done*. The *but* clause is fact and uses the simple past, *invited.*

(39) Wade **would have done** his homework last night, but his friends **invited** him to a movie.

### *Is mixed time confusing to ESL/EFL learners?*

### ▶ *Learner difficulties*

Mixed time is difficult for learners of English because most ESL/EFL grammar texts treat conditional or unreal clauses as separate from real clauses. Thus, when learners encounter sentences with mixed time reference, they are uncertain as to meaning because such forms are often unfamiliar to them. At more advanced levels of proficiency, it is helpful to have learners analyze mixed time clauses in context in order to help them understand these forms.

The next section looks at adverbial clauses of manner, which are related to conditional clauses because they express comparisons to real or unreal situations.

## Adverbial Clauses of Manner

| as if     as though |
| --- |

### *What do you mean by comparisons to unreal situations?*

When speakers want to compare something to something else that is hypothetical or fanciful, they use the phrases *as if* or *as though*, followed by the conditional form. The *as* in these two constructions functions together with either *if* or *though*. It is different from the *as* that introduces an adverbial clause of time or reason.

In Sentence (40) you see the use of *were* to indicate an unreal present situation, or more specifically in this case, a fanciful comparison.

(40) Finally I could see a sort of patch of gray light ahead of us, **as though** there *were* a cleft in the hills.

### *What do you mean by comparisons to real situations?*

*As if* and *as though* can also express comparisons to real situations. Sentence (42) refers to a real possibility or expectation, in contrast to Sentence (41).

(41) It looks **as though** it *is going* snow.

See how well you can identify the time references in the *as if* and *as though* clauses of manner. The answers are at the end of the chapter.

**Discovery Activity 7: *as if* and *as though***

Look at the following excerpts.

1. Underline the examples of *as if* and *as though* that you find.
2. Explain the time reference in the adverbial clause introduced by each example.

*Example*:

She looked at him *as though* he were crazy.
This is an example of *were* referring to present unreal time.

**A.**

Reenie as sucking her thumb and stroking something in her lap with her short, stubby fingers, as if it were a kitten.
[Wood, J. (1995). *When pigs fly* (p. 5). New York: G.P.Putnam's Sons.]

**B.**

Jiniwin's parents had been divorced for three years, and they gave her so little attention it was as though they'd divorced her, too.
[Wood, J. (1995). *When pigs fly* (p. 8). New York: G.P. Putnam's Sons.]

**C.**

He moved so slowly that it scarcely seemed as though he were moving at all, but at last he stood on his feet and then the squirrel scampered back up into the branches of his tree...
[Burnett, F. H. (1911/1982). *The secret garden* (p. 95). New York: Dell.]

**D.**

Starting tomorrow, life is going to be very different for me. I feel as if I'm closing the first chapter on my life as a Traveler and beginning a new and more dangerous one.
[MacHale, D. (2005). *Pendragon, book six: The rivers of zada* (p. 1). New York: Simon & Schuster.]

We have now looked at the different adverbial clauses in English and will now examine adverbial phrases, which are reduced forms of adverbial clauses.

# Section 3: Reduced Adverbial Clauses

## *What are reduced adverbial clauses?*

Reduced adverbial clauses are adverbial clauses that no longer have a full verb phrase. Remember from previous chapters that a verb phrase consists of at least one main verb (e.g. simple present), or of at least one auxiliary + main verb in the appropriate aspect (e.g. present progressive).

***Can all adverbial clauses be reduced?***

Adverbial clauses can be reduced from clauses to phrases under certain conditions:

- These clauses must be adverbial clauses of time beginning with *after, before, while*, and *since*.[2]
- The subject of the adverbial clause and the subject of the main clause must be identical. If there is a different subject for each clause, then the adverbial clause cannot be reduced.

# Reducing Adverbial Clauses

***How do we reduce adverbial clauses to adverbial phrases?***

There are two different ways to reduce the adverbial clauses. How the adverbial time clause is reduced depends upon which verbs are in the verb phrase.

## *A Verb Phrase Including the Auxiliary Verb be*

If the adverbial clause includes a form of the auxiliary verb *be* + present participle, drop the subject and the *be* verb.

| | | |
|---|---|---|
| (42) *While Matt was studying*, he took notes. | → | (42a) *While studying*, he took notes. |
| **subordinator + subject + *be* auxiliary + present participle** | → | **subordinator + present participle** |

In Sentence (42a), we dropped *Matt* and *be*. The sentence now begins with the reduced adverbial clause, *While studying*, followed by the main clause, *he took notes*.

## *A Verb Phrase Including the Main Verb be*

If the adverbial clause includes the main verb *be*, drop the subject and change the *be* form of the verb to *being*.

---

[2] Note that when *since* introduces adverbial clauses of *cause*, these clauses cannot be reduced.

| (43) *After I* **was** late five times, I dropped the class. | → | (43a) *After being* late five times, I dropped the class. |
|---|---|---|
| **subordinator + subject + main verb** *be* | → | **subordinator +** *being* |

## *No be Verb in the Verb Clause*

If there is no form of *be* in the adverbial clause, drop the subject and change the verb in the adverbial clause to a present participle *(-ing)*.

| (44) Since Jason *has graduated*, he has been looking for a job. | → | (44a) Since *graduating* in June, he has been looking for a job. |
|---|---|---|
| **subordinator + subject + main verb (not** *be*) | → | **subordinator + main verb in present participle** |

In Sentence (44a), we dropped *has* and changed *graduated* to *graduating*. The sentence now begins with the adverbial phrase, *Since graduating*, followed by the main clause, *he has been looking for a job*.

## ► *Learner difficulties*

Both learners of English and inexperienced native speakers of English will on occasion use the *–ing* form in the adverbial clause when the subject of the main clause is different from that of the adverbial clause.

*(45) After being late five times, the teacher told me to drop the class.

The subject of the main clause, *the teacher*, is different from the one implied in the reduced adverbial clause, *I*. However, because *the teacher* is the first subject after the reduced adverbial clause, grammatically it acts as the subject of this reduced adverbial clause, even though logically we know it isn't. Similar problems will be discussed in Chapter 12.

This concludes our exploration of the first of the three types of complex sentences we will be investigating in Chapters 9, 10, and 11.

# Summary

| Adverbial Clause Types | | |
|---|---|---|
| **type** | **subordinators** | |
| • **time** | before after until while when since as | *After* we left, the town changed. |
| • **contrast** | although even though though while whereas inasmuch as | *Although* Jack studied, he didn't pass the test. |
| • **place** | where | Many people prefer to live *where* the climate is warm. |
| • **cause** | because since as whereas inasmuch as | They came late *because* the traffic was bad. |
| • **result** | such. . . that so. . . that | There are *so* many cars on the road *that* the traffic is always bad. |
| • **purpose** | so that | She majored in business *so that* she could get a good job. |
| • **conditional**<br>  • **real**<br>    • **present/ future** | If | *If* Jay *comes*, we*'ll have* a party. |
|   • **unreal**<br>    • **present** | | *If* I *were* rich, I *would* travel around the world. |
|     • **past** | | *If* Jenny *had been* rich, she *would have bought* a yacht. |
| • **manner** | as if as though | Melissa petted the wolf cub *as though* it were a puppy. |

| Sentence Types | | |
|---|---|---|
| **Type** | **Example** | **Explanation** |
| | Greg is sleeping | subject + verb phrase |
| **Simple Sentence** | Greg read books. | subject + verb phrase + complement (object) |
| **Compound Sentence** | Cindy is sleeping and Vera is reading. | two simple sentences conjoined by a conjunction |
| **Complex Sentence** | Since it rained last night, the river is flooding. | subordinate clause + simple sentence (main clause) |

# Practice Activities

## *Activity 1: Coordinator Identification*

1. Open any book, newspaper, or magazine.
2. Underline the compound sentences you find.

- Which coordinator or coordinator(s) occur(s) most frequently?
- Which one(s) did you have trouble finding?

## Activity 2: Transition Words and Phrases

Look at the following pairs of sentences.

1. On a separate sheet of paper, join each pair together using as many transition words and phrases as you can (you can change the order of the clauses if you want.)
2. Discuss the differences in meaning when you change the transition words and phrases

*Example*

> It snowed. We left.
> It snowed; **consequently**, we left.
> It snowed; **therefore**, we left.

a) I was extremely hungry. I started eating before you came.
b) My mother left school when she was sixteen. She has had a very successful career as a writer.
c) Jeremy failed the test. He passed the course.

## Activity 3: Complex Sentence Variation

1. Look at the following pairs of sentences.
2. On a separate sheet of paper, try combining each pair into as many different complex adverbial sentences as possible.
3. Think about how the meaning changes when you add different adverbial subordinators.

*Example*

> It snowed. We stayed home.
> **Because** it snowed, we stayed home.
> **When** it snowed, we stayed home.
> **While** it snowed, we stayed home.
> **As** it snowed, we stayed home.

a) I was extremely hungry. I started eating before you came.
b) My mother left school when she was sixteen. She has had a very successful career as a writer.
c) Math is hard for Eva. She had to study to pass the course.

d) Jeremy failed the test. He passed the course.

e) The water boiled over. She was talking on the phone.

## Activity 4: Identifying Types of Adverbial Clauses

1. Underline the subordinate clauses.
2. Label each type of adverbial clause

> Reading and writing grow out of the students' own experiences and interests... As they attempt to express their thoughts to another person in writing, the students are pushed to attempt structures they have not yet mastered... Although they are not composing autonomous text, they are developing abilities essential for writing...
>
> [Johnson, D. & Roen, D. (1989). *Richness in writing* (p. 111). White Plains: Longman.]

## Activity 5: Distinguishing Meaning

Look at the pairs of excerpts below.

- Discuss the differences in meaning between the same subordinators.
- Be careful not to confuse other functions of *as* with *as* functioning as a subordinator.

**A.**

*since*

1.  Since much of our social reality is understood in metaphorical terms, and since our conception of the physical world is partly metaphorical, metaphor plays a very significant role in determining what is real for us.

    [Lakoff, G. & Johnson, M. (1980). *Metaphors we live by* (p. 146). Chicago: University of Chicago Press.]

2.  The Common Application is simpler, more utilitarian—and soaring in popularity. Since a nonprofit consortium of colleges behind it was founded in 1975, membership has swelled from 15 to 298 schools.

    [Springer, K. (2006, December 4). College: A more common application process. *Newsweek*, p. 12].

**B.**

*as*

1.  Mary had liked to look at her mother from a distance and she had thought her very pretty, but as she knew very little of her she could scarcely have been expected to love her or to miss her very much when she was gone. She did not miss her at all, in fact, and as she was a self-absorbed child she gave her entire thought to her self . . .

    [Burnett, F. H. (1911/1982). *The secret garden* (p. 8). New York: Yearling.]

2.  As he made his way into the rehabilitation hospital where Kendra was a patient, Isaac
    Taylor flipped off his cell phone and slid it into the leather holster...

    [Richards, E. (2006). *Lover's knot* (p. 19). Don Mills, Ontario: Mira.]

## Activity 6: Identifying Different Types of Clauses

Look at the excerpts below.

1. Find the compound clauses. Label these CC
2. Find the adverbial clauses. Label these AC

   - Explain what type of adverbial clause each one is.

**A.**

Mr. McGregor was on his hands and knees planting out young cabbages, but he jumped up
and ran after Peter, waving a rake and calling out, "Stop thief!" Peter was most dreadfully
frightened; he rushed all over the garden, for he had forgotten the way back to the gate. He
lost one of his shoes among the cabbages, and the other shoe amongst the potatoes. After
losing them, he ran on four legs and went faster, so that I think he might have gotten away
altogether if he had not unfortunately run into a gooseberry net, and got caught by the large
buttons on his jacket.

   [Potter, B. (1902/1992). *The Tale of Peter Rabbit*. London: Penguin, pp. 26–30].

**B.**

It was a good thing Kerby had warned Fenton not to say anything about the set, because
his mother was in the kitchen when they came inside... Twenty seconds later Kerby had
the chemistry set out on his desk and his visitor was carefully inspecting the special tube.
Fenton Claypool squinted narrowly at the liquid in the tube and pressed his lips together
thoughtfully...

"This set looks very old..."

   "It belonged to Mrs. Graymalkin's little boy, and any little boy *she* ever had must be
pretty old by now..."

   "Then it's very old. So old we can't even read the label any more..."

   [Corbett, S. (1960). *The lemonade trick* (pp. 70–72). New York: Apple Paperbacks.]

## Activity 7: Identifying Conditional Clauses

1. Look at the excerpts from the children's story *If I Were President*.
2. Underline the different conditional clauses.

   - Explain which type of conditional clause each one is.

It would be great to be president of the United States! If I were president, that means after
a big campaign with speeches and posters and TV ads, the people would have chosen me
as their leader. Years of planning and hard work would have prepared me for that day.
If I were president, I'd promise to "preserve, protect, and defend the Constitution of the
United States," because that would be my job... If I were president, I could go bowling
or visit a movie theater without every leaving my house. I'd have my own chef and could

eat whatever I wanted... If I were president, each year I'd give a speech to Congress... All over the country, people would be watching and listening... Congress would present bills... If I didn't like an idea, I'd say no... But if I agreed, I'd sign the bill and make it a law... If I were president, I'd comfort families that had been in an earthquake, hurricane, or flood. Then I'd help them rebuild their towns... If I were president, the people could only elect me twice... Then I'd have to find a new job and a new house... If I were president, they might someday make a statue of me... Or someday my face might show up on the country's money.

[Stier, C. (1999). *If i were president*. Morton Grove, IL: Albert Whitman & Company, No page numbers.]

## Activity 8: Error Analysis A

The following excerpts were written by ESL students. There are errors in compound and complex sentence. Because these are actual excerpts, there are different kinds of errors. However, your job is to evaluate **only the errors related to adverbial clauses.** You may find the other errors distracting, but remember one of your jobs as an ESL/EFL teacher is to be able to pay attention to specific errors in different circumstances.

1. Find the adverbial clause errors. **Only focus on these errors.**
2. Discuss how an explanation of GLUE would be helpful in addressing some of the learners' difficulties.

**A.**
Although studying music and becoming a professional pianist sound good, but I cannot guarantee that you can have a good job. However, if you will study to be a doctor, I can guarantee that you can find a good job. If you will pursue a doctor career, it will enhance your quality of life now and forever.

**B.**
I want to be a policewoman. Because, I like to be. When I'm big I like to be you! My good dream was when I'm a princess. Because I am very beautiful like you!

**C.**
Now, I don't have some children, but if I have a child I want to give a gift for my child, a dog or cat. Dogs and cats help child develop. If a child have a cat or dog, he has to take care of it. If the child didn't take care of the cat or dog, it will be bad for the cat or dog.

## Activity 9: Error Analysis B

The following excerpt was written by an EFL student who was studying the use of transitions.

1. Identify which errors you see. Focus **only on the transition word and phrase problems.**

In an ESL classroom, it will be interesting for students from different cultural backgrounds to have teacher who uses communicative teaching. In an EFL setting, however, because the language teacher and the students are likely to belong to the same language and cultural background. It will be more difficult for meaningful topic discussions to occur in classrooms since students all speak the same language, perhaps having large gaps between their proficiency levels in English and their native language. In addition, there are also usually very big classes with 30 or more students and it makes it very hard for the teacher to give everyone a chance and for everyone not to speak in their native language with everyone, but use English. Nevertheless, it will be a challenge for EFL teachers to use communicative teaching in their classes.

## Answer Key: Chapter 9 Discovery Activities

### *Discussion: Discover Activity 1*

*Excerpt A*

- The two main clauses are conjoined by the coordinator *for.*

  o In modern American English *for* as a coordinator is more used in formal sentences than in spoken or informal written English.

*Excerpt B*

- The two main clauses are conjoined by the coordinator *yet.*

*Excerpt C*

- two coordinators: *but* and *and.*

*Excerpt D*

- two coordinators: *and* and *or.*

  o no subject noun phrases before the verbs *weave, put, catch, string,* or *watch.* When the subject is identical in two clauses of a compound sentence, it is left out to avoid repetition.
  o Likewise, after the last *or* in this sentence the verb *watch* has also been left out because it is the same verb as in the previous clause.

### *Discussion: Discovery Activity 2*

*Excerpt A*

- *as a result* and *thus:* meaning "result"

*Excerpt B*

- *in addition,* and *further:* meaning "addition"

*Excerpt C*

- *moreover:* meaning "addition"
- *nonetheless:* meaning "contrast"

*Excerpt D*

- *thus,* and *consequently:* meaning "result"

## Discussion: Discovery Activity 3

*Excerpt A*

- *when* is the subordinator and *he was young* is the subordinate clause.

*Excerpt B*

- *before* is the subordinator and *grammar came along and ruined things* is a subordinate clause plus a compound clause conjoined by *and.*

*Excerpt C*

- *as* is the subordinator and introduces the subordinate clauses, *you read this* and *you continue to read.*

*Excerpt D*

- *until* and *'til* are the subordinators.

  o *'til* is considered by some stylebooks an incorrect form for till, but is often found in dialogues and informal writing.

## Discussion: Discovery Activity 4

*Excerpt A*

- *even though* introduces an adverbial clause of contrast.

*Excerpt B*

- *wherever* introduces an adverbial clause of place.

*Excerpt C*

- *although* implies an unexpected result.

*Excerpt D*

- *while* conveys the idea of a direct contrast.

*Excerpt E*

- *because* and *since* introduce adverbial clauses of reason.
- *as* introduces an adverbial clause of time.

*Excerpt F*

- *whereas* conveys the idea of contrast.

## Discussion: Discovery Activity 5

*Excerpt A*

- *so that* introduces an adverbial clause of purpose.

*Excerpt B*

- *such* + the noun phrase, *a good story* and *such* + a second noun phase, *an important event*, + the prepositional phrase *in our cultural history* + *that* + the adverbial clause of result.

  - This can be confusing because both *such a good story* and *such an important event in our cultural history* are part of the same result clause with the one *that*.

*Excerpt C*

- *so* followed by two adjectives, *quiet* and *patient* + *she was* + *that* + the adverbial clause of result.
- *so that* introduces an adverbial clause of purpose.

*Excerpt F*

- *so* is followed by *happy* . . . and *so excited* + prepositional phrase (*about your interest in the farm*) + *that* + the adverbial clause of result.
- *so* introduces an adverbial clause of purpose. The *that* has been omitted here.

## Discussion: Discovery Activity 6

*Excerpt A*

- *If I were you, I wouldn't be telling:* present/progressive, unreal clause

*Excerpt B*

- *Calvin won't mind if you finish:* future real clause

*Excerpt C*

- *Had Bianca. . . she might have guessed:* inverted present/unreal clause
- example of mixed time

*Excerpt D*

- *If he is following oral instructions, if someone is "telling him what to do ... we give:"* present progressive, real clause
- *If he is following written instructions:* present progressive/present, real clause

*Excerpt E*

- *If I wanted... + I'd have to:* present unreal

### Discussion: Discovery Activity 7

*Excerpt A*

- *as if* followed by *were:* present unreal
  - ○ In informal spoken and written English *was* is often used instead of *were*.

*Excerpt B*

- *as though:* past unreal situation, *they'd (had) divorced her, too*.

*Excerpt C*

- *as though:* unreal past progressive.

*Excerpt D*

- *as if* followed by a present real condition *I'm closing... and beginning*.
  - ○ The sentence is a compound sentence, conjoined by the coordinator *and* as discussed in Chapter 8.

## Reference

Marshall, H. (1982). GLUE: A useful concept for eliminating run-ons. *TESOL Newsletter, 16*(1).

# Chapter 10
# Complex Sentences Continued Relative Clauses

## Introduction

In Chapter 9 you were introduced to one type of complex clause, adverbial clauses. In this chapter we will be discussing another type of complex clause, relative clauses. We will consider what relative clauses are, the different types of relative clauses and how they are formed. Section 1 focuses on relative pronouns; Section 2 examines relative adverbs, and Section 3 reduced relative clauses.

### What is a relative clause?

A relative clause is a group of words that describes a noun or noun phrase. Relative clauses are also referred to as *adjective* clauses because the function of these clauses is to describe or modify a preceding noun phrase. In other words, relative clauses describe or provide information about someone or something in the main clause, very similar to the modifying function of adjectives. Like adverbial clauses, relative clauses are a type of dependent clause and cannot stand alone. Relative clauses must be accompanied by a main clause.

A relative clause is usually found immediately after the noun phrase it is modifying. At times a relative clause can modify the entire main clause, in which case it will immediately follow that clause.

## The Relative Pronouns

| who | whom | that | which | whose |
| --- | --- | --- | --- | --- |

Relative clauses are generally introduced by relative pronouns. English has five relative pronouns: *who, whom, that, which,* and *whose*. For people, we generally use *who, whom,* and sometimes *that*. For everything else, we use *which* or *that*. We use *whose* to refer to possession.

In formal prescriptive English, *that* should not be used for people, only *who* or *whom*. Nevertheless, it is common for native speakers to use *that* for people both in speaking and less formal writing.

A. DeCapua, *Grammar for Teachers,*
© Springer 2008

*Which* refers to things or concepts, never people. It is important to emphasize and practice with ESL/EFL students that the relative pronoun *which*, unlike *that*, is used only to refer to things or concepts, not to people.

## Section 1: Two Types of Relative Clauses: Essential and Nonessential

### *What is the difference between essential and nonessential clauses?*

There are two types of relative clauses, *essential* and *nonessential*. Different grammar books may call these two types of relative clauses *restrictive* and *nonrestrictive* or *defining* and *non-defining*. Regardless of the label, the distinction between the two types of clauses is based on whether or not a relative clause is necessary for the sentence to have meaning.

Essential clauses include information that gives the sentence meaning. The information in such relative clauses provides key or "essential" information. Nonessential clauses give additional information that is not necessary for the sentence to have meaning. The information in these clauses is extra or "nonessential" information.

| Essential versus Nonessential Relative Clauses | |
|---|---|
| **Example (A)** The teacher who just graduated is the newest teacher in the school. | **Example (B)** The social studies teacher, who is new, is teaching a large class. |
| An **essential** relative clause: | A **nonessential** relative clause: |
| • gives information that is needed in order to identify or limit the noun phrase it is modifying. | • adds extra information or supporting detail about the noun phrase it is modifying. |
| • gives central meaning to the clause by narrowing down the class, group, or category of the noun phrase being modified. | • The main clause still has clear meaning even if the relative clause is taken away. |

In Example (A), the relative clause, *who just graduated*, is specifying which particular teacher is the newest teacher in the school. In Example (B), *who is new*, is merely adding additional information about the social studies teacher, information that is not important to the fact of "teaching a large class."

### *In addition to modifying a noun or noun phrase, what else can a relative clause modify?*

Some relative clauses modify an entire clause, not just a preceding noun phrase. The relative pronoun *which* is used when a relative clause modifies another clause:

(1) He had some ideas about the ballasting of ships, **which** Father admired . . .
    [McKinley, R. (1978). *Beauty: A retelling of beauty & the beast* (p. 9). New York: HarperTrophy.]

(2) When I was not too tired, **which** happened more often as I grew accustomed to the work, I would stay up an extra hour and read by the light of one precious candle.[McKinley, R. (1978). *Beauty: A retelling of beauty & the beast* (p. 38). New York: HarperTrophy.]

- In Sentence (1), the relative pronoun *which* is modifying the entire preceding clause, *He had some ideas about the ballasting of ships.*
- In Sentence (2), *which* occurs within the two parts of the main clause and is modifying, *When I was not too tired.*

### *Can both essential and nonessential relative clauses modify an entire clause?*

Both essential and nonessential relative clauses can modify an entire clause. Essential relative clauses that modify an entire clause are preceded by a comma. These clauses should not be confused with nonessential relative clauses that provide extra information about the noun phrase, as in Sentences (3a), and (3b). Compare the two sentences:

(3a) Jason kept on telling jokes which made all of us really angry.
(3b) Jason kept on telling jokes, which made all of us really angry.

The inclusion or omission of the comma after the relative pronoun *which* in Sentence (3a), and Sentence (3b) changes the meaning of the sentence. In Sentence (3a), *which* is modifying *jokes*. It is specifying or identifying the type of jokes Jason told, namely jokes that angered "us", maybe because they were off-color, sexist, racist, or whatever.

In Sentence (3b), *which* is modifying the main clause *Jason kept on telling jokes*. In this sentence, the relative clause is telling us that the act of telling (versus the jokes themselves as in 3a) angered "us."

### *How do we know whether to use* **which** *or* **that**?

## *Which versus That*

In formal prescriptive grammar, a distinction is drawn between when to use *which* and when to use *that*. According to prescriptive grammar, *which* should be used in nonessential clauses and *that* should be used in essential clauses. However, native speakers will often use *which* in place of *that* in **essential** clauses. On the other hand, native speakers rarely substitute *that* for *which* in nonessential clauses.

### *Should I teach my students this distinction?*

Not using *that* in nonessential clauses is certainly something ESL/EFL students need to be aware of. With respect to whether you should teach the distinction between *which* and *that* in essential clauses depends on the goals of your students. Are the students preparing to take a standardized test based on formal grammar? Are they more interested in becoming better communicators? Are you teaching in an EFL curriculum with a national curriculum and traditional grammar text?

These and more questions relevant to your teaching situation will help you in deciding whether or not to teach this distinction. If you do decide to teach it, keep in mind that not all grammar and stylebooks today agree on whether or not the distinction should be maintained, so your students should be aware of the alternatives they are likely to encounter.

This first Discovery Activity provides practice in identifying essential and nonessential relative clauses. When you have completed all the excerpts, turn to the end of the chapter to the section labeled "Answer Key" and check your answers.

### Discovery Activity 1: Identifying Essential and Nonessential Relative Clauses

Look at the following excerpts.

1. Underline the relative clauses.
2. Label the relative clauses you have identified as either essential or nonessential.

**A.**

When Mattel first broke ground here in 1967, Taiwan was still considered an underdeveloped country. But the Barbie factory, which was quickly followed by three others on the island, helped unleash an astonishing...economic miracle...The island, which is approximately the size of West Virginia, is the fifth largest economy in Asia...

[Dmitri, H. (2005). Barbie's taiwanese homecoming. *Reason, 37*(1), 40–41.]

**B.**

Another surprising find was four miniature silver coffins that had held the king's internal organs...With silver coffins and jewelry rivaling Tutankhamun's, these northern kings were obviously a force to be reckoned with, and were not weak rulers who were barely hanging on to what little power they had.

[Brier, B. (2005, May/June). Treasures of tanis. *Archeology*, 20–21.]

**C.**

The older Vega daughter, Paula, and her new boyfriend, whose name Gail had already forgotten, sat at the far end of the table. Neither of them spoke any English.

[Parker, B. (2005). *Suspicion of rage* (p. 70). New York: Penguin.]

**D.**

My neighbors use the dipthong-rich vowels of the hill accent that was my own first language. After I met, fell in love with, and married the man who was working this land....

[Kingsolver, B. (2002). *Small wonder* (pp. 32–33). New York: HarperCollins.]

*When do we use the relative pronoun* **whose?**

## *Whose*

The relative pronoun *whose* refers to the possession of something by someone. It signals a possessive relationship between two nouns. The relative pronoun *whose* can occur in both essential and nonessential clauses.

(4) The girl *whose* book I borrowed isn't here today.

In Sentence (4) **whose** tells us that the book belongs to the girl. A rule of thumb for understanding the use of *whose* is to consider whether *his, her, its, their* or a possessive form of the noun (apostrophe *'s*) can be substituted:

(5) Eve is the student *whose* grades were the highest in the school.

her grades

Eve's grades

*Can we use* **whose** *for people and things?*

In traditional prescriptive English, *whose* is considered appropriate only for use with persons and animate objects. The construction *noun phrase + of which* is used to refer to possession with inanimate objects:

(6) The tsunami, *the effects of which* are still felt, was devastating.

This *noun phrase + of which* construction is considered formal and found most often in written English. At times this construction can be awkward and unwieldy. Native speakers will generally either avoid the *noun phrase + of which* construction or use *whose* with inanimate objects:

| | |
|---|---|
| (7a) The tsunami was devastating and its effects are still felt. | **alternative construction** |
| (7b) The effects of the devastating tsunami are still felt. | **alternative construction** |
| (7c) The tsunami, *whose effects* are still felt, was devastating. | ***whose*** |

## ▶ *Learner difficulties*

### *whose versus who's*

Both native speakers and ESL/EFL students sometimes confuse the contracted form *who's* with the possessive form *whose* in written English because both forms sound identical in spoken speech.

| | |
|---|---|
| (8) Cindy is the girl *who's* living with Pam. | **contraction of *who* + is** |
| (8a) Ariel is the girl *whose* car Mike bought. | **relative pronoun** |

Students often need practice in recognizing the different functions of these identical sounding structures.

## Relative Pronouns as Subjects and Objects

Relative pronouns can function as **subjects** of a relative clause or they can function as the **objects** of the relative clause. This is an important distinction ESL/EFL students need to learn because the function of the relative pronoun determines several different things.

### *How do we determine the function of a relative pronoun?*

One way to distinguish the function of relative pronoun is to examine what is following the relative pronoun:

- If there is a *verb phrase* following the relative pronoun, it is functioning as the **subject** of the relative clause.
- If there is a *pronoun* or *noun phrase* following the relative pronoun, it is functioning as the **object** of the relative clause.

Look at the two tables below, which illustrate the two functions of relative pronouns.

| Relative Pronoun as the Subject of the Verb Phrase in Relative Clause | | | |
|---|---|---|---|
| main clause | relative pronoun | verb phrase (VP) | complement |
| (9) Jenny wanted a cat | that | purred | a lot. |
| (10) Blair likes students | who | study | hard. |

In Sentences (9) and (10) the relative pronouns are followed by a verb phrase. Both *that* and *who* are functioning as the subjects of their respective verb phrases. Both are the subjects of their relative clauses.

| Relative Pronoun as the Object of the Verb Phrase in Relative Clause | | | |
|---|---|---|---|
| main clause | relative pronoun | pronoun/noun phrase | verb phrase (VP) |
| (11) Astrid saw the movie | that | her friends | had recommended. |
| (12) Cami is the new girl | whom | the class | met. |

In Sentences (11) and (12), the relative pronouns are followed by noun phrases or pronouns. These noun phrases are the subjects of the relative clause and the relative pronoun is the object of the relative clause.

Completing a chart, such as in Discovery Activity 2, is a useful way to help visualize the role of a relative pronoun in a sentence.

**Discovery Activity 2: Distinguishing Relative Pronouns as Subjects versus Objects**

1. Look at the following sentences.
2. Enter each sentence into the chart.

- The first two sentences are done for you as examples.

Completing the chart will help you visualize the function of each relative pronoun

| subject | VP | object | relative pronoun | subject | VP | complement | role of relative pronoun |
|---|---|---|---|---|---|---|---|
| George | saw | the movie | that | | had won | an award. | subject |
| George | saw | the movie | that | I | wanted to see. | | object |

1. George saw the movie that had won an award.
2. George saw the movie that I wanted to see.
3. I found the keys that Sam had lost yesterday.
4. I found the keys that belong to Sam.
5. The big dog barked at the child who was crying hard.
6. The big dog barked at the child who the mother was chasing.
7. The teacher returned the tests that she had corrected.
8. The teacher returned the tests that counted for 50% of the grade.
9. The scientists who discovered the new burial ground became famous.
10. The scientists have discovered the man who they were looking for.

## Discussion: Discovery Activity 2

- In Sentences (1), (4), (5), (8), and (9), the relative pronoun is functioning as the subject of the verb phrase of the relative clause.
- In Sentences (2), (3), (6), (7), and (10), the relative pronoun is functioning as the object of the verb phrase.

From the standpoint of formal prescriptive grammar, in Sentences (6) and (10), the correct form of the relative pronoun is *whom*, not *who* because the relative pronoun is in object position. In addition, in very formal prescriptive grammar, a preposition should not come at the end of a sentence; thus in (10) *for* should precede the relative pronoun *who*:

(10a) The scientists have discovered the man **for whom** they were looking.

*How do I choose between* **who** *and* **whom?**

# Who versus whom

*Who* and *whom* are alternate forms, the choice of which depends on the function of the relative pronoun. In formal prescriptive English, *who* is used when the relative pronoun is the **subject** of the relative clause. *Whom* must be used whenever it is the **object** of the relative clause.

The relative pronoun *who* is commonly used in spoken and informal written English as both the subject and object relative pronoun. Both native and non-native speakers frequently have difficulty distinguishing, or even remembering the distinction, between the subject and object function of the relative pronoun. Choosing between the two forms is often difficult for native speakers because, as we discussed in Chapters 1 & 3, the distinction between the two forms is being lost in modern English

In addition, difficulties in choosing between *who* versus *whom* in relative clauses lies partially in the fact that all relative pronouns occur at the beginning of the relative clause, regardless of their function. In not understanding clearly the difference in use between the two forms, speakers may substitute *whom* for *who* when the relative pronoun is actually in subject position.

One way for native speakers and highly proficient learners of English to evaluate whether or not to use *whom* or *who*, is to try the sentence with *who* left out. If *who* can be omitted, then the relative pronoun is in object position and *whom* is the correct formal form. We will discuss the omission of relative pronouns in greater length after the next Discovery Activity.

See how well you do in deciding between *who* and *whom* by completing Discovery Activity 3.

**Discovery Activity 3: Choosing Between *who* and *whom* in Relative Clauses**

On a separate sheet of paper, complete each sentence with either *who* or *whom*.

1. The doctors _____ had completed their training in Boston earned the most.
2. The bus driver _____ had had his license revoked was soon back on the job.
3. The movie director to _____ the studio had granted $10 million went over budget.
4. The little girl _____ is holding her mother's hand is walking across the street.
5. The business people_____ have become the most successful work long hours.

6. The people _____ the drug company chose for its drug trials were seriously ill.
7. The president and CEO of the company _____ the board had recently elected resigned yesterday.
8. The department elected a new chairperson _____ was known for her leadership abilities.
9. The suit Kelly bought is being altered by a tailor _____ the store had recommended.
10. The students completed evaluations on the teacher _____ was teaching the course that semester.

## Discussion: Discovery Activity 3

- *who:* Sentences (1), (2), (4), (5), (8), and (10)
- *whom:* Sentences (3), (6), (7), and (9).

Remember that if *who(m)* is followed by a verb phrase, this relative pronoun is functioning as the **subject**. If *who(m)* is followed by a noun or noun phrase, then this relative pronoun is functioning as the **object**. If there is a preposition before *who(m)*, then formal English requires *whom* since the relative pronoun is the object of this preposition. In spoken and informal written English, however, many native speakers would use *who* in all instances.

## Omission of Relative Pronouns

### When can we omit a relative pronoun?

As you have already seen, an important point in understanding relative clauses is determining whether or not the relative pronoun is functioning as the subject or object of the relative clause. This is underscored by the fact that we can at times omit the relative pronoun. When the relative pronoun *who, whom, that,* or *which* is the **object** of the relative clause, we can omit the relative pronoun. (The relative pronoun *whose* cannot be omitted). We can omit a relative pronoun only in **essential** relative clauses and only when the relative pronoun is the **object** of the verb phrase).

| Omission of Relative Pronoun | | | |
|---|---|---|---|
| (13) Susan bought the book | *that* | the teacher liked. | • *That* is the object of *liked*.<br>• *The teacher* is the subject of *liked*. |
| (13a) Susan bought the book | Ø | the teacher liked. | • Because *that* is functioning as object in an essential relative clause, *that* can be omitted. |

We cannot omit the relative pronoun in the following sentences because the relative pronouns are the subjects of the verbs:

| No Omission of Relative Pronoun Possible | | |
| --- | --- | --- |
| (14) Susan wanted to buy the book | *that* | **was** on the bestseller list. |
| (15) The teacher | *who* | **taught** us last year has retired. |
| *(14a) Susan wanted to buy the book | | was on the bestseller list. |
| *(15a) The teacher | | taught us last year has retired |

Discover Activity 4 provides an introduction to omitting relative pronouns. If you feel confident in your knowledge of when and when not to omit relative pronouns, move on to Discovery Activity 5. The answers to this Discovery Activity are at the end of the chapter in the Answer Key.

## Discovery Activity 4: Omitting Relative Pronouns

a. Look at the following sentences.
b. Decide whether or not the relative pronoun can be omitted in the following sentences.

1. Last week Gina Giarda stood before her fans who had come from as far away as Japan to applaud her success.
2. Gina Giarda has become a performer who every music lover recognizes.
3. Music was something that she had loved from her earliest days.
4. Barely more than a toddler, Gina learned to play the violin from her parents who were talented musicians.
5. When she was eight, she received a prize that made her famous in classical music circles.
6. Later she began to write songs that she performed all over the world.

Discover Activities 5 and 6 are more challenging than Discovery Activity 4. Discovery Activity 5 asks you to practice identifying omitted relative pronouns in isolated, teacher-created sentences. Discover Activity 6 builds on Discovery Activity 5 and asks you to identity relative clauses with omitted relative pronouns. These relative clauses come from authentic excerpts.

## Discovery Activity 5: Identifying Relative Clauses without Relative Pronouns

Look at the following sentences in which the relative pronouns have been omitted.

a. Underline the relative clause in each sentence.
b. Decide which relative pronoun was omitted and place the symbol ($^\wedge$) where it should go.

*Example*:

Evan sent me a letter $^\wedge$ *I forgot to answer.*
Omitted relative pronoun: that

1. The linguistics textbook Nora bought cost over $100.
2. The new flight attendants the airline had hired quit last week.
3. The children got all the toys they asked for.
4. He finally met the woman he wanted to marry.
5. The animal shelter has many wonderful animals you can adopt.
6. The movie the kids rented was PG13.
7. The science teacher all the students love is retiring at the end of the year.
8. Tina bought the car my brother was selling.

## Discussion: Discovery Activity 5

*Sentence 1*

- We can insert *that* after *textbook*.
- The relative pronoun is the object of the verb phrase *bought*.

*Sentence 2*

- We can insert *whom* or less formally, *who*, after *attendants*. Some people may choose to use *that*, which is acceptable for informal spoken and written English.
- In formal English *whom* is the preferred form because it is the object of the verb phrase *hired*.

*Sentence 3*

- We can insert *that* after *toys*.
- The relative pronoun is the object of the verb phrase *asked for*.

*Sentence 4*

- We can insert *whom* or less formally, *who* after *woman*. Some people may choose to use *that*, which is acceptable for spoken and informal written English.

*Sentence 5*

- We can insert *that* after *animals*.
- The relative pronoun is the object of the verb phrase *can adopt*.

*Sentence 6*

- We can insert *that* after *movie.*
- The relative pronoun is the object of the verb *rented.*

*Sentence 7*

- We can insert *whom* or less formal *who* after *teachers.* Some people may choose to use *that,* which is acceptable for spoken and informal written English.

*Sentence 8*

- We can insert *that* after *car.*
- The relative pronoun is the object of the verb phrase *was selling.*

In completing this activity and in reviewing your answers, you may have noticed that you could use *that* in every case. As we noted in Sentence (4), for instance, *that* is considered acceptable for referring to people in spoken and informal written English. In formal English, *who/whom* should be used to refer to people. In addition, in the sentences where you inserted *that* to refer to animals or things, many native speakers would use *which,* even though formal prescriptive grammar requires *that* in essential clauses.

The next Discovery Activity provides an opportunity for identifying relative clauses with or without relative pronouns. You may find this activity more challenging than the previous two Discovery Activities. This is a long Discovery Activity, so if you find you have no difficulties after the first 3 or 4 excerpts, check your answers in the Answer Key at the end of the chapter. If you had no mistakes, feel free to move on.

---

**Discovery Activity 6: Identifying Relative Clauses with or without Relative Pronouns**

Look at the following excerpts.

1. Underline the relative clause in each sentence.
2. See if you can find relative clauses where the relative pronoun has beens omitted.
3. Provide the omitted relative pronoun.

**A.**

The effort is the force that moves the lever. The load is the weight the lever is trying to move. The fulcrum is the pivot, the point on which the lever moves.
    [Simple Machines: Meet the Levers. (2005). *Kids Discover, 15*(4).]

**B.**

All recent hunter-gatherers are modern human beings (*Homo sapiens*) whose cultures are the products of long histories. They all possess languages, practical skills, beliefs, arts, and values that are fully modern in every sense.
    [Gould, R. (2005). Lessons from the aborigines. The discovery of lucy. *Dig,* 7(4), 18.]

## C.

Mainly, they foraged for plants they could bring back to camp and process in some way to make them edible... Then there were appliances—tools like stone seed-grinding slabs that were too heavy to be carried easily from place to place. These were usually left at campsites that were revisited again and again... While fire is not an object, it is one of the most important kinds of technology we find among modern-day and historic hunter-gatherers.

[Gould, R. (2005). Lessons from the aborigines. The discovery of lucy. *Dig, 7*(4), 19–20.]

## D.

At the next door, García led him into a small foyer whose mosaic-patterned tile walls were barely visible in the light of a bulb...

[Parker, B. (2005). *Suspicion of rage* (p. 122). New York: Penguin.]

## E.

Maddie remembers all too vividly an unfortunate faux pas I committed after I managed to carry on a lengthy conversation with a dark-haired girl I repeatedly called Claire, even though, according to my mortified daughter, Rachel (her actual name) bore absolutely no resemblance to Claire.

[Murphy, A. P. (2004). *The 7 stages of motherhood* (p. 193). New York: Alfred A. Knopf.]

The next Discovery Activity is intended for extra practice. If you had difficulties with Discovery Activity 6, you should also do Discovery Activity 7. If you had no problems, continue on to the next section. The answers to Discovery Activity 7 are available in the Answer Key.

### Discovery Activity 7: More Practice in Identifying Relative Pronouns
### Part I.

Look at the following excerpts.

1. Circle the relative pronouns.
2. Underline what the relative pronoun is modifying.

## A.

Here she was then, Precious Ramotswe, owner of Botswana's only detective agency, The No.1 Ladies' Detective Agency—an agency which by and large had lived up to its initial promise to provide satisfaction for its clients...

[Smith, A. M. (2002). *The kalahari typing school for men* (p. 3). New York: Pantheon Books.]

## B.

In the Arthurian world, the most dangerous foes came in the least likely guises. Heroic knights who slew giants, wizards and even dragons were often entrapped by the frailest maidens.

[Day, D. (1999). *King arthur* (p. 63). New York: Barnes & Noble.]

**C.**

The sword Excalibur was the gift of the Lady of the Lake to King Arthur…Its jeweled scabbard had a magical property that prevented the warrior who wore it from being wounded.
[Day, D. (1999). *King arthur* (p. 82). New York: Barnes & Noble.]

**D.**

Arthur's sword had a scabbard which would not permit any weapon to draw his blood… Arthur was betrayed by Morgan who stole both sword and scabbard, replacing them with counterfeit versions.
[Day, D. (1999). *King arthur* (p. 86). New York: Barnes & Noble.]

**E.**

Camera and light crews followed him, along with people from costume and makeup, and the two extras with whom Marla Valentine had recently conversed.
[Graham, H. (2005). *Killing kelly* (p. 17). Don Mills, Ontario: Mira.]

**F.**

Faulty listening is often responsible for the letter that needs to be retyped time and again, the team that cannot produce results, or the physician who faces a malpractice suit.
[Shafir, R. (2001). *The zen of listening* (p. 14). Wheaton, IL: Quest Books.]

### *Do only relative pronouns introduce relative clauses?*

In addition to the relative pronouns, there are also other words that can introduce relative clauses. These words are called *relative adverbs.*

## Section 2: Relative Adverbs

| when    where    why |
|---|

Like relative pronouns, relative adverbs introduce relative clauses.

- The relative adverb *when* is used to modify a noun phrase of time. Such noun phrases include nouns that denote periods of time such as, *day, week, hour, minute, month, year*, and similar terms.
- The relative adverb *where* is used to modify a noun phrase of place, location, or space.
- The relative adverb *why* is used to modify a noun phrase with the noun *reason.*

| Relative Adverbs | | |
|---|---|---|
| Relative adverb | Meaning | Example |
| when | time | (16) Ian remembered the day **when** he forgot to set his alarm clock. |
| where | place | (17) Is this the house **where** George Washington slept? |
| why | reason | (18) I need to know the reason **why** you were late. |

- In Sentence (16), *when* modifies *the day.*
- In Sentence (17), *where* modifies *the house.*
- In Sentence (18), *why* modifies *the reason.*

***Instead of the relative adverb* when, *can we use relative pronouns to express time and introduce a relative clause?***

The relative pronouns *that* or *on* + *which* can be substituted for the relative adverb *when.* Look at the chart below.

| **(16) Ian remembered the day *when* he forgot to set his alarm clock.** | |
| --- | --- |
| (16a) Ian remembered the day *that* he forgot to set his alarm clock. | **that** |
| (16b) Ian remembered the day *on which* he forgot to set his alarm clock. | **on which** |

***Are there any relative pronouns we can use in place of the relative adverb* where?***

The relative pronouns *which* and *that* can be substituted for the relative adverb *where.* When *which* or *that* is used, a preposition of place must be included. The following chart illustrates these alternatives.

| **(17) Is this the house *where* George Washington slept?** | |
| --- | --- |
| (17a) Is this the house *in which* George Washington slept? | **in which** |
| (17b) Is this the house *which* George Washington slept *in*? | **which. . . in** |
| (17c) Is this the house *that* George Washington slept *in*? | **that. . . in** |

The preposition can come before *which* as in (17a) or at the end of the clause as in (17b). Placing the preposition before *which* is more formal. Placing the preposition at the end of the clause is frowned upon by traditional grammarians, but is commonly found in spoken and even formal written English. With *that* the preposition comes at the end of the clause as in (17c)

***In Chapter 9 we learned that* where *is used to introduce adverbial clauses. Now we are seeing that* where *can be used to introduce relative clauses. Isn't this confusing?***

▶ *Learner difficulties*

The use of *where* as a subordinator in an adverbial clause versus *where* as a relative adverb in a relative clause is often confusing. In Chapter 9 we saw the sentence

(18) The lamb goes *where* Mary goes.

In this sentence *where* is introducing the subordinate clause *Mary goes.* We also saw the sentence

(19) The lamb goes to the school *where* Mary goes.

In Sentence (19), *where* refers to the preposition "to" + the noun phrase *the school*. The two sentences with the different functions of *where* are shown in the chart below.

|                    | preposition | noun phrase |       |            |
| ------------------ | ----------- | ----------- | ----- | ---------- |
| (18) The lamb goes |             |             | *where* | Mary goes. |
| (19) The lamb goes | to          | **the school** | *where* | Mary goes. |

As you see from looking at the chart, only in Sentence (19) is *where* modifying a noun phrase and thus functioning to introduce a relative clause. Remember that a relative clause is also called an adjective clause because it modifies a noun or noun phrase, just as we see in Sentence (19), but not in (18). Thus, if *where* refers to a preceding noun phrase, then *where* is functioning as a relative adverb and not as a subordinator.

Discovery Activity 8 has two parts to it. Part I focuses on identifying relative adverbs. Part II focuses on substituting other words or phrases for a relative adverb. After you complete Part I, check your answers in the Answer Key and then complete Part II.

### Discovery Activity 8: Relative Adverbs
### Part I

Look at the following excerpts.

1. Circle the relative adverbs.
2. Underline what the relative adverb is modifying.

**A.**

> When he was a safe distance from the gatekeeper he trotted up a ramp, where he could see what was going on inside this strange and interesting place.
> [Clearly, B. (1964/1992). *Ribsy* (p. 121). New York: Avon Camelot.]

**B.**

> Mary's lips pinched themselves together. She was no more used to considering other people than Colin was and she saw no reason why an ill-tempered boy should interfere with the thing she liked best.
> [Burnett. F. H. (1911/1982). *The secret garden* (p. 166). New York: Dell.]

**C.**

> Anyone who stands at an urban intersection or in the lobby of a large office building soon senses some pattern in the migration of people. There are times when they flow together, congregating in dense masses, and times when they disperse and flow apart.
> [Barnlund, D. (1987). Verbal self-disclosure: Topics, targets. depth. In L. Luce & E. Smith (Eds.), *Towards internationalism* (2nd ed., p. 147). Cambridge, MA: Newbury.]

**D.**

> Usually they filmed in the studio...[t]onight, however, they were out at Hibiscus Point, a man-made private development where they had been all day, filling every exterior shot they could in a matter of hours.
>
> [Graham, H. (2005). *Killing kelly* (p. 14). Don Mills, Ontario: Mira.]

**E.**

> Ben's luck had not been good, and he had wandered from place to place; but at last he had settled on a ranch in California, where he was at work at the time when Dick became acquainted with Mr. Hobbs.
>
> [Burnett. F. H. (1886). *Little Lord Fauntleroy.* Available through Project Gutenberg at http://www.gutenberg.org]

**F.**

> [Ribsy] wriggled his way through more legs until he came to another gate where another man was taking tickets.
>
> [Clearly. B. (1964/1992). *Ribst* (p. 117). New York: Avon Camelot.]

### Part II

Sometimes it is possible to rewrite the sentence using a relative pronoun instead of a relative adverb.

Look back at the relative adverbs you identified.

3. Consider whether you could rewrite the sentence using a relative pronoun instead of the relative adverb.
4. If you can rewrite the sentence using a relative pronoun, you may need to add other words.

   - Write your new sentences on a separate sheet of paper.


## Adverbial Clause Time "when" versus Relative Clause "when"

*Do ESL/EFL students confuse adverbial clauses introduced by* **when** *with relative clauses introduced by* **when**?

▶ *Learner difficulties*

Learners of English may confuse relative clauses introduced by *when* with adverbial clauses of time introduced by *when* because the clauses look similar. The difference lies in the function of *when* and the type of clause it introduces. Compare:

| | Type of Clause | Function of *when* |
|---|---|---|
| (20) The river sometimes floods *when* it rains. | adverbial | **subordinator:**<br>• introduces the adverbial time clause *it rains* |
| (21) Our street flooded *the year when* we had refinished the basement. | relative | **relative adverb:**<br>• modifies the preceding noun phrase *the year* and<br>• introduces the relative clause *we had refinished the basement* |

- In Sentence (20), *when* is functioning as a subordinator introducing an adverbial clause of time.
- In Sentence (21), *when* is functioning as a relative adverb modifying a preceding noun phrase and introducing a relative clause.

## Building Longer Complex Clauses

As we saw in Chapter 9, more than one adverbial clause can occur in a sentence. Similarly, more than one relative clause can occur in a sentence. Relative clauses can also combine with other adverbial clauses in a sentence.

| Main clause | Subordinate clause 1 | Type | Subordinate clause 2 | Type |
|---|---|---|---|---|
| (22) I was watching the game | *while* they were talking to Jane | **time, adverbial** | *who* lived nearby | **relative** |
| (23) I was watching the game | *that* was being played in the park, | **relative** | *which* is on the corner of Main and Oak. | **relative** |

- In Sentence (22), the main clause is followed by an adverbial time clause, introduced by *while*. This adverbial clause is followed by a relative clause, introduced by the relative pronoun, *who*.
- In Sentence (23), the main clause is followed by two relative clauses. The first relative clause is introduced by the relative pronoun *that*. The second relative clause is introduced by the relative pronoun *which*.

The next Discovery Activity provides practice in identifying different types of clauses within a sentence. See how well you do and then compare your answers to those in the Answer Key at the end of the chapter.

**Discovery Activity 9: Multiple Subordinate Clauses**

Look at the following excerpts.

1. Locate the subordinate clauses.
2. Label each part of the excerpt.

*Example:*

While they were talking to Jane who lived nearby, I was watching the game.

> *While they were talking to Jane, who lived nearby,* I was watching the game.

| subordinate clause | relative clause, |
|---|---|
| adverbial time | *who* modifies *Jane* |

**A.**

A pulley eliminates the friction that would occur if the rope were pulled over a solid shape...

> [Simple Machines: Pulling For You. (2005). *Kids Discover, 15*(4), 9.]

**B.**

I know a man who runs an important media business who suffers terribly before he gives a speech, who in fact for twenty years devoted considerable energy and ingenuity to successfully avoiding ever having to make one...

> [Noonan, P. (1991). *Simply speaking* (p. 6). New York: Regan.]

**C.**

The Pacific Northwest coast is such a dangerous place because it rests on a continental plate that meets... a seafloor plate.

> [Krajik, K. (2005). Future shocks. *Smithsonian, 35*(17), 42.]

**D.**

... in winter waist-high snowfields transform the western steppe into an immense featureless sea that billows and swirls when the Arctic wind whips down from the Siberian tundra. The cartographer's map also ignores the summer sun, which hangs so low over the treeless August plains, a traveler can almost reach up and touch it....

> [Kelly, J. (2005). *The great mortality: An intimate history of the black death, the most devastating plague of all time* (pp. 29–30). New York: HarperCollins.]

*Have we learned all the forms of relative clauses?*

There is still one other type of relative clause, called reduced relative clauses. These are different than relative clauses with an omitted relative pronoun.

## Section 3: Reduced Relative Clauses

*What is a reduced relative clause?*

If the relative clause has the relative pronoun *who, that,* or *which* and the relative pronoun is functioning as the **subject** of the relative clause, we can often reduce the clause. You can think of a reduced relative clause as a short form of a relative clause. We call this reduced form a *phrase*.

## Reducing Relative Clauses

### How can a relative clause be reduced?

In Chapter 9, we saw reduced adverbial clauses. Reduced relative clauses are similar to these. Like adverbial clauses, we have two ways to reduce relative clauses. First, if the relative clause has any form of the verb *be,* delete the relative pronoun, *be,* and any other auxiliaries:

| Reducing Relative Clauses With *be* | | | | |
| --- | --- | --- | --- | --- |
| (24) The man | who | was | interested | in me lived next door. |
| (24a) The man | ~~who~~ | ~~was~~ | interested | in me lived next door. |
| (25) The man | who | had been | working | in the yard lives next door. |
| (25a) The man | ~~who~~ | ~~had been~~ | working | in the yard lives next door. |

We changed our original Sentence (24) from a relative clause to a reduced relative clause by dropping *who* and *was.* The new sentence, Sentence (24a), is *The man interested in me lived next door.*

Similarly, we can change Sentence (25) by dropping *who* and *had been.* The new Sentence (25a) is *The man working in the yard lives next door.*

### What is the second way to reduce a relative clause?

If a relative clause does not have any form of the verb *be,* we delete the relative pronoun and change the verb to a present participle (*-ing*):

| Reducing Relative Clauses Without *be* | | | |
| --- | --- | --- | --- |
| (26) Her CD collection, | which | includes | more than 500 CDs, | fills her bookshelf. |
| (26a) Her CD collection, | ~~which~~ | ~~includes~~ | more than 500 CDs, | fills her bookshelf. |
| | | ⇓ | | |
| | | including | | |

Since Sentence (26) does not include any form of the verb *be,* we changed the verb to the *–ing* participle form.

Discovery Activity 10 provides practice in reducing relative clauses, using teacher made sentences and prepares you for the next activity, Discovery Activity 11, which uses authentic excerpts.

**Discovery Activity 10: Reducing Relative Clauses**

Look at the sentences.

Try to reduce the relative clause in each sentence by crossing out the words you can omit.

*Example:*

She has a sister who is living in Alaska. → She has a sister ~~who is~~ living in Alaska

The food that was prepared by the caterer was delicious. → The food ~~that was~~ prepared by the caterer was delicious.

1. The hockey player who was injured by the puck went to the hospital.
2. The cat went after the dog that was chewing a bone.
3. The trophy that was awarded at the end of the season went to the best new player.
4. I have a friend who is trying to get on reality TV.
5. The movie star who is in Malibu graduated from my high school.

## Discussion: Discovery Activity 10

1. The hockey player ~~who was~~ injured by the puck went to the hospital.
2. The cat went after the dog ~~that was~~ chewing a bone.
3. The trophy ~~that was~~ awarded at the end of the season went to the best new player.
4. I have a friend ~~who is~~ trying to get on reality TV.
5. The movie star ~~who is~~ in Malibu graduated from my high school

Now that you have familiarized yourself with reduced clauses, try Discovery Activity 11 to see how well you do both in identifying reduced relative clauses and in adding the omitted structures. After you try all the excerpts, check your answers in the Answer Key.

### Discovery Activity 11: Reduced Relative Clauses

Look at the following excerpts.

1. Underline the reduced relative clauses.
2. Give the full form.

*Example*:

The boat, caught in the weeds, couldn't move
The boat, (which was) *caught in the weeds*, couldn't move

**A.**

Most of us are not great leaders speaking at great moments. Most of us are businessmen rolling out next year's financial goals, or teachers at a state convention making the case for a new curriculum, or nurses at a union meeting explaining the impact of managed care on the hospitals in which we work.
[Noonan. P. (1991). *Simply speaking* (p. 47). New York: Regan.]

**B.**

Michael Jordan has legs comparable only to those of a whooping crane.
[Bombeck, E. (1995). *All I know about animal behavior I learned in loehmann's dressing room* (p. 191). New York: HarperCollins.]

**C.**

She saw people sitting under a mildewed bus shelter, others walking a path along the side of the road... Closer to the city, they followed a truck laying down a fog of blue smoke through a quivering exhaust pipe... The Vegas lived in a sprawling, flat-roofed tri-level build around 1950 for someone with a great deal of money.
[Parker, B. (2005). *Suspicion of rage* (pp. 39–40). New York: Penguin.]

### *Do ESL/EFL students find relative clauses difficult?*

▶ *Learner difficulties*

Overall, relative clauses pose a number of problems for language learners. First, languages differ in the construction and placement of relative clauses. In Korean, Japanese, and Chinese, for instance, a relative clause comes before the noun it is modifying and there are no relative pronouns. Therefore, some ESL/EFL students, because of their native language, may have difficulty remembering to put a relative clause after the noun phrase it is modifying.

Second, as we have seen in this chapter, a relative pronoun may be omitted when it is functioning as the object in an essential relative clause. ESL/EFL students sometimes omit the relative pronoun in sentences where it is functioning as the subject of the relative clause and therefore cannot be omitted:

*(27) She is the teacher always helps me.

A related problem for many ESL/EFL students is recognizing the function and use of relative clauses without relative pronouns. They may have difficulty interpreting the meaning of relative clauses without the introductory relative pronoun.

Another trouble spot is the tendency of some ESL/EFL students, often as a result of transfer from their native language, to use *what* in place of *that*. Because this use of *what* instead of *that* is also found in some of varieties of nonstandard English, this type of error may be stigmatized by some native speakers:

*(28) That is the book **what** I want.

ESL/EFL students may also reduce nonessential relative clauses when only essential relative clauses can be reduced:

*(29) Annette is working for a company, going broke.

Finally, learners of English may use a relative pronoun and or relative clause where one does not belong because a different structure is required:

*(30) There are some problems caused by culture shock, **which are** anxiety, depression, and ill health.

In sum, relative clauses; can be a problematic area for ESL/EFL students. Like other grammar elements we have discussed, learning to use relative clauses correctly requires practice. After learners have become familiar with the structure of relative clauses, writing assignments that encourage the production of relative clauses in context are essential.

# Summary

## *The Relative Pronouns*

| Type | Relative Pronoun | Refers to |
|---|---|---|
| subject | who, that | person, animal |
|  | that, which | thing, concept |
| object | who, whom, that, Ø | person |
|  | which, that, Ø | thing, concept |
|  | whose | person, animal |
| possessive | whose, of which | thing |
| object of preposition | whom, Ø | person |
|  | which, Ø | thing, concept |

Ø =no relative pronoun necessary; optional

Note 1: *that* is generally used only with essential relative clauses; *which* is generally used with both essential and nonessential clauses.

Note 2: traditional prescriptive grammar allows only *that* in essential clauses and *which* only in nonessential clauses. Most speakers and many writers, however, use *that* and *which* interchangeably in nonessential clauses.

Note 3: In helping learners decide which relative pronoun to use, have them ask themselves questions such as:

* Is the relative pronoun going to refer back to a person or to a thing?
* Is the relative pronoun going to refer a possessive relationship?

Which versus That

| which | that |
|---|---|
| • almost never used with people or animals | • commonly used for people, animals, things |
| • used in both essential and nonessential relative clauses | • not generally found in nonessential clauses |
| • can follow a preposition | • cannot follow a preposition |
| • considered more formal when used to refer to people | • considered less formal when used to refer to people |

Essential versus Nonessential Relative Clauses

| Essential Relative Clause | Nonessential Relative Clause |
|---|---|
| • specifies something necessary to the meaning of the clause | • provides additional or supporting information |
| • identifies or clarifies a specific class or category of something | • extra information not essential to the meaning of the clause |
| • cannot be left out without changing the meaning of the clause | • if left out, the meaning of the main clause does not change |
| • no commas | • must be set off by commas |

# Practice Activities

## *Activity 1: Forming Relative Clauses*

Exercises on relative clauses for ESL/EFL students often consist of sentence combining. In such exercises students are given two sentences and asked to combine them into a relative clause. Such exercises are helpful in helping learners understand the structure of relative clauses.

1. On a separate sheet of paper, combine the following sentences into relative clauses by incorporating the second clause into the first.
2. Discuss whether the relative pronoun is functioning as the subject or object of the relative clause verb phrase.

*Examples*

a. That is a portrait of George Washington. George Washington was the first president of the US.
   That is a portrait of George Washington who was the first president of the US.
   *Who* is the subject of *was*.

b.  That's the house. I grew up in.

That's the house that I grew up in.

*That* is the object of *grew up in* and can be omitted: That's the house I grew up in.

1.  Nellie and Tom have a car. The car has over 100,000 miles.
2.  Samantha bought the dress. She liked the dress.
3.  She showed me a photo of her son. Her son is in the army.
4.  Karen has a friend. Her friend is a drummer in a rock band.
5.  The new movie theater opens next month. The new movie theater holds 600 people.
6.  We saw a person. The person is a famous actress.
7.  The teacher told stories. The stories were funny.
8.  We often visit our friends in Boston. Boston is close.
9.  Her uncle is a politician. Her uncle is famous
10. Marta is one of my closest friends. I've known Marta for eight years.

## *Activity 2: Identifying Relative Pronouns and Relative Adverbs*

1.  Look at the excerpts.
2.  Circle the relative pronouns and relative adverbs.
3.  See if you can tell whether they are essential or nonessential.

**A.**

The Arts Mall is just one of thirty-seven organizations I administer, a chain that stretches from the Anaheim Puppet Theatre to the Title IX Poetry Center in Bangor... It's an old Henny Penny supermarket that we renovated in 1976 when Bicentennial money was wandering around like helpless buffalo, and it houses seventeen little shops... and a watering hole called The Barre. This is one of those quiet little bistros where you aren't driven crazy by the constant ringing of cash registers.

[Keillor, G. (1993/1982). What did we do wrong? In R. Baker (Ed.), *Russell baker's book of American humor* (pp. 41–48). New York: Norton.]

**B.**

What invading species mostly don't do, it turns out, is out-compete native species. Take the case of the American gray squirrel, which was introduced in England in 1876. Dubbed "tree rat" by its detractors, the invader has made a pest of itself in its new land, where it is in the habit of eating flower bulbs and birds' eggs...

[Brudick, A. (2005, May). The truth about invasive species. *Discover, 26*(5), 37.]

**C.**

But in a period of mass death, when enormous amounts of money and property were suddenly being orphaned, notaries, who made out wills and other legal documents, played an essential role in the maintenance of civil order.

[Kelly, J. (2005). *The great mortality: An intimate history of the black death, the most devastating plague of all time* (p. 91). New York: HarperCollins.]

**D.**

"Hope and I heard stories about a monster who lived in the forest, a creature that lived in the forest and ate everything that walked or flew, which is why there is no game in it.
[McKinley, R. (1978). *Beauty: A retelling of beauty & the beast* (p. 76). New York: HarperTrophy.]

## Activity 3: Following the Rules

According to formal prescriptive grammar there are incorrect relative pronouns in the excerpts below.

1. Find and underline the "incorrect" relative pronouns.
2. Explain why each pronoun is "incorrect."

**A.**

"It never occurred to us that the killer could be someone so charming. . ."
"Or so handsome. . ."
"sometimes it's who you least expect." Leatrice cleared her throat. "Appearances can be deceiving"
[Durharm, L. (2005). *Better off wed* (pp. 240–241). New York: Avon Books.]

**B.**

A hundred miles around and guarded by twelve great gates, the city had blue-water canals, fire brigades, hospitals, and fine broad streets lined with houses upon whose doors were listed the names of every occupant.
[Kelly, J. (2005). *The great mortality: An intimate history of the black death, the most devastating plague of all time* (p. 33). New York: HarperCollins.]

## Activity 4: Identifying Relative Clauses without Relative Pronouns

1. Identify the relative clauses
2. Insert the omitted relative pronoun

**A.**

Before the informal talk could turn into a news conference she had no intention of giving, she slipped into her black wool coat.
[Heggan, C. (2005). *The search* (p. 9). Ontario CA: Mira.]

**B.**

The country was flush with military success, awash in French war boot, and best of all, England had a king it could love again. . . [Edward II] was. . . quite handsome, a trait he shared with his son and successor. . .
[Kelly, J. (2005). *The great mortality: An intimate history of the black death, the most devastating plague of all time* (p. 184). New York: HarperCollins.]

**C.**

Anxious as she was to find a clue to her husband's whereabouts, she was equally afaid of the answers she might unearth. For more than eight months, doubt had simmered behind the anger she wore like armor.
[Thompson, C. (2004). *Fatal error* (p. 135). New York: Leisure Books.]

**D.**

> So I went for a hike with a crowd of exceedingly healthy people I had never seen before in my life. It was an easy walk along paths that meandered through the cloud-grass meadows . . .
>
> [Asaro, C. (1995). *Primary inversion* (p. 157). New York: TOR.]

## Activity 5: Identifying the Clauses in a Complex Sentence (optional additional practice and review)

The following excerpts contain examples of adverbial and relative clauses.

1. Label the adverbial clauses AC.
2. Circle the subordinators.
3. Label the relative clauses RC.
4. Circle the relative pronouns.

**A.**

> While the sparkling twenty-somethings in *The Decameron* are fictional, the account of the plague that precedes their conversation in the church is not.
>
> [Kelly, J. (2005). *The great mortality: An intimate history of the black death, the most devastating plague of all time* (p. 105). New York: HarperCollins.]

**B.**

> The upheaval in cosmology that took place in the 1920s was unusual because the established model of an eternal universe came under simultaneous attack on both fronts.
>
> [Singh, S. (2005). *Big bang: The origin of the universe* (p. 268). New York: HarperCollins.]

**C.**

> When I was a college student in the seventies, Transcendental Meditation had become a vehicle of self-discovery and a discipline that brought welcome clarity to eighteen credit hours of graduate work and two part-time jobs.
>
> [Shafir, R. (2001). *The zen of listening* (p. 6). Wheaton, IL: Quest Books.]

**D.**

> Although books are no substitute for firsthand experience, they nevertheless, can provide direct information that is useful in reducing irrational fears and dispelling unfounded myths about people that appear different than themselves.
>
> [Uehara, D. (2005). Diversity in the classroom: Implications for school counselors. *Multicultural Perspectives, 74*, 51].

## Activity 6: Identifying Reduced Relative Clauses

1. Look at the excerpts.
2. Underline the reduced relative clauses. Give the full form.

**A.**

> Eragon's stay is disrupted by news of an Urgal army approaching through the dwarves' tunnel.
>
> [Paolini, C. (2005). *Eldest: Inheritance book 2* (p. xvi). New York: Alfred A. Knopf.]

**B.**

> ... Mendeleyev worked briefly at Heidelberg with Kirchhoff's great partner Robert Bunsen, best remembered today as the inventor of the Bunsen burner, which is still found in every school lab.
>
> [Strathern, P. (2000). *Mendeleyev's dream: The quest for the elements* (p. 268). New York: Berkeley Books.]

**C.**

> A new study by this group, presented at the 2005 World Garlic Symposium in April, found that when heart patients who were already taking cholesterol-lowering statin drugs added aged garlic extract supplements to their regimens, they showed additional improvement over simply taking the medication alone.
>
> [Downey, M. (2005). Garlic. *Better Nutrition, 6,* 8.]

## *Activity 7: Ungrammatical Sentences*

1. Look at the following sentences.
2. Explain why they are ungrammatical according to Standard American English.

a) The mountain who is the highest in the world is Mt. Everest.
b) The book what I liked best was *Harry Potter and the Goblet of Fire.*
c) The man, which my sister decided to marry, she met on the Internet.

## *Activity 8: Error Analysis*

The following excerpts were written by ESL students. There are relative clause errors. Because these excerpts have not been edited, there are other errors also.

- Evaluate the excerpts and **only** identify the problems the learners are having with **relative clauses**.

**A.**

> I think that a hobby, which is reading a book, is a good hobby for children. It doesn't have to be a difficult book. There are lots of people still do not know how to pronounce all words.

**B.**

> In my reading, described the story of the immigrant family, I found the message of hope. The author said that there are some difficulties faced by immigrants caused by language, which is the inability to communicate with the host country people. There are also other problems, that are lack of ability to get a good job, or missing family, or feeling everything strange.

# Answer Key: Chapter 10 Discovery Activities

## *Discussion: Discovery Activity 1*

*Excerpt A*

- *which was quickly followed by three others on the island*
- *which is approximately the size of West Virginia*
- nonessential relative clauses

*Excerpt B*

- *that held the king's internal organs*
- *who were barely hanging on to what little power they had*
- essential relative clauses defining a particular group or class of something or some people

*Excerpt C*

- *whose name Gail had already forgotten*
- nonessential relative clause

*Excerpt E*

- *that was my own first language*
- *who was working this land*
- essential relative clauses

## *Discussion: Discovery Activity 4*

- The relative pronouns can only be omitted in sentences (2), (3), and (6).

  - They can be omitted in these sentences because they are the objects of the verb phrases.

- In (2), the formal form of the relative pronoun is *whom*, not *who* because it is in object position.

## *Discussion: Discovery Activity 6*

*Excerpt A*

- first relative clause: *moves the lever*, introduced by the relative pronoun *that*, modifying *the force*.
- second relative clause: *the lever is trying to move*. The relative pronoun has been omitted. *That* could be inserted between *the weight* and *the lever*. *That* would then modify *the weight*.

- third relative clause: *the lever moves*, introduced by the preposition *on* and the relative pronoun *which*, modifying *the point*.

  o  In this instance, the preposition *on* must occur with the relative pronoun *which* in order to specify place or location.

*Excerpt B*

- first relative clause: *cultures are the products of long histories*, introduced by the possessive relative pronoun *whose*, modifying *modern human beings (Homo sapiens)*.
- second relative clause: *are fully modern in every sense*, introduced by the relative pronoun *that*, modifying the longer noun phrase *languages, practical skills, beliefs, arts, and values*.

*Excerpt C*

- first relative clause: relative pronoun *that* omitted: *they could bring back to camp and process in some way to make them edible*. We can insert *that* between *plants* and *they*, to modify *plants*.
- second relative clause: *that were too heavy to be carried easily from place to place*; *that* modifying *stone seed-grinding slabs*
- third relative clause: *were revisited again and again; that* is modifying *campsites*.

*Excerpt D*

- relative clause: *mosaic-patterned tile walls were barely visible in the light of a bulb* The relative pronoun is *whose*, modifying *a small foyer*.

  o  This is an example of the use of *whose* with an inanimate object *a small foyer*. In formal prescriptive grammar either the construction *noun phrase + of which* or an alternative construction should be used.

*Excerpt E*

- relative clause: *I committed.* We can insert *that* before *I*, to modify *fauxpas*.
- relative clause: *a dark-haired girl I repeatedly called Claire.* The relative pronoun *who(m)* has been omitted. We can insert *whom* (or *who* in informal English) before the relative pronoun. *That* is also used in informal, particularly spoken, English.

## Discussion: Discovery Activity 7

*Excerpt A*

- relative pronoun: *which*, modifying *an agency* and functioning as the subject of the verb phrase *had lived up to*.

  o  This verb phrase is an example of a phrasal verb, *to live up to something* (see Chapter 5).

*Excerpt B*

- relative pronoun: *who* modifying *heroic knights* and the subject of *slew*.

*Excerpt C*

- first relative pronoun: *that*, modifying *magical property* and subject of *prevented*.
- second relative pronoun: *who*, modifying *the warrior* and subject of *wore*.

*Excerpt D*

- first relative pronoun: *which*, modifying *a scabbard* and subject of the verb phrase *would not permit*.
- second relative pronoun: *who*, modifying *Morgan* and subject of *stole*.

*Excerpt E*

- relative pronoun: *whom*, object of the preposition *with* and the verb phrase *had conversed*.
  - Somewhat less formally the preposition *with* can follow the verb phrase *had conversed:... whom Marla Valentine had recently conversed with*.
  - The least formal form would be the use of *who* rather than *whom* in this object position: *who Marla Valentine had conversed with*.

*Excerpt F*

- first relative pronoun: *that*, modifying *the letter* and subject of the verb phrase *needs to be retyped*.
- second relative pronoun: *that*, modifying *the team* and subject of the verb phrase *cannot produce results*.
- third relative pronoun: *who*, modifying *the physician* and subject of the verb phrase *faces*.

## Discussion: Discovery Activity 8

### Part I

*Excerpt A*

- *where,* modifying *a ramp*

*Excerpt B*

- *why* is modifying *reason*

*Excerpt C*

- two instances of *when,* both modifying *times*

*Excerpt D*

- *where,* modifying *a man-made private development*

*Excerpt E*

- *where*, modifying *a ranch in California*
- *when*, modifying *at the time.*

*Excerpt F*

- *where*, modifying *another gate*

## Part II

*Excerpt A*

- *from which* could be substituted for *where*

*Excerpt B*

- *that* could be substituted for *why*

*Excerpt C*

- *that* could be substituted for both instances of *times*

*Excerpt D*

- *at which* could be substituted for *where*

*Excerpt E*

- *at which* or *in which* could be substituted for *where*
- *at which* could be substituted for *when,* and *that* could also be substituted for *when*

  ○ The use of the preposition + *which* is considered to be more formal English; however, it is also wordier and can sound awkward at times, as in *at the time at which Dick became* acquainted. . .

*Excerpt F*

- *at which* could be substituted for *where*


## *Discussion: Discovery Activity 9*


*Excerpt A*

| | |
|---|---|
| relative clause: | that would occur |
| adverbial if clause: | if the rope were pulled over a solid shape |

*Excerpt B*

| | |
|---|---|
| relative clause: | who runs an important media business |
| relative clause: | who suffers terribly |
| adverbial time clause: | before he gives a speech, |

| relative clause: | who in fact for twenty years devoted considerable energy and ingenuity to successfully avoiding ever having to make one. |

*Excerpt C*

| adverbial clause of reason: | because it rests on a continental plate |
| relative clause: | that meets. . . a seafloor plate. |

*Excerpt D*

| relative clause: | that billows and swirls |
| adverbial time clause: | when the Arctic wind whips down from the Siberian tundra |
| relative clause: | which hangs |
| adverbial clause of result: | so low over the treeless August plains, a traveler can almost reach up and touch it. |

- This is an example of where *so* appears without *that*. We could insert *that* before *plains* and *a*.

# Discussion: Discovery Activity 11

*Excerpt A*

Most of us are not great leaders (who are) *speaking at great moments.* Most of us are businessmen (who are) *rolling out next year's financial goals,* or teachers at a state convention (who are) *making the case for a new curriculum,* or nurses at a union (who are) *meeting explaining the impact of managed care on the hospitals in which we work.*

*Excerpt B*

Michael Jordan has legs (that/which are) *comparable only to those of a whooping crane.*

*Excerpt C*

She saw people (who were) *sitting under a mildewed bus shelter,* others (who were) *walking a path along the side of the road.* . . . Closer to the city, they followed a truck (which was) *laying down a fog of blue smoke through a quivering exhaust pipe.* . . . The Vegas lived in a sprawling, flat-roofed tri-level (that/which had been/ or which/that was) *built around 1950 for someone with a great deal of money.*

# Chapter 11
# Complex Sentences Continued: Noun Clauses

## Introduction

In this chapter we explore noun clauses. A noun clause is a subordinate clause that is used in the same ways a noun is. Like a noun, a noun clause can be used as a subject, an object, or a complement.

This chapter is divided into two main sections. Section 1 examines noun clauses in general, their function, the different types of noun clauses, and how they are formed. Section 2 considers a major subclass of noun clauses, reported or indirect speech.

## Section 1: Noun Clauses

Noun clauses usually follow the main clause and are introduced by subordinate conjunctions. These subordinate conjunctions are: *that, whether (or not) if*, or *wh-question* words, depending on the type of noun clause:

- *That* introduces noun clauses following certain verbs, adjectives, or nouns.
- *Whether (or not)* or *if* clauses introduce noun clauses derived from *yes/no* questions.
- *Wh-question* words (e.g. *who, when, what*) introduce noun clauses derived from information questions.

We generally find noun clauses placed after the main clause. They can also be placed in initial position, particularly if the writer or speaker wishes to emphasize the noun clause.

|  | noun clause position | type of noun clause |
| --- | --- | --- |
| The soldiers learned *that a patrol had been attacked.* | after main clause | statement |
| *That a patrol had been attacked* was just announced. | initial position | statement |
| They didn't know *why they had been attacked.* | after main clause | *wh*-question |
| *Why they had been attacked* they didn't know. | initial position | *wh*-question |

## That Noun Clauses

*Which type of noun clauses are the most common?*

## *Verb +* That *Noun Clause*

*That* noun clauses are the most common type of noun clause. Unlike the relative clauses in Chapter 10 introduced by *that*, the *that* in noun clauses does not refer to anything preceding it. The sole function of *that* is to subordinate the noun clause to the main clause. In other words, *that* only serves to introduce a noun clause. Some grammar books refer to the *that* of noun clauses as "complementizer *that*." Certain verbs, especially those expressing mental activities or feelings, are frequently followed by noun clauses. These noun clauses function as objects of the verb.

| Common Verbs Followed by Noun Clauses | | | | | |
|---|---|---|---|---|---|
| admit | claim | doubt | guess | pretend | remember |
| assume | complain | dream | hear | promise | say |
| (dis)agree | conclude | know | imagine | prove | show |
| allege | decide | expect | learn | realize | tell |
| announce | declare | explain | notice | recognize | think |
| assert | deny | feel | observe | regret | understand |
| believe | discover | find out | predict | | |

**Examples:**
Muriel **believes** *that she was right.*
The weather channel **predicted** *that it would rain.*

## *Different Verb + Noun Clause Patterns*

*Is the noun clause pattern the same after all verbs that take noun clauses?*

The verbs in the chart above require only the addition of a *that* noun clause. However, other verbs follow a somewhat more complicated pattern with *that* noun clauses:

- Some verbs **require an indirect object** inserted before the *that* introducing the noun clause.
- Other verbs **may** take an indirect object. The verb can first be followed by an indirect object and then the noun clause. Alternatively, the noun clause can follow the verb directly without an indirect object.
- Finally some verbs **may** take an indirect object, but **it must be preceded by** *to.*

In the following chart you can see the different types of *that* clauses after verbs that take noun clauses.

| Four Types of *that* Clauses After Certain Verbs | | |
|---|---|---|
| | **Pattern** | **Common Verbs** |
| (1) She knew *that she had a problem.* | verb + *that* clauses | see previous chart |
| (2) She convinced **him** *that she had a problem.* | verb + **required indirect object** + noun clause | assure, convince, inform, notify, promise, remind, tell |
| (3a) He wrote **her** *that she needed help.* | verb + (**optional** indirect object) + noun clause | promise, show, teach, warn, write |
| *or* | | |
| (3b) He wrote *that she needed help* | | |
| (4a) He explained **to her** *that he could help.* | verb + (**to + optional** indirect object) + noun clause | admit, complain, explain, mention, point out, prove, reply |
| *or* | | |
| (4b) He explained *that he could help.* | | |

*Is it difficult for ESL/EFL learners to remember the different patterns of noun clauses?*

▶ *Learner difficulties*

Learners of English often have difficulty remembering which verbs take which pattern. For example, ESL/EFL learners may incorrectly insert "to" before the object:

*(5) Roy told **to him** that he had a problem.

Similarly, learners may forget to insert a required "to" before an optional indirect object between the verb and the noun clause:

*(6) He explained **me** that he could help.

## Other Noun Clause Patterns

*Do noun clauses only come after verbs?*

### Be + Adjective + *That* Noun Clause

Noun clauses also follow *be* + certain adjectives. These are adjectives which refer to feelings and mental states.

| *Be* + Common Adjectives Followed by Noun Clauses | | |
|---|---|---|
| afraid | clear | nervous |
| amazed | concerned | obvious |
| annoyed | disappointed | sorry |
| angry | glad | sure |
| aware | grateful | surprised |
| certain | happy | worried |

**Examples:** I am **happy** *that we finished on time.*
She had been **nervous** *that she would miss her flight.*

When a *that* noun clause follows *be + adjective*, the noun clause functions as a complement. Previously, we discussed complements as any sentence constituents needed to complete and/or expand the meaning of the sentence. *That* clauses are sentence constituents that expand the meaning of the *be + adjective* clause. The *that* noun clause provides explanatory information about the main clause. This type of noun clause is often labeled a *noun complement that clause*.

### Noun + *That* Noun Clause

Certain nouns are also followed by noun clauses. These are nouns that express feelings, mental states, or some aspect of possibility.

| Common Nouns Followed by Noun Clauses | | | |
| --- | --- | --- | --- |
| advice | claim | hope | opinion |
| agreement | conclusion | idea | prediction |
| assumption | decision | impression | promise |
| belief | fact | message | threat |
| | feeling | notion | warning |

**Examples:** It was his **idea** *that we go to Rome.*
I have a **feeling** *that the airfare is going to increase.*

Like the *that* noun clause following *+ be +* adjective, the *that* noun clause following a noun functions as a complement to complete or expand the meaning of the sentence.

### *Is* **that** *always used in noun clauses?*

## *Omission of That*

In Chapter 10, we discussed the omission of the relative pronoun *that* when an essential relative clause is functioning as the object of the verb. The *that* introducing noun clauses can also be also omitted when:

* the noun clause is in **object** position
* it comes after *be + adjective,* or
* it comes after one of the nouns that takes a noun clause.

The omission of *that* in noun clauses is especially common in spoken and informal English.

| noun clause with *that* | noun clause without *that* | Type of noun clause |
| --- | --- | --- |
| (7) Dorrie **dreamed** *that* she was flying. | Dorrie **dreamed** she was flying. | after verb |
| (8) Muriel was **glad** *that* she had come. | Muriel **was glad** she had come. | *be + adjective* |
| (9) I have a **feeling** that this is a mistake. | I have a **feeling** this is a mistake. | after noun |

*That* cannot be omitted when the noun clause is in subject position:

      (10) *That* she came early was a surprise.
      *(10a) She came early was a surprise.

### *Should I or shouldn't I teach my students to omit complementizer* **that?**

Different usage or style guides provide additional guidelines for the omission of *that* in object noun clauses. Important considerations include whether or not the omission of *that* could be confusing to the meaning of the sentence or if the inclusion of *that* is too wordy in a given context. You may decide to teach your students not to omit *that;* however, they will need to be able to recognize clauses where the writer has omitted *that.*

In Discovery Activity 1, practice identifying *that* noun clauses. Remember that the *that* introducing a noun clause is often omitted. Try three excerpts and if you find you have no difficulties in identifying *that* noun clauses, feel free to move on to the next section. The answers are at the end of the chapter in the Answer Key.

---

**Discovery Activity 1: *That* Noun Clauses**

Look at the following excerpts.

1. Underline the *that* noun clause.
2. Decide whether the *that* noun clause is following a verb or an adjective.

**A.**

    I remembered that Father's tack had been mysteriously cleaned while it hung on a rack overnight.
      [McKinley, R. (1978). *Beauty: A retelling of the story of beauty & the beast* (p. 103). New York: HarperTrophy.]

**B.**

    Louisa was glad she had not sold the book outright .... *Little Women* brought in thousands of dollars each year and ensured that she and her family would never again experience the hardships of poverty.
      [Ruth, A. (1998). *Louisa may alcott* (p. 100). Minneapolis, MN: Lerner.]

**C.**

    Now I understand the South has a lot of secrets it doesn't want us Yankees to know, but there is no secret to how barbecue is cooked... Thirteen people assured me that they used wood, although in this region wood cooking is usually indirect... A number of owners who were cooking with wood warned me that their way of life was dying out...
      [Richman, A. (2004). *Fork it over: The intrepid adventures of a professional eater* (p. 212). New York: HarperCollins.]

**D.**

> The Jeromes were unhappy that the Marlboroughs did not consider their daughter to be an acceptable bride. Mrs. Jerome was herself disappointed that Randolph was a second son...
>
> [Kehoe, E. (2004). *The titled Americans: Three American sisters and the British aristocratic world into which they married* (p. 51). New York: Atlantic Monthly Press.]

**E.**

> As the *Matthew* set sail for home, Cabot probably believed that his journey had been a success. He thought he had reached northeastern Asia. He believed he had discovered rich fishing waters... Cabot was sure that they would be willing to pay for another voyage. He was also certain that he would find the riches he was looking for on his next voyage.
>
> [Doak, R. (2003). *John cabot and the journey to newfoundland* (pp. 31–32). Minneapolis, MN: Compass Point Books.]

## The Use of the Simple or Base Verb in That Noun Clauses

### What else should I know about noun clauses?

After certain verbs and after certain *it + be + adjective* constructions, English requires the use of the simple or base form of the verb in the *that* noun clause. As we saw in previous chapters, a simple or base verb is the verb without any inflectional endings and a verb that is not part of a "to" infinitive. Many grammar books refer to this noun clause structure as the *subjunctive*.

| verb + noun clause with simple verb | adjective + noun clause with simple verb |
|---|---|
| (11) I *suggest* that he **leave** now. | (13) It is *necessary* that he **be** suspended. |
| (12) I *recommended* that he **leave** now. | (14) It was *essential* that he **complete** the form. |

From the chart above, you will notice that the rule requiring the simple or base form of the verb is evident only in two instances:

- third person singular present tense, as in Sentences (11) and (13)
- past tense, as in Sentences (12) and (14).

As you will remember from earlier chapters, third person singular present tense and past tense are among the few tense inflections English verbs have. However, we do not use either inflection in these special types of noun clauses.

*What are some of the verbs that take the simple or base verb in the noun clause?*

Some of the verbs that are followed by a *that* noun clause with the simple verb are:

| verbs + *that* noun clause + simple verb | | |
|---|---|---|
| advise | direct | require |
| ask | insist | recommend |
| command | propose | suggest |
| demand | request | urge |

Some of the adjectives that are followed by a *that* noun clause with a simple verb are:

| adjectives + *that* noun clause + simple verb | | |
|---|---|---|
| advisable | essential | necessary |
| important | urgent | vital |

### *Is this "subjunctive" common in English?*

This so-called subjunctive form or the use of the simple verb in *that* noun clauses is considered formal English. Native speakers frequently avoid this structure and often prefer to use alternative structures, avoiding verbs from the above list and/or substituting a "to" infinitive verb phrase, e.g.:

(15)  The principal **thought** *that Justin should apply* to Columbia.
(16)  The principal thought that it was *important for Justin* **to apply** to Columbia.

In Sentence (15), the speaker has used the verb *thought* and the modal *should* in the noun clause. Since modals are always followed by a simple verb, for many native speakers this is a more "natural" or "comfortable" use of the simple verb form. In Sentence (16), the speaker has used a "to infinitive" clause, another commonly occurring verb pattern.[1]

## *The Different Functions of That*

### *What are all the different uses of that?*

In different chapters we have discussed that in English form is no guarantee of function—a fact that is underscored by the word *that*. The following chart summarizes the different uses of *that*.

---

[1] Some grammar books classify an infinitive clause as a reduced noun clause.

| Summary of the Different Uses of *That* | |
|---|---|
| | **Function of** *that* |
| I want **that** book | demonstrative adjective |
| I want **that.** | demonstrative pronoun |
| He was *so* excited *that* he dropped his cell phone. It was **such** a good book **that** I couldn't stop reading. | adverbial clauses of result |
| I wanted to borrow that book **so that** I could read it. | adverbial clause of purpose |
| I want to read the book **that** you recommended. | relative pronoun |
| I knew **that** he didn't want the book | noun clause subordinator (complementizer) |

### *Are all these different functions of* **that** *confusing to ESL/EFL learners?*

### ► *Learner difficulties*

ESL/EFL learners, as well as native speakers, generally have the greatest difficulties in distinguishing the relative pronoun *that* from the noun clause complementizer *that*. Distinguishing between these two uses of *that* is particularly difficult for many people because the clauses look similar.

## *Distinguishing Relative Clauses and Noun Clauses with That*

### *How can we distinguish between these two types of clauses?*

In a relative clause, *that* always refers to or modifies a preceding noun phrase. Because in a relative clause *that* is a type of a pronoun, it must refer back to something else. In a noun clause, *that* does not refer to or modifying anything. It does not function as a pronoun, but as a subordinator; it serves only to introduce the noun clause.

To better understand how noun clauses introduced by the subordinator *that* differ from relative clauses introduced by the relative pronoun *that*, we must look at several elements:

- The relative pronoun *that* must have a noun phrase preceding it. It must have something that it can refer back to.
- The *that* of noun clauses is generally preceded by a verb, *be + adjective*, or the certain nouns discussed previously.

| | |
|---|---|
| (17) She found *the book* **that** Jeremy wanted. | **relative pronoun** |
| (18) She *knew* **that** Craig would be late. | **complementizer** |

In Sentence (17), *that* is modifying the noun phrase *the book* and introducing the relative clause *Jeremy wanted*. In Sentence (18), *that* is not modifying a preceding noun phrase, but is a subordinator used to introduce the noun clause *Craig would be late*. The verb *knew*, a verb of mental activity, is one of the group of verbs that takes either an object or a noun clause after it. When a noun clause follows a verb such as *know*, it is functioning as the object of the verb.

The tricky part is that, in some instances, the noun clause *that* is also preceded by a noun phrase. However, such a noun phrase is limited to nouns that express:

- feelings, mental states, or
- some aspect of possibility such as *feeling, idea,* and *fact*.

Important additional clues to help distinguish the *that* introducing noun clauses is that unlike the relative pronoun *that*, the complementizer *that* is **not:**

- functioning as a pronoun
- not the subject or object of the following clause.

See how well you can distinguish the uses of *that* in Discovery Activity 2. The answers are available in the Answer Key.

As you complete this activity, think about what comes before and after *that*.

---

### Discovery Activity 2: *That* as Relative Pronoun and as Complementizer

Look at the following excerpts.

1. Underline all the instances of *that* you can find.
2. Label the function of each instance of *that* that you have underlined.

*Example*:

> Sam knew *that* Barb and Jenny would pay back the money *that* they needed so badly.
>
> *that*: introduces noun clause *Barb and Jenny     would pay back the money*
> *that*: relative pronoun modifying "the money"

It must have been immensely frustrating for them to watch Moreton fritter away capital on schemes that never came to anything. . . . Leonie traveled down to Brede after the auction with the trinkets that she and Jennifer had managed to purchase for Clara, bringing her son with her, the eight-year-old Lionel, who, like all the boys in the family, immediately fell under Uncle Moreton's spell. . . Lionel was entranced by his uncle's sporting tales and, inspired by his feats of derring-do, caught a few large fish, nearly a foot long, in a pool that he came upon in the forest. When he returned with his proud haul, he was met with dismay, as the grown-ups informed him that he had caught rainbow trout from a hatchery that Moreton had established at Brede. . . Moreton, relatively untroubled by the fiasco, merely suggested that they have them for dinner.

[Kehoe, E. (2004). *The titled Americans: Three American sisters and the British aristocratic world into which they married* (p. 258). New York: Atlantic Monthly Press.]

## Noun Clauses Derived from Questions

*In addition to* **that***-type noun clauses, what other kinds of noun clauses are there?*

## *Wh-Question Words*

| who | what | when | where | why | which | how |
|-----|------|------|-------|-----|-------|-----|

There are two types of noun clauses derived from questions, *wh*-question word noun clauses and *yes/no* noun clauses. The *wh*-question words introduce noun clauses derived from information questions. The *wh-question* words, unlike *that*, cannot be omitted in noun clauses.

### Word Order After Question Words

When the *wh-question words* introduce a noun clause, the noun clause follows **normal affirmative sentence word order**. This is a difficult concept for many learners of English to remember, even at advanced levels.

(18) I don't know **where** *Melanie is.*

In Sentence (18) the noun clause is introduced by *where* and then followed by normal affirmative sentence word order:

| where | *Melanie* | *is* |
|-------|-----------|------|
|       | **noun**  | **verb** |

For ESL/EFL learners, even proficient ones, there is a tendency to use question word order after a *wh*-question word:

*(18a) I don't know **where** *is Melanie.*

### What is the sentence position of noun clauses introduced by wh-question words?

Noun clauses introduced by *wh*-question words usually follow a main clause. They can also appear in initial position, with the main clause following. Regardless of the position of the *wh*-noun clause, **normal affirmative word order** follows the *why*-question word.

(19) *What we are doing* is important.

but not:

*(19a) *What are we doing* is important.

## Wh + ever Question Words

*Can the wh-questions words combine with anything?*

We can also combine *wh*-question words with *–ever* to form *whoever, whatever,* and so on to introduce noun clauses.

(20) As the Persians made their progress through a largely empty Attica, they looted **whatever** they could and demolished **whatever** seemed worth the trouble of destruction.

[Strauss, B. (2004), *The battle of salamis: The naval encounter that saved greece—and western civilization* (p. 85). New York: Simon & Schuster.]

# Yes/No Questions and Noun Clauses

*Can yes/no questions function as noun clauses?*

### If/Whether (or Not)

Another type of noun clause is derived from *yes/no* questions. This type of noun clause is introduced by *whether* or *if*. The word *whether* is often followed by *or not*. **Normal affirmative sentence word order follows *whether (or not)* or *if***

The use of *whether*, both with and without *or not*, is more formal than *if*. Examine the following sentences:

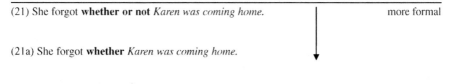

| | |
|---|---|
| (21) She forgot **whether or not** *Karen was coming home.* | more formal |
| (21a) She forgot **whether** *Karen was coming home.* | |
| (21b) She forgot **if** *Karen was coming home.* | less formal |

In spoken and informal written English, speakers will routinely use *if* instead of *whether (or not)* to introduce a noun clause. Neither *if* nor *whether (or not)* can be omitted in noun clauses.

The next Discovery Activity provides practice in identifying different noun clauses derived from questions. You can find the answers at the end of the chapter in the Answer Key.

### Discovery Activity 3: Noun Clauses Derived from Questions

Look at the following excerpts.

1. Underline the noun clauses.
2. Circle the words that introduce the noun clauses originally derived from questions.

**A.**

The next day, Raymond was not at the corner. Herbie wondered what had happened to his buddy.

[Kline, S. (1988). *Herbie jones and the class gift* (p. 36). New York: Putnam's Sons.]

**B.**

This is a story of five little dolls who were left in a box, under a chair, in a park. Why they were left there, I haven't a clue.

[Gardner, S. (2003). *The countess's calamity* (p. 5). New York: Blomsbury Children's Books.]

**C.**

The bright torches they'd followed from the cave entrance had given way to small oil lamps. She didn't know when the change had happened...

[McReynolds, G. (1997). *The chalice and the blade* (p. 11). New York: Bantam.]

**D.**

I'm a very good packer. I know exactly how to save space... As usual, Mom couldn't remember where she had put the tube of sunblock.

[Levy, E. (2001). *Big trouble in little twinsville* (p. 12). New York: Harper-Collins.]

**E**

He wondered if he'd be helping Grandpa hay this summer. He remembered how the chaff stuck to his sweaty body and itched like a thousand mosquitoes and how his arms had ached from lifting and throwing hay bales.

[Kinsey-Warnock, N. (1998). *In the language of loons* (p. 10). New York: Cobblehill Books.]

**F.**

"What's his name?" Mr. Kaspian wanted to know.
I didn't know his name. I didn't even know if any of the cats had names....
"I don't know anything about cats," said Mr. Kaspian. "I don't even know what they eat."

[Sachs, M. (2002). *The four ugly cats in apartment 3D* (pp. 25–26). New York: Atheneum.]

We have now finished our examination of the different types of noun clauses and will move on Section 2, where we explore reported speech, a major subclass of noun clauses. Some grammar books consider reported speech separately from noun clauses; others discuss reported speech as a subcategory of noun clauses. Since reported speech consists of noun clauses, the topic of this chapter, we will explore reported speech here.

## Section 2: Reported Speech

### *What does the term "reported speech" refer to?*

As the term itself implies, reported speech—which some grammar books call *indirect speech*— refers to utterances that are not quotations, but that reflect what someone has said. In contrast to reported speech, direct speech refers to the actual words spoken by a person and is enclosed in quotation marks. Reported speech is commonly found in newspapers, magazines, and fiction. Reported speech includes a noun clause introduced by such verbs as *say, tell, shout, ask,* and *remark.*

| | |
|---|---|
| (22)  Joy said, "I like that book." | direct speech, exact quotation |
| (22a) Joy said that she liked that book. | indirect speech, a report of someone's words. |

These noun clauses report or convey a sense of what someone else has said or written. There are different types of reported speech noun clauses, depending on the type of clause the noun clause is derived from. They are introduced by the same subordinating conjunctions as the noun clauses we have already seen:

- *That* introduces noun clauses that report statements someone has said.
- *Whether (or not)* and *if* introduce yes/no questions someone has asked.
- *Wh-questions* words introduce information questions someone has asked.

## Statements

Noun clauses derived from statements are introduced by *that.* This *that* is often omitted in informal written and spoken English. When **statements** from direct speech are changed to reported speech, there is **no change in word order.**

| Statements in Noun Clauses | | |
|---|---|---|
| **Direct Speech** | **Reported Speech** | **Noun Clause Type** |
| (23) Sue said, "I am hungry." | (23a) Sue said *that* she was hungry. | statement |
| | *or* | |
| | (23b) Sue said she was hungry. | |

## Questions

Noun clauses derived from *yes/no* questions are introduced by *whether (or not)* or *if.* Noun clauses derived from information questions are introduced by *wh-*question words. *Whether/if* or *wh-question* words cannot be omitted in noun clauses.

When we change **questions** from direct speech to reported speech, we must change the question word order to **affirmative sentence word order,** as in Sentences (24a) and (25a).

| Wh-question Words Introducing Noun Clauses | | |
|---|---|---|
| (24) Pam asked, "Is Sue hungry?" | (24a) Pam asked *whether (or not)/if* **Susan was hungry.** | yes/no question with affirmative sentence word order |
| (25) Sue asked, "Where is a restaurant?" | (25a) Sue asked *where **a restaurant was.*** | *wh*-question with affirmative sentence word order |

## Other Patterns in Reported Speech

*Are these all the types of reported speech?*

### Imperatives

There is another type of reported speech, imperatives or commands, which tell someone to do something.

Imperatives in direct speech change to the "to" infinitive form in reported speech, as in Sentence (26a). If it is a negative imperative, we drop the auxiliary *do* and place *not* before the "to" infinitive, as in Sentence (27a).

| Imperatives in Noun Clauses | | |
|---|---|---|
| (26) Pam said, "Eat something." | (26a) Pam said "*to eat* something." | **affirmative** |
| (27) Pam said, "Don't eat anything." | (27a) Pam said *not to eat anything.* | **negative** |

### Exclamations

Exclamations, or interjections, are also found in reported speech. Exclamations refer to expressions of surprise, dismay, pleasure, or other similar emotions. Exclamations in reported speech **retain the same word order** they have in direct speech.

| Exclamations in Noun Clauses | |
|---|---|
| (28) Pam said, "What a mistake I made!" | (28a) Pam realized *what a mistake she had made.* |
| (29) Pam said, "This is a wonderful restaurant!" | (29a) Pam exclaimed *that that was a wonderful restaurant.* |

In Sentences (28) and (28a), both sentences use the same word order, regardless whether the exclamation is in direct speech or in reported speech. You may have noticed that Sentence (28a) uses a different verb, *realized*, than does (28). Generally, writers will use a more descriptive verb than *say* in reported speech to convey the emotional sense of the exclamation.

In Sentence (29), the exclamation is in statement form. In (29a), the reported speech noun clause is introduced by the complementizer *that*. This *that* is followed immediately by the demonstrative adjective *that*. Here it is important to use both types of *that* because each one has a separate function in the sentence. The omission of the complementizer *that* could make the sentence confusing. However, the use of two sequential *thats* can strike native speakers as awkward and they may hesitate when producing such sentences.

*Why do we use the past perfect in Sentence (28a)?*

# Formal Sequencing of Verb Tenses

When changing from direct speech to reported speech, traditional prescriptive grammar requires the *formal sequencing of tenses*. This means that when you change from direct speech to reported speech, you must:

- change verbs in present tense to past tense and
- change past tense verbs to past perfect.

The changes in Sentences (30)–(33) from direct speech to reported speech all follow what is known as the formal sequencing of tenses.

| Formal Sequencing of Tenses | | | |
| --- | --- | --- | --- |
| direct speech | tense | reported speech | time |
| (30) Sue said, "I am hungry." | present → | (30a) Sue said **that** she *was* hungry. | past |
| (31) Sue said, "I was hungry." | past → | (31a) Sue said **that** she *had been* hungry. | past perfect |
| (32) Joe asked, "Can Pat come over?" | present → | (32a) Joe asked **whether** Pat *could* come over. | past |
| (33) Pete asked, "Did Pat come over?" | past → | (33a) Pete asked **whether** Pat *had come* over. | past perfect |

*Do native speakers always observe this formal sequencing of tenses?*

Most native speakers will observe this rule for changing present tense in direct speech to past tense in reported speech; however, many speakers will not observe this rule for changing past tense to the past perfect and will use past tense only, particularly in spoken and informal written English.

Moreover, native speakers will not always follow this sequencing of tenses for actions, events, or facts that are still current and/or true. For example,

(34) "I like to go to the movies," said Meg.
(35) Meg said that she likes to go to the movies.

In Sentence (35), the speaker chose to use present tense because the fact that Meg likes the movies is still true. Similarly,

(36) "The moon revolves around the earth," said the teacher.
(36a) The teacher said the earth revolved around the moon
(36b) The teacher said the earth revolves around the moon.

In Sentence (36a), the formal sequencing of tenses is observed; in Sentence (36b), it is not. Depending on the context, native speakers may prefer to use the present tense in reported speech because they feel it makes more "sense." For them, using the past tense, even though "grammatically" correct, implies that the fact is no longer true.

## Pronoun and Other Changes

*Are there rules for the pronoun changes we see in many of the sentences we have been looking at?*

In addition to understanding the rules governing the sequencing of verb tenses, ESL/EFL learners need to be aware that there are also pronoun and other related changes that may need to occur when changing from direct speech to reported speech:

| Pronoun and Related Changes | | |
|---|---|---|
| **direct speech** | **reported speech** | **change** |
| (37) Blair said, "I have a dog." | (37a) Blair said that *she* had a dog. | I → she |
| (38) Blair said, "My dog likes bones." | (38a) Blair said that *her* dog liked bones | my → her |
| (39) Blair said, "My dog always sleeps here under the porch by this door." | (39a) Blair said that her dog always sleeps *there* under the porch by *that* door. | here → there<br>this → that |

- The subject pronoun *I* in Sentence (37) changes to *she* in Sentence (37a).
- The possessive *my* in Sentence (38) changes to *her* in Sentence (38a).
- *Here* and *this* in Sentence (39) change to *there* and *that* in Sentence (39a).

As you observed in the chart above, pronouns and possessive adjectives change when going from direct speech to reported speech. Expressions of time and place, adverbs, and demonstratives may need to change, depending upon the perspective and distance to the speaker. For instance, if the reference in reported speech refers to a place close to the speaker, *here* can still be used. Similarly, if the reference in reported speech is something near the speaker, *this* can still be used.

*My students are always confusing say and tell. How can I explain the difference to them?*

## Say versus Tell

*Say* and *tell* are similar in meaning but take different sentence patterns, causing ESL/EFL learners to produce sentences such as:

*(40) He said **me** that he was tired.
    *or*
*(41) He told **to me** that he was tired

To help learners, it is important to clarify and practice the two verbs and their respective structures.

After the verb *say*, **an object is optional**. If *say* is followed by an indirect object, it is introduced by *to*, and then followed by the noun clause: We *say something* or *we say to someone something*.

| say | |
|---|---|
| (42) Barney **said** that he was tired. | *said* is followed directly by the noun clause *that he was tired* |
| (43) Barney **said** *to me* that he was tired. | *said* is followed by the preposition *to* + the object pronoun *me*. |

The verb *tell*, on the other hand, **must be followed by an object** and then the noun clause. This object cannot be preceded by *to*. We use *tell* in the sense of we *tell someone something*. The preposition *to* cannot precede the object phrase after *tell*.

| tell | |
|---|---|
| (44) Patti **told** *me* that she had to leave. | *told* is first followed by the object pronoun *me* and then the noun clause *that she had to leave*. |
| *(45) Patti **told** *to me* that she had to leave. | ungrammatical because *to* cannot come before the object *me* after the verb *tell*. |

The object following *say* and *tell* does not have to be an object pronoun, but can be a noun phrase.

(46) Milo **said** *to the new school principal* that he wasn't returning next year.
(47) Milo **told** *the new school principal* that he wasn't returning next year.

- In Sentence (46), *said* is followed by *to* + the noun phrase *the new school principal*.
- In Sentence (47), *told* is followed by the object noun phrase *the new school principal*, which in turn is followed by the noun clause *that he wasn't returning next year*. The *that* can be omitted after both *say* and *tell*.

## Reported Speech as Impression

*Is reported speech always an exact report of what someone has said?*

Up to this point we have discussed reported speech as though it were a mirror of direct speech. Indeed, this is how reported speech is often taught to ESL/EFL learners. In reality, however, reported speech is not always an exact replica of direct speech with the appropriate verb tense and pronoun changes. Very often, reported speech is more an approximation of what someone said. When reported speech is intended to convey a general impression of the words actually spoken, there is usually more than one way to structure the sentences.

| Direct Speech to Reported Speech | | |
|---|---|---|
| (48) "Is there any new information about the murderer?" asked Sophie. | (48a) Sophie asked whether there was any new information about the murderer | **reported speech: exact replica** |
| (49) "He is thought likely to be either a student or a Master in the Faculty of Arts," he replied. "Who else would think of setting us a philosophical riddle?" | (49a) He replied that he was thought likely to be either a student or a Master in the Faculty of Arts because who else would think of setting them a philosophical riddle. | **reported speech: approximation** |

[Gross, C. (2004/2002), *Scholarium*. H. Atkins, Transl. New Milford, CT: Toby Press. p. 70].

- In Sentence (48a), the reported speech is an exact replica of the actual quote of Sentence (48).
- In Sentence (49a), the reported speech is similar to, but not identical to the original quote of Sentence (49). The reported speech begins with the main clause *He replied*, which is followed by a noun clause introduced by *that*.
- An important difference between Sentences (49) and (49a) is the change of the question *Who else...* to an adverbial clause introduced by *because*.

Still another way to reformulate Sentence (49) is:

(49c) He replied that he was thought likely to be either a student or a Master in the Faculty of Arts. After all, who else would think of setting them a philosophical riddle.

Reported speech may also reflect the writer's or speaker's interpretation of what was said by using certain verbs to introduce the noun clause. These verbs include *claim, demand, insist,* and *allege*. Compare, for example, the following reported statements, Sentences 50a–50c, with the original direct statement, Sentence (50):

| | |
|---|---|
| (50) "The man grabbed my purse and ran through the lobby," said the woman. | **exact quotation** |
| (50a) The woman *said* that the man had grabbed her purse and had run through the lobby. | |
| (50b) The woman *claimed* that the man had grabbed her purse and had run through the lobby. | **variation** |
| (50c) The woman *insisted* that the man had grabbed her purse and had run through the lobby. | |

Although Sentences (50a), (50b), and (50c) all convey essentially the same information as the original sentence, there is a different nuance to each sentence in reported speech:

- In Sentence (50a), the sentence is an exact mirror of the quote.
- In Sentence (50b), because of the use of the verb *claim*, there is a slight element of doubt cast on the truth of the woman's statement. Perhaps she is issuing a false report. Perhaps it is not clear that the man ran through the lobby instead of down the hall.
- In Sentence (50c), by using the verb *insist*, the writer conveys something of the strength of emotion the woman was feeling.

Discovery Activity 4 provides practice in changing from direct speech to reported speech. When you do this activity, practice following the formal sequencing of tenses.

---

**Discovery Activity 4: Changing Direct Speech to Reported Speech**

A common activity for English language learners is to give them sentences in direct speech and to ask them to rewrite these sentences in reported speech, observing the rules of traditional prescriptive grammar. Look at the following quotes.

1. On a separate sheet of paper, change the sentences in direct speech to reported speech, observing the formal sequencing of tenses.
2. As you complete this Discovery Activity, consider what different elements ESL/EFL learners have to remember to do such an activity correctly.

   - Some of these require some extra thought because of punctuation and word order.

*Example*

"The idea was to create as many modern interventions as we could," said Kenneth Drucker
Kenneth Drucker said that the idea had been to create as many modern interventions as they could.

In changing this quotation, learners need to remember to begin with the subject noun phrase and verb (Kenneth Drucker + said). Then learners need to remember to change *was* to *had been* and *we* to *they*. The modal *could* is already a past form and does not change.

**A.**

"I have to add a little more water to the stew," [Melinda] said.
[McKinley, R. (1978). *Beauty: A retelling of beauty & the beast* (p. 34). New York: HarperTrophy.]

**B.**

"You won't see your roses bloom," [said] Hope. "I'll plant them tomorrow".... [Beauty] said.
[McKinley, R. (1978). *Beauty: A retelling of beauty & the beast* (p. 79). New York: HarperTrophy.]

**C.**

Elmer [asked], "Was she murdered?".... "It's hard to say after all this time," Ben answered.
[Emerson, K. L. (2007). *No mortal reason* (pp. 92–93). Coronal del Mar, CA: Pemberly Press.]

**D.**

"Why did the telegram come addressed to Mrs. Spaulding?" Mrs. Ellington asked.... "That is the name which appears as my byline," [Diana replied].
[Emerson, K. L. (2007). *No mortal reason* (p. 98). Coronal del Mar, CA: Pemberly Press.]

**E.**

Diana [said], "I never intended to write anything negative about the Hotel Grant. My editor, I admit, likes sensational stories. And I have written about crime in the past"...
[Emerson, K. L. (2007). *No mortal reason* (p. 98). Coronal del Mar, CA: Pemberly Press.]

## *Discussion: Discovery Activity 4*

*Excerpt A*

Melinda said that she had to add a little more water to the stew.

- The present verb changes to the past. The pronoun *I* changes to *she*.

*Excerpt B*

Hope said that she wouldn't see her roses bloom. Beauty said that she would plant them tomorrow.

- *Will* (and its corresponding negative form *won't*) change to *would(n't)*.
- The pronouns *you* and *I* need to change to *she*.

*Excerpt C*

Elmer asked whether (or not)/if she had been murdered. Ben answered that it was hard to tell after all that time.

- The past verb changes to past perfect.
- The present verb changes to the past.

*Excerpt D*

Mrs. Ellington asked why the telegram had come addressed to Mrs. Spaulding. Diana replied that that was the name, which appeared as her byline.

- When a *wh*-question becomes a noun clause, we use affirmative word order, not question word order.
- The past verb changes to past perfect.
- The present verb changes to the past.

*Excerpt E*

Diana said that she had never intended to write anything negative about the Hotel Grant. She admitted that her editor liked sensational stories and that she had written about crime in the past.

- The past verb changes to past perfect.
- *My* changes to *her.*
- The present perfect verb changes to the past perfect.

In completing Discovery Activity 4, you will have noticed that reported speech is not always an exact replica of direct speech. It is important for teachers to help their ESL/EFL learners go beyond memorizing the formal sequencing of tenses in order to gain an understanding of the use and meanings of reported speech.

### Do ESL/EFL student have trouble with reported speech?

▶ *Learner difficulties*

> The greatest difficult for learners of English is using affirmative sentence word order in noun clauses after *wh* –question words and *whether/if*.
>
> *Last night, my friend asked me *where* **was I** going.

Another area of difficulty is the formal sequencing of tenses. They will often produce sentences such as:

*Last night, my friend **asked** what I **am** doing.

ESL/EFL learners may combine both problems and produce sentences such as:

*Last night, my friend asked me *where* **am I** going.

In addition, as we reviewed earlier, ESL/EFL learners confuse *say* and *tell* and their structures.

It is important not to rely exclusively on exercises that simply ask learners of English to mechanically change direct quotations to reported speech. Such exercises are useful in practicing structures at the beginning levels and for later review. However, ESL/EFL learners also need opportunities to recognize and understand the roles of direct speech and reported speech. Advanced ESL/EFL learners should have opportunities to examine exceptions to the rules in order to understand when and where they are likely to encounter variations to these rules.

## Summary

| Noun Clause Types | | |
|---|---|---|
| **statement** | Emma heard *that we were coming.* Emma heard *we were coming.* Emma wondered *whether or not we were coming.* | *that* may be omitted in object position From most formal to least formal |
| **embedded yes/no question** | Emma wondered *whether we were coming.* Emma wondered *if we were coming.* | |
| **embedded wh- question** | Emma wondered *when we were coming.* | affirmative word order, not question word order |

| Say versus Tell | |
|---|---|
| **say + (to + object) + (that) + noun clause** | **tell + object + (that) + noun clause** |
| Kay said *to Mary she wasn't coming.* Kay said *she wasn't coming.* | Kay told Mary *she wasn't coming.* Kay told Mary *she wasn't coming.* |

## Formal Sequencing of Tenses in Reported Speech

|  | present |  | past |
|---|---|---|---|
| April said, "I know you." | simple | April said that she knew me. | simple |
| April said, "I'm talking to you." | progressive | April said that she was talking to me. | progressive |
| April said, "I've met him before." | perfect | April said that she had met him before. | perfect |
|  | past |  | past |
| April said, "I wrote you." | simple | April said that she had written me. | perfect |
| April said, "I was talking to you." | progressive | April said that she had been talking to me. | progressive |
| April said, "I had never heard of him." | perfect | April said that she had never heard of him. | perfect (no change) |

## Formal Sequencing of Tenses in Reported Speech: Modals

| present | past | change in form | no change in form |
|---|---|---|---|
| can | could |  | should<br>should have<br>could have |
| may | might | *may* in the sense of possibility | must have |
| must | had to |  |  |
| will | would |  |  |

# Practice Activities

## *Activity 1: Identifying Noun Clauses*

1. Look at the following excerpts.
2. Underline the noun clauses.
3. Remember, *that* is often omitted in noun clauses.

**A.**

For years, we've been told how bad the sun is for our skin, our eyes, our looks, our you-name-it... But it's also true that some sun exposure is absolutely necessary for good health... Recent studies have found that vitamin D helps lower the risk of breast, colon, prostate and other cancers.

[Cherry, R. (2005, June). For once, there's some good sun news. *Vegetarian Times,* p. 23.]

**B.**

When researchers are interested in finding out whether an individual factor such as motivation affects second language learning, they usually select a group of learners and give them a questionnaire to measure the type and degree of motivation. The learners are then given a test to measure their second language proficiency. The test and the questionnaire are both scored and the researcher investigates whether a learner with a high score on the proficiency test is also more likely to have a high score on the motivation questionnaire.

[Lightbown, P., & Spada, N. (1993). *How languages are learned* (p. 35). Oxford: Oxford University Press.]

**C.**

I had not expected Emerson would have any difficulty in persuading Mr. Salt to violate a visitor's privacy. We found the manager more than eager to oblige. The chambermaid had reported that the lady's bed had not been slept in, nor the towels in the bath changer used.

[Peters, E. (2005). *The serpent on the crown* (p. 211). New York: Harper Collins.]

**D.**

"Would you join us at the hotel for a little refreshment. I believe that is customary after a funeral." I assumed the invitation included me, though she had looked only at Emerson and Ramses.

[Peters, E. (2005). *The serpent on the crown* (p. 195). New York: Harper Collins.]

## *Activity 2: Changing from Direct Speech to Reported Speech*

1. Look at the following quotes.
2. On a separate sheet of paper, change the sentences in direct speech to reported speech, observing the rule of sequencing of tenses

- When you change from direct speech to reported speech, you may want to combine some of the sentences together.
- When you change the quotes to noun clauses, note which introductory words you need to add. Also note what happens to word order in quotes that include questions.

**A.**

"Stay away from those Morelli boys," my mother had warned me.
[Evanovich, J. (1994). *One for the money* (p. 3). New York: Charles Scribner's Sons.]

**B.**

Ramirez shook his head. "I don't know Joe Morelli. I only know he shot Ziggy."
[Evanovich, J. (1994). *One for the money* (p. 48). New York: Charles Scribner's Sons.]

**C.**

Nate [asked], "Where's the ball?"
"Don't tell anybody." Mike said. "I kicked it"...
[Peterson, P. J. (1997). *Can you keep a secret?* (p. 5). New York: Dutton Children's Books.]

**D.**

"Can I pet him?" Carla asked.
"Why does everything have to happen to me?" Brenda [asked]...
[Peterson, P. J. (1997). *Can you keep a secret?* (p. 61). New York: Dutton Children's Books.]

## *Activity 3: Exploring Direct Speech versus Reported Speech (optional additional practice)*

1. Choose a dialogue excerpt of about 5–8 sentences from a work of fiction.
2. Rewrite the quotes to reported speech.
3. Bring both the excerpt and your version to class.
4. Exchange the excerpt only with a partner.
5. Rewrite the quotes from the excerpt your partner gave you into reported speech.
6. When you finish, compare and discuss your versions of both excerpts:

   • What changes did you have to make and why?
   • Were you able to change all the quotes verbatim to reported speech?
   • What kinds of changes did you have to make?
   • How did you keep the "flavor" or tone of the quotes?

## *Activity 4: Multiple Subordinate Clauses (optional additional practice)*

As we have seen in previous chapters, sentences can consist of more than one subordinate clause of any type.

1. Look at the excerpts.
2. Underline the different subordinate clauses
3. Label each one:

   • AC = adverbial clause
   • RC = relative clause
   • NC = noun clause

4. Be careful. Some relative clauses and noun clauses have an omitted relative pronoun.

**A.**

Most cultural exploration begins with the annoyance of being lost. The control systems of the mind signal that something unexpected has arisen, that we are in uncharted waters and are going to have to switch off the automatic pilot and the help ourselves. There's a reef where we least expect it... People in real-life situations don't actually see it this way, because the almost inevitable response is to deny that the reef is there until one has run aground.

[Hall, E. T. (1976/1981). *Beyond culture* (p. 46). New York: Anchor Books.]

**B.**

With the war mostly over, aid officials warn that thousands of displaced persons and refuges might venture back to their former homeland only to be greeted by an environment that can no longer support them.

[Fink, S. (2005). Saving eden. *Discover, 26*(7), 54.]

**C.**

> It was not inevitable, said Columbus, that Eastern goods should arrive from the East; nor that Westerners should pay such a premium... The world being round, was it not simple logic that spices might also come around the other way: round the back of the globe, from the west? (Contrary to one hoary myth, hardly any well-informed medieval Europeans were flat-earthers. That the earth was spherical had been accepted by all informed opinion since ancient times).
>
>     [Turner, J. (2004). *Spice: The history of temptation* (pp. 5–6). New York: Knopf.]

**D.**

> The first law states that any floating object will displace a volume of water whose mass equals the object's mass. An iceberg that is 90 percent as dense as seawater, for instance, displaces 90 percent of its volume, so 90 percent of it lies below the surface. The second law determines how objects of different shapes and densities orient themselves as they float.
>
>     [Mackenzie, D. (2005). Tilt! *Discover, 26*(7), 85.]

## Activity 6: Error Analysis

The following excerpts were written by EFL students. There are noun clause errors. Because these are authentic excerpts, there are other errors as well. Only focus on **noun clause errors.**

1. Read the excerpts and identify the problems the learners are having with noun clauses.

**A.**

I know that someone who had an accident when he was in the traffic because of the construction. I'm suggesting the mayor improves the transportation.

**B.**

The teacher was telling us a joke. I was the only one who was quiet in the room. At the end of the class I asked my friend Rosa what was the joke about.

**C.**

My mother suddenly fell down and the other people who work in the factory immediately called the ambulance. I talked with the doctor and he told that her blood pressure was high. Then the doctor told I have to take care of mother. He said don't worry, if she takes care, she is going to be alright.

**D.**

A book can contribute to a child's development. It helps develop their knowledge. There are lots of different examples that show children what is the right thing and what should do they for that age.

## *Activity 7: Error Analysis in the Classroom*

The following sentences were heard in an ESL classroom.

- Explain the learners' problem(s).
- Discuss why the student may be making such error(s).

1. The teacher, she say me I got to write again.
2. He never told how old he is.
3. One group taught us what was asthma was.
4. In my chart I have the phases of the moon, and how does it change.
5. Lee told to me he got to go early so he can't finish with me.

## Answer Key: Chapter 11 Discovery Activities

## *Discussion: Discovery Activity 1*

### *Excerpt A*

noun clause: *that Father's tack had been mysteriously cleaned*

- follows the verb *remembered*.
- The remainder of the sentence, *while it hung on a rack overnight*, is an adverbial clause introduced by *while*.

### *Excerpt B*

noun clause: *she had not sold the book outright,*

- *that* omitted
- follows *be* + the adjective *glad*

noun clause: *that she and her family would never again experience the hardships of poverty*.

- follows verb *ensured*

### *Excerpt C*

noun clause: *the South has a lot of secrets it doesn't want us Yankees to know.*

- *that* omitted

noun clause: *that they used wood*

- follows the verb *assured* + the indirect object *me*
- The rest of the sentence is an adverbial clause introduced by *although*.

noun clause: *that their way of life was dying out*

- follows the verb *warned* + indirect object *me* + the noun clause

*Excerpt D*

noun clauses: *that the Marlboroughs did not consider their daughter to be an acceptable bride*

- follows *be* + the adjective *unhappy*

noun clause: *that Randolph was a second son*

- follows the adjective *disappointed*

*Excerpt E*

noun clause: *that his journey had been a success*

- follows the verb *believe*

noun clause: *he had reached northeastern Asia*

- *that* omitted
- follows the verb *thought*

noun clause: *he had discovered rich fishing waters*

- *that* omitted

noun clause: *that they would be willing to pay for another voyage*

- follows *be* + adjective *sure*

noun clause: *that he would find the riches he was looking for on his next voyage*

- follows *be* + adjective *certain*

## Discussion: Discovery Activity 2

| | |
|---|---|
| . . . on schemes **that** never came to anything. | relative pronoun |
| . . . with the trinkets **that** she and Jennifer had managed to purchase | relative pronoun |
| . . . in a pool **that** he came upon in the forest | relative pronoun |
| . . . as the grown-ups informed him **that** he had caught | noun clause |
| . . . from a hatchery **that** Moreton had established | relative pronoun |
| . . . merely suggested **that** they have them | noun clause |

## Discussion: Discovery Activity 3

*Excerpt A*

noun clause: *what happened to his buddy.*

*Excerpt B*

noun clause in initial position: *Why they were left there.*

*Excerpt C*

noun clause: *when the change had happened*

*Excerpt D*

noun clauses: *how to save space; where she had put the tube of sunblock.*

*Excerpt E*

noun clauses: *if he'd be helping; how the chaff stuck; how his arms ached.*

*Excerpt F*

noun clauses: *if any of the cats; what they eat.*

# Chapter 12
# Verbal Constructions

In this chapter we look at some structures that you have already been introduced to at various times in the text. The chapter is divided into three parts, each one of which explores a different type of verbal construction. Section 1 examines gerund phrases; Section 2 delves into participial phrases, and Section 3 considers the "to" + verb or infinitive phrases.

## Introduction

### What are "verbals?"

Certain structures are called verbals because they are derived from verbs but do not inflect for person and tense, nor combine with an auxiliary verb to form verb phrases. Verbals include *gerunds, participles,* and *infinitives.* The important element to focus on in this chapter is the form and function of the verbal constructions. Compare:

| | |
|---|---|
| (1) Ray wants to go home | main verb **wants** + infinitive **to go** |
| (2) I am going home. | auxiliary **be** + **-ing** present participle |
| (3) They like going home early. | main verb **like** followed by **-ing participle** functioning as a gerund |

- In Sentence (1), the main verb *want* inflects for person (third person singular) and tense (present). The infinitive, *to go,* does not inflect for person or tense.
- In Sentence (2), we know that *going* is part of a verb phrase. As we saw in Chapter 6, *am* is the auxiliary verb be for *going* and is inflected for person (first person singular) and tense (present). Together, *am* and *going* form the present progressive.
- In Sentence (3), *going* occurs after the main verb *like.* It occurs without an auxiliary verb, so it cannot be part of a progressive verb phrase.

The verbals—gerunds, participles, and infinitives—combine with other elements to form verbal phrases, specifically gerund phrases, participial phrases, and infinitive phrases.[1] We begin by examining gerunds and gerund phrases. You were introduced to gerunds in Chapter 5.

## Section 1: Gerunds and Gerund Phrases

In Chapter 5, we examined how certain verbs are followed by an *-ing* form of the verb. We observed that this *–ing* form is also known as the *gerund*.

### What is a gerund phrase?

A gerund is a verbal that functions as a noun. A gerund phrase consists of a verbal, modifier(s), object(s), and/or complement(s). Because a gerund, and by extension a gerund phrase, functions as a noun, it occupies some of the same positions in a sentence that a noun does: subject, direct object, object of the preposition, and complement.

| Gerunds | |
| --- | --- |
| | **function of the gerund** |
| (4) *Studying* is hard work. | **subject** |
| (5) Some students enjoy *studying*. | **object** |
| (6) Nothing stops Lucy from *studying*. | **object of the preposition** *from* |
| (7) Lucy's favorite activity is *studying*. | **subject complement** |

In Sentences (4) through (7) we see the different uses of *studying* as a gerund:

- In Sentence (4), *Studying* is the subject of the verb *is*. Because *Studying* functions as a noncountable noun (see Chapter 3), it is followed by the singular verb *is*.
- In Sentence (5), *studying* is the object of the verb *enjoy*, a verb that is followed by a gerund form of another verb (See Appendix D).
- In Sentence (6), *studying* is the object of the preposition *from*.
- In Sentence (7), *studying* is a subject complement because it is renaming or identifying the subject of the verb. *Studying* tells us what Lucy's favorite activity is.

The sentences below are identical to the ones in the previous chart with one exception. Instead of using simple gerunds, each sentence now includes a gerund phrase.

| Gerund Phrases | |
| --- | --- |
| **studying + English + grammar = -gerund phrase** | **function of the gerund phrase** |
| (4a) *Studying English grammar* requires patience. | **subject** |
| (5a) Everyone enjoys *studying English grammar*. | **object** |
| (6a) Nothing stops Lucy from *studying English grammar*. | **object of the preposition** *from* |
| (7a) Lucy's favorite activity is *studying English grammar.* | **subject complement** |

---

[1] Some grammar books call verbal phrases non-finite phrases.

# Negation and Gerunds

*Can we use gerunds in a negative sense?*

Gerunds are often used negatively. Both gerunds and gerund phrases are made negative by the addition of *not* before the verbal:

(8) *Not studying* can be a problem.
(9) *Not studying English grammar* can be a problem.

Both Discovery Activities 1 and 2 focus on helping you distinguish between gerund phrases and verb phrases. Discovery Activity 1 is easier than Discovery Activity 2 because it uses short, teacher-made sentences. Discovery Activity 2 is more difficult because it uses authentic material. Try both and see how well you do. The answers to both these Discovery Activities are at the end of the chapter in the Answer Key.

---

**Discovery Activity 1: Gerund Phrases versus Verb Phrases**

Look at the sentences below.

Underline the *–ing* form.

- If the *–ing* is a gerund, underline and label only this form.
- If the *–ing* is part of a progressive verb phrase, underline and label the entire verb phrase.

*Example*:

gerund

Lucy's favorite activity is *studying*.

Pres. Prog VP

Lucy *is studying* at the library.

1. Her sole occupation was writing short stories.
2. Their grandmother was vacationing in Florida when the storm hit.
3. The club is holding a social next month.
4. To be a dedicated teacher is a special calling.
5. The long trip with her young children was driving her crazy.
6. Joseph's hobby is rebuilding antique cars.

---

This second Discovery Activity is similar to the previous one, but uses authentic excerpts. You may find this Discovery Activity more challenging than the first one. Remember that the answers are in the Answer Key.

**Discovery Activity 2: Identifying the Different Functions of Gerunds and Gerund Phrases**

Look at the following excerpts.

1.  Underline all the gerunds and gerund phrases you can find.
2.  Identify the function of each gerund and gerund phrase you underlined.

**A.**

I worked the last shift at Dave's Dogs, and I was supposed to start shutting down a half hour before closing so I could clean up for the day crew.
[Evanovich, J. (2005). *Eleven on top* (p. 1). New York: St. Martin's.]

**B.**

A North Carolina law mandated hanging for taking a fugitive out of the state, while captains outbound from Louisiana faced up to ten years in prison if they were caught aiding a fugitive.
[Bordewich, F. (2005). *Bound for canaan* (p. 273). New York: HarperCollins.]

**C.**

Challenging each other's opinions comes so naturally to Americans that most of the time they aren't even aware that they are doing it.
[Sakamoto, S., & Naotsuka, R. (1982). *Polite fictions: Why Japanese and Americans seem rude to each other* (p. 56). Tokyo: Kinseido.]

**D.**

Knowing the rules is not at all the same thing as playing the game. Even now, during a conversation in Japanese I will notice a startled reaction, and belatedly realize that once again I have rudely interrupted by instinctively trying to hit back the other person's bowling ball.
[Sakamoto, S. & Naotsuka, R. (1982). *Polite fictions: Why Japanese and Americans seem rude to each other* (p. 85). Tokyo: Kinseido.]

*Are gerund difficult for ESL/EFL learners?*

▶ *Learner difficulties*

ESL/EFL learners are sometimes confused by sentences where a gerund is functioning as a subject complement after the verb. In Sentence (7), *Lucy's favorite activity is studying,* for instance, *is studying* looks identical to the present progressive verb phrase.

Low proficiency ESL/EFL learners may be confused by words that end in *–ing,* but that are not gerunds or participles. Such words include *during, nothing, wedding,* and *morning.*

## Possessive Gerunds

### Since gerunds function as nouns, can we also use them in a possessive sense?

Since gerunds function as nouns, they can take possessive pronouns or be preceded by nouns with the possessive 's inflection.

| | |
|---|---|
| (10) **His** *coming late* created problems. | possessive pronoun before the gerund phrase |
| (11) *Jude's writing* was very good. | possessive 's inflection on a proper noun before the gerund phrase |
| (12) *The cat's purring* soothed the baby. | possessive 's inflection on a noun before the gerund phrase |

### Is the possessive gerund structure in Sentence (10) unusual?

Although the possessive gerund as used in Sentence (10) is not the most common gerund construction, it is found in both written and spoken English,. Consider this excerpt, taken from an interview with actress Julia Louis-Dreyfus in a popular magazine, *Entertainment Weekly*.

(13) To Louis-Dreyfus, Moore embodied a strong 1970s career woman who wasn't perfect—far from it. "**Her being** able to play humiliation as well as she did was very appealing," says the actress, 45, no stranger to self mockery.
> [Stack, T. (2006, December 1). Julia Louis-Dreyfus' inspiration: Mary tyler moore. *Entertainment Weekly*, p. 44]

## Section 2: Participial Phrases

### What is a participial phrase?

A participial phrase consists of a participle, either *–ing* or *–ed*, modifier(s), object(s), and/or complement(s). Participial phrases function to modify nouns in sentences. Consider the sentence:

(14) *Driving all day*, Tony arrived home in time for the party.

In Sentence (14), *Driving all day* is a participial phrase modifying the noun *Tony*, which is the subject of the verb *arrived*.

### What do you mean by "modifying Tony?"

*Driving all day* is telling us something about Tony. In this case it is describing what he did. We will see more examples of participial phrases and what they modify in this section.

*We've looked at so many participles and their different functions. Could you review what the different functions of participles are before exploring participial phrases?*

## Types of Participles

In Chapter 4, we looked at adjectives that ended in *-ing* and *-ed*, which we called participial adjectives. As you will recall, we labeled these types of adjectives participial adjectives because they are derived from verbs, but are not part of full verb phrases (auxiliary + past or present participle).

In Chapters 5 and 6, we discussed participles as being the *-ing* or *-ed* form of the main verb that accompanies an auxiliary verb in order to form a verb phrase. As you will remember, *present participle* refers to the *-ing* form used with present progressive forms of the verb phrase. *Past participle* refers to the *-ed* form used with past progressive forms of the verb phrase or with passive voice.[2]

In Chapters 9 & 10, we looked at adverbial and relative clauses, which we saw can be reduced. When these clauses are reduced, they become participial clauses.[3]

The chart below summarizes the different functions of participles and underscores once gain how in English form does not equal function.

| Participles | |
|---|---|
| | **Function of the Participle** |
| (15a) I read a *boring* book. <br> (15b) The *embarrassed* child hid her face. | **participial adjective** modifying *book* |
| (16a) I am *reading* a good book. <br> (16b) I was *reading* a good book. | **present participle**, part of a progressive verb phrase (*be* + V + ing) |
| (17a) The mother has *scolded* her child. <br> (17b) The mother had *scolded* her child. | **past participle**, part of a perfect verb phrase (*have* + V + ed) |
| (18) *Running too quickly*, the child fell. | **participial phrase**, modifying *the child* |

- In Sentence (15a), *boring* is an *-ing* participial adjective modifying the noun *book*. In Sentence (15b), *embarrassed* is an *-ed* participial adjective modifying the noun *child*.
- In Sentence (16a), *reading* is part of the present progressive verb phrase *am reading*. In Sentence (16b), *reading* is part of the past progressive verb phrase *was reading*. In order to be complete sentences, (15a) and (15b) require both parts of the verb phrase: the auxiliary *be* and the present participle of the main verb *read*.

---

[2] The *-ed* participles also include *-en* forms such as *chosen, drunk,* and *forgotten.*

[3] Note, however, that not all participial phrases are reduced relative or adverbial clauses.

- In Sentence (17a), *scolded* is part of the present perfect verb phrase *has scolded*. In Sentence (17b), *scolded* is part of the past perfect verb phrase *had scolded*. As in Sentences (16a) and (16b), these sentences would not be complete sentences without both parts of the verb phrase: the auxiliary *have* and the past participle of the main verb *scold*.
- In Sentence (18), we see an example similar to Sentence (14). In both (18) and (14), the initial participial phrase is modifying the noun immediately following it.

*Are participial phrases always at the beginning of a sentence as in Sentence (13)?*

## Sentence Position

We find participial phrases in three positions. Participial phrases can come before a main clause (initial position), after a noun phrase they are modifying (middle position), or after a main clause (final position).

| Participial Phrases | | |
|---|---|---|
| | **position** | **function** |
| (19) *Wanting to improve her grade,* the student asked the teacher for help. | initial | modifying **the student** |
| (20) The children's mother, *insisting on their cooperation,* asked them to clean their rooms. | middle | modifying **the children's mother** |
| (21) The neighbor noticed the man *talking on his cell phone.* | final | modifying **the man** |

*What kind of punctuation do we need to use when participial phrases occur in different positions?*

- When the participial phrase comes before a main clause, it is followed by a comma, as in Sentence (19).
- When the participial phrase follows a main clause, a comma must come before the participial phrase, as in Sentence (20).
- When the participial phrase occurs in mid-sentence position, we use two commas. One comma comes before the participial phrase and the second comma comes after it, as in Sentence (21).

## Function

*What is the function of participial phrases and when do we use them?*

As we saw in Sentences (14) and (18), participial phrases generally modify nouns and noun phrases. Participial phrases function primarily as adjectives. A participial phrase is often a reduced relative clause (see Chapter 10). Participial phrases can also function as adverbs. These are often reduced adverb clauses (See Chapter 9). Because participial phrases are a more formal form of sentence structure, we usually use them in writing rather than in speaking.

| Different Types of Participial Phrases | |
|---|---|
| | **Function** |
| (22) The passengers, *waiting for takeoff*, began to complain. | participial phrase functioning as **adjective** modifying *the passengers* (from a reduced *relative* clause) |
| (23) *While waiting for takeoff*, the flight attendants passed out magazines. | participial phrase functioning as **adverb** expressing time (from a reduced *adverb* clause, with adverb still included) |

- In Sentence (22), *waiting for take off,* is a participial phrase functioning as an adjective. This participial phrase is modifying *the passengers* and is a reduced relative clause. The full relative clause is *"The passengers, who were waiting for the plane to take off, became restless."*
- In Sentence (23), *While waiting for takeoff,* is a participial phrase functioning as an adverb. It is a reduced adverbial clause. The full adverb clause is *"While they were waiting for takeoff, the flight attendants passed out magazines."*

## Gerund Phrases versus Participial Phrases

*How can I tell the difference between gerund phrases and participial phrases?*

The key to distinguishing gerund and participial phrases is to consider their function in a sentence. An *-ing* participle is functioning as a **noun** and part of a **gerund phrase** if it is:

- the subject,
- the direct object,
- the object of a preposition, or
- the subject complement

An *-ing* participle is functioning as an **adjective** and part of a **participial phrase** if it is:

- describing a noun or a noun phrase

*Is there anything that will help me distinguish the* **-ing** *participle in a gerund phrase versus a participial phrase?*

An easy way to help you differentiate between the two structures is to try substituting "it." If the gerund or gerund phrase is functioning as a noun, as in Sentence (24), you can substitute "it" and the sentence is still grammatical, as in Sentence (24a).

> (24) *Doing crossword puzzles* relaxes Lyle.
> (24a) *It* relaxes Lyle.

If, on the other hand, the participle is part of a participial phrase and functioning as an adjective, substituting "it" will give you a nonsense sentence. Compare Sentences (25) and (25a).

> (25) *While waiting for takeoff,* the flight attendants passed out magazines.
> *(25a) *It,* the flight attendants passed out magazines.

Discovery Activity 3 practices identifying gerund and participial phrases. This activity uses teacher-generated sentences. Discovery Activity 4 also practices identifying gerund and participial phrases, but uses authentic excerpts. The answers to both Discovery Activities are at the end of the chapter in the Answer Key.

### Discovery Activity 3: Distinguishing Between Gerund and Participial Phrases

Look at the following excerpts.

1. Decide whether the underlined phrases are participial phrases or gerund phrases.
2. If you are unsure, try substituting "it" for the underlined phrase.

*Example:*

> participial phrase
> *Concerned about the cost of gas,* Geraldine decided to carpool.

1. The candidate contested the outcome of the election, *claiming voter fraud.*
2. *Working even after retirement age,* George has been indispensable to the company.
3. You should consider *doing your homework more carefully.*
4. *Exhausted by the climb,* Taylor collapsed by the side of the road.
5. *Taking a vacation* is important for all of us.
6. Brenda, *taking a deep breath,* continued her talk.
7. *Getting up early* is hard when you're tired.

Try two or three excerpts in this next Discovery Activity. Compare your answers to those in the Answer Key. If you have no mistakes, you may with to move on to the next section.

### Discovery Activity 4: Gerund Phrase or Participial Phrase?

a. The gerund phrases and participial phrases have been underlined in the following excerpts.
b. Label each one.

- If it is a gerund phrase, label it **GP**.
- If it is a participial phrase, label it **PP**.

1. *Drawing conclusions from chimpanzees and gorillas* overlooks an important point: at some moment back then, we got language (and all that goes with it) and *they* did not.

   [Lakoff, R. (2004). *Language and women's place: Text and commentaries* (p. 117). In M. Bucholtz (Ed.), New York: Oxford.]
2. *Looking back over three years of magazines*, we found twenty-three articles hyping plastic surgery, and one hundred more whose tone presumed or implied that their readers were unhappy with aging.

   [Blyth, M. (2004). *Spin sisters* (p. 101). New York: St. Martin's Press.]
3. *Using the backside of its bucket*, the loader awkwardly patted the reeking mass into one solid rectangular cube.

   [Royte, E. (2005). *Garbage land: On the secret trail of trash* (p. 45). New York: Little, Brown & Company.]
4. *Frowning in his dress shirt and polished brown shoes*, Apuzzi picked is way over a sofa cushion, across the slippery frame of a foldout bed, and in between two black garbage bags.

   [Royte, E. (2005). *Garbage land: On the secret trail of trash* (p. 46). New York: Little, Brown & Company.]
5. *Achieving a rich, moist brown humus in a sanitary landfill* is nothing but a romantic fantasy!

   [Royte, E. (2005). *Garbage land: On the secret trail of trash* (p. 89). New York: Little, Brown & Company.]
6. *Watching Twla Tharp and her dancers*, I was reminded that business managers routinely complain that they don't have time to "practice" being leaders.

   [Bennis, W., & Thomas, R. (2002). *Geeks & Geezers* (p. xiv). Boston: Harvard Business School Press.]

# Past Participles (*-ed*) in Participial Phrases

### *Do we only have –ing participles in participial phrases?*

In addition to the *–ing* present participle, the *–ed* past participle also occurs in participial phrases. *–ed* participial phrases that function as adjectives are closely related to verbs in passive voice:

| | |
|---|---|
| (26) The teacher *was annoyed* by the students' behavior. | **past passive voice** |
| (27) *Annoyed by the students' behavior*, the teacher gave them extra work. | **participial phrase** |

- In Sentence (26) *was annoyed* is a past passive verb phrase.
- In Sentence (27) the *be* auxiliary verb has been dropped and *annoyed* has become a participle in a participial phrase.

### *How can I tell the difference in function between the different -ed participles?*

## *Distinguishing the Different -ed Participles*

An *-ed* participle is functioning as an **adjective** and is part of a **participial phrase** if it is:

- describing a noun or a noun phrase and
- comes before a noun or noun phrase

*the **annoyed** teacher*
   An *–ed* participle is functioning as part of a **passive verb phrase** if it:

- co-occurs with any tense and form of the auxiliary *be* + (optional *by* phrase)

*The teacher **was annoyed** by the students.*
   An *–ed* participle is functioning as part of a **perfect verb phrase** if it:

- co-occurs with any tense and form of the auxiliary *have*

*The students **have annoyed** the teacher all day.*

   In Discovery Activity 5, practice identifying the various functions of the *–ed*. The answers are available in the Answer Key.

---

**Discovery Activity 5: Identifying the Different Types of *-ed***

Look at the following excerpts.

1. Underline all the *-ed* forms you find.

2. Identify each -*ed* form you have underlined.
3. Remember that there are numerous irregular forms that do not end in –*ed*, such as *eaten* or *drunk*.

*Example*:

The *tired* scientist had *finished* the research *praised* by his peers when he *retired*.

tired:     participial adjective
finished: part of past perfect verb phrase *had finished*
praised:  part of participial phrase *praised by his peers* modifying *the research*
retired:  regular past tense verb

**A.**

> Unexpected questions have tripped up many a liar. What is wrong, for example, with the lie: "I tried calling twice from a pay phone, but the line was busy"?
> [Sullivan, E. (2001). *The concise book of lying* (p. 88). New York: Farrar, Straus and Giroux.]

**B.**

> Case studies, supplemented by simulations, are not the cornerstone of business school education. Revered above all else are the lessons to be learned from "just going out and doing it." Entrepreneuring. . . has become the avocation of young men and women raised to believe they can do anything and convinced that they live in an era without precedents.
> [Bennis, W. & Thomas, R. (2002). *Geeks & Geezers* (p. 64). Boston: Harvard University Press.]

**C.**

> Through the years, the Schwartz topics addressed behind closed doors have been as disparate as the hospitals involved. One session at Massachusetts General focused on the stresses that spouses and other family members face when hospital clinicians bring their jobs home with them.
> [Huff, C. (2006, December 15). Under pressure and coping. *American Way*, p. 15]

Discovery Activity 4 practices identifying some of the different types of participles, both -*ed* and –*ing*, and their functions. If you feel confident in your ability to distinguish the different participles, try just Excerpt D. After you have checked your answers in the Answer Key and if you have no problems, you can ignore the rest and move on to the next section.

**Discovery Activity 6: Identifying the Different Participles**

Look at the following excerpts.

1. Underline all the examples of participles you can find.
2. Identify the function of each participle you have identified.

*Example*:

*Sitting* by the lake, I was *watching* the *diving* loons.

*Sitting:*   part of a participial phrase *by the lake*.

*watching:* present participle, part of the past progressive verb phrase *was watching*.

*diving:*    participial adjective modifying the noun *loons*.

**A.**

> I opened the door and there was Mel, standing in the hallway, with a tall gentlemen standing behind him.
>
> [Wilder, G. (2005). *Kiss me like a stranger* (p. 95). New York: St Martin's.]

**B.**

> President Johnson watched the developing demonstrations in St. Augustine warily. Just a year earlier, as vice president, he had attended a dinner in preparation for the upcoming anniversary.
>
> [Kotz, N. (2005). *Judgment days* (p. 126). New York: Houghton Mifflin.]

**C.**

> I wish I could report that letters from people who read my column on butchering a monkfish reflected the response I was hoping for.
>
> [Trillin, C. (1995). *Too soon to tell* (p. 24). New York: Warner.]

**D.**

> The biggest problem I had during the seven weeks of filming was trying not to break up laughing when I was acting in a scene with Bob Newhart... I always felt like saying, "Well, Bob started it... " On the last day of filming... we were outside in downtown Los Angeles, which was supposed to be New York. We finished filming at midnight, and the producer sent Bob and me home in the same fake Yellow Cab, along with a pile of our own clothing that we had loaned to the production... When we got to Bob's home in Beverly Hills, we both got out of the cab, carrying a bundle of Bob's clothes.
>
> [Wilder, G. (2005). *Kiss me like a stranger* (p. 111). New York: St Martin's.]

## Time

*Since participles don't inflect for time, do all participial phrases refer to the same time?*

As we discussed in the beginning of this chapter, one reason participles are called verbals is because they do not inflect the way verbs do. However, participles, unlike gerunds, do have two different forms for a type of time reference. The two different forms participles take to indicate time reference are the **basic** (Sentence 28) and the **perfect** (Sentence 29).

(28) **Wanting** *to end the argument,* Peter left the room.
(29) **Having reached** *a decision,* the jurors returned to the courtroom.

- In Sentence (28), the basic participle indicates "general" or "non-specific" time.
- In Sentence (29), we have a sequencing of events. The perfect participle indicates that this event or action occurred prior to the event or action expressed by the main verb, *returned.*

## Passive Participial Phrases

### Are there also passive participial phrases?

Participial phrases can be in the passive (see Chapter 8). These passive participles can also express two different types of time references. Passive participial phrases referring to general time consist of *being* + past participle, as in Sentence (30). Sentences referring to the earlier of two actions or events consist of *having* + past participle, as in Sentence (31).

(30) *Being watched by millions of viewers,* the newsman became a household name.
(31) *Having **been** sequestered for two weeks,* the jurors were happy to return home.

### Do ESL/EFL learners have difficulties with participial phrases?

► *Learner difficulties*

Advanced ESL/EFL learners, especially those enrolled in writing courses, are often encouraged to use participial phrases to add variety to their writing and to avoid short, choppy sentences. For practice, they are frequently given sentences and asked to rewrite or combine them to include participial phrases. While learners may have little trouble with such exercises, in their own writing they may avoid the use of participial phrases or use them incorrectly, especially if these structures are not found in or are different from those in their own language. For example, instead of using a participle, ESL/EFL learners may use an inflected verb:

*(32) The girl *sits* over there is a student in Professor Danik's class.

Another problem both ESL/EFL learners and inexperienced native speakers may have is writing sentences with what are called *dangling modifiers.* After a participial phrase, the noun or noun phrase immediately following refers to the preceding participial phrase. At times, however, when the participial phrase is in initial sentence position, writers will use a noun or noun phrase in the main clause that cannot logically be the one the participial phrase is supposed to refer to.

*(33) Walking to the store, a bucket of paint fell on his head.

Although the sentence may initially sound correct, the question to ask oneself is whether or not a bucket of paint can walk. Since an introductory participial phrase modifies the noun or noun phrase immediately following it, the answer here is "no." The sentence needs to be re-written as:

(33a) While Andrew was walking to the store, a bucket of paint fell on his head.
*or*
(33b) Walking to the store, Andrew had an accident. A bucket of paint fell on his head.

# Section 3: Infinitives

The last type of verbal we will look at is *infinitives*. The infinitive, as we have seen previously, is the "to" + base or simple verb. Infinitives can combine with other words to form *infinitive phrases*. You may be puzzled why many grammarians categorize infinitives as verbals. The reason for this is that infinitives do not inflect for person and number and can fulfill different functions in sentences.

# Function

## What are the functions of infinitives and infinitive phrases?

Infinitives can function as nouns, adjectives, adverbs, and complements. When infinitives function as nouns, they can be in subject or object position. The following chart illustrates the different functions of infinitives:

| Infinitives and Infinitive Phrases | |
|---|---|
| | **Function** |
| *To find a good job* is an important goal | **subject** of the verb *is* |
| Most people want *to find a good job*. | **object** of the verb *want* |
| The teacher has a lot of work *to do*. | **adjective** modifying *work* |
| The teacher is leaving now *to get to her class*. | **adverb** modifying *now* |
| Her class is difficult *to teach*. | **adjective complement** modifying *difficult* |

As you can see from the chart, infinitives and infinitive phrases can take a variety of patterns. These patterns are the focus of this section of Chapter 12.

## Infinitives as Direct Objects of Verbs

*What is the most common position and function of infinitives and infinitive phrases?*

The most common sentence position of infinitives and infinitive phrases is after a main verb. When infinitives and infinitive phrases follow verbs, they are functioning as objects. We examined this pattern in Chapter 5 when we discussed which verbs are followed by gerunds, which by infinitives, and which by a gerund or an infinitive. In this chapter, we focus on the verbs that are followed exclusively by infinitives.

| Common Verbs Followed by Infinitives | | | | |
|---|---|---|---|---|
| afford | consent | hope | proceed | tend |
| agree | decide | learn | profess | threaten |
| arrange | deserve | manage | prove | volunteer |
| ask | determine | mean | refuse | want |
| care | fail | offer | resolve | wait |
| claim | forget | prepare | seem | wish |
| come | happen | pretend | struggle | |

The verbs in this chart are generally followed immediately by an infinitive or an infinitive phrase, although at times adverbs may come between the main verb and an infinitive or an infinitive phrase.

(34)   He agreed *to come* for the interview.
(34a)  He agreed **immediately** *to come* for the interview.

In formal prescriptive grammar, an adverb should not come between the "to" and simple verb of an infinitive. When this does occur, it is referred to as a "split infinitive."

(35)   He prepared *to* **immediately** *come* for the interview.

Although the split infinitive is frowned upon in formal prescriptive grammar, many native speakers ignore this prohibition.

## Other Patterns

*Does anything besides an adverb ever come between the verb and the infinitive?*

### *Verb + Indirect Object + Infinitive as Direct Object*

Some verbs in English follow a slightly different pattern. These verbs require an indirect object between the main verb and the infinitive or the infinitive phrase. The indirect object may be either a noun or pronoun.

   (36)  The teacher allowed **her students** *to drink in class.*
   (37)  The sergeant commanded **them** *to leave.*

| Common Verbs Followed by Indirect Object + Infinitive | | | |
|---|---|---|---|
| advise | convince | inspire | remind |
| allow | direct | instruct | request |
| authorize | encourage | invite | require |
| appoint | forbid | motivate | teach |
| cause | force | order | tell |
| challenge | get (=cause) | permit | urge |
| command | hire | persuade | warn |

*Does this rule always apply?*

The exception to the rule that these verbs must have an indirect object inserted between the main verb and the infinitive or the infinitive phrase is when the main verb is in the passive. When we change one of these verbs to the passive, the **original indirect object becomes the subject** of the passive sentence. Thus, there is no indirect object between the verb and the infinitive.

   (38)  Her students **were allowed** *to drink in class.*
   (39)  They **were commanded** *to leave.*

*Are there any other patterns?*

### *Verb + (indirect object) + Infinitive as Direct Object*

Some verbs may or may not take an indirect object before the infinitive. The difference lies in the meaning. When the verb is followed only by an infinitive or an infinitive phrase, it is being used intransitively (see Chapter 5). When it is followed by an object + infinitive, it is being used transitively

(40)  The teacher expected *to leave* late.
(41)  The teacher expected **me** *to leave* late.

- In Sentence (40), the verb *expect* is being used **intransitively**. In this sentence it is the teacher who is expecting to leave.
- In Sentence (41), the verb *expect* is being used **transitively**. In this sentence the teacher is expecting someone else (*me*) to leave.

| Some Common Verbs Followed by Infinitives *or* Indirect Object + Infinitive | | |
| --- | --- | --- |
| ask | expect | prepare |
| beg | like | want |
| choose | need | wish |
|  | prefer |  |

### How do we make infinitives negative?

Infinitives can be made negative by placing *not* before "to" + the simple or base verb.

(42)  She decided **not** *to go* home.

### Can we make infinitives passive?

In Discovery Activity 5, Excerpt B, we observed that infinitives can be used passively. The structure is "to" + *be* + past participle. Because *be* follows "to," it always remains in its simple or base form.

(43)  Revered above all else are the lessons **to be learned** from "just going out and doing it."
       [Bennis, W., & Thomas, R. (2002). *Geeks & geezers* (p. 64). Boston: Harvard University Press.]

### What other sentence position and function do infinitives and infinitive phrases have?

## Infinitives as Subjects

Infinitives and infinitive phrases can be the subject of a sentence:

(44)  *To do one's homework* is important.

### Is it common to use infinitives and infinitive phrases as subjects?

Placing the infinitive at the beginning of the sentence is considered formal and generally not found in informal spoken or written English.

# Infinitives After Be + Certain Adjectives

*Where else do we find infinitives and infinitive phrases?*

Infinitives or infinitive phrases can follow *be* +certain adjectives. These adjectives generally express mental states or emotion:

(45)  She was **eager** *to hear* the news.

| *Be* + Common Adjectives Followed by Infinitives | | | |
|---|---|---|---|
| amazed | difficult | glad | relieved |
| angry | delighted | happy | reluctant |
| anxious | determined | hesitant | sad |
| ashamed | disappointed | likely | shocked |
| astonished | disturbed | lucky | sorry |
| careful | eager | pleased | surprised |
| certain | eligible | proud | upset |
| content | fortunate | ready | wrong |

Many of the *–ed* participial adjectives in this chart have *–ing* participial adjective counterparts that can also be followed by an infinitive or an infinitive phrase. When the *–ing* participial adjective is used, the sentence must then include the filler or dummy *It* subject, as in Sentence (47).

(46)  Hannah was *surprised* **to learn** she had been accepted at Harvard.

(47)  **It** was *surprising* **to see** how quickly he recovered after the accident.

# Infinitives as Adjectives and Adverbs

*How does the infinitive or infinitive phrase function as an adjective or adverb?*

Infinitives and infinitive phrases function as adjectives when they modify a preceding noun. They function as adverbs when they modify a verb or an entire sentence. When infinitives and infinitive phrases function as adverbs, they are expressing a purpose:

| Infinitives | Function |
|---|---|
| (48) The students have a lot of homework *to do*. | **adjective** |
| (49) The students came *to learn English*. | **adverb** |
| (50) *To learn* English better, the students came to the US. | **adverb** |

- In Sentences (48), the infinitive is modifying the noun *homework*, and thus functioning as an adjective.
- In Sentence (49), the infinitive phrase is modifying the verb *came*, and thus functioning as an adverb. The infinitive phrase *to learn English* is explaining "why" *the students came*.
- In Sentence (50), the infinitive phrase is modifying the entire sentence *the students came to the US*, and thus also functioning as an adverb.

*How can I decide if the infinitive or infinitive phrase is functioning as an adverb?*

Crucial to deciding whether or not an infinitive or infinitive phrase is functioning as an adverb is to ask the question "Why?" For example, in Sentence (49), the infinitive phrase *to learn English* is explaining "why" *the students came*. In Sentence (50), the infinitive phrase *To learn English better* is again telling us the "why" of the main clause.

## Other Structures with Infinitives

*What kind of other structures use infinitives and infinitive phrases?*

## It and Infinitives

In English we often avoid using infinitives or infinitive phrases as subjects except in formal situations or for specific emphasis. Instead, we use the "filler" or "dummy" subject *it*. Previously we saw this sentence:

(47) **It** was *surprising* **to see** how quickly he recovered after the accident.

In Sentence (47), the subject pronoun *It* is followed by *be* + *adjective*. This structure is followed by the infinitive phrase *to see*. The infinitive phrase is not the subject of the sentence, but the complement of *surprising*.

The subject pronoun *It* is referred to as a "filler" or "dummy" subject because it does not refer to anything. This *It* simply fulfills the grammatical requirement of English that every main verb must have a subject.

## Base Verbs or "Bare Infinitives"

*What is a "bare infinitive?"*

Certain verbs are followed by the verb without the "to." This type of verb is frequently referred to as a *bare* or *simple* infinitive or just the "simple" or "base verb." These verbs include two groups of words, the so-called causatives verbs and the sensory verbs.

| Verbs Followed by the Base or Simple Verb | | | |
|---|---|---|---|
| **causative verbs** | | **sensory verbs** | |
| have | let | feel | observe |
| help | make | hear | see |
| | | notice | watch |

## Causative Verbs

### What is a causative verb?

In Chapter 8 we discussed the causative verb *get*. The label *causative* is also commonly used with the verbs *help, have, let,* and *make* because they express the idea that "X" causes "Y" to do something. The verb *make* when used in a causative sense implies that "X" compels "Y" to do something.

   (51) Marcia's dad *made* her *do* her homework this afternoon.

The verb *let* when used in a causative sense implies that "X" allows "Y" to do something.

   (52) Marcia's dad *let* her *watch* a movie last night.

The causative verbs are followed by an object and the base verb, as in Sentences (51) and (52).
   The verb *help* may be followed by either a base infinitive or the full infinitive:

   (53) They *helped **clear*** the yard of debris.
   (54) They *helped **to clear*** the yard of debris.

The sensory verbs are followed by a noun or pronoun + base verb:

   (55) Dave *felt* **the girls** *watch* him.
   (56) I *heard* **him** *open* the door.

After a sensory verb + a noun or pronoun, a gerund may be used instead of a base verb:

   (55a) Dave *felt* **the girls** *watching* him.
   (56a) I *heard* **him** *opening* the door.

## Time

### Can infinitives have different time reference?

Infinitives, like participles, do not inflect for person or number, but can indicate different time references.

## *Basic Infinitive*

Sometimes referred to as the present infinitive or the general infinitive, this is the "to" + base verb form we have examined up to now. This infinitive form expresses time that is simultaneous with or future from the time expressed by the main verb of the sentence. The basic infinitive is the most common form of the infinitive.

Occasionally, a speaker may wish to emphasize duration, and will use a *progressive infinitive*. This construction consists of "to" + *be* + present participle.

(57) The toddler constantly wants *to be sitting on* her mother's lap.

## *Perfect Infinitive*

To express time preceding that of the main verb, the infinitive takes a perfect form: "to" + *have* + past participle.

(58) The parents were lucky *to have found* this specialist for their sick child.

The perfect infinitive can be used with *progressive aspect* to emphasize duration. This construction consists of "to" + *have* + *been* + V-ing.

(59) He was too scared of the police *to have been telling* lies all the time.

The perfect infinitive can also be used in *passive voice*. This construction consists of "to" + *have* + *been* + past participle:

(60) Shelly was surprised *to have been offered* the job.

See how well you do in identifying infinitives in Discovery Activity 6 and then check your answers in the Answer Key.

**Discovery Activity 7: Finding Infinitives**

Look at the following excerpts.

1. Underline the infinitives

**A.**

> Practice and performance come to be viewed as inseparable... The key to practicing in the midst of performance is to identify where opportunities exist... Find ways to notice yourself in action, to experiment with different ways of behaving in real time, and to adjust your behavior...
> [Bennis, W., & Thomas, R. (2002). *Geeks & geezers* (p. 178). Boston: Harvard University Press.]

**B.**

Since one man's patron is generally another man's client, a chain of such relationships extends from the top to the bottom of society... The anthropologist Julian Pitt-Rivers coined the term "lopsided friendship" to describe this bond between social unequals. To call such an arrangement friendship may seem to stretch the word beyond all recognition.

[Bellow, A. (2003). *In praise of nepotism: A natural history* (p. 37). New York: Doubleday.]

**C.**

References to *The Godfather* permeate popular culture... Real gangsters are even said to have adopted the rituals and language of the Corleone family...

[Bellow, A. (2003). *In praise of nepotism: A natural history* (p. 29). New York: Doubleday.]

*What kinds of problems do ESL/EFL learners have with infinitives and infinitive phrases?*

▶ *Learner difficulties*

Low proficiency ESL/EFL learners at times confuse infinitives with prepositional phrases beginning with "to." For such ESL/EFL learners, it is helpful to stress that the "to" of an infinitive is followed by a verb describing an action, event, or state, such as *to write, to walk, to teach*. Prepositional phrases beginning with "to," in contrast, have a noun or noun phrase after the "to." Compare, for instance:

| | |
|---|---|
| (61) The girl wants *to walk.* | **infinitive** |
| (62) The girl is walking *to the store.* | **prepositional phrase** |
| (63) The girl wants *to walk to the store.* | **infinitive + prepositional phrase** |

- In Sentence (61), "to" is followed by the verb *walk*. We know that it is not the noun *walk* because of sentence position and the lack of other preceding words that indicate noun function, such as articles.
- In Sentence (62), "to" is followed by *the* + a noun. This indicates that "to" is functioning as a preposition and part of a prepositional phrase.
- In Sentence (63), the *to walk* is an infinitive followed by a prepositional phrase. We know this because:
  - the sentence position of *to walk* after the verb *wants* and
  - the words following the second "to" (article *the* + noun *store*). This tells us that the first "to" is part of the infinitive and the second "to" a preposition.

A related area of difficulty for many ESL/EFL learners is remembering which verbs require an indirect object before the infinitive and which ones do not:

*(66)  The teacher arranged *me* to have a tutor.

Still another area of difficulty for ESL/EFL learners, particularly at lower levels of proficiency, is remembering to include the "to" before an infinitive when an object comes between it and the main verb.

*(67)  Her friend encouraged her *study* for the university.

At lower levels of proficiency, ESL/EFL learners tend to include the "to" after verbs that take only the base verb.

*(68)  The teacher made me *to do* my homework over again.
*(69)  Allison saw the teacher *to give* the students help.

## Summary

| Verbals |
|---|
| • There are three types of verbals: gerunds, participles, and "to" infinitives. |
| • They are called verbals because they lack inflections for person, number, and in the case of gerunds, time. |

| Gerunds | Participles | Infinitives |
|---|---|---|
| • Gerunds are *–ing* forms of verbs<br>• Gerunds function as nouns; can therefore can be in subject, object, or complement position | • There are two types of participles that form participial phrases, *-ing* and *–ed*.<br>  ○ Only transitive verbs can form *–ed* participles<br>• Participial phrases generally function as adjectives and sometimes as adverbs<br>• Participial phrases can indicate time: general time or prior time<br>• Participial phrases can be used in passive voice | • Infinitives are the "to" + base verb.<br>• Infinitives function as subject, object, adjective, adverb, and complement<br>• Infinitives can indicate time: general time or prior time<br>• Infinitives can be used in passive voice |

| Participles as Verbals | | |
|---|---|---|
| | active | passive |
| general form | requiring | required |
| progressive form | Ø | being required |
| perfect form | having required | having been required |
| perfect progressive form | having been requiring | Ø |

## Infinitive Patterns

- main verb + infinitive
  - I offered *to help*.
- main verb + required object + infinitive
  - She convinced **him** *to leave*.
- main verb + (optional object) + infinitive
  - I wanted **him** *to leave*.
  - I wanted *to leave*.

## Practice Activities

### *Activity 1: Identifying the Different Types of –ing*

Look at the following excerpts.

1. Underline all the -*ing* forms you find.
2. Label each -*ing* form you have underlined.

*Example*:

The people are sitting in a speeding bus.

| present participle of verb phrase | present participial adjective | participle verbal |
|---|---|---|

The people are *sitting* in a *speeding* bus, *enjoying* the view.

**A.**

I remember my mother telling me when my kids were small and I was working hard that it was the best time of my life.
   [Blyth, M. (2004). *Spin sisters* (p. 78). New York: St. Martin's Press.]

**B.**

Walking home after the party, I also realized that I had to acknowledge from the start that I was part of the Girls' club whose members are experts at telling and selling stories to American women.
   [Blyth, M. (2004). *Spin sisters* (p. 3). New York: St. Martin's Press.]

## C.

Watching playful dolphins keep up with speeding boats, diving and leaping near the front,
or bow, you'd think that these marine animals must be incredibly fast swimmers.
> [Gordon, D. (2005, June/July). 10 Cool things about dolphins. *National Geographic
> Kids*, p. 18]

## *Activity 2: Identifying Gerund Phrases and Their Functions*

a. Underline each gerund phrase.
b. Label the function of each gerund phrase.

*Example:*

The boss carefully considered *hiring a new office manager*. object

1. Swimming laps is vigorous exercise.
2. Avery gave up smoking last year.
3. Candidates for public office do not object to releasing their tax returns.
4. Winning the Tour de France more often than any other bicyclist has made Lance
   Armstrong a legend.
5. The mayor insisted on providing housing for the needy.
6. Demanding satisfaction, the customer insisted on seeing the manager.

## *Activity 3: Identifying Different Functions of Participles*

a. Underline each participle of a verb phrase, participial adjective, or participial
   phrase.
b. Label each participle you underlined.

*Example:*

The *crying* baby is *teething*.

crying = participial adjective; teething = present participle, part of the present progressive verb phrase *is teething*.

1. I was sleeping soundly when I was awakened by the howling wind and heavy
   thunder.
2. The city was evacuated as the broken levees let polluted water pour through the
   streets.
3. The chef is becoming famous for his dishes, which use locally grown vegetables.
4. A storm of protest has been unleashed over the proposed tax hikes.
5. The yard of the abandoned house is filling with rusting toys, broken machinery,
   discarded bottles, and decaying vegetation.
6. She had been planning a visit to an unspoiled beach in the Caribbean until she
   was told about a relaxing mountain resort in the Rockies.

## Activity 4: Identifying Participles and Their Functions (optional additional practice)

Look at the following excerpt.

1. Label the type and function of each underlined participle.
2. The first one has been done for you.

*Example*

Said:    Past participle; part of past perfect verb phrase

When you paraphrase what's been **said,** or repeat the specifics of what you have *heard,* there can be no doubt that you have *listened* and *understood* the speaker. This is especially effective when you are *disagreeing* with your conversation partner or have *listened* to her explain something highly complex or technical. *Paraphrasing* the speaker clarifies that you understood correctly. Or it can help the speaker recognize that you misunderstood what she was *attempting* to communicate... In an emotionally *charged* situation, you gain a side benefit of *defusing* anger when you repeat the specifics of what the other person stated... *Skilled* customer service managers know that by *repeating* what an angry customer is *saying,* they can reduce the level of hostility. *Remaining* calm while doing so sends a message about your own professionalism and poise.

[Fine, D. (2002). *The fine art of small talk* (p. 52). Englewood, CO: Small Talk Publishers.]

## Activity 5: Identifying Infinitive Phrases versus Prepositional Phrases with "To"

a. Underline each infinitive and prepositional phrase.
b. Label each phrase you have underlined. PP for prepositional phrase and IP for infinitive phrase.
c. Explain what clues there are at help you identify the function of "to"

*Example:*

They go *to the school around the corner.* PP
Some students like *to study.* IP

1. Some residents ignored official orders to leave their homes.
2. The risk of widespread contamination and disease had left the police with no choice but to use force, if necessary, to evacuate any resident who refused to leave.
3. Those who had lost their homes in the storm were forced to go to relatives or to shelters.
4. The sick and elderly asked the police to help them move to other safer areas.
5. In a move to defend himself, the politician prepared to come back to his home state to face his accusers.

## *Activity 6: Distinguishing Verbals (optional additional practice)*

1. Look at the following excerpts.
2. Underline the verbals.
3. Label the function of each verbal you have identified.

**A.**

> Mr. Collins was not left long to the silent contemplation of his successful love for Mrs. Bennet, having dawdled about in the vestibule to watch for the end of the conference, no sooner saw Elizabeth open the door and with quick step pass her to the staircase, than she entered the breakfast room and congratulated both him and herself in warm terms on the happy prospect of their nearer connections.
>
> [Austen, J. (1813/1988). *Pride and prejudice* (p. 110). New York: Oxford University Press.]

**B.**

> Having now a good house and very sufficient income, he intended to marry and in seeking a reconciliation with the Longbourn family he had a wife in view as he meant to choose one of the daughters if he found them as handsome and amiable as they were represented by common report.
>
> [Austen, J. (1813/1988). *Pride and prejudice* (p. 79). New York: Oxford University Press.]

**C.**

> Occupied in observing Mr. Bingley's attentions to her sister, Elizabeth was far from suspecting that she was herself becoming an object of some interest in the eyes of his friend.
>
> [Austen, J. (1813/1988). *Pride and prejudice* (p. 23). New York: Oxford University Press.]

## *Activity 7: Dangling Modifiers*

Both inexperienced native speakers and advanced learners of English are often given exercises to help them practice avoiding dangling modifiers. One common exercise is to ask students to rewrite sentences with dangling modifiers.

a. Examine each sentence below.
b. On a separate sheet of paper, rewrite each sentence to avoid dangling modifiers.
c. Discuss what benefits such an activity might or might not have for learners of English.

1. Having successfully completed the paper, the grade was excellent.
2. Sipping margaritas in the bar, the band sounded off-key.
3. Unwilling to evacuate in time, the Red Cross couldn't save all the stranded refugees.
4. Walking along the beach, the wind was blowing sand into their faces.

# Answer Key: Chapter 12 Discovery Activities

## *Discussion: Discovery Activity 1*

*Sentence (1)*

*writing* is part of the gerund phrase *writing short stories.*

- The gerund phrase is functioning as a complement because it is naming or describing the subject of the verb, *Her sole occupation.*

*Sentence (2)*

*vacationing* is part of the past progressive verb phrase *was vacationing.*

- An important clue in this sentence is the adverbial clause *when the storm hit,* which describes a past action that interrupted another ongoing past action, *was vacationing in Florida.*

*Sentence (3)*

*holding* is part of the progressive verb phrase, *is holding*

*Sentence (4)*

*calling* is part of the gerund phrase *special calling.*

- An important clue is the use of the article *a.*
- Gerunds, but not progressive verb phrases, can be preceded by an article because gerunds function as nouns.

*Sentence (5)*

*was driving* is the past progressive verb phrase describing an action of some duration.

*Sentence (6)*

*rebuilding antique cars* is a gerund phrase.

- The gerund phrase is functioning as a complement because it is naming or describing the subject of the verb, *Joseph's hobby.*

## *Discussion: Discovery Activity 2*

*Excerpt A*

- *shutting down:*

  - gerund after *start*, a verb that can be followed by either gerund, as here or an infinitive
  - object of *start*

- *closing:*

  - gerund, after the preposition *before*
  - object of *before*

*Excerpt B*

- *hanging:*

  - gerund after *mandated*: a verb that must be followed by a gerund.
  - object of *mandated*.

- *taking a fugitive out of the state:*

  - gerund phrase
  - object of the preposition *for*

- *aiding:*

  - gerund after *caught*, a verb that must be followed by a gerund.

*Excerpt C*

- *Challenging each other's opinions:*

  - gerund phrase
  - subject of the verb *comes*

- *doing* is part of the present progressive verb phrase *are doing*.

*Excerpt D*

- *Knowing the rules:*

  - gerund phrase
  - subject of *is*.

- *Playing the game:*

  - gerund
  - complement of *is*

- *trying*:

    - gerund
    - object of the preposition *by*
    - the adverb *instinctively* has been inserted between *by* and *trying*

- *bowling*

    - gerund
    - modifying *ball*, telling us what kind of ball

## Discussion: Discovery Activity 3

- Participial phrases: Sentences (1), (2), (4), and (6)
- Gerund phrases: Sentences (3), (5), and (7)

## Discussion: Discovery Activity 4

- Gerund phrases: Sentences (1) and (5)
- Participial phrases: Sentences (2), (3), (4), and (6)

## Discussion: Discovery Activity 5

*Excerpt A*

| | |
|---|---|
| unexpected | participial adjective |
| tripped | past participle, part of present perfect verb phrase *have tripped* |
| tried | past tense of the verb *try* |

*Excerpt B*

| | |
|---|---|
| supplemented | participle, part of the participial phrase, *supplemented by simulations* |
| revered | participle, part of the participial phrase, *Revered above all else* |
| learned | past participle, part of passive infinitive *to be learned* (see following section on infinitives) |
| raised, convinced | part of participial phrase, reduced relative clauses who were/have been |

*Excerpt C*

addressed  participial phrase, reduced relative clause
              *that/which were/had been addressed*
involved   participial phrase, reduced relative clause
              *that/which were/had been involved*
focused   regular simple past tense


## *Discussion: Discovery Activity 6*

*Excerpt A*

* *standing*: participles in participial phrases *in the hallway* and *behind him*


*Excerpt B*

* *developing*: participial adjective modifying *demonstrations*
* *attended:* past participle, part of the past perfect verb phrase *had attended.*
* *upcoming:* participial adjective modifying *anniversary.*


*Excerpt C*

* *Butchering:* gerund, object of the preposition *on*
* *Reflected:* past participle, part of the participial phrase *reflected the response I was hoping for*


*Excerpt D*

* *filming:* gerund, naming an activity, similar to *swimming, driving, bowling* and so on
* *trying:* present participle, part of the past progressive verb phrase *was trying*
* *laughing:* a gerund, after the phrasal verb *break up*, which consists of a verb + particle (preposition)
* *acting:* present participle, part of the past progressive verb phrase *was acting*
* *saying:* gerund, after the idiom *feel like*, which is always followed by a noun or gerund form of a verb
* *started*: regular past tense
* *supposed*: part of the idiom *be supposed to*
* *finished:* regular past tense
* *filming:* gerund
* *filming:* gerund, direct object of the verb *finish*, which is always followed by a noun or gerund form of a verb
* *clothing*: noun that happens to end in *ing*, similar to *morning*, or *shilling*. It is not a participle, but less proficient ESL/EFL learners may confuse this word with a participle.

- *loaned*: past participle, part of the past perfect verb phrase *had loaned*
- *carrying:* part of a participial phrase *a bundle of Bob's clothes*

## Discussion: Activity 7

*Excerpt A*

*be viewed* (passive), *to identify, to notice, to experiment, to adjust*

- In the second sentence of this excerpt we see *to* functioning as a preposition and followed by a gerund *practicing*

*Excerpt B*

*to describe, To call. . . friendship* (functioning as the subject of the main clause), *to stretch*

*Excerpt C*

*to have adopted* (perfect infinitive)

# Glossary

**abstract noun**: A noun that denotes an abstract or intangible concept, such as *happiness* or *anger.*

**active (voice):** In an active sentence, the person or thing that is performing or causing the action is the subject of the verb; also, there is an object that receives the action. For example, in the sentence, *The boy hit the ball, The boy* performs the action *hit* and *the ball* receives the action.

**adjective:** A word that describes or modifies the meaning of a noun. An adjective provides lexical or semantic meaning. It is one of the major word class categories.

**adjective phrase:** A phrase with an adjective.

**adjective clause:** A clause that modifies the noun or noun phrase it follows. Because a relative clause modifies a noun or noun phrase, it functions as an adjective. Relative clauses are also known as *adjective clauses.* A relative clause is usually introduced by a relative pronoun.

**adverb:** A word that describes or modifies a verb, an adjective, another adverb, a phrase, or a sentence. An adverb provides lexical or semantic meaning. It is one of the major word class categories.

**adverb phrase** A phrase with an adverb.

**affirmative sentence**: A sentence that does not have a negative verb; often referred to as a *positive sentence.*

**affix:** A term including both suffixes and prefixes.

**agreement:** The subject and verb must agree in number. If the subject is singular, the verb form must also be singular. *Jane likes books.* If the subject is plural, the verb must also be plural: *The girls **like** books.*

**article:** The words *a/an*, and *the*. They signal nouns and are members of one of the minor structure word categories.

**aspect:** Refers to a choice in the verb phrase expressing time meanings that are related to the duration, repetition, or completion of the action or state of the verb, e.g. *am writing* vs. *have written.*

**attitude adverb:** An adverb that conveys an evaluation or judgment of what is said, e.g. *frankly, surprisingly.*

**auxiliary verb:** *Have, be, do.* A verb that "helps" and or "supports" a main verb.

**base verb**: The simple form of a verb to which inflections can be attached, e.g. *walk* → *walks*.

**bound morpheme:** A morpheme that must be attached to another morpheme. It cannot stand alone. For example *un* as in *unhappy* or the plural *–s* as in *boys*.

**causative verb:** a verb that indicates a thing or person causes or brings about another thing or person to do something or a new state of affairs.

**closed word class:** Function or structure words to which new words are very rarely added. e.g. prepositions or pronouns. A closed word class is a minor structure word class category.

**collective noun:** A noun that refers to a group, e.g. *committee, team, government*.

**comparative:** A form of an adjective or adverb that is used to describe differences between two persons, things, or situations. Adjectives or adverbs consisting of one syllable or ending in *–ly* generally add *–er*. Adjectives or adverbs consisting of two or more syllables generally use *more*.

**complement:** Anything that comes after the verb to complete a sentence. See also subject complement.

**complementizer:** Used in this text to refer to *that* when it introduces a noun clause.

**complex sentences:** A sentence that has a main clause and one or more subordinate clauses.

**compound sentence:** A sentence that has two or more main clauses but no subordinate clause. The main clauses are conjoined by coordinators.

**conditional:** A sentence that refers to something real or unreal, and that generally has an *if* clause and a clause with *would, could,* or *might*.

**conjunction:** A word that connects clauses. There are two types of conjunctions: coordinators and subordinators.

**conjunctive adverb:** A transition word that connects two ideas between two main clauses, e.g. *therefore, however*.

**constituent:** The basic unit of a sentence, including noun, adjective, adverb, prepositional, and verb phrases. Sentence constituents are combined in meaningful ways to form sentences.

**coordinator:** A type of conjunction that connects two or more main clauses, phrases, or words: *and, but, or, for, yet*.

**count noun:** A noun that refers to something that can be counted, e.g. *pencil, book, job*.

**crossover noun:** A noun that has both a count meaning and a noncount meaning. e g. *hair* or *water*. Generally the two meanings are related, although not always.

**definite article:** The word *the*. It is used when speakers want to refer to something that is known to the speaker and the hearer.

**degree adverb:** An adverb that increases or decreases the effect or intensity of that which it is modifying.

**demonstrative:** *this, these* and *that, those*. A demonstrative indicates whether something is near or far in relation to the speaker There are two types of demonstratives: demonstrative adjectives and demonstrative pronouns. **Demonstrative**

adjectives occur before a noun, e.g. *this book*. **Demonstrative pronouns** occur without a noun, e.g. *I want this*.

**dependent clause:** A subordinate clause; a clause that cannot stand alone, but that must occur with a main clause and that is introduced by a subordinator.

**derivational morphology:** The process of creating new words by adding affixes to a stem, e.g. *sad* → *sadness* or *happy* → *unhappy*.

**descriptive grammar:** An approach to grammar that focuses on describing or examining how people use language.

**determiner:** A structure word that occurs before a noun and specifies or limits it in some way, e.g. *the, those, some*.

**direct object:** Something that receives the action of the verb, usually a noun, pronoun, or noun phrase, but can also be a clause.

**direct speech:** Quoted speech; the exact words someone has said or written.

**"do" support:** Refers to the function of the *do* auxiliary in questions and negatives in simple present and simple past.

**di-transitive verb:** A verb that has both a direct and indirect object.

**downtowner:** An adverb that lessens the meaning or intensity of an adjective or another adverb, e.g. *slightly nervous*.

**dummy "it":** When "It" is used as the subject but has no meaning, e.g. *It is cold*.

**essential relative clause:** A relative clause that is necessary for meaning.

**expression of quantity:** A word or words that occur before a noun to indicate an amount or quantity, e.g. *a slice of, a pound of, a lot of, some*.

**filler verb:** A verb that has no semantic meaning, but is necessary for grammatical reasons, e.g. *"do" support*.

**focus adverb:** An adverb that draws attention to that which it is modifying, e.g. *frankly*.

**form:** The construction of a particular word. In English, form is no guarantee of function.

**free morpheme:** A morpheme that does not need to be attached or bound to another morpheme.

**frequency adverb:** An adverb that tells us *how often* an action occurs, e.g. *always, sometimes, never*.

**function:** The role of a word, phrase, or clause. In English, form is no guarantee of function.

**function word:** Structure word; a word that expresses a grammatical relationship but has no semantic meaning, e.g. *the, to, and*, from.

**future:** Time that is yet to come. Usually expressed in English by *will* or *be going to*.

**gradable adjective:** An adjective that can be compared using *–er* or *–est* or *more/most*.

**gerund:** *-ing* form of a verb that functions as a noun.

**gerund phrase:** A phrase with a gerund.

**idiom:** A fixed or set expression that cannot be determined from the individual parts, e.g. *eat crow, kick the bucket*.

*if* **clause:** A subordinate clause that begins with *if* and that express a real or unreal situation. See conditional.

**imperative:** A command. A verb in simple form without a subject telling someone to do something, e.g. *Eat your vegetables.*

**indefinite article:** The word *a* or *an*. It is used when speakers want to refer to indefinite or undefined meaning. e.g. *back seat driver, a cock and bull story.*

**independent clause:** A main clause. A clause that can stand alone and does not need to be attached to another clause.

**indefinite pronoun:** A pronoun without specific reference, e.g. *anybody, someone.*

**indirect object:** Something that follows verbs such as *give* or *take,* and that refers to the person or thing receiving the action.

**indirect speech:** Reported speech. A type of sentence that expresses what someone has said or written, but that is not a direct quote.

**infinitive:** A verb form that includes "to" + the simple or base form of the verb.

**inflection:** a morphological change in verbs, nouns, adjectives, and adjectives that signals some kind of grammatical information, e.g. *book* → *books* (the –*s* shows plural); or *walk* - → *ed* (the –*ed* shows past tense.) There are only 8 inflections in English, but these cause many difficulties for ESL/EFL learners.

**intransitive verb:** A verb that does not take an object.

**inversion:** The process of moving the first auxiliary to the front of a sentence to form a question, e.g. *He is walking* → *Is he walking?*

**irregular verb:** A verb that does not follow the normal inflectional patterns of English for form the simple past and/or past participle.

**lexical:** A word that has meaning rather than just a grammatical function.

**linking verb:** A verb that "links" or joins the subject and complement. Sometimes referred to as a *copula* verb.

**main clause:** Independent clause. A clause that can stand alone and does not require another clause. The minimum clause in English consists of a subject + verb.

**main verb:** A verb that has lexical or semantic meaning, not an auxiliary verb. It can be used as the only verb in a sentence.

**major category:** This consists of the word classes that have lexical or semantic meaning: nouns, verbs, adjectives, and adverbs.

**mass noun:** A noun that refers to a substance or abstract concept not divisible into countable units, e.g. *water, thunder.* A mass noun is a noncount noun and cannot be used in the plural or with the indefinite article *a/an* or a number.

**minor category:** This consists of the word classes that have grammatical meaning, e.g. prepositions, conjunctions, and pronouns.

**modal/modal auxiliary:** A special class of auxiliary verbs that convey semantic meaning. A modal occurs with a main verb and modifies the meaning of the main verb by expressing ability, politeness, possibility, necessity, and the like.

**modify:** To add to, or specify. The meaning of a word. For example, in *beautiful house,* the adjective *beautiful* modifies the noun, *house.*

**morpheme:** The smallest unit of meaning. It is not the same as a syllable. A morpheme can be a single word, e.g. *hippopotamus,* or it can be a grammatical unit such as the past tense –ed inflection attached to a regular verb. Affixes are also morphemes, e.g. *un* as in *unhappy*.

**morphology:** the study of how morphemes are put together to form words (derivational morphology) and how morphemes provide grammatical information (inflectional morphology).

**noncount noun:** A noun that cannot be counted, e.g. *happiness*. It cannot be used in the plural or with the indefinite article *a/an* or a number.

**nonessential relative clause:** A relative clause that is not necessary for meaning but that provides extra or additional information about the noun it is modifying.

**nonstandard:** A form of the language not accepted in general usage, e.g. *He don't know me*.

**noun:** A word that is generally thought of as referring to people, animals, places, ideas, or things. A noun provides lexical or semantic meaning. It is one of the major word class categories.

**noun clause:** A subordinate clause that functions in the same way a noun, pronoun, or noun phrase does. Noun clauses begin with *that, wh-question word,* or *whether or not/if*.

**noun phrase:** A phrase with a noun or pronoun.

**object:** A noun, pronoun, or noun phrase that receives the action of the verb. Only transitive verbs take objects.

**open word class:** A category of lexical or semantic words to which new words are easily added, e.g. nouns. An open word class is a major word class category.

**participial adjective:** An adjective that has an –*ing* or –*ed* form.

**participle:** The –*ing* or –*ed* form of a verb, e.g. *I am writing; I have walked*.

**particle:** A preposition or adverb that forms part of a phrasal verb. As part of a phrasal verb, the preposition or adverb loses its meaning.

**past participle:** The third form of the English verb, e.g. *walk, walked (past)* and *have walked (past participle)*. Sometimes referred to as the –*en* participle to distinguish it from the past tense –*ed* and because many common English participles end in –*en*, e.g. *write, wrote, written*.

**part of speech:** A traditional way of referring to word class.

**passive (voice):** In a passive sentence the doer or agent of the action is either unimportant, unknown or the speakers wants to emphasize the original object, e.g. *A flying object hit John* versus *John was hit by flying object*. The passive is formed with a form of *be* + past participle (+ optional *by* phrase). Only transitive verbs can be used in the passive.

**past perfect:** A verb form used to express a relationship between two past events or situations. The past perfect indicates the first of these two. The past perfect is formed with *had* + past participle.

**past perfect progressive:** Similar to the past perfect, the past perfect progressive is a verb form used to express a relationship between two past events or situations. The past perfect progressive, however, emphasizes the ongoing nature of the event or situation. The past perfect progressive is formed with *had* + *been* + present participle.

**past progressive:** A verb form used to express an ongoing, continuous action or situation in the past. The past progressive is formed with a past form of *be* + present participle. Also called the past continuous.

**perfect infinitive:** Used to show an earlier action than that of the main clause. The perfect infinitive is formed with "to" + *have* + past participle.

**phrasal verb:** A verb with one or more prepositions/adverbs (or particle) where the verb and preposition/adverb function as a semantic unit. The verb + adjective/adverb have a meaning that cannot be determined from looking at the separate parts.

**phrase:** A group of words that form a grammatical unit or constituent, e.g. noun phrase, verb phrase, adjective phrase.

**place adverb:** An adverb that answers the question *Where?*, e.g. *here, there.*

**possessive adjective:** Possessive determiner. Modifies a noun to indicate possession or ownership: *my, your, our, his, her.*

**possessive pronoun:** Indicates possession or ownership and substitutes for a noun phrase, e.g. *mine, yours, ours, his, hers, its.*

**prefix:** A morpheme attached to the beginning of a word, e.g. *un* in *unhappy.*

**preposition:** A structure class word, e.g. *in, from, to, on.* A preposition introduces a prepositional phrase and links the phrase to other words in a sentence.

**prepositional phrase:** A phrase with a preposition followed by a noun or noun phrase.

**prescriptive grammar:** An approach to grammar that focuses on the rules for correct and incorrect use of the language.

**present participle:** a main verb + *ing* with any necessary spelling changes, e.g. *walking* or *sitting.*

**present progressive:** A verb form used to express an ongoing, continuous, incomplete action or situation. The present progressive is formed with the present form of *be* + present participle. Also called the present continuous.

**present perfect:** A verb form used to express a relationship between past and present time. It indicates recent past time, time that began in the past and continues into the present and into some time in the future, and indefinite time. It is formed with the present form of *have* + past participle.

**present perfect progressive:** Similar to the present perfect, the present perfect progressive is a verb form used to express a relationship between past and present time. The present perfect progressive, however, emphasizes the ongoing nature of the event or situation. The present perfect progressive is formed with a present form of *have* + *been* + present participle.

**primary auxiliary:** *have, be,* or *do* used as an auxiliary verb.

**pro-form:** A word that functions to substitute for something else, e.g. *Did you see Jane? Yes, I did.* In this example *did* substitutes for *I saw Jane.*

**pronoun:** A structure word that functions to substitute for a noun or noun phrase.

**quantifier:** A word or words that occurs before a noun to indicate a quantity or amount, e.g. *a slice of, a pound of, a lot of, some.* Also called an expression of quantity.

**quoted speech:** Direct speech; the exact words someone has said or written.

**reduced clause:** A clause that has been reduced from its full form, e.g. *The woman who was living next door moved away→ The woman living next door moved away.*

**redundancy:** The inclusion of more grammatical information than necessary for meaning, e.g. *two teachers* or *these teachers.* The use of *two* or *these* already tells us that "teacher" consists of more than one; the use of the plural *–s* inflection is redundant.

**reflexive pronoun:** A pronoun that usually refers back to the subject of the sentence, e.g. *She bought herself a new car.*

**regular plural:** A noun that forms the plural by adding *–s*, with any necessary spelling changes.

**regular verb:** A verb that forms the simple past by adding *–ed*, with any necessary spelling changes.

**relative adverb:** One of the adverbs *where, when,* or *why* used to introduce a relative clause.

**relative clause:** A clause that modifies the noun or noun phrase it follows. Because a relative clause modifies a noun or noun phrase, it functions as an adjective. Relative clauses are also known as *adjective clauses.* A relative clause is usually introduced by a relative pronoun.

**relative pronoun:** A pronoun that introduces a relative clause and that refers back to the noun or noun phrase of the main clause. *That, which, who(m),* and *whose* are relative pronouns.

**reported speech:** A type of sentence that expresses the meaning of what someone has said. Reported speech sentences are noun clauses, which may be introduced by *that, wh-questions,* and *whether (or not)/if.*

**semantic:** Having to do with meaning. The major class words, verbs, nouns, adjectives, and adverbs, all have lexical or semantic meaning.

**semi-modal:** A structure that is related to the modal auxiliaries in terms of meaning and some grammatical properties. Semi-modals consist of more than one word, e.g. *have to, be able to.*

**simple verb:** The base form of a verb to which inflections can be attached, e.g. *walk → walks.*

**standard:** The language forms generally accepted by most users in formal and informal contexts; the forms that are found in grammar texts and in foreign/second language texts.

**stative verb:** A verb that refers to mental states, attitudes, emotions, and conditions. A stative verb is usually not used in the progressive forms.

**stigmatized language:** A non-standard form of language that is negatively regarded by users of the standard variety.

**structure word:** Function word; a word that expresses a grammatical relationship but has no semantic meaning, e.g. *the, to, and.*

**style book:** A reference book for native speakers providing guidance for punctuation, research paper guidelines, grammatical issues of concern and/or confusion, and so on.

**subject:** The part of the sentence, usually a noun or noun phrase, that acts as the agent, doer, or experiencer of the verb.

**Subject complement:** A word or phrase following a linking verb such as *be* and that describes or modifies the subject of this linking verb.

**subjunctive:** Used to refer to the use of the simple form of the verb in clauses following certain verbs. Also used in traditional grammar to refer to the form of the verb used to indicate hypothetical, contrary-to-fact situations.

**subordinate clause:** A dependent clause that cannot stand alone, but that must occur with a main clause and that is introduced by a subordinator.

**subordination:** The linking together of a main clause and another clause so that this clause is subordinate or dependent upon the main clause. The subordinate clause is introduced by a subordinator.

**subordinator:** A word that subordinates a clause to a main clause. A subordinator introduces a subordinate or dependent clause.

**suffix:** A bound morpheme that occurs at the end of a word, e.g. *rude* → *rudeness.*

**superlative:** A form of an adjective or adverb that is used to rank a person, thing, or situation in the last position. Adjectives or adverbs consisting of one syllable or ending in *–ly* generally add *–est*. Adjectives or adverbs consisting of two or more syllables generally use *most.*

**syllable:** A unit of language consisting of a single sound, that is a single sound without interruption or breaks. The word *man*, for instance, consist of one syllable; the word *woman* of two.

**tense:** Refers to an inflectional morpheme attached to the verb related to time, e.g. *kicks and kicked* → present and past.

*that*-**clause:** A type of noun clause.

**time adverb:** An adverb referring to time, e.g. *since.*

**transition word/phrase:** Words used to connect one idea to another. A transition word or phrase can continue a line of reasoning (e.g. *furthermore, in addition*), show order of ideas or arguments (e.g. *first, finally*), indicate a contrast (e.g. *however, on the other hand*), and more.

**transitive verb:** A verb that takes an object.

**verb:** A semantic class of words that refer to actions, situations, states, attitudes, mental conditions. A verb shows tense by taking the present *–s* and the past *–ed* inflection. In the case of an irregular verb, it may change its form in the past (e.g. *brought*), or not change at all (e.g. *cut*).

**verb phrase:** A phrase containing a main verb.

**verbal:** A form derived from a verb but having another function, e.g. *crying baby*. Here *crying* is a participial adjective.

**verbal phrase**: A phrase containing a verbal, e.g. *Crying loudly, the baby woke us up.* There are three types of verbal phrases: gerund, participial, and infinitive.

**voice**: Active or passive type sentence construction, e.g. *Shakespeare wrote Hamlet* versus *Hamlet was written by Shakespeare.*

*wh*-**question word:** a word such as *what, who, when, why* used for questions and to introduce noun clause questions.

**word class:** A group of words that are classified together on the basis of semantic meaning and/or grammatical function.

**yes/no question:** A type of question that can be answered with "yes" or "no."

# Appendices

## Appendix A: Irregular English Verbs in Alphabetical List[1]

| Base Form | Simple Past | Past Participle |
|-----------|-------------|-----------------|
| arise | arose | arisen |
| awake | awoke | awoken |
| be | was/were | been |
| beat | beat | beaten |
| become | became | become |
| begin | began | begun |
| bend | bent | bent |
| bet | bet | bet |
| bid | bid | bid |
| bite | bit | bitten |
| bleed | bled | bled |
| blow | blew | blown |
| break | broke | broken |
| breed | bred | bred |
| bring | brought | brought |
| broadcast | broadcast | broadcast |
| build | built | built |
| burn | burned | burned (AmE) |
| burst | burst | burst |
| buy | bought | bought |
| catch | caught | caught |
| choose | chose | chosen |
| cling | clung | clung |
| come | came | come |
| cost | cost | cost |
| creep | crept | crept |
| cut | cut | cut |

[1] There are some differences between American and British English. Only the American irregular verbs are listed here.

(continued)

| Base Form | **Simple Past** | **Past Participle** |
|---|---|---|
| deal | dealt | dealt |
| dig | dug | dug |
| dive | dived/dove* | dived/dove* |
| do | did | done |
| draw | drew | drawn |
| dream | dreamed/dreamt* | dreamed/dreamt* |
| drink | drank | drunk |
| drive | drove | driven |
| eat | ate | eaten |
| fall | fell | fallen |
| feed | fed | fed |
| feel | felt | felt |
| fight | fought | fought |
| find | found | found |
| flee | fled | fled |
| fling | flung | flung |
| fly | flew | flown |
| forbid | forbade | forbidden |
| forget | forgot | forgotten |
| forgive | forgave | forgiven |
| freeze | froze | frozen |
| get | got | got |
| give | gave | given |
| go | went | gone |
| grind | ground | ground |
| grow | grew | grown |
| hang | hung | hung |
| have | had | had |
| hear | heard | heard |
| hide | hid | hidden |
| hit | hit | hit |
| hold | held | held |
| hurt | hurt | hurt |
| keep | kept | kept |
| kneel | knelt | knelt |
| know | knew | known |
| lay | laid | laid |
| lead | led | led |
| leave | left | left |
| lend | lent | lent |
| let | let | let |
| lie | lay | lain |
| light | lighted/lit* | lighted/lit* |
| lose | lost | lost |
| make | made | made |
| mean | meant | meant |
| meet | met | met |
| mistake | mistook | mistaken |
| pay | paid | paid |
| prove | proved | proved/proven* |

(continued)

| Base Form | Simple Past | Past Participle |
|-----------|-------------|-----------------|
| put | put | put |
| quit | quit | quit |
| read | read* | read* |
| rid | rid | rid |
| ride | rode | ridden |
| ring | rang | rung |
| rise | rose | risen |
| run | ran | run |
| say | said | said |
| see | saw | seen |
| seek | sought | sought |
| sell | sold | sold |
| send | sent | sent |
| set | set | set |
| sew | sewed | sewn |
| shake | shook | shaken |
| shave | shaved | shaved/shaven* |
| shine | shone | shone |
| shoot | shot | shot |
| show | showed | shown |
| shrink | shrank | shrunk |
| shut | shut | shut |
| sing | sang | sung |
| sink | sank | sunk |
| sit | sat | sat |
| sleep | slept | slept |
| slide | slid | slid |
| slit | slit | slit |
| speak | spoke | spoken |
| speed | sped | sped |
| spend | spent | spent |
| spin | spun | spun |
| spit | spat | spat |
| split | split | split |
| spread | spread | spread |
| spring | sprang | sprung |
| stand | stood | stood |
| steal | stole | stolen |
| stick | stuck | stuck |
| sting | stung | stung |
| stink | stank | stunk |
| strike | struck | struck |
| strive | strove | striven |
| swear | swore | sworn |
| sweep | swept | swept |
| swim | swam | swum |
| swing | swung | swung |
| take | took | taken |
| teach | taught | taught |
| tear | tore | torn |

| | (continued) | |
|---|---|---|
| Base Form | **Simple Past** | **Past Participle** |
| tell | told | told |
| think | thought | thought |
| throw | threw | thrown |
| understand | understood | understood |
| uphold | upheld | upheld |
| upset | upset | upset |
| wake | woke | woken |
| wear | wore | worn |
| weep | wept | wept |
| win | won | won |
| wind | wound | wound |
| write | wrote | written |

*either form is acceptable

# Appendix B: Some Patterns of Common Irregular Verbs

Some ESL/EFL learners find it helpful to learn irregular verbs based on patterns. While this is not a comprehensive list of all the irregular English verb patterns, it does illustrate some of the more common patterns. Note also that there are different ways to group irregular verbs, so do not be surprised if you find patterns other than these in different sources.

| **No Change in Base Form** | | |
|---|---|---|
| bet | hit | shed |
| bid | hurt | shut |
| broadcast | let | split |
| burst | put | spread |
| cast | quit | thrust |
| cost | rid | wed* |
| cut | set | wet* |
| forecast | | |

* alternate forms possible: wedded, wetted

| **Verbs that end in "d" and change to "t" for both Simple Past and Past Participle** | |
|---|---|
| bend | bent |
| build | built |
| lend | lent |
| send | sent |
| spend | spent |

### Similar Vowel Changes in Simple Past and Past Participle (short i, æ, short u)

| Base Form | Simple Present | Past Participle |
|---|---|---|
| begin | began | begun |
| drink | drank | drunk |
| ring | rang | rung |
| shrink | shrank | shrunk |
| sing | sang | sung |
| sink | sank | sunk |
| spring | sprang | sprung |
| stink | stank | stunk |
| swim | swam | swum |

### Same Vowel Change; thus Same Past and Present Participle Forms (long e to short e)

| Base Form | Simple Present | Past Participle |
|---|---|---|
| bleed | bled | bled |
| breed | bred | bred |
| feed | fed | fed |
| meet | met | met |
| read | read* | read* |
| lead | led | led |
| speed | sped | sped |

*no spelling, only pronunciation change

### Same Vowel Change, thus Same Past and Present Participle Forms (short i to long u)

| Base Form | Simple Present | Past Participle | |
|---|---|---|---|
| cling | clung | clung | dug |
| dig | dug | flung | |
| fling | flung | hung | |
| hang | hung | slung | spun |
| sling | slung | stuck | |
| spin | spun | stung | |
| stick | stuck | struck | |
| sting | stung | swung | |
| strike | struck | won | |
| swing | swung | | |
| win | won | | |

### Same Vowel Change, thus Same Past and Present Participle Forms (long i to au)

| Base Form | Simple Present | Past Participle |
|---|---|---|
| bind | bound | bound |
| find | found | found |
| grind | ground | ground |
| wind | wound | wound |

**Same Vowel Change, thus Same Past and Present Participle Forms (long e to aw)**

| Base Form | Simple Present | Past Participle |
|---|---|---|
| bring | brought | brought |
| buy | bought | bought |
| catch | caught | caught |
| seek | sought | sought |
| teach | taught | taught |
| think | thought | thought |

**Same Vowel Change, thus Same Past and Present Participle Forms (long e to short e)**

| Base Form | Simple Present | Past Participle |
|---|---|---|
| creep | crept | crept |
| deal | dealt | dealt |
| feel | felt | felt |
| flee | fled | fled |
| keep | kept | kept |
| leave | left | left |
| mean | meant | meant |
| sleep | slept | slept |
| sweep | swept | swept |
| weep | wept | wept |

**Past and Present Participle Forms Have Same Vowel (long o), but Past Participle ends in -n or-en**

| Base Form | Simple Present | Past Participle |
|---|---|---|
| break | broke | broken |
| choose | chose | chosen |
| freeze | froze | frozen |
| speak | spoke | spoken |
| swear | swore | sworn |
| steal | stole | stolen |
| tear | tore | torn |
| wake | woke | woken |
| wear | wore | worn |
| weave | wove | woven |

# Appendix C: Essential Spelling Rules

## *Doubling Final Consonants*

- When a one-syllable word ends in **b, d, g, l, m, n, p, r** and **t,** double the final consonant when adding *–ed, -ing, -er,* or *-est:*

  rob      robbed
  slip     slipping
  big      bigger      biggest

- If a word ends in **b, d, g, l, m, n, p, r** and **t**

  - and consists of more than one syllable
  - and the final syllable is stressed

- double the final consonant when adding *–ed*, or *-ing*:

      prefer    prefe**rr**ed
      begin     begi**nn**ing


## *Forming Plurals*

- If the noun ends in **s, ss, sh, ch, z,** or **x,** add *-es*

      gas       gas**es**
      press     press**es**
      cash      cash**es**
      church    church**es**
      buzz      buzz**es**
      fax       fax**es**

- If the noun ends in a **consonant** + y, change the y to i and add *–es*.

      lady      lad**ies**
      fly       fl**ies**

- If the noun ends in a **vowel** + y, just add *–s.*

      toy       toy**s**
      bay       bay**s**


## *Final "e"*

- If a word ends with a silent "e," drop the "e" before adding a suffix if the suffix begins with a vowel:

      make      mak**ing**
      have      hav**ing**

- Do not drop the "e" when the suffix begins with a consonant:

      state     state**ment**
      hate      hate**fully**


### Words Ending in "y"

- For plurals or for a third person singular present tense verb, if the word ends in a consonant + y, change the "y" to "i" and add "es." Do not change the "y" if the "y" is preceded by a vowel.

      lady      lad**ies**
      hurry     hurr**ies**
      boy       boy**s**

- When changing adjectives to adverbs or adding the comparative and superlative suffixes *–er* or *–est*, change the "y" to "i"

    happy        happ**ily**        happ**ier**        happ**iest**


## Appendix D: Gerunds and Infinitives After Verbs

### Common Verbs Followed by a Gerund

| | | | | |
|---|---|---|---|---|
| acknowledge | defer | enjoy | miss | resent |
| admit | delay | escape | postpone | resist |
| anticipate | deplore | finish | quit | resume |
| appreciate | deny | imagine | recall | risk |
| avoid | detest | keep* | recommend | suggest |
| consider | dislike | mention** | recollect | stop |
| complete | discuss | mind | regret | tolerate |
| defend | endure | | | |

*in the sense of *continue*
**in the sense of *object to* or *dislike*

### Common Verbs Followed by Gerund or Infinitives: No Change in Meaning

| | | | |
|---|---|---|---|
| attempt | deserve | intend | prefer |
| begin | dislike | like | propose |
| cease | dread | love | start |
| can't stand | hate | neglect | undertake |
| continue | hesitate | prefer | |

### Common Verbs Followed by Gerund or Infinitives: With Change in Meaning

| | | |
|---|---|---|
| attempt | propose | stop |
| forget | regret | try |
| mean | remember | |

### Sensory and Perception Verbs Followed by Object + Gerund

| Verb | | object | gerund | Complement |
|---|---|---|---|---|
| **feel** | We felt | the waves | crashing | into the pier. |
| **see** | We saw | the seagulls | flying | over us. |
| **smell** | We smelled | the fishermen | gutting | fish. |
| **notice** | We noticed | tourists | coming | by bus. |
| **observe** | We observed | the fishermen | fishing | on the pier. |
| **watch** | We watched | the boats | sailing | in the distance. |

## Common Expressions Followed by a Gerund

| | |
|---|---|
| Be used to | It's no use |
| Get used to | It's no good |
| Can't help | It's not worth |
| How about ___? | Look forward to |
| What about ___? | |

## Common *Be* + Adjective Expressions Followed by a Gerund

| | | | |
|---|---|---|---|
| be accustomed to | be concerned with | be famous for | be nervous about |
| be afraid of | be critical of | be glad about | be proud of |
| be angry about | be discouraged from | be good at | be responsible for |
| be ashamed of | be enthusiastic about | be interested in | be sad about |
| be capable of | be familiar with | be known for | |

These *be + adjective expressions* are all followed by prepositions. It is helpful to point out to ESL/EFL learners that prepositions are followed by the gerund form of a verb and not the infinitive form.

# Appendix E: Common Adverbial Subordinator

| Relationship (meaning) | Subordinators |
|---|---|
| **Condition** | if, unless |
| **Contrast** | although, even though, though, while, whereas |
| **Manner** | as if, like |
| **Place** | where, wherever |
| **Reason** | because, since |
| **Result** | so, so that |
| **Time** | after, as, before, since, until (till), when(ever), while |

# Appendix F: The Eight Inflectional Morphemes of English

| The 8 English Inflectional Morphemes | | | |
|---|---|---|---|
| Morpheme | Grammatical function | Attaches to | Example |
| -s | plural | noun | desks, chairs, boxes |
| -'s | possessive | noun | the boy's hat the cat's tail |
| -s | third person singular | verb present tense | She drives. He talks. It walks. |
| -ed | regular past tense | verb | He talked. |
| -ed | regular past participle | verb | She has walked. |
| -ing | present participle | verb | She is driving. |
| -er | comparative | adjective | taller, higher |
| -est | superlative | adjective | tallest, highest |

# Appendix G: The Minor Categories, The Structure Words

| Some Common English Prepositions: One word | | | | | |
|---|---|---|---|---|---|
| aboard | (as in "act as a child") | but | inside | onto | toward |
| about | at | by | near | opposite | towards |
| above | atop | despite | nearest | out | under |
| across | before | down | (as in | outside | underneath |
| after | behind | during | "call for | over | unlike |
| against | below | except | the store | since | until |
| along | beneath | following | nearest | than | up |
| amid | beside | for | you.") | through | upon |
| amidst | besides | from | of | throughout | with |
| among | between | in | off | till | within |
| around | beyond | into | on | to | without |

| Some Common English Prepositions: Two words | | | |
|---|---|---|---|
| according to | aside from | inside of | out of |
| ahead of | because of | instead of | outside |
| along with | close to | near | prior to |
| apart from | due to | to | subsequent to |
| as for | except for | next to | up to |
| as to | far from | of | |

| Determiners: Tell us how many or which items noun or noun phrase is referring to | |
|---|---|
| Examples | Type |
| the, a/an | articles |
| my, your, his, her, its, our, their | possessive adjectives |
| this, that, these, those | demonstrative adjectives |
| some, many, much, few, a few, little, a little, a lot of, no | quantifiers |
| one, two, three, fifteen, forty, one hundred | ordinal numbers |
| first, second, twentieth, | cardinal numbers |

| Conjunctions | | | | | | |
|---|---|---|---|---|---|---|
| and | for | but | nor | or | so | yet |

# Appendix H: Summary of Major Learner Difficulties

- Correct use of the 8 inflectional endings (plural *−s*, posses-           Chapters 3,
  sive '*s*, present tense third person singular *–s*, past tense *–ed*,     4, 5, and 6
  past participle *–ed*; present participle *–ing*, comparative *-er*,
  and superlative *–est*).

  1. book  →  book**s**
  2. Jane  →  Jane**'s**

(continued)

---

3. walk   →   (he, she, it) walks
4. walk   →   walk**ed**
5. walk   →   walk**ed** (as in *I have walked*)
6. walk   →   walk**ing**
7. small   →   small**er**
8. small   →   small**est**

- Distinguishing between count, non-count, and crossover nouns, and the use of appropriate accompanying modifiers, such as *much, many, some, a/n, the, little,* and *few.*  **Chapter 3**

  **a** cat
  | | |
  |---|---|
  | **some** cats | **some** advice |
  | **many** cats | **much** advice |
  | **few** cats | **little** advice |
  | **fewer** responsibilities | **less** responsibility |

- Choosing the correct pronoun for the noun to which it is referring/replacing.  **Chapter 3**

- Placing adjectives in the correct position and in the correct order  **Chapter 4**

  She bought a **big beautiful wooden** box.

- Remembering to include all parts of the verb phrase when there is more than one element and putting these elements of the verb phrase in the correct form.  **Chapters 5 and 6**

  **1 auxiliary + participle**
  is walking, has walked
  **2 auxiliaries + participle**
  will be walking, has been walking
  **3 auxiliaries + participle**
  will have been walking, has been walked (as in *the dogs have been walked*)

- Inserting the *do* auxiliary for questions and the negative in simple present and simple past, and remembering the correct forms of *do* and the main verb.  **Chapters 5, 6, and 7**

  I **do not walk** home everyday.
  Pam **does not walk** home everyday.
  We **did not walk** home everyday.

- Distinguishing between transitive and intransitive verbs.  **Chapter 5**

  **intransitive**
  I walked around the block.
  I slept.
  **transitive**
  I hit the ball.
  I ate an ice cream cone.

- Placing direct and indirect noun phrases, and pronouns correctly after transitive verbs.  **Chapter 5**

  | | |
  |---|---|
  | I hit the ball. | I hit **it**. |
  | I hit the ball to Mary. | I hit **it to her**. |

(continued)

---

- Differentiating between verbs followed by gerunds, infinitives, or either.                    Chapter 5

  I enjoy **walking**
  I want **to walk**.

  She stopped **smoking**.
  She stopped **to smoke**.

- Understanding and using phrasal verbs and the different possible patterns for object noun phrases and pronouns.                    Chapter 5

  Kari **turned in** her homework.
  Kari **turned** her homework **in**.
  Kari **turned** it **in**.

  Henry **comes across** as rude.

  They **entered into** negotiations last week.
  They **entered into** them last week.

- Remembering the different forms of the verbs and auxiliaries in the different tenses.                    Chapter 6

- Mastering the different time references of the different tenses, especially the present perfect versus the simple past.                    Chapter 6

- Comprehending and using the modal auxiliary verbs and related structures, which often convey subtle nuances of meaning.                    Chapter 7

- Forming *wh-* questions, especially when the *do* auxiliary must be inserted.                    Chapters 5 & 6

  **Who** lives in this house?
  **What** was her name?
  **What does** she do?
  **How much** does this cost?
  **How many** cars have they owned?
  **Where** are you going?
  **Where did** she go?
  **When** will they come?
  **Why** hasn't he answered his phone?

- Understanding the meaning and use of transition words and phrases.                    Chapter 9

  **thus, consequently, therefore, in spite of, moreover,** and so on.

- Understanding the meaning and use of the different subordinators in adverbial clauses.                    Chapter 9

  She has lived here **since** she was a little girl.
  They decided to buy a house **since** their rent was raised again.
  Liz has **so many** problems with her boss that she is looking for a new job.
  Joe has **so much** free time that he is looking for another job.

(continued)

|  | Chapter 10 |
|---|---|

- Mastering the use and placement of relative pronouns and relative clauses.

> I e-mailed the woman **who** called me.
> They sold the house **that** they had renovated.

- Differentiating between essential and non-essential relative clauses                                          Chapter 10

**essential**

> We lost the pictures that we took of our Florida vacation.
> The people whom we had met were disappointed that we lost our pictures.
> A nurse is someone who is dedicated to helping people.

**nonessential**

> Florida, which is a peninsula, has many beaches.
> The nurse, who is wearing street clothes, has finished her shift.

Chapter 10

- Understanding when the relative pronoun can be omitted.

> We lost the pictures we took of our Florida vacation
> The people we had met were disappointed that we lost our pictures

- Using correct word order in noun clauses                                          Chapter 11

**say versus tell**

> Gerry *said* that he was leaving.
> Gerry *told me* that he was leaving.

**with embedded questions, which requires regular affirmative sentence word order**

> Gerry asked when *we were leaving*.
> Gerry asked how *we had gotten* to his house.

# Index

Breinigsville, PA USA
04 January 2010
229918BV00001B/1/P